Stoicism

Traditions and Transformations

Stoicism is now widely recognized as one of the most important philo-sophical schools of ancient Greece and Rome. But how did it influ-ence Western thought after Greek and Roman antiquity? The ques-tion is a difficult one to answer because the most important Stoic texts have been lost since the end of the classical period, though not before early Christian thinkers had borrowed their ideas and applied them to discussions ranging from dialectic to moral theology. Later philosophers became familiar with Stoic teachings only indirectly, often without knowing that an idea came from the Stoics.

The contributors recruited for this volume include some of the leading international scholars of Stoicism as well as experts in later periods of philosophy. They trace the impact of Stoicism and Stoic ideas from late antiquity through the medieval and modern periods. The story that emerges testifies to the power of Stoic philosophy – its ability to appeal even when the voices of the original thinkers are silent. The volume documents one of the most important minority reports in the history of Western philosophy.

Steven K. Strange is Associate Professor of Philosophy at Emory University.

Jack Zupko is Associate Professor of Philosophy at Emory University.

Stoicism

Traditions and Transformations

Edited by

STEVEN K. STRANGE

Emory University

JACK ZUPKO

Emory University

CAMBRIDGE
UNIVERSITY PRESS

PUBLISHED BY THE PRESS SYNDICATE OF THE UNIVERSITY OF CAMBRIDGE
The Pitt Building, Trumpington Street, Cambridge, United Kingdom

CAMBRIDGE UNIVERSITY PRESS
The Edinburgh Building, Cambridge CB2 2RU, UK
40 West 20th Street, New York, NY 10011-4211, USA
477 Williamstown Road, Port Melbourne, VIC 3207, Australia
Ruiz de Alarcón 13, 28014 Madrid, Spain
Dock House, The Waterfront, Cape Town 8001, South Africa

http://www.cambridge.org

First published 2004

Printed in the United States of America

Typeface   ITC New Baskerville 10/13 pt.   *System* LATEX 2ε   [TB]

A catalog record for this book is available from the British Library.

Library of Congress Cataloging in Publication data

Stoicism : traditions and transformations / edited by Steven K. Strange, Jack Zupko.
      p.   cm.
Includes bibliographical references (p.) and indexes.
ISBN 0-521-82709-4 (hb)
1. Stoics.   I. Strange, Steven K.   II. Zupko, Jack.
B528.S6785   2004
188 – dc22   2003056919

ISBN 0 521 82709 4 hardback

Contents

Contributors

Lawrence C. Becker, William R. Kenan, Jr., Professor of Humanities and Professor of Philosophy, Emeritus, College of William and Mary

Firmin DeBrabander, Adjunct Assistant Professor of Philosophy, Boston College

Sten Ebbesen, Professor, Institute for Greek and Latin, University of Copenhagen

Troels Engberg-Pedersen, Professor, Institute of Biblical Exegesis, University of Copenhagen

Brad Inwood, Professor of Classics and Canada Research Chair in Ancient Philosophy, University of Toronto

Jacqueline Lagrée, Professor of Philosophy, Université de Rennes 1

A. A. Long, Professor of Classics and Irving Stone Professor of Literature, University of California, Berkeley

Calvin Normore, Professor of Philosophy, University of California, Los Angeles

Martha Nussbaum, Ernst Freund Distinguished Service Professor of Law and Ethics, University of Chicago

Donald Rutherford, Associate Professor of Philosophy, University of California, San Diego

Richard Sorabji, Professor of Ancient Philosophy, King's College, University of London, and Fellow of Wolfson College, Oxford

Steven K. Strange, Associate Professor of Philosophy, Emory University

Jack Zupko, Associate Professor of Philosophy, Emory University

Acknowledgments

Most of the essays in this volume originated as papers delivered at the biennial Leroy E. Loemker Conference at Emory University on 31 March– 2 April 2000. The editors would like to thank the sponsors whose financial support made that gathering possible: the Leroy E. Loemker Lecture Fund; the Emory University Department of Philosophy; the Hightower Lecture Fund of Emory College; and the Emory University College of Arts and Sciences and Graduate School of Arts and Sciences.

We would also like to thank our production editor at Cambridge, Brian R. MacDonald, for his assistance in bringing a complex manuscript into final form.

Abbreviations

CAG	*Commentaria in Aristotelem Graeca*
CCL	*Corpus Christianorum, Series Latina*
CSEL	*Corpus Scriptorum Ecclesiasticorum Latinorum*
FDS	Karlheinz Hülser (ed.), *Die Fragmente zur Dialektik der Stoiker*
LS	A. A. Long and David Sedley (eds.), *The Hellenistic Philosophers*
PG	*Patriologiae Cursus Completus, Series Graeca,* ed. J.-P. Migne
PL	*Patriologiae Cursus Completus, Series Latina,* ed. J.-P. Migne
SVF	H. von Arnim (ed.), *Stoicorum Veterum Fragmenta*

Stoicism

Traditions and Transformations

Introduction

Steven K. Strange and Jack Zupko

Stoicism remains one of the most significant minority reports in the history of Western philosophy. Unfortunately, however, the precise nature of its impact on later thinkers is far from clear. The essays in this volume are intended to bring this picture into sharper focus by exploring how Stoicism actually influenced philosophers from antiquity through the modern period in fields ranging from logic and ethics to politics and theology. The contributing authors have expertise in different periods in the history of philosophy, but all have sought to demonstrate the continuity of Stoic themes over time, looking at the ways in which Stoic ideas were appropriated (often unconsciously) and transformed by later philosophers for their own purposes and under widely varying circumstances. The story they tell shows that Stoicism had many faces beyond antiquity, and that its doctrines have continued to appeal to philosophers of many different backgrounds and temperaments.

In tracing the influence of Stoicism on Western thought, one can take either the high road or the low road. The high road would insist on determining the ancient provenance of Stoic and apparently Stoic ideas in the work of medieval and modern thinkers, using the writings of the ancient Stoics to grade their proximity to the genuine article; this would require paying close attention to the particular questions that exercised thinkers such as Zeno and Chrysippus, in order to determine the extent to which later figures contributed to their solutions. The low road, on the other hand, would focus less on questions that interested ancient Stoics and more on broader tendencies and trends, looking at the way Stoic doctrines were employed in new settings and against different competitors, becoming altered or "watered-down" in the process. The high road is the one traditionally taken by historians of philosophy; the low road is sometimes referred to, derisively, as "intellectual history".

The present volume takes the low road. But that is not just because we believe it to be the right approach. Where the history of Stoicism is concerned, it turns out to be the only approach. Because no corpus of writings or teachings by a major Stoic figure survived antiquity, later authors tended to learn about Stoicism in a piecemeal fashion, through fragments of texts and secondhand reports. There was no genuine article for them to be acquainted with, as there was for both Aristotle after the twelfth century and Plato after the fourteenth. Later authors read the surviving materials as best they could, which is to say that they recontextualized them, borrowing Stoic distinctions to solve their own problems, usually in complete innocence of the way they had been originally used. Needless to say, this has methodological implications. Our assumption throughout this volume is that we are going to have to adjust to the nature of the evidence if we are to have any hope of tracking Stoicism beyond ancient Greece and Rome. In particular, we are going to have to shift our criteria for what counts as Stoic away from the possession of a definitive set of doctrines or their use in certain well-defined contexts to a looser, somewhat more impressionistic reading of Stoicism and what it means to be a Stoic. Hypotheses will be confirmed along the low road, though perhaps not well confirmed, and certainly not decisively demonstrated. But the looser approach will make it possible for us to understand what it was about Stoicism that gripped some later authors but not others, and why Stoic ideas have continued to resonate in Western philosophy despite the predominance of more recognized schools and approaches. That there are Stoic notes in the writings of medieval, modern, and contemporary philosophers is undeniable to anyone who reads them. The problem with taking the high road is that there is no clearly discernible path of transmission to connect the Stoic subtexts of the medieval and modern periods to the main text in antiquity, such as it is. As a result, such an approach would leave the history of Stoicism after antiquity exactly as it is today: a series of vaguely familiar echoes.

That said, the essays collected here approach the question of the impact of Stoicism from multiple angles, some of which do follow the high road while others happily depart from it, again as the nature of the evidence dictates. They are organized chronologically because a thematic approach seemed misleading – as if to suggest that later authors simply picked up where the ancient Stoics left off and added to the topics they discussed. Hence, our subtitle emphasizes the tradition*s* of Stoicism, in the plural. There are essays addressed to how Stoic doctrines were understood in different historical periods and within specific philosophical traditions, as well as essays on the way Stoic ideas were transformed by historical and political circumstances, a process of appropriation that continues to this day, as the essays by Martha Nussbaum and Lawrence Becker suggest. We hope that the present volume helps to set historical parameters for further discussion of the traditions of Stoicism, or, rather, of its traditions and transformations.

It is well known that the Stoics were the first philosophers to call themselves "Socratics," but there has been relatively little study of the influence of Socrates on individual Stoic philosophers. In "The Socratic Imprint on Epictetus' Philosophy," A. A. Long investigates the importance of Socrates as portrayed in Plato's early dialogues for Epictetus' *Discourses*. Socrates is Epictetus' favorite philosopher, whom he treats as a model for his students not only for the Stoic theory of the preeminence of virtue over all other values but also for the practice of life, in self-examination, and in methodology. It is especially in the appropriation of Socrates' characteristic method that Epictetus stands apart from earlier Stoics, as Long shows. He is able to provide numerous illustrations from the *Discourses* of Epictetus' use of the figure and method of Socrates, and especially of the striking portrait of Socrates and his protreptic and dialectic in Plato's *Gorgias*. This allows us to see that the theory of preconceptions (*prolepseis*) or natural notions in Epictetus' epistemology can help provide a solution to some notorious problems about the workings of Socratic elenchus, along the lines of the interpretation proposed by the late Gregory Vlastos.

Steven K. Strange, in "The Stoics on the Voluntariness of the Passions," provides a fresh reconstruction and defense of Chrysippus' view of the emotions and his unitary philosophical psychology. This defense is important, he maintains, if we are to properly understand the dispute between Posidonius and Chrysippus about the passions and its implications for Stoic ethics and psychotherapy. The rejection of Chrysippus' unitary psychology, which holds that the only motivational function of the human soul is reason, is common to almost the whole tradition of moral psychology, but some of its virtues may have been missed, and its influence, especially on the history of the concept of the will, may have been obscured. Strange argues that the Chrysippean view is that the motivating factor in human action is always the judgment of reason, an assent to something's being good or bad in relation to the agent, but at the same time, an emotion – either a passion or, in the case of the wise person, a "good emotion." This judgment of reason, of course, may be, and often is, false and even irrational (in which case it is also a passion), in the sense that it goes against things that the agent has good reason, and even knows that he has good reason, to believe. The element of self-deception in such passional judgments is crucial. The nature of passions such as anger or grief as due to such passional judgments is illuminated by comparing them with the so-called good feelings, the emotions of the sage, and by examining the Stoic account of incontinence, which turns out to lie much closer to Aristotle than has generally been appreciated.

In "Stoicism in the Apostle Paul: A Philosophical Reading," Troels Engberg-Pedersen shows how important it is to read between the lines when looking for Stoic influences in a text. For the Apostle Paul, like his younger contemporary Philo Judaeus, uses Stoic ideas to articulate his Jewish message, although its powerful, apocalyptic character makes the influence of Greek philosophy harder to see. Engberg-Pedersen focuses on Galatians 5:13–26 as his proof text, wherein Paul tells the Galatians that they have no need of Mosaic law because Christian faith and possession of the spirit are sufficient to overcome the selfish, bodily urges that would otherwise enslave them. The influence of Stoicism emerges in the structural similarity between Paul's notion of faith (*pistis*) and the Stoic conception of wisdom (*sophia*): just as the Christ-person is free in his obedience to the will of God – an obedience that is, paradoxically, self-willed – so in *oikeiōsis* the Stoic comes to see himself as a person of reason, liberated from the body in his agreement with "the will of him who orders the universe." In both cases, the person who is truly free is able to reject the bonds of external law because the law has in an important sense been fulfilled in him. Engberg-Pedersen concludes with the suggestion that Paul is best understood as a "crypto-Stoic" thinker because, although he did not think of himself as a philosopher, he used Stoic ideas very effectively in presenting the gospel of Christ.

In his essay "Moral Judgment in Seneca," Brad Inwood investigates Seneca's use of the metaphors of judicial deliberation and legal judgment to illustrate the concept of moral judgment. He is able to show that this is a particularly rich analogy in Seneca's moral thought, which he develops in an original way. It has been argued that Stoics developed different codes of moral conduct for sages and for ordinary moral progressors, but Seneca's use of the juridical metaphor strongly suggests that this may be a misinterpretation. For, in a number of places, as Inwood shows, Seneca contrasts a strict or severe judge with a more flexible and merciful one, and claims that only a sage or wise person could be justified in imposing judicial severity, because everyone else (and indeed the sage herself before gaining wisdom) could be held guilty of infringing upon the law in some way, were it to be strictly enforced. By analogy, one is obligated to apply the same moral standards to oneself as one does to others in making moral evaluations, and if one does so fairly, and one is not a sage, one will have to grant that one is a moral sinner like everyone else. The same standards therefore apply to all, sages and fools, but mercy or clemency, a looser application of the same moral laws, to ordinary nonsages. Inwood demonstrates the importance of the juridical metaphor for Seneca by pointing to and discussing a number of key passages in his *Dialogues* and *Letters*.

Richard Sorabji's essay, "Stoic First Movements in Christianity," is concerned with the transformation, by a new tradition, of a particular moment of Stoic influence. Emotions are judgments for the Stoic, acts of rational assent to involuntary first movements of the soul (*ictus* in Seneca), such as shivering, blushing, sexual irritation, and so on. The Stoic sage trained himself to interrogate these movements so that he could decide whether it would be appropriate to assent to them (most non-Stoics, by contrast, were thought to assent readily to appearances without realizing that assenting is distinct from appearing). Some two centuries after Seneca, however, the Christian thinker Origen borrowed the expression "first movements" and gave it a fateful interpretation by connecting it not with involuntary appearances but rather with the "bad thoughts" mentioned in Mark 7:21 and Matthew 15:19. As Sorabji points out, this blurred the original Stoic distinction so that it was "no longer clear whether a beginning of emotion is distinct from emotion or whether it is a little bit of emotion." A little more than a century later, the Christian writer Evagrius discusses eight such bad thoughts, including gluttony, fornication, and avarice (the list, slightly modified, was to reemerge as the seven deadly sins of the Western tradition). But bad thoughts could not be viewed as mere incitements. Rather, they were temptations, and sin became our assent to them, or to the pleasure of having them. Thus, Sorabji concludes, the Stoic doctrine of how to combat emotion developed into the Christian doctrine of how to resist temptation.

Sten Ebbesen examines the medieval fate of a number of Stoic teachings in "Where Were the Stoics in the Late Middle Ages?" The Stoics, he argues, were everywhere and nowhere during the scholastic period – everywhere in the sense that their tough-minded rationalism and analytic methods became the hallmark of scholastic philosophy, nowhere in the sense that hardly anyone during the Middle Ages understood what Stoicism was or recognized particular doctrines as having come from the

Stoics. This makes it difficult to trace Stoic influences. Still, Ebbesen shows that Stoicism is unmistakably present on several fronts: in the widespread use in medieval logic and grammar of the distinction between a "signifying thing" and "thing signified," which shaped the eleventh- and twelfth-century debate between the "thing-people" and "word- or name-people" (a.k.a. realists and nominalists); in certain "un-Aristotelian" additions to Aristotelian logic, such as the properties of syncategorematic words and the notion of logical consequence, the terminology of which is almost certainly derived from the Stoics; and in the Stoic doctrine of assent, which emerges in a variety of places, from Peter Abelard's account of moral goodness to John Buridan's definition of knowledge. Like the Stoics, scholastic thinkers also had a penchant for "crazy examples" that tested the limits of their philosophical systems and, by the late thirteenth century, a conception of the sage-philosopher as embodying the life of virtue. In the end, though, it was what Ebbesen calls their "community of spirit with the Stoics" that best explains the preservation and development of Stoic ideas by medieval philosophers in the absence of authoritative texts and teachings.

In "Abelard's Stoicism and Its Consequences," Calvin Normore identifies an important strand of Stoic ethical theory preserved in Abelard's idea that the locus of sin is intention or consent. Just as the Stoics were drawn by their assumption of a world determined by fate to hold that moral responsibility consists in assent, so Abelard, recognizing that the world cannot be otherwise than God willed it, ascribes moral goodness and badness primarily to intentions and only secondarily or derivatively to actions. The prescription is similar in both cases: for the Stoics, we should live in accordance with nature; for Abelard, we should will what is objectively pleasing to God. Normore takes Abelard's Stoicism to be embodied in the Philosopher of the *Dialogue between a Philosopher, a Jew, and a Christian*. Although his internalist conception of sin proved unpopular in the thirteenth century, it was kept alive by critics such as Peter Lombard, eventually to be taken up again in the fourteenth century by William of Ockham – although this time without the crucial Stoic idea that the actual world is in itself the best possible.

The Reformation brought tremendous social and political upheaval to Western Europe, and in its wake Stoic ethics enjoyed a brief, but intense, revival in the late sixteenth and early seventeenth centuries. Jacqueline Lagrée's essay, "Constancy and Coherence," is addressed to this encounter between Christianity and Stoic ethics. For Renaissance thinkers inspired by Seneca, constancy was a virtue pertaining to the

military man in the heat of battle, not to the private citizen. But everything changed with the appearance in 1584 of the treatise *On Constancy*
by the Flemish philosopher Justus Lipsius. Lipsius showed that Stoicism
was compatible with Christianity and that Stoic constancy manifests itself in the coherence and immutability of truths in the soul of the wise
man, who, in the midst of political turmoil, cleaves to universal law in the
form of divine providence. This kind of Stoicism fit with the austere, rationalistic conception of religion being advanced by the reformers. The
resonance was probably not accidental – John Calvin had himself published a commentary on Seneca's *De Clementia* in 1532. In any case, Lipsius
must have struck a chord in many of his readers, weary of decades of religious conflict, because he soon became the most popular author of his
time. Other thinkers followed in his footsteps, the most successful being
Guillaume du Vair (1556–1621). Du Vair took Stoicism in a decidedly
more Christian direction, transforming pagan constancy into Christian
consolation by means of the theological virtues of faith, hope, and charity. But Christians always viewed the paganism of ancient Stoicism with a
certain ambivalence. Eventually, Christian Stoicism fell out of favor and
the Stoic virtue of constancy came to be seen as illusory and idolatrous,
completely put to shame by the virtue of patience with hope that fortified
the Christian martyrs. In the end, modern Stoicism became more of an
ethical and juridical attitude than a philosophy properly speaking.

In his essay "On the Happy Life: Descartes vis-à-vis Seneca," Donald
Rutherford looks at the reaction to Seneca's work *On the Happy Life* in
Descartes' correspondence with Princess Elisabeth, and the light that it
throws both on Descartes' attitude to the ancient Stoics and on the influence of their eudaimonism on his ethical thought. Descartes develops the
latter at length in his letters to Elisabeth in critical reaction to Seneca's
work, claiming that his ethical theory represents a compromise between
Stoicism and Epicureanism. By identifying happiness with tranquillity and
distinguishing it from virtue and its cultivation, Descartes is led to abandon eudaimonism in favor of a proto-Kantian view, although his claim
that the crucial component in the exercise of virtue is not rationality but
freedom differs both from the Stoics and Kant. Importantly, Descartes
also breaks ethics free from the dependence on divine providence that
one finds in Stoicism, for an important factor in human freedom is that
divine providence is inscrutable to us, a theme familiar from Descartes'
rejection of Stoic providentialism in science. Descartes also rejects the
Stoic ideal of extirpation of the passions, both in this correspondence
and in *The Passions of the Soul*.

"Of all the great classical philosophers," writes Alexandre Matheron, "Spinoza is the one whose teaching best lends itself to a point-by-point comparison with Stoicism." Firmin DeBrabander follows up on Matheron's suggestion by comparing the concept of moral perfection in Spinoza's *Ethics* with traditional Stoic views in his essay, "Psychotherapy and Moral Perfection: Spinoza and the Stoics on the Prospect of Happiness." He finds that despite numerous similarities in their conception of the natural order as an expression of divinity, their insistence that the instinct for self-preservation is the seat of virtue, and their recognition of a cognitive element in the passions, Spinoza ultimately rejects the kind of moral perfectionism embodied by the Stoic sage because his tranquillity seems more otherworldly than natural. According to Spinoza, self-control is an ideal we would do well to avoid because it prevents us from seeing ourselves as we truly are: aspects of Nature absolutely and ineluctably determined by its laws. Paradoxically, he would insist that "individual power is augmented by the recognition of impotence, and that freedom is attained in the acceptance of necessity." Likewise, the Stoic notion of freedom of judgment is an illusion. Unlike the Stoic sage, the resignation of Spinoza's philosopher is complete; indeed, he is "only separated from the unhappiness of the common people by a few degrees of intellectual clarity, and he is certainly no stranger to their sufferings."

In "Duties of Justice, Duties of Material Aid: Cicero's Problematic Legacy," Martha Nussbaum compares Cicero's views on justice in his Stoic-influenced work *On Duties* to modern discussions of the justice or injustice of the distribution of basic human goods such as clean water, health services, sanitation, and adequate nutrition in societies around the world. She mentions some contemporary accounts of the just distribution of goods in theories of international law and morality but admits that this topic has not been much discussed by philosophers, in contrast to questions of international law and justice in relation to commerce, treaties, and warfare. She lays part of the blame for this situation at the door of Cicero, and particularly his distinction in *On Duties* between duties of justice and duties of material aid to needy persons, particularly foreigners. Cicero thinks the latter duties are much less demanding than duties of justice and require us to give more consideration to the needs of family, friends, and fellow citizens than to citizens of other societies. Cicero's influence is very real because of his role in shaping the thoughts of both philosophers and statesmen down through the centuries. Nussbaum provides a spirited critique of the Stoic theory she sees lying behind Cicero's pernicious and, in her judgment, indefensible distinction between duties of justice and of material aid, which also helps illuminate some obscure areas of Stoic social thought. She closes with some interesting remarks about the relevance of this dispute for the notion of property rights in international justice.

In his essay, "Stoic Emotion," Lawrence C. Becker reinforces and completes the argument of his important recent book, *A New Stoicism*, with an account of how his contemporary revival of a Stoic ethics would deal with the important topic of emotion. Becker maintains that the proper Stoic position, going back to the ancient Stoics, is that one's ethical perspective should be shaped and determined by the best available scientific account of the natural world and of human nature. He grants that advances in science require the Stoic to give up some important elements of the ancient Stoic world view, in particular providentialism and a teleological conception of the universe, but argues that this does not really undercut the Stoic approach to ethics and the good life. It may even reinforce it. He compares ancient Stoic accounts of the nature of emotion with those of contemporary psychological research and shows that they are not incompatible. Chrysippus' claim that emotions are judgments will have to be modified in the direction of Posidonius' claim that there are standing irrational sources of motivation in humans, but this does not undermine Stoic cognitive therapy of the emotions. A proper Stoic view of the emotions would incorporate the best available account of their role in human psychological health. And such an account might well be more compatible with a fundamentally Stoic approach to emotional life than the more popular "romantic" view, which tends to overvalorize the emotions.

1

The Socratic Imprint on Epictetus' Philosophy

A. A. Long

The honorable and good person neither fights with anyone himself, nor, as far as he can, does he let anyone else do so. Of this as of everything else the life of Socrates is available to us as a paradigm, who not only himself avoided fighting everywhere, but did not let others fight either. (1.5.1–2)

Now that Socrates is dead, the memory of what he did or said when alive is no less beneficial to people, or rather is even more so. (4.1.169)

The Stoic *Discourses* of Epictetus are conspicuously marked throughout by the figure of Socrates. No other philosopher, not even Zeno or Diogenes, is named nearly so frequently. Epictetus views Socrates as the *single* figure who best authorizes and exemplifies everything he is trying to give his students in terms of philosophical methodology, self-examination, and a life model for them to imitate. This strikingly explicit coincidence between Epictetus' objectives and Socrates makes the Stoicism of the *Discourses* particularly distinctive.

In order to take the measure of this point, we need to start from the role of Socrates in the preceding Stoic tradition. The earliest Stoic philosophers had drawn so heavily on Plato's and, to a lesser extent, Xenophon's Socrates that members of the school were happy to be called Socratics.[1]

A version of this chapter has already appeared as chapter 3 of my 2002 book. Permission from Oxford University Press to reprint this work is gratefully acknowledged. For my excerpts from Plato's *Gorgias* I adopt (with ocasional changes) the translations of T. H. Irwin (Plato 1979). The translations of Epictetus are my own and, except as noted, are from the *Discourses*. I also draw on some material included in my article Long 2000; this article formed the basis for the paper I read at Emory University's Loemker Conference on Stoicism in April 2000.

The details cover numerous Stoic doctrines in ethics, moral psychology, and theology, including the priority of the soul's good over everything else, the unity of the virtues, the identity of virtue with knowledge, and divine providence. Such famous Stoic paradoxes as the confinement of real freedom and wealth to the sage had already been adumbrated in earlier Socratic and Cynic literature. The Stoics' hardest and most notorious thesis was that genuine and complete happiness requires nothing except moral virtue. And on this, above all, they looked to Socrates who had famously said at his trial: "No harm can come to the good man in life or in death, and his circumstances are not ignored by the gods" (Plato, *Apology* 41d).

The Stoics had also treated Socrates' life as a near paradigm of Stoic wisdom's practical realization, and they were especially impressed by accounts of Socrates' fortitude, self-control, and imperviousness to physical and emotional stress. When Epictetus aligns Stoic doctrines with Socrates or when he asks his students to reflect on Socrates' equanimity at his trial, imprisonment, and death, he is doing just what earlier Greek and Roman Stoics had done.

What seems to be completely missing from this earlier Stoic appropriation of Socrates is the dialectic Socrates practices in Plato's dialogues, including interpersonal discussion by question and answer, exposure of ignorance and inconsistency by means of the elenchus, and irony.[2] The great interest and the apparent novelty of Epictetus' dependence and reflection on Socrates consist in his adaptation of Socratic dialectic in the ways just described. Although we cannot simply assert that he was the first and only Stoic philosopher to do this, I shall suggest reasons besides the silence of our sources for thinking this likely.[3] In adopting this interpretation, I do not mean that Epictetus regarded Socratic dialectic as more important than everything else in the Socratic record; his Socrates has a unity that helps us to understand why he made that figure the principal model of his own teaching method. But Epictetus' recourse to Socratic dialectic is my main theme in this chapter. Up to now it has been so little studied that standard accounts of the discourses have lacked a crucial dimension.

Epictetus quotes or paraphrases or alludes to around a hundred passages from sixteen of Plato's dialogues, nearly all of which are spoken there by Socrates.[4] He was drawn to Plato not out of interest in Plato's speculative philosophy but because the Platonic dialogues were the richest source on Socrates' life, thought, and conversation. Epictetus concludes a discourse entitled "What Is the Rule for Living?" with these words: "In the case of theory it is easy to examine and refute an ignorant person, but in the business of life no one submits to such testing and we hate the one who puts us through it. But Socrates used to say that an unexamined life is not worth living" (1.26.17–18). Here as elsewhere (see 3.12.15) Epictetus quotes one of the most memorable of Socrates' concluding sentences from the *Apology* (38a). His remarks about the hatred "we" extend to anyone who makes us give an account of our lives are a gloss not only on this context of the *Apology* but also on Socrates' explanation of his elenctic mission and the Athenian prosecution to which it has brought him.

REFLECTIONS OF PLATO'S *GORGIAS*

The Platonic dialogue to which Epictetus attends most closely is the *Gorgias*. That is hardly an accident, for in this dialogue Socrates makes his most explicit statements about the rationale of his dialectic in general and of the elenchus in particular. The *Gorgias* also contains Plato's clearest and strongest statements of what many modern scholars take to be the core of Socratic ethics, more or less uninfluenced by Plato's own metaphysics and psychology. Here are some key examples, all of them echoed by Epictetus:

A. Nothing is worse than false beliefs about goodness and justice (458a; Epictetus 1.11.11).
B. It is worse to do wrong than to suffer wrong (474c ff.; Epictetus 4.1.122–23).
C. The paradigm wrongdoer, the tyrant, has the least power and freedom (468b; Epictetus 4.1.51–53).
D. Every action is motivated by a desire for what the agent thinks is good (468b; Epictetus 1.18.1–2; 3.3.2–4).
E. [As a corollary of D]: No one does or wants what is bad, knowing or thinking that what he does or wants is bad (i.e., wrongdoing is involuntary) (468d; Epictetus 2.26.1–2).
F. [As a further corollary of D]: The wrongdoer does not what he wants but what (mistakenly) "seems good to him" (468; Epictetus 4.1.3).
G. Untended diseases of the soul leave ineradicable imprints (525a; Epictetus 2.18.11).

The Stoic tradition had endorsed all of these propositions, but Epictetus formulates them in ways that recall their original Socratic contexts in the *Gorgias*. Why would he do this? I propose two closely related reasons.

First, Socrates' three interlocutors in this dialogue, mutatis mutandis, have great resonance and relevance for Epictetus' students: Gorgias, the celebrated professor of rhetoric, who (as presented by Plato) cares nothing for the ethical effects of his words on his audience; Polus, an overeager discussant who cannot defend his conventionalist morality against Socratic challenges; and, finally, Callicles, the ambitious politician, whose "might is right" concept of justice and extreme hedonism are pitted against Socrates' claims for the cultivation of a well-tempered soul. Epictetus' discourses include or allude to contemporary equivalents to Gorgias, Polus, and Callicles, each of whom, in his own way, is antithetical to the ideal Epictetus offers his students.

Second, Socrates in the *Gorgias* does not simply announce the startling propositions I have numbered A–G. He puts most of them forward within the context of his elenctic discussion with Polus. Shortly before Polus replaces Gorgias as Socrates' discussant, Socrates tells Gorgias:

> What kind of man am I? One of those who would be pleased to be refuted [*elenchthentōn*] if I say something untrue, and pleased to refute if someone else does, yet not at all less pleased to be refuted than to refute. For I think that being refuted is a greater good, insofar as it is a greater good for a man to be rid of the greatest badness in himself than to rid someone else of it; for I think there is no badness for a man as great as a false belief about the things which our discussion is about now. (458a = proposition A)

In the course of his discussion with Polus, Socrates advances propositions C–F against Polus' attempts to defend the value of sheer rhetorical power untempered by moral integrity. When Polus objects that Socrates' position is absurd, Socrates gives him a lesson in elenctic discussion, contrasting that with the kind of rhetoric practiced in a court of law where defendants are often condemned on the basis of false witnesses. He acknowledges that Polus can adduce numerous witnesses who will attest to the falsehood of his own position, but he dismisses them as irrelevant to the kind of argument he and Polus are involved in: "If I can't produce you, all alone by yourself as a witness agreeing on the things I'm talking about, I think I have achieved nothing of any account in what our discussion is about. And I don't think you'll have achieved anything either unless I, all alone, bear witness for you, and you let all the others go" (472bc). As the discussion proceeds, Socrates secures Polus' agreement to premises that support his own position and conflict with Polus' initial support for sheer rhetorical power. Although Polus is scarcely convinced, he admits that Socrates' conclusions *follow from* the premises that he himself has accepted (480e).

Socrates' procedure in his final argument with Callicles is similar. At the outset he tells Callicles that, unless he can refute Socrates' thesis that doing injustice with impunity is the worst of evils – the thesis that Callicles vehemently opposes – Callicles will be discordant with himself throughout his life (482b). This prediction anticipates the outcome of their argument; for, after eliciting a series of reluctant admissions from Callicles, Socrates tells him:

Those things which appeared true to us earlier in the previous arguments are held firm and bound down, so I say . . . by iron and adamantine arguments; so at least it appears thus far. And if you, or someone more vigorous than you, doesn't untie them, no one who says anything besides what I say now can be right. For my argument is always the same, that I myself don't know how these things are, but no one I've ever met, just as now, is able to speak otherwise without being ridiculous. (508e–509a)

The ridiculousness, Socrates explains, is conditional on the validity of his argument and the truth of its premises. If these conditions are met, the inability of an opponent to refute his argument exposes such a person to the diagnosis of holding radically false beliefs about what is good for himself – beliefs, moreover, that actually conflict with his (and every person's) wish to flourish to the greatest extent possible.

Whether Socrates in Plato's *Gorgias* is entitled to claim these results need not concern us here. All we require is an outline of his elenctic strategy in order to compare it with Epictetus' procedural statements about the method. We may begin with passages that register his unmistakable allusions to Plato's dialogue.

Epictetus (almost certainly with heavy irony) thanks a certain Lesbius for "every day proving to me [*exelenchein*] that I know nothing" (3.20.19). On two occasions, when recommending Socrates' elenctic methodology to his students, he cites Socrates' remark to Polus that the only witness he needs is his fellow disputant (2.12.5; 2.26.6). He picks up Socrates' observation that his elenctic methodology, far from being adversarial, benefits the questioner as well as the respondent, and turns the method into a striking metaphor about the way a philosopher should "write" dialogues – not by literally inscribing different speakers but by examining himself, all alone:

Socrates didn't write? Who wrote so much as he? But how? Because, since he couldn't always have someone to test [*elenchein*] his judgments or to be tested

by him in turn, he made a habit of testing and examining himself and was forever trying out the use of some particular preconception. That is how a philosopher writes. But trifling phrases like "he said" and "I said" he leaves to others.
(2.1.32–33)[5]

Epictetus characterizes elenctic discussion as the essence of what it means
to meet a philosopher, taking it to involve, just like Socrates, the pre-
paredness of the participants to expose their beliefs to mutual scrutiny
and susceptibility to refutation (3.9.13). He recognizes too the hostility
that the practice frequently evokes (2.14.20; 3.1.19–23), and its lack of
effectiveness in some instances (4.1.146).[6]

  With this by way of introduction, we may now turn to passages that
illustrate Epictetus' interpretation of the Socratic elenchus and his own
practice of it.

THE SOCRATIC ELENCHUS IN THE *DISCOURSES*

Our best place to start is the discourse where Epictetus introduces
Socrates as his paradigm for the protreptic and elenctic style (2.26):

(1) Every error involves a [mental] conflict [*machē*]. For since the erring person doesn't want to err but to be right, it's clear that he isn't doing what he
wants. (2) For what does the thief want to achieve? His own interest. Therefore,
if thieving is contrary to his interest, he is not doing what he wants.

(3) Further, every rational soul is naturally averse to conflict; but as long as
someone is unaware of being involved in a conflict, there is nothing to prevent
him from acting inconsistently. Yet, once he is aware, he is strongly constrained to
abandon and shun the conflict, just as one who perceives that something is false
is forcibly constrained to renounce the falsehood, though until it shows itself he
assents to it as true.

(4) The person who can show an individual the conflict responsible for his
error and clearly make him see how he is not doing what he wants to do and is
doing what he does not want to do – that is the person who combines expertise
in argument, exhortation [*protreptikos*], and refutation [*elenktikos*]. (5) For if a
person can show this, the erring individual will concede of his own accord; but
as long as you fail to show it, don't be surprised if the other persists, because he
is acting under the impression that he is right.

(6) That is why Socrates put his faith in this faculty and used to say: "I make a
habit of invoking no other witness to what I say; instead, I am always content with
my interlocutor and call for his vote and summon him as a witness, and all on his
own he is enough for me in place of everyone."[7]

(7) That is because Socrates understood the motivations of a rational soul,
and the way it inclines like a scale, whether you want it to or not. Show a conflict
to a rational soul, and it will give it up. But if you don't point it out, blame yourself
rather than the person who remains unpersuaded.

When Epictetus associates "expertise in argument" (section 4) with the ability to expose a person's mental conflicts and reorient his volitions, we should not take him to be specifying a skill additional to elenctic and protreptic.[8] These are rather the manifestation of Socrates' argumentative expertise. It is interesting, though, to note that the Greek I have translated by "expertise in argument" (*deinos en logōi*) recalls Gorgias' chief claim to fame, which it is the purpose of Plato's so-named dialogue to transfer from the sophist to Socrates. Our passage may appear naive in its presumption that no one is prepared to live with awareness of mental conflict. However, Epictetus acknowledges elsewhere (see *Discourse* 1.5) that some hard-line skeptics are impervious to elenctic argumentation. For now, we should concentrate on how he implements the theory about exposure to mental conflict and the consequential reorientation of volition.

Epictetus' conception of philosophy and its psychological foundations relies on a whole series of claims that are explicit or implicit in 2.26. These claims include the need to start from awareness of one's own ignorance about ultimate values, the desire to understand and resolve discrepant opinions concerning these and, above all, the assumption that human beings in general are lovers of truth and consistency and hostile to contradiction.[9] He also relies on a further assumption, which is not only fundamental to his entire outlook but also crucial for understanding why he drew on the Socratic elenchus for his own pedagogy. It may be stated as follows: human beings are innately equipped with the motivation to seek their own good (i.e., happiness) and to choose whatever means they think will promote that good. I will comment on this assumption after we have observed his use of it in two elenctic passages.

First, a short but very telling instance:

Can't people think that something is advantageous to themselves, and not choose it? – They cannot.

What about the woman [Medea] who says: "I understand the harmful things I intend to do, but passion rules my decisions."[10]

The exact point is: she thinks that gratifying her passion and avenging herself on her husband is more advantageous than saving her children.

Yes; but she is deceived. – Show her clearly that she is deceived and she will not do it. – But until you point this out to her, what can she follow except what appears to her [to be more advantageous]? (1.28.6–8)

Medea presents herself as *knowingly* doing what is harmful (killing her children) under the influence of passion, but Epictetus, like Socrates, denies that such an analysis of one's motivations can ever be correct; he takes Medea, notwithstanding what she says, to be motivated by completely mistaken beliefs concerning where her own advantage really lies. The passage says nothing explicitly about Medea's error being due to her suffering from conflicting beliefs or desires, but that is the clear implication. We could summarily rewrite as follows:

MEDEA. I want and therefore choose what is most advantageous to myself.
EPICTETUS. So does everyone.
MEDEA. Killing my children to spite Jason is what is most advantageous to me.
EPICTETUS. That is a gross error. Nothing could be less advantageous to you than killing your children. Your anger is causing you the following conflict: wanting what is most advantageous to yourself, and choosing what is least advantageous to yourself.

The Medea excerpt shares the lesson of the previous passage: that persons suffering from conflicting beliefs will only abandon the conflict when it is convincingly pointed out to them. Both passages endorse the central Socratic proposition (which I numbered D earlier) that actions are always motivated by what the agent (however mistakenly and self-deceptively) thinks will be good for him or her. This intellectualist account of human motivation is, of course, extremely controversial, but it was absolutely central to Socratic ethics and completely endorsed by Epictetus. They were equally adamant that what is truly advantageous for any person must always coincide with what is morally right.

Next, I take a discourse (1.11) actually composed as a dialogue between Epictetus and an unnamed government administrator, who has come to talk with him. In the course of conversation the man tells Epictetus that he was recently made so distraught by an illness affecting his young daughter that he could not bear to remain at home until he got news of the child's recovery. The point of the ensuing dialogue is to discover whether the father was really motivated, as he professed to be, by love of his daughter. The text is too long to be cited in full, so I offer this translation of sections 5–15, flagging the most recognizable Socratic features in brackets:

EPICTETUS. Do you think you acted correctly [*orthōs*]?
FATHER. I think I acted naturally [*phusikōs*]. [This is the belief to be examined.]
EPICTETUS. Well, convince me that you acted naturally, and I will convince you that everything that occurs in accordance with nature occurs correctly.
FATHER. This is the way all, or at least most, fathers feel.
EPICTETUS. I don't deny *that*; the question we are disputing is whether it is correct. For by this reasoning we would have to say that tumors are good for the body because they occur, and that erring is absolutely in accordance with

nature because nearly all of us, or at least most of us, err. Show me, then, how your behavior is in accordance with nature. [Pressure on the interlocutor to clarify his terms.]

FATHER. I can't. Rather, you show me how it is not in accordance with nature and not correct. [Confession of ignorance; inducement of *aporia*.]

EPICTETUS. Well, if we were investigating light and dark, what criterion would we invoke to distinguish between them?

FATHER. Sight.

EPICTETUS. And if the question were about temperature or texture?

FATHER. Touch.

EPICTETUS. Accordingly, since our dispute is about things in accordance with nature and what occurs correctly or incorrectly, what criterion do you want us to adopt? [Socratic style of analogical or inductive inference.]

FATHER. I don't know. [Further confession of ignorance, and *aporia*.]

EPICTETUS. Ignorance about the criterion of colors and smells and flavors may not be very harmful; but do you think that someone ignorant of the criterion of things good and bad and in accordance with or contrary to nature is only slightly harmed?

FATHER. No, that is the greatest harm.

EPICTETUS. Tell me, is everyone's opinion concerning what is fine and proper correct? Does that apply to all the opinions that Jews and Syrians and Egyptians and Romans hold on the subject of food?

FATHER. How could that be possible?

EPICTETUS. Presumably it is absolutely necessary that if the Egyptians' opinions are correct, the others' are not, and if the Jews' are fine, the others' are not?

FATHER. Certainly.

EPICTETUS. Where ignorance exists, there also exists lack of learning and lack of training concerning essentials.

FATHER. I agree.

EPICTETUS. Now that you are aware of this, in future you will concentrate your mind on nothing else than learning the criterion of what accords with nature and using it in order to make judgments concerning particular cases.

Epictetus now gets the father to agree that love of one's family and good reasoning (*eulogiston*) are mutually consistent, with the implication that if one of them is in accordance with nature and correct, the other must be so too. Pressed by Epictetus, the father accepts that abandoning his daughter was not a well-reasoned act. Could it, then, have been motivated, as he claimed, by love? Through a further induction, the father is led to agree that if the child's mother and others responsible for her welfare had acted like himself, their behavior would not have been loving. Thus, Epictetus concludes, the father, contrary to his initial belief, was not motivated by an *excusably natural* love for his daughter, but by erroneous reasoning about the *properly* natural and right thing to do. The father ran away, he concludes, because that was what mistakenly "seemed good to him."[11]

The Socratic features of this elenchus are too obvious to need full articulation. By the end, the father has been brought to agree that (1) his protestations of love for his daughter conflict with the standards of love he would apply to other people and (2) his initial appeal to the naturalness of his action is incompatible with what he acknowledges to be natural in the sense of being the normative and properly rational behavior. The point of the exercise is also thoroughly Socratic – not to blame or criticize the father but to show him how his judgment and will went astray, failing to fit the affection that he had taken to be his motive.

In order to understand the rationale behind Epictetus' Socratic mode of argumentation, we need to clarify his claim that, although (1) human beings are innately motivated to seek their own happiness and to prefer right to wrong, (2) they typically hold beliefs that conflict with the attainment of these objectives. Here is one of his clearest statements, taken from the beginning of the discourse entitled "The Starting Point of Philosophy" (2.11):

To make an authentic start on philosophy and to enter it at the front door, a person needs to be aware of his own weakness and incapacity concerning absolute essentials. For in regard to a right-angled triangle or a half tone, we came into the world without any natural concept; it was through some expert instruction that we learned each of these, and consequently people who don't know them don't think that they do. But, on the other hand, who has entered the world without an innate concept [*emphutos ennoia*] of good and bad, fine and ugly, fitting and unfitting, and of happiness, propriety, and what is due and what one should and should not do? For this reason, we all use these terms and try to adapt our preconceptions [about them] to particular instances, saying: "He has done well, or as he should, or as he should not; she has been unfortunate, or fortunate; he is just, or unjust." Which of us is sparing in using these terms? Which of us holds back his use of them until he learns to do so like those who are ignorant of lines or sounds? (6) The explanation is that we came into the world already instructed in this area to some extent by nature, and starting from this we have added on our own opinion. – By Zeus, you are right; I do know by nature, don't I, what is fine and ugly? Have I no concept of them? – You do.

Don't I apply the concept to particular instances? – You do.

Don't I apply it well?

That's where the whole question lies, and that's where opinion comes to be added. Because, starting from those concepts they agree on, people get into conflict as a result of applying them to instances where the concepts don't fit.

Epictetus' essential point is that everyone is *innately* equipped with a predisposition to form concepts that furnish the basic capacity to make value judgments. Because people are born with this equipment, they tend to

think, like his interlocutor here, that they *know* the specifics of goodness and happiness, or right and wrong, and can therefore make correct
value judgments in particular cases. When Epictetus draws attention to
the "conflicts" that arise from misapplication of the natural concepts, he
is referring not only to disagreements between persons but also to conflicts or contradictions that arise for the same reason within one person,
like Medea.

How does Epictetus' theory about innate concepts of value relate
to the Socratic elenchus, and what does Epictetus mean by positing
these concepts? I will approach these questions by taking the second
first.[12]

The innate concepts or "preconceptions" (*prolepseis*), as he often calls
them, are explained as follows (1.22.1–2; and see 4.1.44–45):

> Preconceptions are common to all people, and one preconception does not
> conflict with another. For which of us does not take it that a good thing is ad-
> vantageous and choiceworthy, and something to be sought and pursued in every
> circumstance? Which of us does not take it that justice is something honorable
> and fitting? When, then, does conflict occur? In the application of preconceptions
> to particular instances, as when someone says:
> > He acted in a fine way; he is courageous.
> But someone else retorts:
> > No, he's crazy.

Here Epictetus makes two big claims concerning people's innate concepts
of value: first, any two people have the same preconception about the
same item; or to put it logically, they agree about the connotation of a
term such as "good". Second, people's stock of preconceptions forms
a mutually consistent set of evaluative concepts or meanings. We may
recall his comment in the preceding passage about starting from agreed
concepts.

These are obviously very bold claims. However, their boldness is tempered by a very important qualification. What gives preconceptions their
universality and mutual consistency is their extremely general or formal content: everyone conceives "good" things to be advantageous and
choiceworthy, and "bad" things to be harmful and undesirable, irrespective of what they actually take to be good or bad in particular instances.

More controversial, it may seem, is the claim that such universal and
mutually consistent attitudes also pertain to the moral realm of justice,
propriety, and so forth. Epictetus could reasonably respond that people in
general do agree on the positive connotations of justice and the negative
connotations of injustice, taking these concepts or terms quite generally.

Further, in claiming that these preconceptions are innate, his point is presumably not that infants are fully equipped with them but that our basic evaluative and moral propensities are hard-wired and genetically programmed, as we would say today; they are not, in their general content, a cultural accretion.

He is emphatically not saying that preconceptions are sufficient criteria on their own to guide our judgments. We do not know what particular things are good simply by having the preconception that goodness is profitable. All we know is an essential property of goodness. We need Stoic doctrine in order to learn that conventional goods such as health or wealth are not strictly good or their opposites strictly bad because they are not unequivocally profitable or harmful respectively, or to learn that happiness does not consist in a succession of pleasurable sensations and an absence of painful ones. Our preconceptions need to be articulated by definitions far more precise than their innate content involves; and we need unremitting training in order to make our conduct consonant with these refinements. The role of preconceptions is nonetheless fundamental and primary in Epictetus' philosophy.

If he is right, human beings all agree in wanting to flourish, to have their desires for happiness fulfilled, to possess what is really good and to avoid what is really harmful, and to favor justice over injustice. His task, as he sees it, is to show how people's particular value judgments are typically in conflict with their ethical preconceptions, and thus people fail to achieve the happiness and correct behavior they naturally want.

We can now identify a quite precise role for the Socratic elenchus to play in Epictetus' educational agenda. The Socrates of the *Gorgias* does not talk about innate and universal preconceptions of happiness and so forth, but, if Gregory Vlastos was broadly correct in his brilliant analysis of the Socratic elenchus in Plato's *Gorgias*, Socrates' confidence in this mode of argument presumes that his interlocutors do have true beliefs that the elenchus can bring to light.[13]

Vlastos asked why Socrates could claim, as he does in the *Gorgias*, that the outcome of his elenctic arguments was not simply a demonstration of the interlocutor's inconsistency but also an endorsement of Socrates' counterproposal (for instance, that doing injustice is worse than suffering it). The answer, Vlastos proposed, requires a twofold assumption: first, that any set of entirely consistent beliefs must be true; second, and still more important, that whoever has a false moral belief will always have at the same time true beliefs entailing the negation of that false belief. Socrates finds that his own moral beliefs, because their consistency has been exhaustively tested, satisfy the first assumption; and in the elenchus he elicits from his interlocutor *latent* but true moral beliefs that are found to cohere with Socrates' own judgments.

Vlastos' interpretation of the Socratic elenchus in Plato's *Gorgias* is controversial.[14] What matters for my purpose is not its exegetical correctness as regards interpretation of the Platonic Socrates, but its affinity to Epictetus' methodology. As a Stoic philosopher, he takes himself to have a set of true moral beliefs which he can employ as premises, and he appeals to his interlocutors' innate preconceptions as resources equipping them to endorse those beliefs and thereby recognize the inconsistency infecting the particular desires and judgments with which they started. In Epictetus, innate preconceptions play a role very similar to the role of latent but true beliefs in Vlastos' interpretation of elenctic argument in Plato's *Gorgias*.[15]

The criterial role and natural origin of preconceptions goes back to early Stoicism, but Epictetus was probably unique in making them equivalent to an *innate* moral sense. Platonism has previously been suggested as an influence on him, and that may be so in part; but Epictetus is not invoking Plato's fully fledged theory that a learner *after* birth can *recollect* prenatal acquaintance with everlasting truths. The Plato that interests Epictetus is the author of what we today call the Socratic dialogues.

Early in this chapter I noted the importance Epictetus attaches to the Socratic injunction on the worthlessness of living an unexamined life. Both in Plato and in Epictetus elenctic discussion is a methodology that gets its participants to examine their beliefs by exposing unrecognized inconsistencies and involuntary ignorance. Plato's Socrates regularly asks his opinionated interlocutors to answer questions about what some moral concept (piety or courage, for instance) is, with a view to subjecting their responses to elenctic examination.

Epictetus follows suit. He characterizes Socrates as the person who said that the beginning of education is the scrutiny of terms (1.17.12), and in hyperbolical but authentically Socratic style he labels anyone who fails to know what basic values are as going around deaf and blind, thinking he is someone when he is nothing (2.24.19). More particularly, he connects the standard Socratic question "What is X?" with his own diagnosis of the way people typically err: by heedlessly applying their preconceptions to particular instances (4.1.41; cf. 2.11, quoted earlier):

This . . . is the cause of everyone's miseries. We differ in our opinions. One person thinks he is sick; no way, but he is not applying his preconceptions. Another thinks he is a pauper, another that he has a harsh mother or father, and another that Caesar is not gracious to him. This is one thing only – ignorance of how to apply preconceptions. For who does not have a preconception of badness, that it is harmful, to be avoided, to be banished in every way? (4.1.42–43)

Epictetus repeats his point that preconceptions themselves do not conflict with one another, and proceeds:

What, then, is this bad thing that is harmful and to be avoided? A person says he is not Caesar's friend.[16] He has gone off the right track, missed the right application, he is ailing. He is seeking what has nothing to do with the matter in hand. Because if he succeeds in being Caesar's friend, he has no less failed in his quest. For what is it that every person is seeking? To be serene, to be happy, to do everything as he wants, not to be impeded or constrained. So when someone becomes Caesar's friend, has he ceased to be impeded or constrained? Is he serene and flourishing? (4.1.45–46)

We are now in a position to see that Epictetus does not simply parrot the Socratic elenchus but adapts it to his own didactic purposes, assisted by his special concept of universal and innate preconceptions. He may, as I noted in his refutation of the would-be loving father, use interpersonal dialogue that exactly mimics the procedures and goals of Socratic dialectic, and he offers his students a lesson in how to practice that, as we shall see. But his preferred procedure in his intimate dealings with students is to show them how to practice the elenchus on themselves by giving them such examples as the one preceding rather than engaging them directly in dialogue. In just the same way, he urges them to interrogate their own impressions of particular things: "For just as Socrates used to say we should not live an unexamined life, so we should not accept an unexamined impression, but should say: 'Wait, let me see who you are and where you are coming from. . . . Do you have your guarantee from nature, which every impression that is to be accepted should have?" (3.12.15). Epictetus repeatedly expresses his cardinal rule of life in the formula: "making correct use of impressions."[17] That formula and the model of the mind to which it belongs are neither Socratic nor Platonic. However, the material I have discussed here shows that Epictetus had an extraordinarily precise understanding of the methodology and goals of the Socratic elenchus. His main departure from Plato's Socratic practice was in training his students to engage in dialogue with their individual selves and to use this as their principal instrument of moral progress.

A LESSON IN THE USE AND ABUSE OF SOCRATIC DIALECTIC

Some of Epictetus' students had the ambition to become professional teachers of Stoicism. For their benefit he delivered a fascinating discourse on how to engage in discussion with a lay person (2.12). This provides a further perspective on his interpretation of the Socratic paradigm in general and the Socratic elenchus in particular.

Our Stoic authorities have been quite precise in specifying the knowledge necessary for engaging in discussion; but we are quite untrained in our proper application of it. Give any of us a layman as our interlocutor, and we are at a loss in dealing with that person. Having stirred him a little ... we are unable to handle him further, and either we abuse him or mock him, saying:
He's a layman; it's impossible to deal with him.
Yet, when a real guide finds someone going astray, he leads him to the right path instead of mocking or abusing him and going away. You yourself, then, should show him the truth, and you will see that he does follow; but as long as you don't show him, don't mock him, but rather be aware of your own incapacity.
How did Socrates act?
He made a habit of compelling his interlocutor to be his witness, and did not need another witness ... [Epictetus refers to *Gorgias* 474a] because he exposed the implications of that person's concepts [*ennoiai*] so clearly that whoever it was became aware of his inconsistency and gave it up....[18]
Socrates did not say: "Define malice for me," and then, when it had been defined, respond with the words: "A bad definition – for the *definiens* [definition] is not extensionally equivalent to the *definiendum*."[19] Laymen find such technical jargon tiresome and difficult, but *we* can't give it up. Yet, we are quite unable to stir them when we do use terms that enable them, by focusing on their own impressions, to respond yes or no. Understandably, then, at least those of us who are cautious, recognize our inability and give up the matter. But when the impatient ones, who are more numerous, are involved in it, they get flustered and cause fluster, and finally walk away, after an exchange of abuse.
The first and chief thing about Socrates was that he never got worked up in a discussion, never uttered anything abusive or aggressive, but put up with others' abuse.... What then? Well, nowadays the thing isn't very safe, especially in Rome. (2.12.1–17)

Epictetus explains that any current practitioner of Socratic dialectic "had clearly better not do it in a corner."[20] Rather:

He needs to approach a wealthy man of consular rank, as it might be, and ask him [such typical Socratic questions as]:
I say, can you tell me to whom you have entrusted your horses? – I can.
To some random person unacquainted with horsemanship? – Certainly not.
And to whom have you entrusted your gold or your silver or your clothes? – Again, not to just anyone.

Have you already thought of entrusting your own body to someone, to look after it? – Of course.

Presumably to somone experienced in physical training or medicine? – Yes.

Are these your chief possessions, or do you have something else superior to all of them? – What sort of thing do you mean?

That which uses them, for heaven's sake, and judges and deliberates each thing. – You mean the soul, I suppose?

Correct; that's just what I mean.

For heaven's sake, I regard this as far superior to the rest of my possessions.

Can you say, then, in what way you have cared for your soul? For it's not likely that as wise and politically prominent a man as you should carelessly and randomly let your chief possession be neglected and ruined? – Certainly not.

But have you yourself cared for it? Did you learn to do so from someone, or did you discover that by yourself?

So now there's the danger that, first, he will say:

What business is it of yours, my fine fellow? Are you my master?

And then, if you persist in bothering him, he may raise his hand and box your ears. There was a time when I myself was very keen on this activity, before I fell into my present situation. (2.12.17–25)

What are we to make of this discourse? Is it a recommendation to imitate Socrates or the reverse? Is the conclusion an honest confession of Epictetus' own shortcomings as a discussant with a lay person? How are we to interpret the praise of Socrates for his effectiveness in using ordinary language, the remark that we can't dispense with technical terms, and the injunction about having to engage a prominent person out in the open?

The answer to all of these questions, I believe, requires us to interpret the entire text as a lesson to the students in how to apply, or rather how *not* to apply, the Socratic elenchus in the everyday world of their own time.

As regards the statement, we can't dispense with technical terms, Jonathan Barnes has proposed that Epictetus is criticizing his fellow Stoics for their penchant for jargon: he is not beating his own breast; the first-person plural indicates a polite complicity rather than an honest confession.[21] I am sure this is right. But if Epictetus is recommending that his students imitate Socrates' use of ordinary language, what does he expect them to make of his parody of Socratic questions in the conversation with the prominent Roman, the angry response it evokes, and his apparent admission of such an encounter's applicability to his youthful self at Rome?

Maybe Epictetus did have such a cautionary experience before his exile under Domitian's collective expulsion of philosophers in A.D. 95, but

I take him in any case to be saying: try to converse with your interlocutors on their own ground, and even in your use of Socratically leading questions, be careful not to proceed in a peremptory manner that will simply antagonize them. The advice to engage a big official is almost certainly ironical. That is to say, Epictetus is telling his students that they shouldn't try to outdo Socrates or worry about Callicles' taunt of Socrates for preferring conversation with young men to engaging in politics. We should think of Epictetus as recommending his students to use discourse that is appropriate to their interlocutor's mind-set and social status.

Readers of Plato are familiar with the way Socrates' dialectical style changes in relation to his discussants; the *Gorgias*, as it moves from Gorgias to Polus to Callicles, is a prime example. Similarly we find Epictetus varying his dialectic in relation to the age and background of the individuals he talks to. When he meets Maximus (3.7), an administrator and an Epicurean, he converses with him, as one philosopher to another, and does not avoid technicalities. In contrast, when a rhetorician on his way to Rome for a lawsuit consults him about his business (3.9), he informs the man at the beginning of their conversation that the kind of advice he is qualified to offer him cannot be provided in a brief encounter.

Here we observe Epictetus drawing on the Platonic idea of dialectic as a cooperative undertaking, wherein the questioner or philosopher no less than the respondent submits his judgments to examination. Viewed in the light of this passage, the mock questioning of the prominent Roman was bound to fail because the conversation lacked the give-and-take and the mutual respect and encouragement of a properly Socratic encounter.

SELF-EXAMINATION AND SELF-DISCOVERY

It is misleading to call Epictetus' discourses diatribes or sermons, as is frequently done. These labels treat his pithy anecdotes, vivid and abrupt sentences, hyperbole, and exhortation as if they were the core and goal of his didactic style. Although Epictetus constantly uses these devices, his purpose in doing so is a rhetorical instrument of his fundamental project. That is to get his students to see for themselves, first, that they potentially have all the resources they need for a good and fulfilling life and, second, that their own reasoning, self-scrutiny, and discipline are necessary to activate these resources.

Every discourse has this probative purpose. The proofs rarely have a strict logical form, but they contain at least implicit premises and explicit conclusions. Their cogency is dialectical rather than formal. What I mean is that the discourses are addressed to individuals under the condition that they want to live lives free from frustration and emotional disquiet. Epictetus does not think that his arguments can be effective universally or in the abstract. He presupposes that he is addressing people who want to live free from error and distress. His proofs are conditional on these wants. They are not addressed to persons who choose to live, in his stark apostrophe, as slaves.

By his time, Stoicism had become a highly scholastic system. Stoic philosophers were notorious for their interest in logical paradoxes, and their ethics and physics involved numerous fine distinctions with their own technical terminology. Epictetus does not object to these refinements, but he does not deal with them in the surviving discourses. The reason, as he constantly explains, is that such technicalities should be the province of very advanced students. His own chief concern is with what he calls the first topic of philosophy – desires and aversions – which has as its goal to ensure that a person does not fail in his desires or have experiences he does not want (3.2.1). His focus on Socrates is a very strong sign of his determination to return Stoicism to its primary goal of radically reshaping people's values and goals.

Epictetus' warnings against confusing scholastic learning with genuine philosophical progress can give the impression that he disparages logical expertise or careful argument. Against this, it is only necessary to read 1.17. Here he justifies the criterial and critical functions of logic by appealing not only to the old Stoic authorities but also, by reference, to Socrates, who insisted on beginning with the examination of words and asking what each means (1.17.12). The logic that Epictetus regards as fundamental is any normal person's capacity to reflect on the grounds and consistency of his individual beliefs and desires and motivations. This explains why he largely avoids the technical terms of traditional Stoicism. He does not expound doctrines that are expressed in these ways. Instead, as he urges in the dialectical lesson of 2.12, he tries to engage his audience by means of everyday terms such as desire, purpose, freedom, and happiness, with a minimal reference to esoteric theory.

His discourses are dialogical lessons – invitations to his audience to examine themselves by thinking about these everyday terms and comparing what they take them to mean with the proposals Epictetus offers himself. Thus, he takes it to be self-evident that people want their desires to be fulfilled. Yet, their actual desires are frequently frustrated and consequently cause them distress. The problem here, he suggests, is not in wanting a desire to be fulfilled; human beings naturally seek the fufillment of their desires. Accordingly, the remedy for frustration is to focus one's desires exclusively within the mental domain, where success can be assured.

There is much more to Epictetus' reflection of Socrates than I have treated in this chapter. Socrates' imprint is present on almost every page of the discourses; for, apart from appropriating and adapting Socratic methodology, Epictetus constantly mentions the exemplary moments of Socrates' behavior at and after his trial. In addition, he likes to idealize and update Socrates by insisting, against the historical record, that Socrates was a great family man (3.26.23) and even a model of cleanliness (4.9.19). In the *Manual*, Arrian appeals to Socrates in citing two of Epictetus' constant themes: judgments, not things, are what disturb people (*Encheiridon* 5); and the imperative never to relax attention to one's reason (*Encheiridon* 51).

In view of all this, it is curious that scholars have hitherto paid so little attention to the Socratic paradigm in Epictetus. One reason must be the authority exercised by the books of Adolf Bonhöffer, where Epictetus is presented as an orthodox Stoic through and through with little attention given to the style of the discourses.[22] Another reason is the fact that the discourses, for the most part, are very different from the Socratic conversations composed by Plato and Xenophon, which involve a cast of distinct and clearly drawn characters. A third reason, deeper than either of these, could be the perception that Epictetus cannot be authentically Socratic because he does not repeatedly declare his own ignorance or engage in apparently open-ended exploration of ethical questions.

Actually, however, Epictetus is consistently reticent and self-deprecating about his own competence and identity as a philosopher. I have also referred to his insistence on puzzlement and confession of ignorance from any really promising student. Like Plato's Socrates, he professes no interest in speculation about the exact details of the physical world.[23] Whether Plato's Socratic dialogues are as open-ended as some of them appear to be on the surface, and whether his Socrates is quite sincere or unqualified in his confessions of ignorance – these are matters of scholarly controversy. Even if we opt for the first alternative in responding to both questions, we cannot obscure the fact that Plato's Socrates, even in the so-called Socratic dialogues, strenuously argues for such doctrines as those I set out when outlining the *Gorgias*.

Epictetus was obviously aware that Stoicism, however much it was prefigured by Socrates, was a subsequent development. Under his Stoic identity he presents himself as a pedagogue with a range of definite lessons to teach his students. Given his time and place, as a Greco-Roman philosopher training Greco-Roman youths, Epictetus had to adapt the Socratic paradigm to some extent. And so his Socrates, like himself, is a paternalist rather than a pederastic mentor, which would not have suited the mores of his day. What we are left with, when all due qualifications are made, is the most creative appropriation of Socrates subsequent to the works of Plato and Xenophon.

Notes

1. For the influence of Socrates on Stoicism, see Long 1988 and Sedley 1993, and chapters in van der Waerdt 1994. Socrates' importance to Epictetus is barely mentioned in the classic works by A. Bonhöffer (see note 22). Studies that deal with it in some detail include Döring 1979 and Gourinat 2001, whose article includes reference to my present paper.

2. Zeno is the only Stoic who is attested to have written a work entitled *Elenchoi* (Diogenes Laertius 7.4), and no form of the word occurs in the surviving fragments of Chrysippus or other Stoics. They did include in their dialectic knowledge of how to discourse correctly on arguments in question and answer form (see Long 1996: 87), as Epictetus himself acknowledges (1.7.3); but by their time this specification had become too standard to allude specifically to Socratic discussion. As for irony, it was officially excluded from the sage's character (whose virtues include irrefutability [*anelenxia*]) and treated as a mark of inferior persons (*SVF* 3:630).

3. It has been suggested to me that Epictetus was probably influenced by his teacher Musonius. Maybe. But in the record of Musonius' discourses the allusions to Socrates are commonplace and do not in the least recall Socratic dialectic.

4. See Jagu 1946: 161–65.

5. The text continues: "either those who are blessed with leisure or those who are too stupid to calculate logical consequences." With some hesitation, I suggest that the first group refers to the likes of Plato, who as a literal writer of dialogue understands the progression of the arguments he records, and the second group to people who merely parrot the form of Platonic dialogues. Epictetus may well be alluding to Socrates' definition of solitary thinking as "writing in one's soul" (*Philebus* 39a). Special thanks to David Sedley for advice on this passage.

6. As a further allusion to the *Gorgias*, I note 4.1.128 where, in reminiscence of Socrates at 506c, Epictetus formally reviews the premises to which his imaginary interlocutor has agreed.

7. Epictetus paraphrases *Gorgias* 474a.

8. At 3.21.19 Epictetus says that Socrates was appointed by God to hold the elenctic position. For further discussion of this passage and for Epictetus' association of elenctic with protreptic, see Long 2002: 54–57.

9. See Long 2002: 98–104.

10. Medea was one of the Stoics' favorite mythological paradigms for a noble nature gone wrong: see Gill 1983. Epictetus refers to her again at 2.17.19 and 4.13.15. The lines he cites here are from Euripides, *Medea* 1079–80.

11. Throughout Epictetus' refutation, he is careful to describe the father's wrongly chosen act by the expression "what seemed good to you" (*hoti edoxen soi*). Thus he explicitly registers Socrates' fundamental distinction in the *Gorgias* (see proposition F) between doing what one thinks (perhaps mistakenly) will bring about one's good (the universal human desideratum) and doing what one "wants" (getting that desideratum).

12. The classic study of Stoic concepts (*ennoiai*) and preconceptions (*prolēpseis*) is F. H. Sandbach, in Long 1971: 22–37, who argues for Epictetus' novelty in treating the latter as 'innate' ideas in the moral domain. Epictetus devotes an entire discourse (1.22) to preconceptions; see also 2.17.

13. See Vlastos 1991: ch. 4, and Vlastos 1994: ch. 1.

14. See Benson 1995.

15. After first proposing affinity between Vlastos' and Epictetus' Socrates, I subsequently discovered that in late Platonism the role I assign to innate preconceptions in Epictetus' adaptation of the Socratic elenchus is played by common notions (*koinai ennoiai*). Olympiodorus, in his commentary on Plato's *Gorgias*, describes common conceptions (from which all demonstrative proof should start) as including God-given foundations for acting rightly (Olympiodorus 1970: 51). According to Olympiodorus, Socrates refutes Gorgias by showing that Gorgias' admission that an orator may do wrong is inconsistent with Gorgias' endorsement of the common notion that an orator knows what is right (63). Tarrant 2000: 116–17 finds that "[w]hile Olympiodorus has actually anticipated many of Vlastos' claims about Socrates' arguments, in particular about the presence of true moral beliefs residing within questioner and interlocutor, he explains this with reference to one's awareness (conscious or unconscious) of common notions."

16. On the semiofficial status of being Caesar's friend, see Millar 1977: 110–22. Epictetus satirizes the danger and enslavement it might involve at 4.1.47–50.

17. See 1.1.7; 1.3.4; 1.6.13; 1.7.33; 1.12.34; 1.20.15, with discussion in Long 1996: ch. 12, 275–82.

18. Here Epictetus engages in a made-up example of Socratic dialogue, to illustrate how to expose a person's contradictory beliefs about malice (*phthonos*). The text is too condensed to make the argument thoroughly clear. I conjecture that it should have the following structure:

    The interlocutor starts by taking malice to be pleasure taken in someone else's misfortunes (cf. Plato, *Philebus* 48c). Under challenge, he accepts that malice is a painful emotion, contradicting his initial claim. He then agrees that it cannot be a pain aroused by others' misfortunes. So he is prompted to redefine malice as pain taken in someone else's good fortunes (cf. *SVF* 1:434), a complete reversal of his starting point.

19. I draw on Barnes 1997: 29, for this skillful translation of Epictetus' logical jargon.

20. See Plato, *Gorgias* 485d, where Callicles charges Socrates with "twittering in a corner with three or four young men."
21. Barnes 1997: 29.
22. Bonhöffer 1890 and 1894.
23. Fr. 1, cited by Stobaeus (1974: 2:13–14. For discussion of this text, see Long 2002: 149–52.

2

The Stoics on the Voluntariness of the Passions

Steven K. Strange

One of the most characteristic and, to the contemporary mind at least, bizarre theses of orthodox Chrysippean Stoicism is its insistence on the wholly rational character of the human mind or soul. The whole of the soul, or at least the whole of the *hēgemonikon* or "leading part" of the soul, is said to be reason (*logos*): there are no irrational parts or powers within the soul, no independent sources or faculties of emotion or nonrational desire, and all cases of apparent irrationality are supposed to be referred to the operations of thought itself (*dianoia*, another name for the mind). This seems to fly in the face of much of what we assume or feel sure we know about human psychology: not only do modern psychological theories tend to stress the role of irrational or subrational factors in human motivation, but we seem to be clearly aware in ourselves of major nonrational or irrational aspects of our own behavior and thought processes. Thus when confronted with Stoic claims such as that all emotions and desires are really just judgments or beliefs, or that passions or emotions are unnatural conditions that ought to be extirpated, we find these not only hard to swallow but difficult and nearly impossible even to grasp. However, there is nothing about this sort of difficulty with Stoicism that is specifically modern. Every major theory of moral psychology since the Hellenistic period has taken for granted the originally Platonic-Aristotelian separation of reason from the passions against which the strict rationalism or intellectualism of the Stoics was a reaction: I need only mention such examples as Plotinus, Augustine, Aquinas, Hume, and Kant. Indeed, this held true even during the brief but important revival in popularity of Stoic moral thinking in the seventeenth century: both Descartes and Spinoza, each in his own way quite sympathetic to Stoicism in ethics, accept in some form the standard division of passive affections of the soul from active judgments. No doubt the dominance of this distinction between reason and the passions in the history of philosophy contributes to our feeling that it is just philosophical common sense, as well as to the perceived uncongeniality of the Stoic view and our failure to comprehend it.

But even though later philosophy, as well as historical common sense, seems to have wholly rejected this part of the Stoic view, at least one aspect of it has continued to be deeply influential, the part of it that concerns responsibility and the human capacity for moral choice. We have a concept of the will as a faculty of choice or of deciding to perform or not to perform certain actions. Such a concept in fact represents a rather late development in the history of philosophy, and its origins remain obscure.[1] It is well known that the standard Latin term for the will, *voluntas*, was originally just the Latin translation of the Greek term *boulēsis* or (as I shall be rendering it) "wish," translated this way by Cicero in his discussion of the Stoic theory of the emotions in the *Tusculan Disputations* (4.12), and taken over from Cicero by Seneca and later writers, such as Lactantius.

The Stoics, of course, did not invent the term *boulēsis*: it is used by Plato, among other places, in the fourth book of the *Republic* to designate the kind of desire proper to the rational part of the soul, that is, desire for the good, as contrasted to *thumos* or spirit, desire for respect, fame, and more generally one's personal interests, and *epithumia* or bodily appetites, paradigmatically the desires for food, drink, and sex and their associated pleasures. Aristotle uses the term *boulēsis* in the same way as Plato, as the desire (*orexis*) for the good, in his *Ethics* and in the *De Anima*. In both Plato and Aristotle, wish is a function of the rational part of the soul, not of the nonrational or "lower" parts – which by the way indicates that Platonic-Aristotelian moral psychology is itself perhaps not as familiar or commonsensical (by our lights) as we might at first have supposed: the separation between the rational and nonrational soul in Plato and Aristotle is not the, for us, expected distinction between pure thought or belief on one side and feelings and desires on the other, because wish, which belongs essentially to the rational part of the soul, counts as a type of desire.

The concept of wish or *boulēsis* in Stoic moral psychology has affinities with that in Plato and Aristotle, and indeed they probably took over the use of the term from the Old Academy, while adapting it for their own use. *Boulēsis* for the Stoics is defined as reasonable desire or pursuit (*eulogos orexis*),[2] reasonable because it is desire that aims at what is in fact good

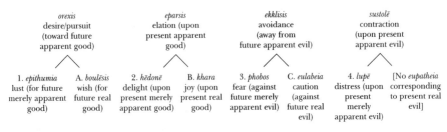

(1)–(4) are passions (*pathē*)

(A)–(C) are rational affections (*eupatheiai*). No *eupatheia* corresponds to the passion of distress or *lupē*.

FIGURE 1. Psychological responses to perceived good or evil

and is not merely apparently so. As such, wish belongs to the class of the *eupatheiai* or "rational affections" in Stoic theory – that is, it is one of the emotions or analogues of emotion that are possessed solely by the sage or wise person, which in his case have come to replace the normal passions or *pathē*, which according to the Stoics are diseased conditions of the vicious soul, and which they insist on calling by separate names to bring out the crucial difference between the two kinds (see Figure 1). It is nevertheless a species of the same genus, pursuit or desire (*orexis*), as *epithumia* or lust, bad or irrational desire (which aim at things that seem to be good but are not). Wish, as opposed to will, is thus a kind of desire, not a faculty, and has no obvious connection with the notion of choice; moreover, it is by definition aimed at the genuine good, so that the idea of a *bad* wish or will makes no sense. Indeed, it is only possessed by the fully morally good person: a bad person cannot be said to have *boulēsis*.[3] As far as I am aware, it seems to be Saint Augustine, in his *De Libero Arbitrio*, who first clearly introduces the notion of a bad *voluntas* – but even Augustine's bad *voluntas* is aimed at things, namely earthly or corporeal goods, that are good considered in themselves, just not good for the spiritual beings that he considers us to be. Augustine, even if he does not – as some might want to suggest – create the modern notion of the will, is a much less remote ancestor of it than are the Stoics. (Yet his notion of *voluntas* seems to owe something to the Stoic conception of *boulēsis*, as well as to Plato's and Aristotle's.)

The Stoic notion of *boulēsis* thus lies fairly far from its descendant, the later and familiar notion of the will. The specific contribution of Stoic moral psychology to the history of the notion of moral choice does not seem, therefore, to lie in the term used for its faculty. Of greater importance here is the Stoic conception of what makes someone's action, or someone's emotion or desire, voluntary or a locus of responsibility, so that it may be evaluated in terms of praise or blame. The key notion here is that of assent (*sunkatathesis*), which Cicero, usually eager to play down Stoic originality and to portray the Stoics as mere deviationists from the Old Academy, identified as one of Zeno's most important innovations in philosophy.[4] Assent is the acceptance of a proposition (*axiōma*) presented to us in experience or thought as the content of a *phantasia* or impression and as being true: assenting to such a proposition is what we would call an act of judgment.[5] According to the Stoic view, it is primarily assent that is "in our power" or "up to us" (*eph' hēmin*), and it is only because this lies in our control that anything at all does. So if we are responsible for any of our actions, for any of our desires, or for any of our passions or emotions, it is because these all depend upon our capacity to give or withhold our assent in particular cases. Similarly, if we are to bear any responsibility for our own moral character, this too will be due to our capacity for assent. But responsibility for desires and emotions is primary here, for our actions and our moral character are functions of them, of what we want and how we respond to the world. And our desires, in a fairly clear sense, just *are* emotions, for the Stoics, for they are the impulses to pursue or avoid, to accept or reject, certain objects (technically, certain prospective or actual properties applying to ourselves) as being respectively good or bad. Therefore, according to the Stoics, they are also immediately dependent on our value judgments and views about the good. So, in the end, everything will depend on what we take to be good and evil.

Of course, what we *should* take to be good or evil according to Stoicism – as is well known to anyone even minimally acquainted with the tenets of Stoic ethics – is only our own moral condition, our own virtue and vice, respectively. This is the attitude to the world adopted by the Stoic sage or *sophos*, which she has attained through the excellence of her understanding of the cosmos and her place in it, due to the perfection of her reason and proper *oikeiōsis* or accommodation to the world. Ordinary people such as we are, however, as the Stoics were aware, do not look upon the world and the good and evil in it in this way, and seemingly cannot help taking things such as pleasure and pain, health and sickness, wealth and poverty, the life and death of themselves and loved ones as good and evil, respectively. They cannot help, it seems, being grieved at the death of a friend, or elated at the success of whatever enterprise they may have been engaged in. It seems to us not only natural but inevitable that human beings should have such feelings. Yet the Stoics want to insist that we *can*, in principle, avoid experiencing such feelings, and that because they are bad and harmful to ourselves (as well as to others), and are impediments to our happiness and freedom, that we should and must strive to and learn to avoid feeling them.

Now, even if we might be inclined to concede the first of these claims, the great majority of us would surely, at least initially, strongly resist the second, namely that we would be much better off with all of our passions extirpated. I do not propose to defend this thesis here, although it is well worth reflecting upon in the course of a close and careful study of Epictetus' *Discourses* or Seneca's *Letters*. My concern is rather with the first claim, that passions are voluntary and that we therefore can in principle learn to avoid having them. This seems generally taken to be a rather straightforward if paradoxical claim on the part of the Stoics. However, it seems to me to be very closely bound up, in interesting ways, with the rationalism and monism of their moral psychology and to merit closer discussion for this reason. Moreover, I think consideration of their views about this can throw some interesting light on the general Stoic conception of responsibility and the nature of their compatibilism (by which I mean the compatibilism of Chrysippus). Perhaps the discussion might even throw some light on the antecedents of the original notion of the will.

THE PASSIONS AS *HORMAI PLEONAZOUSAI* AND STOIC INTELLECTUALISM

We first need to go over some ground that has already been well covered in recent studies, namely the basic outline of the Stoics' conception of the emotions within the general context of their philosophy of action.[6] It is important to remind ourselves of the details in order not to be misled by the oddity of Stoic moral psychology into drawing false analogies with more familiar theories. I cannot deal in detail with all controversial points, so I restrict myself to a few crucial observations. My main focus is the passions or *pathē* that are experienced by ordinary people, that is, "fools" or nonsages; but we need to compare these with the *eupatheiai* or rational affections of the good person or sage. In genus, both passions and rational affections in human beings (rational animals) are the proper motions (*kinēseis*) of the mind or *hēgemonikon*, that is, impulses (*hormai*),[7] intentional motions of the soul, that is, of thought (*dianoia*), toward or away from some object (again, technically, toward or away from some predicate or *katēgorēma* taken as worthy of being sought or avoided – crudely, practical evaluative predicates that may (right away) or do (now) affect the evaluating subject. *Hormai*, the intentional motions of the soul, are not dispositional states of desire or aversion, but actual occurrent motions of the soul toward or away from prospective or actual valued or disvalued objects. The theory can countenance dispositional desiderative states as *tendencies* to pursue or avoid certain kinds of objects,[8] but *hormai* themselves are always actual movements occasioned by the (also actual) positive or negative evaluation of some practical property.

The *summa genera* of passions are four (lust or appetite, fear, delight, and distress), depending on whether the associated object is present or prospective, and conceived as good or bad, with three *summa genera* of rational affections (wish, caution, and joy – there is no rational affection having as its object a present evil, briefly because the only real evil is vice, which can never be present for a sage) (see Figure 1). Passions differ from these latter, fully rational *hormai* in being *disturbances* of the soul: they are referred to by Stobaeus' source (*SVF* 3:378) as "flutterings" (*ptoiai*), and a similar thought may lie behind Cicero's somewhat misleading translation in the *Tusculan Disputations* of *pathos* by *perturbatio* and *commotio*.[9] We may thus think of them as analogous to the disorderly and disturbing motions of soul that have been eliminated in the competing Epicurean ideal of *ataraxia*. The usual Stoic term for the analogous state, attained by their sage, is *apatheia* or absence of passion. ("Dispassionateness" is perhaps the best available translation.) The sage experiences instead of passions the calm or orderly motions of the soul that are the *eupatheiai* (which are still a type of *hormai*).

Connected with the notion of passions as disturbances within the soul is Zeno's description of them as irrational and excessive impulses. According to Diogenes Laertius (7.110; cf. Cicero, *Tusculan Disputations* 4.11), Zeno defined passion as an irrational or unnatural motion of the soul, and as a *hormē pleonazousa*, an "excessive impulse," one that goes beyond the bounds or reason.[10] It appears from the parallel with the Cicero passage that "going beyond the bounds" here means turning away from (or, elsewhere, disobeying) "right" or correct reason.[11] This is captured in Chrysippus' famous comparison of a walking person, who is able to stop moving immediately any time he wants, with a runner, who is unable to stop himself right away. This disobedient violation of the appropriate bounds set by reason for the relevant motion of the soul is presumably the same as the "certain voluntary intemperance" that Cicero says Zeno declared to be the mother of all emotions (i.e., passions, *Academica* 1.39). Passions represent disturbances in the soul – more precisely, in the soul's *hēgemonikon* or controlling part – precisely because they exceed rational bounds. For the soul's *hēgemonikon* is the mind or thought (*dianoia*), and a disturbance in it is a disturbance of its rationality. We can come to see this by reflecting on what is meant by the Stoic talk of a "motion of the soul." The Stoics, of course, do not conceive of the soul as an immaterial entity: the soul, and in particular the *hēgemonikon* or controlling portion of the soul, which is also the mind (*dianoia*), is a bit of *pneuma*, a mixture of corporeal air and fire that is concentrated about the main organ of the body, which for the Stoics is the heart.

So the motion of the soul, under one aspect, is a literal movement within this *pneuma*, which is itself a part of the active element in the universe, which the Stoics identify with Zeus or God. Under another aspect, the motion of the soul is intentional: in the case of appetite and fear, it is a movement of thought toward what is judged to be an apparently good object, or away from an apparently bad one. These movements are also called desire or pursuit (*orexis*) and aversion (*ekklisis*). In the case of delight or pleasure and distress, where the material movement corresponding to the passion is an actual physical swelling (elation, *eparsis*) or contraction (*sustolē*) of the soul, presumably again to be considered as the region of *pneuma* around the heart, the intentional aspect is an opinion (*doxa*) about the presence of some good or evil object. So while *hormē* quite literally is a motion in the *pneuma* constituting the *hēgemonikon* either outward, toward something that is desired or welcomed, or away from something unwanted or rejected, it is also at the same time a movement of thought, as I said earlier. These two aspects of the movement which is the *hormē*, the literal, spatial movement toward the object, and the intentional movement of thought, are not in any way separate: they are quite literally two ways of looking at the very same phenomenon – from the outside and from the inside, as it were, from the third-person and from the first-person perspective, respectively.

Note that passions have been defined not only as pursuits and avoidances but as out-of-bounds *impulses* (*hormai*).[12] This applies in the first instance to lust and fear (corresponding to the *eupatheiai* wish and caution), which are the primary forms of passion: delight and distress (and joy) are said to supervene (*epigignesthai*) on these,[13] perhaps as the results of satisfaction of lust (or, respectively, wish) or its opposite. Officially, *orexeis* and *ekkliseis* are species of *hormai* (or, respectively, *aphormai*), impulses: strictly, they are impulses toward actual, occurrent pursuits and avoidances of immediately available objects, as opposed to ones expected to be pursued or avoided in the future.[14] Most discussions naturally focus on the case of *orexis* or desire (or, sometimes, *ekklisis* or avoidance), though presumably one could also have an excessive (or, respectively, nonexcessive and fully rational) occurrent impulse toward the object of some future plan – for example, that one will be prepared to do whatever is necessary when one reaches the age of thirty-five to become president of the United States. Some notion of moral evaluation of future plan or intention, if that is what *orousis* is, would seem to be required, as Inwood notes, and *orousis* will clearly also be "up to us." Nonrational animals also have impulses, but in this discussion we are only concerned with rational impulses, that is, the impulses of rational animals, all of which are either actual or future pursuits (or avoidances) on the basis of judgments.

I have focused so far on the standard Old Stoic definitions given in our texts of passions as motions, that is, impulses of soul, and have brought in the intentional element, and the element of judgment, as consequent upon this – though, as I have stressed, these should not be seen as two separable aspects of the phenomenon but two ways of looking at the same thing. Chrysippus, however, notoriously seems to have given definitions of the passions *merely* in terms of judgment (*krisis*) and opinion (*doxa*) – as the judgment, which is also an opinion, that there is a good or evil in the offing, or now present, which good or evil is of a certain particular sort – without making a reference to motion or impulse a part of this definition. For this he was notoriously criticized by Galen, who accused him of contradicting the Zenonian definitions of passions in terms of the soul's motion or *hormē*. Galen probably is following Posidonius on this point, because it appears from some of the evidence in Galen's *Doctrines of Hippocrates and Plato* that Posidonius was concerned not only to refute what he saw as Chrysippus' extreme monistic rationalism in psychology but to claim Stoic orthodoxy for his new, more moderate (and Platonically influenced) moral psychology by arguing that it was more in line with the moral psychology of Zeno and Cleanthes,[15] the canonical founders of Stoicism, than was Chrysippus' own. (To what extent Posidonius' alternative, less rationalistic moral psychology might have also involved a rejection of psychological monism is a question I wish to leave to one side.)[16]

I agree with the those scholars who argue that this criticism of Chrysippus' definitions is not well grounded. For one thing, it is clear from Galen's evidence that Chrysippus attempted to defend Zeno's definitions in terms of his own. This sort of phenomenon is not unknown elsewhere in Stoicism. Every important Stoic tried to give his own individual definition of the *telos* or happiness, for instance, but we should not think that in so doing that they meant to imply that Zeno's definitions in terms of consistency (*homologia*) or the well-flowingness of life were to be rejected: rather, they should be seen as expanding and commenting upon Zeno's definitions, the acceptance of which was probably seen as defining orthodoxy, or at least one's adherence to the Stoic school.

It will be clear, I hope, why I do not think that Chrysippus' definitions of the passions in terms of evaluative judgments need conflict with the standard definitions (which he apparently also defended) of passions as excessive impulse and as irrational movements of the soul *caused* by such judgments. For one thing, the two sorts of definitions are often found together (e.g., at Pseudo-Andronicus, *On Passions*, init.), which is what we should expect, if indeed they are supposed to express the same basic Stoic viewpoint. The judgment, given the Stoics' dual-aspect metaphysics, should also have a physical correlate that is intentionally directed in the same way that it is (one is reminded here of the direct connection made by Aristotle between the intentional experience of fears, confidences, and sexual stimulations and heatings and chillings of the *pneuma* in the body in *De Motu Animalium* 8).[17] The judgment and the motion are conceptually inseparable; besides, if the *hēgemonikon* or controlling part of the soul is just supposed to be thought (*dianoia*), then any motion of it will presumably be a thought. Chrysippus fixes on the judgment as the key element in the phenomenon of emotion because it is the cause of the motion or impulse as effect – necessarily so, because the impulse in the soul is continuous with the visible bodily action (actually reaching for the food, say), and thus is the link that explains how the value judgment manages to cause the action that it is held to motivate (again, we are reminded of the chain of psychic and bodily events that result in the action to be explained in Aristotle's *De Motu Animalium*). And because the judgment is the locus of responsibility, what is "up to us," it is what accounts for why the action itself is voluntary and responsible.

What of the nature of this judgment, which is supposed to constitute the passion? The sources for Chrysippus' moral psychology present a distinction between two moments in the judgment that is cause of a passion, as I have already noted. The subject judges (assents to the impression that) a certain object is good or evil (and that it is either present or in the offing), but also that it is appropriate for one to react to this realization in the way specified, by pursuing or avoiding the prospective object, or contracting or expanding (i.e., feeling elated or depressed) at the thought that one has or has not got it. The hormetic reaction of the passion then follows automatically, once these requisite judgments have been made – the motions are not under *independent* conscious control.

The dual nature of the judgment is particularly clear in the case of delight and distress, where the material movement corresponding to the passion is an actual physical elation or contraction of the soul, which one judges to be appropriate in the circumstances. The link between the two opinions is sometimes expressed merely by specifying that the original evaluative judgment is "recent" or "fresh" (*prosphatos*): this term is apparently intended to account for the transitory and unstable nature of passions, or at least for the fact that they tend to diminish in intensity monotonically over time, even though the person in question has not ceased to believe in the goodness or badness of the object.[18] It seems clear that there was a corresponding secondary moment of judgment in the case of lust and fear as well. This is sometimes expressed by talking of the prospective object being taken to be a very great good or evil, even "the greatest good," so great that one would be justified in taking it to be one's primary or only object of concern (more so than one's virtue or the overall good of the universe, for instance, which are really and in truth what is good). It also appears that there was a similar duality in the judgment that was held to be the cause of desire or *orexis* (i.e., wish as well as lust or appetite), since Galen in *On the Doctrines of Hippocrates and Plato* (4.2.3–4) reports that Chrysippus defined *orexis* as "rational *hormē* [i.e., the *hormē* of a rational animal] to something appropriately pleasant [*hoson khrē hēdon*]," which must mean something *judged* to be appropriately pleasant to pursue.[19] Despite the reference to the pleasant here, the context in Galen seems to make clear that this was Chrysippus' definition of *orexis* as a genus.

The two opinions or judgments are, however, clearly distinguished in direct quotations from Chrysippus, and it seems clear that he stressed that both were in principle under the voluntary control of the agent. For he advocated trying to influence the secondary judgment rather than the primary one sometimes in therapy of passions. The two judgments are logically related, however, in that the second constitutes a further observation on the sort of good or evil that the object of the primary judgment is taken to be.

Once we notice that the rational affections differ from the passions in that their objects actually *are* good, rather than just seeming so, whereas in the case of passions the objects actually *are not* good, although they may seem so, we are entitled to conclude that the upshot of this complicated classification (which is actually a good deal more complex than I have made out) is that the class of Stoic emotions actually *coincides* with the class of what we would call human desires and their respective satisfactions,

and their opposites – that is, with every valued and disvalued experience.
That emotions are at base desires is not an idea that is new with the
Stoics: Aristotle defines emotions in terms of desires, for instance in his
well-known definitions of anger in the *De Anima* and the *Rhetoric*. What
is significant about the Stoic theory is that it allows us to see how *all*
desires – or at least all practical desires, ones capable of being put into
action (for I could desire that some purely theoretical claim be true,
for instance that there be life on Mars)[20] – can be conceived along the
lines of emotions. For all such desires will be either rational or irrational
pursuits or avoidances. Moreover, all actions have such desires as their
motivations. So the scope and role of the emotions and passions in Stoic
theory turn out to be very broad.

THE PASSIONS NOT OPPOSED TO REASON

Now we come to the crucial question of how the Stoics suppose that all
emotions and desires (and thus actions) can be fully under the *control*
of reason (and that they are in fact functions of reason). This, I take
it, is because they are all the direct results of evaluative judgments, and
judgments for the Stoics are acts of assent, which are supposed to be
wholly voluntary, and in fact the primary case of what counts as voluntary.
It is up to me what appearances or impressions (*phantasiai*) I should
accept or reject, at least in doubtful cases. This is *all* that is up to me, but
it is enough.[21]

The point here is not merely that the emotions are "cognitive" – that
is, that they essentially involve judgments. This is true of Aristotle's conception of the emotions as well, as can be seen, for example, from the
definition of anger that he gives in *Rhetoric* 2.2.[22] But one would not wish
to claim that for Aristotle that the emotions in any way *are* the judgments,
as the Stoics claim – despite the fact that for Aristotle, as well as for the
Stoics, they are all by definition types of desire or *orexis*. In Aristotle,
following Plato, emotions and judgments reside in distinct and separate
parts or faculties of the soul, even if emotions are caused or occasioned by
certain judgments – for example, that one has been unjustly or inappro-
priately harmed. On the Stoic view, however, the emotion is a movement
of the soul necessarily consequent upon an evaluative judgment and occurs in one and the same *hēgemonikon* or controlling part of the soul as
the judgment, and there is full continuity between a particular occurrence of a type of evaluative judgment (that a certain future available
object is good or appropriate, say) and the particular resulting motion

(that I pursue it on that occasion: see Cicero's careful explanation of the Zenonian position in *Academica* 1.39). The cause (the particular act of judgment) and effect (the particular pursuit of the object) are always present together, and there are no grounds for separating them.

Plato and Aristotle, on the other hand, thought that emotions (with the exception, at least in Plato, of wish) and reasoning must be separated in the soul. They held this on the basis of the argument that Plato gives in *Republic* 4 (436–39), which is endorsed by Aristotle in *Nicomachean Ethics* 1.13. According to this argument, reason and appetite (alternatively, for Plato at least, spirit and appetite) can oppose one another as faculties, in the sense that one can spur us to pursuit and the other to avoidance of the very same object at the very same time: for example, a particular opportunity to drink that presents itself – appetite, in the form of thirst, spurring us to drink, while reason impels us not to do so. (The pursuit and avoidance in question seem to be conceived as actual movements in the soul, as is suggested by Plato's physical examples of the application of his principle concerning opposites, for example, the case of the archer. In fact, the argument seems to depend on this.) The argument is intended to show that this is only possible if this particular judgment of reason and this particular thirst occur in distinct parts or aspects of the soul.[23] As Plato sees and notes in the passage, the argument can only get off the ground if we assume that thirst is for drink unqualified, not for good drink (438a), but as we have already seen, the Stoics (presumably following Socrates) reject such an assumption: lust for them is precisely for what *seems* good, and not as in the *Republic* for unqualified sorts of objects, or objects *qua* pleasant, even if the reason that a particular object seems good to me on some occasion is the obviously inadequate one that I believe that it would serve to quench my raging thirst, that is, merely that it is a potential drink, irrespective of whether it may be poisoned or otherwise unhealthy. The Stoics have other reasons for rejecting the argument as well, besides this one that is invited by Plato's text itself: the oscillation model, which involves the denial that the opposite movements in the soul appealed to in Plato's argument are really simultaneous,[24] and the insistence that the mental acts labeled by Plato as "pursuit" and "avoidance" may not really be contrary to one another, as assumed by the argument.

It appears to be this same form of argument that Aristotle alludes to in *Nicomachean Ethics* 1.13, when he cites his reason for positing a non-rational element in human moral psychology (1102b16–21). Aristotle makes explicit what is implicit in Plato's presentation of the argument, that the phenomenon appealed to is that of *akrasia* or weakness of will, where notoriously appetite or emotion does appear to go against reason. (Note Aristotle's reference to the opposite *hormai* of the *akratic* and the paralytic: here, as in Stoic terminology, *hormai* would seem to denote, if not actual opposed motions, at least opposed forces operating within the soul. As we have seen, some such opposition seems required by Plato's formulation of the argument, which Aristotle is summarizing here.)

Now, if we mean by *akrasia* or "weakness of will" acting or doing something knowingly or intentionally against one's better judgment, it seems clear, as Engberg-Pederson has argued in his book on *oikeiōsis*,[25] I believe correctly, that for the Stoics the passions are cases of *akrasia* or, more precisely, the classes of passions and cases of *akrasia* are coextensive with one another. The Stoics do not therefore wish to deny the existence of *akrasia*, as has often been maintained – nor could they reasonably have defended the Socratic Paradox, which declares that no one does wrong *willingly*. On the contrary, they wish to maintain that wrong actions and their motivations (i.e., passions) are all voluntary and open to moral evaluation. In this they resemble Aristotle, who likewise holds that *akrasia* is voluntary and blameworthy, and who likewise seems to allow *akrasia* (along with its opposite *enkrateia*) an important role in the formation or modification of character. Passions are genuinely akratic because the *logos* that they are disobediences to is one's own dominant or hegemonic *logos*, not merely the "right reason" which states the objective prescription that applies to the particular situation in which one finds oneself. This is because all rational animals have bestowed on them and continue to possess natural preconceptions about what is good, however confused or inarticulate these may be in the case of an individual person. (*Oikeiōsis*, or anyway proper *oikeiōsis*, involves the process of coming to articulate these preconceptions properly, and to fit them correctly to particular situations.) Thus one will always possess, or at least have available to one, a correct and relevant *doxa* about the good – unless, of course, one has attained sagehood, in which case one will possess *epistēmē* or knowledge about the good.

For the Stoics it is this *doxa* that is overcome by *epithumia* (which is in effect another *doxa*) in the case of *akrasia*, a position that Aristotle explicitly tries to refute. Aristotle holds, at least in the *De Anima*, rather that *akrasia* is *orexis* overcoming *orexis* (3.11), which fits with his general view that desire is the primary cause of action, and that thought is subordinate to it (3.10; *De Motu Animalium*). The focus on the role and function of practical reason in Aristotle's "physical" discussion of *akrasia* in *Nicomachean Ethics*

7.3 is due to it being Socrates' views on *akrasia* that are there being discussed. But Aristotle's "physical" solution to the Socratic puzzle about *akrasia* is remarkably similar to the Stoics' own picture, as I have developed it, especially in attributing *akrasia* to beliefs that conflict, but not per se (logically).

For the Stoics, in cases of (real or apparent) weakness of will, it is not passion that is opposed to reason: rather, reason is opposing itself, reason is as it were disobeying reason. If one decides to do something against one's better judgment, as we say, what is occurring is that there are *two* judgments in the soul that are opposed to one another, the one declaring that it is appropriate to perform a certain action A, and the other that it is not right to do so.[26] Logically, these two judgments are, of course, contradictory, but this only entails that they cannot both be entertained, or in Stoic terms assented to, by the same mind at the same time. One will find oneself wavering between them. Copious evidence in the form of literal quotations from Chrysippus' treatise on the passions cited by Galen in the central books of his work *On the Doctrines of Hippocrates and Plato* (evidence that Galen himself seems often willfully to misunderstand) reveals that Chrysippus tried to show in detail the sorts of psychological mechanisms a person may engage in so as to accommodate the presence of such a contradiction in her practical commitments. He compares this kind of situation, for instance, with a person's refusal to believe anything bad about his lover, even though one may possess the incriminating report on unimpeachable authority. That is, one may decide not even to entertain a certain proposition, in the knowledge that if one did entertain it, one would be compelled to assent to it. Chrysippus, as reported by Galen, quotes a fragment of the comic poet Menander: "I got my mind in hand and stuck it in a pot."[27]

Chrysippus also seems to have undertaken an elaborate exegesis of Medea's famous monologue in Euripides' play (*Medea* 1021–80), where she addresses her own *thumos* or anger at her husband as the motive for her prospective murder of her children, and utters the famous lines:

> I know what kind of evils I am about to do
> but anger [*thumos*] is strongest among my deliberations.[28]

Traces of this exegesis are no doubt to be found in Epictetus' discussion of the same scene in his *Discourses* (1.28.7). Contrary to what Galen insists, Chrysippus need not have been compelled to see here a direct opposition between Medea's reasoning and her *emotion* of anger, as something separate from reason. Rather, the source of her anger, according to

Epictetus and Chrysippus, is her *judgment* that it would be an overwhelmingly good or appropriate thing for her to take the most terrible revenge upon her husband for his abandonment of her. Of course, she also thinks that it would also be a good thing to spare her children's lives. If she also thinks that *this* would be an *appropriate* action, then we would find her in the sort of akratic situation mentioned earlier: the overwhelming power of her positive evaluation of revenge would cause her just to refuse to think about the wrongness or moral inappropriateness of the murder of the children, at least until after the savage act has been carried out. But this does not seem to be Epictetus' analysis of the situation. On his interpretation, Medea thinks that these two goods are in conflict but that revenge in the present situation is "more profitable" (*sumphorōteron*) for her than saving her children (1.28.7). Of course, this belief is false: the gratification of anger is never a real good, only an apparent one, and as Epictetus repeatedly insists throughout his *Discourses*, real goods actually cannot conflict: the world and human life are so constructed that true goods form a single, coherent, mutually realizable structure. But Medea, not being a Stoic and trapped in the confusion of ordinary human moral beliefs, fails to realize these facts. Given her beliefs, she must do what she thinks she must do. Epictetus even pretends to admire her for the strength of her soul (2.17.21). This is odd, since it seems we should analyze Medea's *akrasia* as the species of it that Chrysippus called "from weakness" rather than "from rashness."[29]

To express admiration for Medea may seem a strange thing for a Stoic moralist to say, but in fact it is quite consistent with the general Stoic attitude about the moral evaluation of wrongdoing. I return to this point in closing. For now, I want to point to another important feature of Medea's situation, namely the relative intensity of the evaluative judgment involved in the passion. Chrysippus emphasizes that in the case of a strong passion at least, the object is taken by the agent as being overwhelmingly good or bad (as being the greatest good or evil). I suggested earlier that this was the gist of the second in Chrysippus' analysis of the two judgments that found emotion. We know that in his psychotherapy he emphasized against Cleanthes the importance not only of trying to persuade people of the Stoic doctrine that nothing outside the mind is actually really good or evil and hence that no *pathos* can be justified, since all passions involve positive or negative evaluative judgments about external objects but, first, that external things are *less* important than we ordinarily think, and less than virtue and vice (a view, of course, that Peripatetics and Platonists agreed upon with the Stoics).

ASSENT AND THE VOLUNTARINESS OF PASSIONS

Passions, and the emotions more generally, thus depend on the Stoic view entirely on the judgments of reason concerning the goodness or badness of particular objects, or the appropriateness or inappropriateness of particular actions, that is, pursuits or avoidances of objects. There is an additional complication here that deserves to be mentioned. In the case of the truly morally good acts of the sage, the object pursued seems actually to be what the Stoics sometimes call the proper "selection" (*eklogē*) of external objects, and this forms the practical content of virtuous action (this is the notion of *kathēkon* or obligation). This is what should be meant by the idea that the sage pursues only his own moral virtue. The sage is nevertheless said to have *hormē* toward the external objects, as when from obligation he acts to preserve his health (rather than because it is good in itself to do so). In this case the objects are said and seen by the sage to possess positive value (*axia*) rather than goodness. But the object of his *orexis* or pursuit will be the goodness of the action of proper or appropriate selection.

Nevertheless it is always the goodness or perceived apparent goodness of an object (or its badness, in the case of aversion) that motivates an action. This in turn will form the content of an evaluative judgment or act of assent. Actions, emotions, and desires are all subject to praise and blame or moral evaluation, the Stoics think, for precisely the same reason: because this sort of act of assent lies in our power to perform or not to perform. This is true not only in the case of evaluative judgments: whether we believe that *any* given proposition is true or false will be an act of assent, which will be up to us in the same way.[30] For instance, even perceptual beliefs or *aisthēseis* involve acts of assent, as is evident when we reflect on the fact that we sometimes do not accept what our senses seem to be telling us – for example, that the pencil in the glass of water is actually bent, or that the sun is a relatively small object up in the sky. The example of perception also helps make clear the important fact that it is not *always* within our power to withhold a particular act of assent: the Stoics hold that we cannot refuse to believe the clear evidence of our senses – for instance, I cannot fail to believe that I am now speaking to you or that you are now listening to me. (In fact, our very word "evidence" seems to derive from this Stoic view about what they call *enargeia*, obviousness, although the proximate source is Cicero's use of the term in his discussion of skeptical epistemology in the *Academica*.)[31] This is their famous doctrine of the *katalēptikē phantasia* or compellingly clear-and-distinct (cataleptic) impression, which we are unable to resist assenting to.

The same holds in the practical or moral case. Here the *phantasia* or impression is of the appropriateness or inappropriateness of an act, of the pursuit or avoidance of a particular object as being good or bad for us (cf. Epictetus, *Discourses* 1.28.5–6). We cannot fail to pursue what we grasp as obviously good or to avoid what is obviously bad, which is to say that there are practical cataleptic impressions as well as theoretical ones. But in normal circumstances (which is to say, as long as we have not yet attained to sagehood) these are not the sort of practical (or hormetic) impressions we are characteristically presented with. Fortunately, the Stoics think, the world is so providentially arranged that all irresistible (cataleptic) impressions are, in fact, true. (The sage assents only to cataleptic impressions: if not the cataleptic impression that a certain action is either good or bad, at least the impression that it is *reasonable* that it is good or bad.) The purpose and, indeed, the very nature of our reason is to distinguish (*krinein*) between true and false impressions (i.e., between those that present us with true as opposed to false propositions) – in the practical case, between true and false impressions that it would be good or bad to pursue or avoid certain things. Because all cataleptic or irresistible impressions are in fact true, nature never leads us completely astray. In the case of noncataleptic impressions, it is wholly up to us to assent or not.

Besides, the Stoics argue, there is naturally available to us a way to train ourselves so that we never assent to false propositions or impressions – this is apparently what the method of Stoic moral education, of making progress toward wisdom, principally consists in. Hence it is always *possible* that we could assent only to true propositions, that is, if we had properly (and voluntarily) trained ourselves to do so. Hence it follows that virtue and vice, and the complete avoidance of passions, which all involve false evaluative judgments, lies completely within our power.[32]

If our assent, emotion, desire, and action are all up to us in the way specified, then clearly our characters will be up to us too. Despite the persuasiveness of the hormetic impressions signifying pleasures, and the seductive power of our bad companions (the two sources of moral perversion, according to the Stoics), we have in principle the possibility of resisting them – in the precise Chrysippean sense of possibility, that this ability could have naturally occurred in us in this situation and that nothing external prevents its having done so.

Aristotle in the second part of *Nicomachean Ethics* 3.5 strives to answer an objection, based on the Socratic Paradox,[33] that we cannot be held responsible for our own bad characters, because it is not up to us how the good appears to us. But Aristotle's position in that chapter – that we can be held responsible for our bad moral characters because we are responsible for the voluntary actions that went into our habituation that produced those characters – won't do, because by Aristotle's own lights how the good appears to us, that is, whether we possess a concept of the good that is at all adequate, *already* depends on our character. Hence, Aristotle is committed to saying that a person can be held responsible for her conception of the good if she is *already* assumed to be responsible for her character, so that Aristotle's argument is circular. It is clear what the Stoics' way of dealing with this sort of problem will be: to insist on the basic principle that we are responsible for how the good appears to us. This also means that they reject Aristotle's further claim that a vicious person has irretrievably lost the proper conception of the good and hence is a morally hopeless case. This is not true for the Stoics – fortunately so, since all of us, at least nowadays, are vicious fools.

The notion of power or possibility appealed to here must be understood within the context of Stoic (i.e., Chrysippean) determinism. Chrysippus holds that everything that happens, happens in accordance with fate (*heimarmenē*), and thus must occur in exactly the way that it does both because it is causally determined to happen in just that way, and because in so doing it makes a contribution to the overall perfection of the universe (universal teleological determinism). Included in everything that happens are, of course, all human assents, pursuits and avoidances, and emotions, which are just as fated as is anything else. Nevertheless, these are held by the Stoics to be open to moral evaluation and praise and blame. Important passages from Cicero (*De Fato* 40–44), Aulus Gellius (*Noctes Atticae* 7.2.1–14), and Plutarch (*De Stoicorum Repugnantiae*), supplemented by some others (perhaps, for instance, Origen *De Principiis* 3.1–6) show us Chrysippus' way of constructing a compatibilist defense against objectors who claim that Stoic determinism undermines the legitimacy of any attribution of responsibility. I think we are now in a position to see how this defense works. It crucially depends on the voluntariness of the passions, our control over our evaluative attitudes and judgments.

Notes

1. Its origins have often but usually unconvincingly been discussed. They have in recent years been the subject of a set of Sather Lectures by Michael Frede, which will hopefully soon be published.

2. Cf. Cicero, *Tusculan Disputations* 4.12, Diogenes Laertius 7.115, and *SVF* 3:173, also Inwood 1985: appendix 2, p. 237.

3. Compare the conditions of the vicious persons described in Plato's *Republic*, books 7 and 9, where *boulēsis* seems to be, even if present, at least not operative in the preferred way, as a desire for the person's true good.
4. In Varro's speech in *Academica* 1.40–41.
5. This is somewhat of an oversimplification, since we do not know the precise details of the Stoic view of practical judgment (cf. Bobzien 1998: 240–41); however, it seems safe to assume that it involved assent to or approval of a practical impression, analogous to assent to the truth of an impression in the theoretical case.
6. One could mention here, among others, Frede 1986, Engberg-Pedersen 1990, Nussbaum 1994 (and Nussbaum 2001), Brennan 1998, and the relevant section of Long and Sedley 1987.
7. See Inwood 1985: 228–29. Epictetus makes *orexis* or desire or pursuit and *hormē* distinct genera, the former seemingly directed at the good (and away from evil), and the latter directed at appropriate or preferred objects. I assume that this represents a later development in the Stoic theory.
8. Perhaps this what is meant by *hexis hormētikē* at Stobaeus 2.86.17 = *SVF* 3:169.
9. But perhaps *commotio* is just a translation of *kinēsis*.
10. Cf. *huperteinousa ta kata ton logon metra*, Clement of Alexandria in book 2 of the *Stromateis* (*SVF* 3:377).
11. Cf. Chrysippus in LS 65J4 for both expressions.
12. Recall again that the *eupatheiai*, by way of contrast, are properly restrained impulses.
13. LS 65A4.
14. Here the contrast term to *orexis* is *orousis*; on all this, see Inwood 1985, appendix 2.
15. Galen 1981: 4.3.2, 4.4.38, and 5.6.33–38, respectively.
16. See Cooper 1999, following the lead of Fillion-Lahille 1984.
17. Cf. also the "boiling of the blood around the heart" in his "physicist"'s definition of anger in Aristotle, *De Anima* 1.1 fin., corresponding to the intentional "dialectician"'s definition as a desire for revenge.
18. The details are complex and controversial. It is, however, clear that the term *prosphatos* applied to the value judgment causing an emotion was originally due to Zeno. The secondary judgment seems to have been brought in by Chrysippus to explicate this term of Zeno's.
19. I assume the accusatives *ti* and *hēdon* are to be retained; cf. also 250.9 and 342.30 Müller.
20. Cf. LS 53Q4.
21. Epictetus (*Encheiridion* 1 init.) lists as what is up to us is *hupolēpsis*, supposition (which includes belief), impulse, desire, and aversion, "and what are our doings [*erga*]." All the items on the list are, in terms of the Old Stoic classification, either assents or *hormai*, and thus depend on assent.
22. Compare Seneca, *De Ira* 3.3, and Posidonius as reported by Lactantius, *On the Anger of God* 17.13 (reporting the contents of the lacuna at Seneca, *De Ira* 1.2).
23. Galen 1981: 5.7, claims that the argument establishes indifferently *either* that there are different parts *or* different faculties (of reason and appetite, or appetite and spirit) within the soul (cf. 5.7.49–50). He does not seem to

think it matters which. His interpretation certainly seems to gain support from the fact that Aristotle, who uses the same argument for dividing the soul, seems to think that reason and the desiderative part may only be different faculties, not different parts, of the soul. But this is so, it seems to me, only if a difference of faculty is enough to allow simultaneous opposite intentional *movements* having the same object in a unitary soul. I am unsure as to whether this is, in fact, the case.

24. Plutarch, *De Virtute Morali* 446f–447a = LS 65G.

25. Engberg-Pedersen 1990.

26. Again, cf. Engberg-Pedersen 1990 for a clear exposition of the correct idea here.

27. *Ton noun ekhōn hupokheirion / eis ton pithon dedōka,* Galen 1981: 4.6.34.

28. Alternatively, "Anger is stronger *than* my deliberations": *kai manthanth' men hoia dran mellô kaka / thumos de kreissōn tōn emōn bouleumatōn* (1078–79).

29. See also Chrysippus' analysis of Menelaus' failure to carry out his resolve to kill his faithless spouse Helen in the sack of Troy, Galen 1981: 4.6.

30. See note 6 on the analogy between theoretical and practical judgments (assents) for the Stoics.

31. For discussion, see Zupko 2003: 360, n43.

32. See Origen, *De principiis* 3.1.4–5, a very Chrysippean-sounding passage, fortunately preserved in Greek, in which Origen is responding precisely to the objection that in at least some cases of immoral choices (the example is of a monk being seduced to violate his vow of chastity) "the impression from without is of such a sort that it is impossible to resist it."

33. Probably, however, as this was maintained by Plato in the *Laws*, and not as held by the historical Socrates.

3

Stoicism in the Apostle Paul

A *Philosophical Reading*

Troels Engberg-Pedersen

In 1949 Max Pohlenz, the doyen of early twentieth-century German scholarship on Stoicism, published an article, "Paulus und die Stoa," in which he discussed the first few chapters of the apostle's letter to the Romans and the Christian historian Luke's account of Paul's speech on the Areopagus in chapter 17 of the Acts of the Apostles. Pohlenz was asking about the Stoic credentials of various ideas in the two texts. He concluded that in Paul there was nothing that went directly back to Stoicism. Instead, any Stoic-sounding ideas had come to Paul through Jewish traditions that would rather reflect some form of middle Platonism. In Luke, by contrast, there is a direct reminiscence of Posidonius.

In 1989 Abraham J. Malherbe, Buckingham Professor of the New Testament at Yale Divinity School, published a book, *Paul and the Popular Philosophers.*[1] He argued that in a number of individual passages in the letters, Paul was interacting directly with specific motifs derived from the moral exhortation of philosophers like the Cynics, Stoics, and Epicureans. Paul need not have read, for instance, Chrysippus. But he had an easy familiarity with the moral discourse of the "popular philosophers" of his own time, as exemplified to us by his near contemporaries Seneca, Dio Chrysostom, and Epictetus.

In *Paul and the Stoics* (2000), I argued that Paul is relying on central ideas in Stoicism even when he states the core of his own theological thought. This development should be of some interest to students of Stoicism. If we follow Pohlenz, we would say that while direct interaction between Christianity and Stoicism did begin in the New Testament, it is only reflected in a relatively late text that may be no earlier than A.D.100. Also, we would point out that the Stoic ideas that Luke ascribes to his Paul in the major part of the Areopagus speech (Acts 17:22–29) are only to be understood as a foil for his distinctively Christian claims made toward its end (17:30–31). Furthermore, the speech is followed by partial rejection by some of those present (17:32), including some Epicurean and Stoic philosophers (17:18–20). When they heard about the "resurrection of the dead," they laughed (17:32). So, even if Luke relied on Posidonius, the difference between Stoicism and Christianity was apparently felt to be more important than the similarity.

If we follow Malherbe, we would move the time of direct interaction between nascent Christianity and Stoicism back by about fifty years to Paul's own letters. And we would not presuppose any basic contrast between Paul's use of the specific motifs of moral exhortation and what we find in his contemporaries. Instead, we would see him as acting within a shared context. No one belonging to that context said exactly the same thing. But they all drew on a common pool of hortatory ideas and practices, modifying and adapting them for their own purposes.

If we are persuaded by my own work, we would agree with Malherbe but now also claim direct interaction between nascent Christianity and Stoicism at the earliest stage that is available to us, not only in the hortatory practices, which in themselves constitute a very important part of the Pauline letters but also at the center of his theological ideas. To put the point succinctly, Stoicism helps Paul articulate his own message of faith in Jesus Christ.

How may we account for the change from Pohlenz to the present? As often happens, a change of this kind is basically one of interest and perspective. Pohlenz was operating within a framework that presupposed a fundamental contrast between Jewish ways of thinking and Greek ones. And Paul belonged with the Jews. Thus, with only superficially disguised distaste, Pohlenz could describe Paul's central theological "construction" in Romans (the term is Pohlenz's own: "Diese theologische Konstruktion") as "completely un-Hellenic" and claim that "Greek ideas might at most have any influence at the periphery."[2] Pohlenz's treatment in the same article of the Jewish philosopher Philo, Paul's contemporary, is also highly revealing. Philo does far better than Paul because there is no question whether he was influenced by the "Greek ideas." He evidently was. But how was that kind of engagement at all possible if it had the character of crossing a cultural gap? Answer: Philo was "a compromiser" (*ein Kompromissler*)![3] Surely the case of Philo should have led Pohlenz to question his own presuppositions.

The change to Malherbe is quite striking. Here there is no longer any basic contrast between Jewish ways of thinking and Greek ones. Jews in Philo's and Paul's time were living in a world that was Hellenistic or Greco-Roman. Like anybody else they certainly had traditions of their own, and they may well have cherished these more than most others cherished theirs. But in the form these traditions had in the first century A.D., they had lost any of their pristine character. Instead, they should be seen as interacting with other comparable traditions in what was basically a shared context. Early Christianity was a part of Judaism, which was a part of the Greco-Roman world and culture.

There is a methodological rule of thumb involved in this which is relevant for the study of Paul in any dimension. It is also the single most important element in the paradigm shift – short of a revolution – that has been taking place in Pauline studies over the past twenty-five years. It is this: in contextualizing Paul, always begin by looking for similarities; only later, if at all, may one attempt to formulate differences. This holds for Paul in relation to Judaism. And it holds for Paul in relation to the wider Greco-Roman context. Paul was a Jew. And Pauline Christianity was a Jewish religion; indeed, Pauline Christianity differs sharply from "Christianity" – it is only Christianity in the making. But Judaism was *already* a part of the Greco-Roman world. So don't look for differences because you think beforehand that they are there.[4]

What lies behind this rule is a concerted effort on the part of the most influential modern Pauline scholars to distance themselves from a traditional, theological reading of the apostle – Paul and his religion as being seen from the outside. Initially, at least, any question of the validity of any particular aspect of his thought and practice is placed in brackets. What scholars are concerned to find is historical truths about Paul, not his own theological truths. It does not matter, therefore, whether the scholar likes what he or she finds. Paul is being analyzed historically and with critical distance from any later theological or dogmatic use of his ideas.

This perspective is directly relevant to the present essay. I am writing here specifically for students of ancient philosophy. But what I am presenting is a reading of Paul in relation to Stoicism that has also been presented – and far more extensively – to New Testament scholars. That is a sign of the drastic change in Pauline scholarship: a reading that belongs squarely within New Testament scholarship may also be presented to students of ancient philosophy without in any way demanding that they share Paul's own perspective and subscribe to any of his truths. For neither does the reading itself.

I emphasize this here because the gap between ancient philosophy and Christianity is still quite often felt to be a wide one. Curiously, that is not the case on the side of the most enlightened New Testament scholarship. Here there is a strong interest in ancient philosophy and its overlaps with early Christianity. Malherbe is a witness to this. On the other side, that of students of ancient philosophy, the situation is rather different. Quite often, Christian texts arc viewed with a degree of distaste and distancing that matches that of Pohlenz. This attitude is wholly understandable in view of the way theologians have traditionally claimed superiority over philosophy. But it no longer matches the way these texts are treated by New Testament scholars. To put it bluntly: students of ancient philosophy who approach early Christian texts like the Pauline letters differently from the way in which they would read, say, Seneca or Epictetus, only show that in this particular respect they are reflecting perspectives that have been obsolete for thirty years or more.

This is not to deny that one needs to perform a number of intellectual somersaults in order to connect with the Pauline text in a manner that will appear philosophically satisfactory. In addition to placing the truth question in brackets, one must also bracket a wide range of ideas within Paul's own thought world. Who, for instance, will be able to do anything with Paul's apocalyptic conviction that Christ will soon reappear in the sky and bring believers, dead or alive, up to his heavenly abode (1 Thessalonians 4:13–18)? In principle, however, that situation is not different from the one encountered by any student of ancient philosophy. Again, who will be able to do anything with the cosmologies of Plato, Aristotle, or the Stoics? And who will feel confident that these cosmologies are entirely unrelated to what the philosophers say in the rest of their various systems?

Intellectual somersaults are required by any student of Paul, and a certain amount of explanation is necessary in the exposition of his thought to people who come to it from the outside. It is up to the individual to decide whether the benefit is likely to repay the cost. But there is no benefit unless one is willing to pay the cost in the first place.

This sets the task for the present essay: I shall show by a single example in what way it is correct to claim that Stoicism helps Paul formulate the core of his theological thought. That may be historically interesting in itself. But if it is just a matter of Paul using Stoicism, there is perhaps little excuse for spending much time on him. We shall see, however, that Paul had enough of a philosophical mind to add an interesting thought or two to what he took over from Stoicism. As it happens, these are thoughts that he might have found in Aristotle, had he ever been acquainted with him. The result is that in the passage we analyze, Paul comes out as arguing in a manner that combines Aristotelian and Stoic insights to produce something of at least some independent philosophical interest. That is perhaps no mean feat for somebody who basically felt that he had too little time for philosophy.

To set the scene for the analysis of Paul, we shall spend a few moments on Philo, Paul's great contemporary and fellow Jew, who more overtly than Paul did the same as he: employed Greek philosophy to articulate his Jewish message.

PHILO AND PAUL

Within Philo's extensive oeuvre we shall pick up two themes from his thoroughly Stoic treatise *Every Good Man Is Free* that show Philo's difference from Paul on two relevant issues, but also, and more important, his similarity to him.[5]

One issue concerns the relationship between Philo's interest in Greek philosophy, and here in particular Stoicism, and his basic Jewish outlook. How do the two things fit together at a general level? What role does Greek philosophy play for him? Philo's interest in Greek philosophy is quite overt, whereas Paul's, as we shall see, is covert. That is a difference. But they agree on assigning a kind of ancillary role to Greek philosophy only. They use it to bring out what they take to be their own Jewish or Jewish-Christian message. It is an interesting question whether *we* should say behind their backs, as it were, that their use of Greek philosophy has ended up transforming their own message. In Philo's case, where we have a whole range of Jewish material to compare it with, the answer should probably be yes. In Paul's case it is unclear whether there is any real question here since there is almost no contemporary or earlier material with which to compare his articulation of the Christian message. Thus, if Paul's message is in the end importantly shaped by the kind of Greek philosophy (including Stoicism) that can be seen to underlie it, that only shows that from the very beginning of Christianity as we know it there was a symbiosis of that religion with Greek philosophy.

The other issue concerns the relationship between a couple of important concepts that Philo discusses in *Every Good Man Is Free*: freedom and law. The two concepts are also in focus in the Pauline text we shall analyze. Philo provides an account that is explicitly Stoic and in complete conformity with Stoic dogma. But he also connects that perspective smoothly with his basic Jewish outlook, in effect taking "law" to stand for the Mosaic law. Paul's handling of the two concepts is more complex and creative. But here, too, the Stoic perspective can be seen to lie just below the surface. Thus there is a difference in the detailed way they use Stoic material. But again the similarity will turn out to be more important.

THE USE OF GREEK PHILOSOPHY IN PHILO

Every Good Man Is Free stands somewhat apart in Philo's oeuvre. It is not a commentary on Jewish scripture, as so much else is in Philo. Indeed, it is strikingly reticent on Judaism, only mentioning a few times the "lawgiver of the Jews," Moses. By contrast, it is a strongly Hellenistic, almost Hellenizing, treatise throughout. And, of course, it argues a thesis – the one in its title – that is distinctly Stoic. So should we conclude that this is just a rhetorical exercise, possibly even a youthful one, that has little to do with what really mattered to Philo, his great commentaries on scripture? Far from it! The treatise is certainly strongly Hellenizing and indeed steeped in Stoicism. One finds in it almost all the usual Stoic motifs that went into the Stoic argument for the freedom of the good man. But it also completely shares the basic intention behind Philo's more obviously Jewish writings of showing that Judaism, and the Jewish law, is the very best philosophy. In *Every Good Man*, Philo as it were moves *from* Greek, and here specifically Stoic, philosophy *to* "the Jewish lawgiver," whereas in the allegorical interpretation of his great commentaries he reads Moses in the light of Greek philosophy (including Stoicism). But the aim is the same throughout: to show that in the law of Moses you find *the best* philosophy. In both types of writing, Greek philosophy (including Stoicism) is used to articulate that best philosophy which is found elsewhere, in the Jewish law. Philo certainly did not see any contrast between Greek philosophy and his own Jewish religion. And if we pressed him, he would probably agree that he had used Greek philosophy to articulate his Jewish religion. But he would also hasten to point out that what had been articulated in that way was more powerfully present in the Jewish law itself. We may disagree on the latter point. But that only shows the extent to which the former is true.

Let us note a few places in *Every Good Man* that bear out this double-sided relationship with Greek philosophy. The ostensive philosophical hero of the treatise is the founder of Stoicism, Zeno, who is characterized

as having "lived under the direction of virtue to an unsurpassed degree."
This is in section 53, where Zeno is actually being quoted. Zeno turns up
several times throughout the treatise and is always treated with courtesy.
But a page later, Philo shows his hand when he goes on like this: "We may
well suppose that the fountain from which Zeno drew this thought was
the law-book of the Jews" (§57).

The same picture is drawn at the very end of the work (§160). Philo
has been speaking of the need to instill in the young first "the soft food of
instruction in the school subjects [*ta enkuklia*]" and only later "the harder,
stronger meat, which philosophy produces." He concludes: "Reared by
these to manhood and robustness, they will reach the happy consummation [*telos*] which Zeno, *or rather an oracle higher than Zeno*, bids us seek,
a life led in accordance with nature [*to akolouthōs tēi phusei zēn*]." End of
treatise! Clearly, Philo intends to remain on Stoic ground but also to insist
that the famous Zenonian tag, "to live in accordance with nature," *really*
derives from elsewhere: it is *puthochrēston*, or uttered by an oracle higher
than him.

The basically Jewish direction of this thoroughly Stoic treatise comes
out particularly clearly in the famous description in sections 75–91 of
the Essenes. Greece, says Philo, may produce some examples of good
and free people (§73). Persia may do the same, and India too (§74).
And then there is "Palaestinian Syria," where you will find "more than
four thousand" members of "the very populous nation of the Jews," those
called Essenes (§75). The description of these, too, is steeped in Stoic
ideas. They are after all introduced as the best example of the Stoic
thesis that only a good man is free. But Philo's somewhat hidden aim
of pointing beyond Stoicism to Jewish law remains alive. Thus he says
the following of the Essenes' relationship with Greek philosophy: "As
for philosophy they abandon the logical part to quibbling verbalists as
unnecessary for the acquisition of virtue, and the physical to visionary
praters as beyond the grasp of human nature, only retaining that part
which treats philosophically of the existence of God and the creation of
the universe. But the ethical part they study very industriously, taking for
their trainers *the laws of their fathers* [!, evidently the Mosaic law], which
could not possibly have been conceived by the human soul without divine
inspiration" (§80). Or, again, a few pages later: "Such are the athletes of
virtue produced by a philosophy [!] free from the pedantry of Greek
wordiness, a philosophy which sets its pupils to practise themselves in
laudable actions, by which the liberty which can never be enslaved is
firmly established" (§88).

Thus, while being thoroughly Stoic, *Every Good Man Is Free* is also intended to provide the best description of what Judaism is all about. Stoicism is here employed extensively and overtly, though not for itself but to articulate the essence of Judaism.

FREEDOM AND LAW IN PHILO

Among Philo's arguments for the freedom of the good man is the well-known Stoic motif that the good man is free of the tyranny of the passions. "Our inquiry is concerned with characters which have never fallen under the yoke of desires, or fears, or pleasures, or pains; characters which have as it were escaped from prison and thrown off the chains which bound them so tightly" (§18);[6] "let us examine the veritable free man, who alone possesses independence [*to autokrates*], even though a host of people claim to be his masters" (§19). That claim is false, however. "For in very truth he who has God alone for his leader, he alone is free" (§20); "no two things are so closely akin as independence of action [*autopragia*] and freedom, because the bad man has a multitude of encumbrances, such as love of money or reputation or pleasure, while the good man has none at all, . . . inspired as he is by his ardent yearning for the freedom whose peculiar heritage it is that it obeys no orders [*to autokeleuston*] and works no will but its own [<*to*> *ethelourgon*]" (§21–22). That man alone has an "unenslaved character [*adoulōton ēthos*]" (§23).

In these few paragraphs, Philo well displays his Stoic aptitude for finding the proper terms: *to autokrates, autopragia, to autokeleuston kai ethelourgon, to adoulōton ēthos*. But he also manages to bring in how a person may reach such a state: by having God alone for one's leader. That phrase, of course, fits perfectly both with Stoicism and with Philo's own law-abiding Judaism.[7]

In a later passage Philo brings in the notion of law: "Those (men) in whom anger or desire or any other passion, or again any insidious vice holds sway, are entirely enslaved, while all who live with law are free. The infallible law is right reason [*orthos logos*], a law engraved not by this mortal or that and, therefore, perishable as he, nor on parchment or slabs, and, therefore, soulless as they, but by immortal nature on the immortal mind, never to perish" (§§45–46).[8] Everybody should agree, therefore, that "right reason, which is the fountain head [*pēgē*] of all other law, can impart freedom to the wise, who obey all that it prescribes or forbids" (§47).

Which law is Philo talking about? Obviously the Stoic universal law – but also the Jewish law. This comes out in section 62 where Philo introduces his list of examples of good men who are free. The introduction is phrased in purely Stoic terms. But we already know that the list will culminate in the long description of the Jewish Essenes. Here is the introduction to Philo's list: "[I]n the past there have been those who surpassed their contemporaries in virtue, who took God for their sole guide [cf. earlier] and lived according to a law of nature's right reason [*kata nomon ton orthon phuseōs logon*], not only free themselves, but communicating to their neighbours the spirit of freedom; also in our own time there are still men [e.g., the Essenes!] formed as it were in the likeness of the original picture supplied by the high excellence of sages" (§62).

The point is this: Philo, who was a good Jew, took over everything found in Stoicism concerning freedom and the law and applied it wholesale to the Jewish law. Taking God for one's sole guide means letting right reason govern and extinguish the passions. That is the same as living "with" (*meta*) law, not just in accordance with it. One who does this *obeys* everything the law and right reason prescribe or forbid. But he is at the same time also one who "obeys no orders and works no will but his own." For he *wills* the law and nothing but that. In him the passions have been extinguished. His is therefore a completely "unenslaved character." He is "independent" and displays total "independence of action." All of this, Philo implies, will come about if one lets oneself be guided by the will of the *Jewish* God as expressed in the *Jewish* law.

Paul too, in the passage we shall discuss, treats of freedom and law. His treatment is more complex and not at all rigidly in accordance with Stoic dogma, where the two are so closely connected. Paul certainly speaks for freedom but does not immediately connect that with law. For Paul was not merely a good Jew, but one who also believed in Christ Jesus. And that meant a certain distance in relation to the Jewish law. At first it will even appear as if Paul opposed freedom and the (Mosaic) law. Freedom, for him, was freedom *from* that law. In the end, however, Paul will come out as being, once more, far closer to Philo than one might immediately expect. Even though Pauline freedom was freedom from following the Mosaic law in favor of following Christ, the apostle ends up using the law again in the peculiar notion of "Christ's law," which is the Mosaic law with Christ prefixed. And following *that* law *is* a matter of freedom and, indeed, in the best Stoic manner of freedom from the passions.

In short, just as Paul's use of Greek philosophy is more complex than Philo's, so is his handling of the Stoic conceptual pair of freedom and law. But the similarity is closer than the difference. Both employ Greek philosophy (including Stoicism) creatively to articulate their own Jewish or Jewish-Christian message.

PAUL: GALATIANS 5:13–26

My specimen text from Paul is the passage 5:13–26 toward the end of his letter to the Galatians.[9]

(13) You, brothers, were called for freedom. Only do not use your freedom as a starting point for the flesh, but be slaves [*douleuete*] to one another through love [*agapē*]. (14) For the whole (Mosaic) law [*ho pas nomos*] is fulfilled in the one word: *Thou shalt love thy neighbour as thyself.* (15) But if you bite and devour one another, take care lest you be consumed by one another. (16) What I mean is this: walk by the spirit, then you shall not fulfill the desire of the flesh. (17) For the flesh desires against the spirit and the spirit against the flesh. For these are opposed to one another in order that you may not do what you wish. (18) But if you are being led by the spirit, you are not under the (Mosaic) law. (19) Now the works of the flesh are well known: adultery, uncleanness, licentiousness, (20) idolatry, witchcraft, cases of hatred [*echthrai*], strife, emulation, cases of anger [*thumoi*], ambitions, seditions, factions, (21) envyings, cases of drunkenness [*methai*], revellings and the same kind of things. Of these I tell you in advance, as I have also told you previously: those who do such things shall not inherit the kingdom of God. (22) But the fruit [*karpos*] of the spirit is love, joy, peacefulness, forbearance, kindness, goodness, faithfulness, (23) mildness, temperance. Concerning such things there is no law. (24) Those who are Christ's have crucified the flesh together with its passions [*pathēmata*] and desires [*epithumiai*]. (25) If we live by the spirit, let us also walk by the spirit. (26) Let us not become puffed up, provoking one another, envying one another.

In this section of the letter Paul provides what New Testament scholars usually call "general *paraenesis*" or moral exhortation that is not specifically directed toward local issues in the congregations to which he is writing. It is followed in 6:1–10 by *paraenesis* that is of more direct relevance to specific issues among the Galatians. And the letter is concluded in 6:11–18 by a summary of the argument of the first four chapters, a summary that in certain ways recapitulates a section just before 5:13ff., 5:2–12. Thus our passage might initially be construed as having a somewhat parenthetical role in the letter: sliced in between two summaries of all the material that has been presented *before* the first summary. As we shall see, such a conclusion would be completely mistaken.

The letter as a whole is addressed to a group of people who lived somewhere in the interior of ancient Turkey and were non-Jewish. They had been converted to the Christ faith by hearing Paul's message. They had also been baptized. And they had received "the spirit" (*pneuma*). Later, certain other Christ-believing missionaries of a more strongly Jewish orientation and with roots back to the Jerusalem church had turned up trying to persuade the Galatians to go the whole Christ-believing way and place themselves under the Jewish law. Paul will have none of that. Christ faith, baptism, and possession of the spirit should be enough. He therefore employs the first four chapters of the letter to argue the negative case that the Galatians *must not* enter under the Mosaic law and try to live in accordance with its rules.

That argument is over by 5:1, where Paul states that Christ has "*liberated*" Christians "for *freedom*" and urges the Galatians to stick to that. Here, at the climax of Paul's argument, we encounter the term "freedom" (*eleutheria*) of which Philo made so much in his rehearsal of Stoic ideas. Paul goes on to formulate, in 5:6, a kind of general maxim or "rule" – later (6:15–16), Paul will himself call it a *kanōn* – that also sounds somewhat Stoic: "In Christ Jesus neither circumcision [that is, being under the Jewish law] nor uncircumcision [that is, *not* being under it] has any force (or matters), only faith that is active through love." It is difficult not to hear in the first part of this rule the point that circumcision and uncircumcision are "indifferent" in the Stoic sense. In fact, systematic theologians from time to time do employ the concept of *adiaphora*. They probably have it from this text.

The second part of Paul's rule, however, gives the line for the argument of 5:13–26. That fact is of great importance. It shows that 5:13ff. is no mere parenthesis. On the contrary, having previously argued purely negatively and in various intricate ways based on Hebrew scripture what the Galatians must not do, he now provides the positive content of life "in Christ Jesus" already hinted at in 5:6 (a life of faith that is active through love). As it turns out in 5:13ff., a life "in Christ Jesus" is also a life "in the spirit." And the passage is intended to show that it is living in the spirit as *opposed* to living under the law that will yield the kind of life that constitutes the positive content of life "in Christ Jesus." The spirit will provide what the law cannot. Paul even intends to produce a reasoned argument why that is so. Thus 5:13–26 formulates the ultimate reason, now stated in wholly positive terms and thoroughly argued for, why Paul produced his various intricate arguments against entering under the law. It is *because* only the spirit and not the law may yield the proper life "in Christ Jesus" that the Galatians must not enter under it. Galatians 5:13–26 is no mere parenthesis.

I emphasize that Paul is arguing here. His intellectual arsenal was larger than most of us would be comfortable with. His basic outlook was apocalyptic, relying strongly on a two-world conception (of a present evil time frame, *aiōn*, or world, *kosmos*, e.g., Galatians 1:4 and 6:14 – and another, more splendid one). He can also speak of direct bodily participation (e.g. "in Christ Jesus") in a manner that was probably to be taken quite literally, where we would speak of metaphor. But he can also argue far more philosophically, as we shall see in our passage. That is fortunate because it may help us to get at the sense of what he means to say when he speaks in the other types of vocabulary. Take his talk of the "spirit" (*pneuma*). It probably belongs to both his apocalyptic and his body-oriented language. The spirit is at home in the "other" world. But it is literally infused into the hearts of believers in baptism: "Because you are sons [namely, of God – this reflects their having faith], God *sent out* his son's spirit *into* our hearts [namely, in baptism] crying: Abba! Father!" (Galatians 4:6). Well and good. But how should we understand this highly picturesque language? By seeing how Paul also gives cognitive content to his notion of spirit. That is what happens in our passage.

Galatians 5:13–16: Two Paradoxes and a Thesis

Paul begins from two apparent paradoxes. The Galatians have been called, so he says, for freedom (namely, from the law; cf. 5:1 paraphrased earlier). Only, they must not let that freedom work as a basis for "the flesh." Instead, they must "be slaves to one another" in love (5:13). That, surely, is a peculiar form of freedom! The next paradox comes with Paul's explanation for his first paradoxical claim: "*For* the whole law [meaning the law of Moses] is *fulfilled* in the one word: Thou shalt love thy neighbour as thyself" (5:14). Why speak of the fulfillment of the Mosaic law when everything up to then has been aimed at saying that one should discard it? One is thankful that Paul goes on with a *Legō de*, "What I mean is this" (5:16).

What does he mean? Answer: the Galatians should "walk" or live in accordance with the spirit that is already theirs; if they do, they never will, indeed, *can*not, fulfill any "desire of the flesh." The last thesis, stated in 5:16b, is then argued for in 5:17–24. We have three questions to answer. What is the overall shape of that argument? How does what is said in 5:16ff explain the first paradox we noted, that as free (from the law) the Galatians are required to serve one another in love? How does it explain the second paradox to the effect that in so doing they will fulfill the law?

Galatians 5:17–23 in the Argument

Paul begins in a manner that has exasperated New Testament scholars:
"For the flesh desires against the spirit"; and vice versa: "[F]or these are
opposed to one another, in order that you may not do what you wish"
(5:17). "But if you are being led by the spirit..." (5:18). Students of
ancient philosophy will immediately – and rightly – see a reference in
5:17 to *akrasia*. They will not feel so comfortable with the rest. How is
the fight between the flesh and the spirit to be understood? In 5:17 itself
it might initially appear as if Paul is speaking of both the flesh and the
spirit as entities internal to the psyche in the manner, say, of Aristotle in
Nicomachean Ethics 1.13. But if 5:17 is taken to refer to an internal fight in
which even the opposition of the spirit to the flesh will only result in cases
of *akrasia*, then 5:17 will not provide a reason (cf. *gar*, "for") for 5:16 –
that if they do live in accordance with the spirit, then they most certainly
will *not* follow the desires of the flesh. Nor will 5:17 provide a proper
background to 5:18: "But *if* you are being led by the spirit, *then*..." –
once more signifying that then the situation of *akrasia* envisaged in 5:17
will no longer apply. Thus an alternative reading of 5:17 seems required.

Suppose Paul is speaking in 5:17 in his apocalyptic dress. The Flesh
and the Spirit may stand for powers external to individuals – though evidently of the highest relevance to them. The two powers are at war with
one another (wherever they are to be found), one trying to prevent individuals from doing what they wish to do in accordance with the other.
Crucially, however, that leaves something over to the individuals themselves. Something is up to them. So *if* they will walk in accordance with
the Spirit (*including* the spirit in themselves), *then* ... the risk of *akrasia*
will be overcome (5:16). Or again, *if* they let themselves be led by the
Spirit/spirit, *then* ... (5:18).

On this reading we already have two ideas that will turn out to be
important: first, the idea of *akrasia* or risking to do what one does not
wish to do; and, second, the idea that if one lets oneself be taken over by
the Spirit/spirit that is already one's own, then the risk of *akrasia* will be
overcome.

Next Paul introduces a distinction between being under the law
(5:18b–21) and living with the spirit (5:22–23). Initially it is rather puz-
zling that he should bring in the law once more as something that belongs
on the bad side. For as we know, he is arguing, among other things, for
the second paradox that Christian love fulfills the law. But Paul even
gives the new puzzle an extra twist when he connects being under the law

intimately with doing "works of the flesh." Usually, "works" (*erga*) in Paul are those of the law, in the often used phrase "works of the law" (*erga nomou*). Here they are of the flesh. Moreover, this is given in *explanation* of how one will live when one is under the law. What is Paul up to? Is he suggesting that the law somehow leads people to do fleshly acts? A strange idea![10]

A solution suggests itself when one considers the difference in ontology between the works of the flesh listed in 5:19–21 and the "fruit" of the spirit listed in 5:22–23.[11] In 5:19–21 Paul provides what is normally called a vice list. In fact, he is not speaking of vices proper in the sense of certain bad states of mind and character. Rather, his theme is acts in the form of act types: illicit sexual activities (*porneia*), unclean acts (*akatharsia*), and so forth. By contrast, the list that exemplifies the fruit of the spirit is a genuine virtue list. Love (*agapē*), joyfulness (*chara*), peacefulness (*eirēnē*), patience (*makrothumia*), and the like are states of mind and character.

This difference suggests a valid phenomenological point about living under the law. The law consists of rules that tell one what to do (type) and what not to do (again type). In the latter group belong the various types of fleshly act listed in 5:19–21. But no matter how much one oneself in principle applauds the law and wishes to follow it, the law itself can never secure that it is actually being followed. The risk is always there that one acts against the law's rules and against what one oneself basically wishes to do. In other words, there is always a risk of – *akrasia*.

It is quite different with living in accordance with the spirit. For the spirit's fruit consists of proper states of character, virtues in the full, Greek sense of the term (even though they are not explicitly identified as such by Paul). If you have the spirit, then you also have those full states of character, and then you will not be able (psychologically) to act against them; you will always and only do the good.

If this is the basic distinction that Paul is drawing on, then one can see the point of his argument in 5:17–23 in relation to 5:16. If having the spirit consists in having the full states of character listed in 5:22–23, then if one walks by it (5:16a) and lets oneself be led by it (5:18a), one will in fact never fulfill the desires of the flesh (5:16b). By contrast, if one is under the law, then since the law is related in the suggested way to the act types listed in 5:19–21, one will always run the risk of *akrasia*, of acting in accordance with the flesh and against the law that one basically wishes to follow. What Paul is bringing out is the phenomenology of having the spirit and living by that in contrast with the phenomenology of living under the law. If the flesh is the great opponent, then it is the spirit and not the law that constitutes the solution. For only the spirit will provide the *kind* of thing that is required to vanquish the flesh.

This last point is explicitly made at the end of 5:23 when Paul states that the law is not *kata* the "kind of thing" (*ta toiauta*) he has just listed, the spirit's virtues. Most New Testament scholars translate *kata* here as "against." The law is not against love, joy, peacefulness, and so forth. That seems exceedingly lame in itself. Also, did Paul not say in 5:14 that the whole law was *fulfilled* in the love command? A few scholars therefore translate *kata* as "about." That is far better in itself. But will this not run afoul of 5:14, too? No. For whereas in 5:23 Paul is saying that the law is not about love (etc.) understood as a state of character, the love command given in 5:14 is in principle a command to do certain types of act, not to be or become psychically structured in some specific way.

So far we may reasonably claim that in 5:17–23 Paul has provided a respectable phenomenological argument for the thesis stated in 5:16b. The risk of *akrasia*, of fulfilling the desires of the flesh, will be overcome if one lets oneself be led by the spirit. For the spirit's fruit is the kind of thing that will have that effect – as opposed to anything engendered by the law.

But then, why is that so?

Galatians 5:24–25 in the Argument

Why is there the difference we have discovered in the relationship of the law and the spirit to the flesh? Or better, why may the spirit generate full moral virtues? Paul in effect answers this question in 5:24 when he states that "those who belong to Christ Jesus have crucified the flesh together with the passions and desires." To see what he means we should consider what it is to belong to Christ (literally "to be Christ's") and what is referred to by the flesh. The latter question may be answered by looking again at the list of fleshly act types given in 5:19–21.

At first, the list looks like a very mixed bag. But the appearance is misleading. In addition to a few act types that are specifically religious (idolatry, magic), the rest are divided up almost evenly between acts that are specifically body-oriented (e.g., adultery, uncleanness, wantonness) and others that are of a distinctly social kind (e.g., enmities, strife, emulation, fits of anger, and ambitious intrigue). Moreover, some of the latter are tied to individuals in certain specific ways no matter how much they are *directed* toward others and may also be *shared* by others – for example, fits of anger (*thumoi*) and ambitious intrigue (*eritheiai*) and fits of ill will (*phthonoi*). These types of act directly reflect states or events in the psyche of individuals. Furthermore, they derive from a fundamental desire to give the individual more of any coveted goods than others will get. With such an emphasis on the body and the individual it will be immediately clear to anybody who is acquainted with the ancient ethical tradition, and the Stoic theory of *oikeiōsis* in particular, that the root idea that serves to define the flesh in Paul is that of selfishness: basing one's external behavior exclusively on one's own individual perspective, which includes that of one's own individual body. Call this the bodily I-perspective. The flesh in Paul corresponds closely with the bodily I-perspective that constitutes the essence of the first stage of Stoic *oikeiōsis*, before the change to the rational, distancing view "from above" upon the individual.[12] This suggestion fits Paul's delimitation of the flesh in 5:24 by reference to "passions and desires" (*pathēmata kai epithumiai*). While these may certainly be distinctly body-oriented phenomena (e.g., *epithumia* for bodily pleasure), they may also include such phenomena as fits of anger that are not so much oriented toward the body as toward the individual's own desires irrespective of their object.

The contrasting idea of belonging to Christ may be elucidated by a couple of intriguing verses much earlier in the letter, which serve to set the parameters for everything that follows. In 2:19–20 Paul says this: "(19) For I [*egō*] have through the law died to the law in order that I might live for God. I am crucified together with Christ. (20) It is no longer I [*egō*] who live: Christ lives in me. To the extent that I now live in the flesh, I live in the faith(fulness) of God's son who felt love for me and gave himself over for my sake." Putting these verses together with 5:24 we may say that belonging to Christ (5:24) is a matter of defining oneself (2:19–20), not by the characteristics that would normally serve to define the specific individual (*egō*) that one is, but exclusively by Christ: one is a "Christ-person," nothing more – just as in the Stoic theory of *oikeiōsis* one comes to see oneself as a person of reason. The I-perspective (2:19–20) that is tied to the body (both together constitute the flesh of 5:24) has been "crucified." The bodily based I-perspective has been set completely apart and is allowed no role in defining who one is. How does that come about? Through "faith" (2:20) or by aligning oneself with the faithfulness (toward God) shown by Christ in his act of giving himself over to be crucified for the sake of human beings. More on faith later.

The details of the Christ myth need not concern us here. What matters is this: 5:24 taken together with 2:19–20 explains why the spirit may bring about what the law could not. Apparently, having the spirit as a result of having the faith that makes one identify exclusively with Christ *means* having "crucified," eradicated, extinguished the flesh with its passions and desires: everything, that is, that is based in the bodily I-perspective. In that case, the problem of living under the law – the constant risk of *akrasia* – will in fact be dissolved. No room will by now be left for any exercise of the bodily I-perspective that lay behind the various types of vicious acts.

Understood in this way in the light of 2:19–20, 5:24 *explains* the difference between living in the spirit and living under the law (5:18–23). It therefore also explains why the thesis stated in 5:16b holds, that *if* the Galatians will live by the spirit, there is complete certainty that they will not fulfill the desires of the flesh. The spirit and its fruit (full virtues of character) is the kind of thing that will necessarily issue in the corresponding practices (5:18–23). It therefore excludes the possibility of fulfilling the desires of the flesh (back to 5:16b). But the reason for this is that it is based on faith and belonging to Christ in the sense of identifying completely with him (5:24).

With all these things settled, it is wholly appropriate that Paul should conclude the argument begun in 5:16 by stating in 5:25: "If we live by the spirit [as they of course do], let us also walk by the spirit." This piece of exhortation brings the argument back full circle to where it began. In 5:16a Paul employed an imperative in the second-person plural. In 5:25b he uses a hortatory subjunctive in the first-person plural. The difference matches the development of the intervening argument. Through that argument we now know that having the spirit *means* being in a state that altogether excludes the risk of *akrasia* and fulfilling the desires of the flesh. Then the most appropriate form of exhortation is not an injunction in the imperative, as if some new situation was being envisaged, but a shared reminder of where believers in Christ ("we") already are.

DISSOLVING THE PARADOXES

Let us move back from here to the two paradoxical points from which Paul began. Why should the Galatians employ their freedom from the law to be slaves to one another in love? Because on Paul's radical interpretation of crucifying the flesh, that is what one will do once one gives up the bodily I-perspective. In other words, freedom from the law in Christ – understood as Paul goes on to describe it in the argument we have been looking at – *implies* slavery to one another.

Further, why does Paul suddenly speak of fulfilling the Mosaic law? Several answers are both possible and apposite. An important one is that Paul did not see the Christ faith for which he was arguing as being in opposition to Judaism. On the contrary, it was the true Judaism. To match this, Paul's Christ faith was a state (of mind) that would indeed fulfill the Jewish law instead of abrogating it. Another answer pertains more directly to the issue treated in the letter as a whole. If Paul's Jewish-oriented opponents advocated that the Galatians should take the whole step and become Jews by adopting the Mosaic law, one central argument in their armory will have been that only in that way would they have any chance of getting completely away from the kind of sinfulness that Jews normally took to be characteristic of non-Jews (Gentiles). Paul takes this up. Yes, the law should be fulfilled. But the law is fulfilled in love. And love is what comes with the Christ faith (as construed by Paul) *without* the law. Indeed, if one lives primarily by the law, one will only get so far as to live with the constant risk of akratic sinning. Complete freedom from that risk requires something different: Christ faith and the spirit. *That*, to conclude the line of Paul's argument, is the reason why they should remain in the freedom from the law for which Christ has liberated them (5:1).

In this manner Paul succeeds – to his own satisfaction, at least – in both having his cake and eating it. There is freedom *from* the law for Paul's non-Jewish addressees. In that way they will *fulfill* the law. Indeed, Christ faith and living by the spirit is the *only* way of fulfilling it.

Can we base as much as this on Paul's superficially very paradoxical claim in 5:14 about fulfilling the Mosaic law? Indeed, yes. For in 6:2 he makes the point wholly explicit when he states that by carrying one another's burdens (cf. "be slaves to one another in love"), the Galatians will "fulfill in full measure [*anaplēroun*]" – "*Christ's* law," or the "Christ law," that is, the (Mosaic) law as seen from within the Christ perspective that Paul has just developed. The law itself cannot make people do it always and everywhere. Christ faith and possession of the spirit can. In acting in accordance with the spirit, Christ people – and they alone – fulfill the law, "Christ's law."

GALATIANS 5:13–26 IN ITS ANCIENT PHILOSOPHICAL CONTEXT: ARISTOTLE AND THE STOICS

I have claimed that there is a genuine argument in Galatians 5:13–26, not just a series of disjointed injunctions. A certain degree of explication has been required to show this, but the argument is there. What one needs to see in the argument is an easy acquaintance with certain basic ideas in Aristotelian and Stoic ethics.[13] Let us take note of these ideas.

Paul began from the claim (5:6) that "in Christ Jesus neither circumcision nor uncircumcision has any force, only faith that is active through love." We noted the use here of the basic Stoic idea of *adiaphora*. We shall also see in a moment that Paul's notion of faith (*pistis*) is closely comparable in structural terms with the Stoic one of wisdom (*sophia*). The idea that faith is "active [*energoumenē*] through love," however, is Aristotelian in its basic ontology of a state (*hexis*) – here the one of love – that issues in acts or actualizations (*energeiai*). Of course, the Stoics would take over that bit of ontology and elaborate it further.[14] But that is part of the point. Paul's use of the philosophical tradition is not always very distinct, nor is distinctness required to claim that he is in fact drawing on it. In the present verse, Paul's use of the idea of *adiaphora* is sufficiently distinct to allow us to claim derivation – at least at second hand – from Stoicism. His use of the Aristotelian-sounding term *energeia* is hardly sufficiently distinct to back up a claim for derivation from Aristotle. But the distinction itself between a *hexis* and an *energeia* is of great importance to Paul's actual argument, as we have seen. Paul's philosophy is there, albeit just below the surface.

Later (5:13), when Paul identifies the Galatians' present state as one of freedom (*eleutheria*), he is clearly drawing on an idea that had a special force within Stoicism. We have seen this already in our remarks on Philo, who made so much of the same idea. Paul's further point that the Galatians should employ their freedom to enslave themselves to one another initially looks distinctly un-Stoic. Did the Stoics (and Philo) not precisely emphasize the *un*enslaved character of the good and wise? However, we also saw that Philo was not at all averse to ascribing obedience to the wise, at the same time that he also stressed that the freedom that is theirs is distinguished by *not* obeying any orders and working *no* will but its own. There is something like a genuine Stoic paradox here, of an obedience that is totally self-willed.[15] It is not at all impossible that Paul is playing on the same idea.

In Paul's actual argument from 5:16 onward, the focus on the risk of *akrasia* and how that may be overcome in full virtues that will always and everywhere be actualized in acts of love certainly reflects knowledge of the ancient ethical tradition. Is it Aristotelian or Stoic? The theme itself is, of course, absolutely central to Aristotelian ethics. But there is one consideration that suggests that it is the Stoic elaboration of it that is most germane to Paul. In Aristotle it is a crucial idea that acquisition of the proper moral *hexis* requires training of the desiderative part of the mind, which is noncognitive in itself. Such training will come about through practice, upbringing, or, as we shall see, living under good laws. In Stoicism, by contrast, the proper moral state is itself through and through cognitive. And it may come about through a change that is cognitive, too. That fits Paul far better than the Aristotelian picture. For in Paul the change is described as having a distinctly cognitive component.

What I have in mind is Paul's understanding of faith (*pistis*) as described in Galatians 2:19–20. Faith is a conviction or belief *that* something has happened, which radically alters one's self-understanding, one's sense of where one "belongs" and hence who and what one is. What one believes has happened is stated in a mythic story about Christ (that he, God's son, in faithfulness toward God felt love for human beings and gave himself over to death on their behalf; cf. 2:20). This story is taken to be literally true. When one lives "in the faith(fulness)" of Christ, one has a belief that this set of events has occurred. But one will also understand what occurred as being directly relevant to oneself: "Paul" lives in the faith(fulness) of God's son who felt love for "*me*" and gave himself over to death on "*my*" behalf. That additional element in the belief is what explains the sense one now has of "belonging" to Christ (cf. 5:24) in the radical form of being dead as the person one was but alive by having Christ live "in one" (2:20). As we saw, one "belongs" to Christ in the sense that one now identifies oneself exclusively as a "Christ person," neglecting every individualizing trait that previously went into one's self-identification.

Extreme as this line of thought is, there can be no doubt that it is presented by Paul as an essentially cognitive one. It is therefore in line with Stoicism, rather than Aristotle. As already hinted, it is in fact closely similar structurally to the Stoic account of "conversion" to a grasp of the good, as given in Cicero's *De Finibus* 3.20–21. There too we find, at the end of the gradual development of Stoic *oikeiōsis*, a grasp that something is the case, which has radical consequences for one's sense of where one "belongs" and who and what one is. This realization of the one and only good strongly relativizes the value previously ascribed to everything that belongs to the bodily I. Indeed, the bodily I-perspective is now in principle left totally behind. One has reached the stage of Stoic *apatheia*.[16] When we then further note that *apatheia* is also what Paul describes in Galatians 5: 24, we may confidently claim that the structural homology between Paul and Stoicism is a very tight one here.

So far we have seen Paul to be more directly at home within Stoicism than with Aristotle. There is one remaining philosophical theme that fits Aristotle better than the Stoics, although even here Paul mixes motifs from both philosophies. The theme is Paul's handling of the law. On the one hand, the law is insufficient to make people do what it enjoins. That is similar to Aristotle's claim toward the end of the *Nicomachean Ethics* that "words" cannot by themselves effect the proper practice.[17] Aristotle, however, went on to say that for the very same reason there was a need for laws.[18] In Paul, by contrast, the law shares the ineffectual character of "words." Thus there is both similarity and difference.

Paul is again very Aristotelian, however, when he goes on to claim that law is not directly concerned with such things as states of character (5:23). Aristotle has the same idea – and literally the same words – in *Politics* 3.13.[19] Law, he says, is not "about" (*kata*), or relevant to, a special kind of moral hero he has just presented, one whose moral virtue is so far above that of the rest that he is "like a god among human beings."[20] Law, for Aristotle, is concerned with fallible human beings. Paul agrees. But then that is precisely what shows the *in*sufficiency of the law. For, like the Stoics, Paul went directly for *in*fallibility.

Stoicism too might provide some input for Paul's handling of the law, though not with regard to the insufficiency thesis of the law. To my knowledge nothing similar to that can be found in Stoicism. That should not surprise us. For in Stoicism "words" in principle do have the ability to effect the proper practice. Where Paul is critical of the law, he is more Aristotelian than Stoic. But we also saw that he may be very positive toward the law: when it is, as it were, prefixed by "Christ" (6:2). Now if the experience of Christ functions in a way that is similar to reaching the rational grasp of the good in Stoicism, then operating in accordance with "Christ's law" (*ho nomos tou Christou*) in Paul will be similar to wise acting in Stoicism, living in accordance with nature or "the law common to all things [*ho nomos ho koinos*], identical with right reason, which pervades all things and is the same as Zeus, who in his turn is the leader of the ordering of everything."[21] In Stoicism, of course, the law common to all things is closely tied to an ontology (nature), but also to God (Zeus). In Paul, by contrast, Christ's law is a local one (the Mosaic law) – though certainly understood by Paul as having universal reach – tied to nothing other than Christ (and God). But the Stoics brought out in their own way and vocabulary exactly the point that Paul is also after when he reintroduces the law in its positive guise and prefixes it with "Christ": the point that once human beings have grasped the one thing that ultimately matters, they will be in perfect subjective agreement with what is objectively required, with the will of God. Thus the Stoics continued as follows immediately after the quotation given: "And the virtue of the happy man and smooth current [*euroia*] of his life is just this: when everything is being done in accordance with a harmony [*sumphōnia*] of the spirit [Stoic *daimōn*] dwelling in each person with the will [*boulēsis*] of him who orders the universe."[22] Paul has exactly the same idea when he speaks of fulfilling the Christ law. His vocabulary, however, is quite different.

CONCLUSION

Was Paul a Stoic? That depends. He was – and saw himself as – an "apostle of Christ." And he was not quite – and certainly did not see himself as – a philosopher. A fortiori he was not a Stoic.

I have argued, however, that Paul did make use of notions that are distinctly Stoic to formulate his own message: the *adiaphora, oikeiōsis, apatheia,* and more. He did not directly quote those notions or bring in Stoicism with flying colors. For that he was probably too preoccupied with his own agenda. Indeed, elsewhere he contrasts the "wisdom [*sophia*] of the present world" with his own "wisdom" (*sophia*), which was kept apart for "those who are perfect [*teleioi*]" (1 Corinthians 2:6). Nevertheless, Paul did use Stoic notions to formulate his message.

Nor was this use of merely peripheral importance. It lies at the heart of the argument of Galatians 5:13–26. And that passage itself lies at the heart of what Paul was trying to communicate in this letter as a whole. In 5:13–26 Paul brought out the positive point of the Christ faith he had preached to the Galatians. And that point explains why, in the rest of the letter, he argued so strongly against supplementing the Christ faith with adherence to the Mosaic law. The former was sufficient in itself. Adopting the latter in addition would only lead in the wrong direction: back to a state where the risk of *akrasia* had not been eradicated.

So, was Paul a Stoic? Not in the direct way stated here, of one who is and sees himself as a philosopher. But in his own, hidden way he was. Once we look just below the surface, we see that Paul brings in central Stoic ideas and employs them to spell out the meaning of his own message of Christ. Paul was a crypto-Stoic.[23]

Thus Paul was far closer to Stoicism than Max Pohlenz would allow. Pohlenz never got near to seeing those hidden, but real and important similarities that we have discovered. To get there he should have attempted to read Paul's texts in some philosophical depth as an exercise well worth undertaking on its own. But his presupposed belief in a basic contrast between Jewish (religious) and Greek (philosophical) ways of thinking stood against that.

Paul was also more of a Stoic than has been allowed by Abraham Malherbe. His use of Stoic ideas is in no way peripheral to his own most central concerns. Rather, he uses philosophical ideas, and Stoic ones in particular, to articulate the meaning of his own core message.

In this he is in line with Philo, who did exactly the same. The comparison with Philo is in fact quite revealing. These two Jews, I have argued, are far closer to one another in their use of Greek philosophy than is normally allowed. Whereas the one flaunts his knowledge, however, and makes it part of his message, the other hides it away. But it is still there.

Notes

1. Malherbe 1989 collects a number of his papers on the topic. For other relevant writings, see Malherbe 1986, 1987, 1992, and 1994.
2. Pohlenz 1949: 70.
3. Pohlenz 1949: 76.
4. The point underlies a collection of essays edited by the present writer in Engberg-Pederson 2001. It is well expressed by Philip S. Alexander in one of those essays, "Hellenism and Hellenization as Problematic Historiographical Categories": "[W]e need an intellectual paradigm shift so that the presumption now is always in favour of similarity rather than dissimilarity" (79).
5. All references to *Every Good Man Is Free* are to the Loeb edition (Philo of Alexandria 1929), following the numbered divisions of that text.
6. The Loeb translation has been slightly modified here.
7. For Stoicism cf., for example, Diogenes Laertius 7.88 (quoted later).
8. The Loeb translation has been slightly modified here.
9. The following account relies on chapters 6–7 of *Paul and the Stoics*, in which I discuss the passage and its position within the letter extensively and in constant interaction with the relevant New Testament scholarship (Engberg-Pedersen 2000: 131–77, with notes on 324–50). It should be noted that the reading I propose is not the *communis opinio* within the guild (to the extent that one can speak of such a thing). My claim is that it makes better overall sense of the passage as a whole and its role within the letter than alternative readings.
10. Readers who know their Paul may reply that the apostle seems to say something like this in Romans 5:20. However, Paul's claims in Romans about the effect of the law need careful sifting. See Engberg-Pedersen 2000: 240–46.
11. This is one of the points where the present reading of Galatians 5:13–26 is heterodox.
12. I am relying here on my own account of the initial stages of Stoic *oikeiōsis* as reflected in Cicero, *De Finibus* 3.16. See Engberg-Pedersen 1990: 64–71.

13. This is the single most important point where I feel I have been able to add to New Testament scholarship on Paul. It is not that New Testament scholars know nothing about Stoicism or Aristotelianism. Some definitely do. But one very rarely comes across attempts to read Paul (in the light of ancient philosophy) *as if* he were a philosopher intent on drawing philosophical distinctions like those one finds in the Stoics or Aristotle.

14. Cf., for example, *SVF* 3:104.

15. Cf. *SVF* 3:615 (Stobaeus): "[T]he good man alone rules [*archei*] . . . and the good man alone is obedient [*peitharchikos*] since he follows [is *akolouthētikos* of] one who rules [*archōn*]."

16. I am relying here on my own account of the last stage of Stoic *oikeiōsis* as reflected in Cicero, *De Finibus* 3.20–21, for which, see Engberg-Pedersen 1990: 80–97.

17. Aristotle, *Nicomachean Ethics* 10.9, 1179b4–5 and 1179b26–31.

18. Ibid., 9.8, 1168b31ff.

19. Aristotle, *Politics* 3.13, 1284a14.

20. Ibid., 3.13, 1284a10–11.

21. Diogenes Laertius, *Lives of Eminent Philosophers* 7.88.

22. Ibid.

23. I owe this happy formulation to my friend, Sten Ebbesen.

4

Moral Judgment in Seneca

Brad Inwood

We are all familiar with the notion of a moral judgment. In the vocabulary
of ethical debate, this term is so common as to be a cliché. While we have
different theories about how we make such judgments, it would seem distinctly odd to observe that "judgment" is a term transferred from another
semantic domain and to attempt to sort out its meaning by scrutinizing its
source or to impugn the clarity or usefulness of the term on the grounds
that it began its conceptual career as a mere metaphor. Whatever origins
the term may have had, they now seem irrelevant.

But is this really so? I want to argue that moral judgment has not always
been taken as a bland general synonym for moral decisions and that it
need not be; to see that, we can consider uses of the terminology of moral
judgment in which the original semantic sphere for such language (the
judicial sphere) is still relevant to understanding how it is used.[1] One
such use comes from the Stoic Seneca, and I argue that he did take the
notion of moral judgment as a live metaphor, one that he used to develop
his own distinctive Stoic views on moral thinking.

That the particular language we use in talking about moral decision
and moral assessment should matter is not surprising. Even for us, this is
not the only way to talk about such matters; we also invoke the notions of
deduction, calculation, and analysis, for example. Perceptual language is

Versions of this chapter were also read to audiences at the University of Toronto and at
the Chicago area conference on Roman Stoicism in the spring of 2000, as well as at the
University of Victoria and the University of Calgary in March 2001. I am grateful to a number
of people for helpful comment, but especially to Miriam Griffin who heard the Chicago
version.

also familiar – we speak of discernment, moral intuition, even perception itself. Such terminology can have an influence on our moral theory, for it may well be more than mere terminology; it may reflect a model or paradigm for moral reasoning. (Of course, the causal relationship may also run the other way; if we are self-consciously critical about our theory, we may well make a deliberate choice of terminological model.) If our model for moral decisions is, for example, calculation, we might be drawn unwittingly to certain substantive views in moral theory, such as the notion that there is a single commensurable value at the core of our reasoning. If our model is deduction, we search (perhaps in frustration) for a satisfactorily universal rule under which we might subsume our experience and our deliberations. If we are in the habit of talking about moral discernment or perception, we no doubt tend to seek moral truth in the details. The effect of such models is evident in the ancient tradition, too. The so-called practical syllogism of Aristotle is one such model, and so is his use of geometrical analysis in discussions of moral deliberation. At other times he uses the language of perception. Our interpretation of his theory is to some extent guided by our choice of which model to treat as central to his theory.[2]

To speak of moral decision in the language of passing judgment is to adopt one model in place of other possibilities. It is significant for one's moral theory. Yet the term moral judgment seems not to carry this kind of significance any more. I don't know when it ceased to do so, but that would be a question for historians of a later period in the history of philosophy. My attention was drawn to this theme for a simple reason. There is a remarkable absence of this model, based on the activity of legal decision making, characteristic of a judicial decision maker, in most ancient texts dealing with moral decisions or moral theory. Not a total absence, of course, just the presence of a quiet whisper to contrast with the noisy omnipresence of this idea in our own discourse.

I only became aware of how scarce this kind of language is in most ancient texts when I began reading Seneca – reading him for his own sake rather than as a source for earlier Stoic ideas. For I was struck by how very frequent the language of judging is in his works. The nouns *iudex* and *iudicium* abound, and not in trivial or trivially metaphorical senses; the verb *iudicare*, which is certainly common in a broadly extended sense in Latin generally, occurs frequently in contexts that invite (or even demand) that we consider the import of the underlying notion of judicial determination. Latin writers do draw on such language more than Greek authors, for the Roman elite seems to have dealt more consistently with judicial experience than its Greek counterparts did, if for no other reason then because every *paterfamilias* held the position of judge and magistrate with regard to his own household.[3] But even the lawyer Cicero does not, in my reading, show such a propensity for thinking and talking about moral assessment and decision in terms of judging and passing judgment.

I doubt that the facts support the extravagant claim that Seneca invented the idea of moral judgment. But his elaboration of the metaphor of judges and judging is pervasive and insistent; its use is both original and illuminating. So I do want to suggest that whatever its origins, we find in Seneca an intriguing, influential, and creative exploitation of this notion in the service of his own moral philosophy.[4] In this provisional discussion I can neither explore Seneca's exploitation of this concept thoroughly, nor can I explore the possibility of its influence on later uses of the idea. It will, I hope, suffice if I draw attention to the interest and complexity of his thinking on the topic.

The verb *iudicare* and the noun *iudicium* are common, and while I hope to show that Seneca self-consciously uses them to develop his own original views, it would be difficult to start from those terms. In considering his usage we would certainly find far too much noise and nowhere near enough signal. A more effective entrée into the topic comes from consideration of the agent noun *iudex*. For Seneca says some striking things about judges – moral judges, in particular – and if we can come to an understanding of those oddities we will be well on the way to an understanding of his thoughts on the topic of moral judgment more generally. From the outset I want to make a confession, though. The notion of a moral judge equivocates between two distinguishable ideas: the demands on an actual judge to act by relevant moral standards in carrying out his or her duties as a judge; and the notion that someone making a moral decision or evaluation is to be conceptualized as a judge. My main interest is, of course, in the latter notion. But the morally proper behavior of a real judge would tend to show many of the same features as the morally proper behavior of any moral agent acting on the model of a judge; hence I propose to allow these two ideas to blend together for the purposes of this chapter.

Several works are of particular importance for Seneca's exploration and exploitation of the idea of a moral judge: *On Clemency, On Anger,* and *On Favors* stand out for their close connections, though there does not seem to be a planned coordination with regard to the theme.

In *On Clemency* Seneca naturally deals with the proper behavior of a judge. For much of what the young emperor whom he is advising will have to do will involve acting in his capacity as a judge of other men, indeed a judge from whom appeal is impossible. In 1.5 he argues for the exercise of leniency on the grounds of the extraordinary power of the emperor, but in 1.6 his tack shifts. He asks Nero to consider that his great city would be reduced to a wasteland if its population were thinned out by the judgments of a *severus iudex*, an obvious consideration in favor of not being unduly *severus*. The stern judge is one who never relaxes his judgment in the light of important mitigating factors. (I quote throughout, except as noted, from the excellent translation of John Procopé in Seneca 1995):

Think what an empty waste there would be if nothing were left of it save those whom a stern judge would acquit! How few investigators there are who would not be found guilty under the very law by which they make their investigation! How few accusers are blameless! Is anyone more reluctant, I wonder, to grant pardon than he who has all too often had reason to seek it? We have all done wrong, some seriously, some more trivially, some on purpose, some perhaps under impulse or led astray by the wickedness of others. Some of us were not firm enough in our good intentions, losing our innocence unwillingly, clutching at it as we lost it. Nor have we merely transgressed – to the end of our lives we shall continue to transgress. Suppose, indeed, that someone has so purged his mind as to be beyond further reach of confusion or deception. His innocence has been reached, none the less, through doing wrong.

The stern judge, then, is someone who judges others as harshly as the law permits, despite the fact that such judgment would, if exercised consistently, lead to his own condemnation under the same laws. And even if he is now morally perfect, it remains the case that, at some point in his past, a stern judge could have brought his career, if not his life, to an end. A *severus iudex*, then, would be undermining his own credibility as a judge by implicitly relying on a double standard. He would, then, be weakening his own authority and so compromising his effectiveness as well as behaving unreasonably. Further light on the propriety of passing judgment comes from the closing sections of this fragmentary work, in 2.7. Seneca is discussing the topic of forgiveness:

"But why will he not forgive?" Come now, let us make up our minds as to what pardon is, and we shall realize that a wise man ought not to grant it. Pardon is the remission of deserved punishment. The reason why the wise man ought not to grant this is given at greater length by those whose theme it is. [Here Seneca refers to Stoic philosophers acting in their doctrinally official capacity.] I for my part, as though to summarize a case that is not my own,[5] would say: a person can only be forgiven if he deserves to be punished. But the wise man does nothing that he ought not to do and omits nothing that he ought to do. So he will not excuse a punishment which he ought to exact. But what you want to achieve through pardon [*venia*] can be granted to you in a more honourable way. The wise man will spare men, take thought for them, and reform them – but without forgiving, since to forgive is to confess that one has left undone something which ought to have been done. In one case, he may simply administer a verbal admonition without any punishment, seeing the man to be at an age still capable of correction. In another, where the man is patently labouring under an invidious accusation, he will order him to go scot-free, since he may have been misled or under the influence of alcohol. Enemies he will release unharmed, sometimes even commended, if they had an honourable reason – loyalty, a treaty, their freedom – to drive them to war. All these are works of mercy [*clementia*], not pardon. Mercy has a freedom of decision. It judges not by legal formula, but by what is equitable and good. It can acquit or set the damages as high as it wishes. All these things it does with the idea not of doing something less than what is just but that what it decides should be the justest possible.

The wise man is here envisaged as a judge acting in pursuit of the just outcome in every case. Mercy is a factor internal to the determination of the just decision, whereas pardon is external to that decision. The wise man judges with freedom of decision (*liberum arbitrium*), not constrained by the *formula* that would guide a judge in the courtroom.[6] This latitude makes it possible for his consideration of relevant factors to be based *ex aequo et bono* rather than on more mechanical considerations. The reformative goal of punishment remains paramount.

Evidently the wise man does not play the role of a *severus iudex* in his dealings with others, whether or not he is an actual judge presiding at a tribunal, and we may infer that the stern judge neglects the broad range of relevant factors because he fails to acknowledge his own human fallibility and its relevance for his own judgments. The wise man of *On Clemency* 2 will have become wise after having erred, and awareness of that personal history will enter into his subsequent judgments. This is in itself an interesting insight into moral judgment, and one that militates vigorously against some models of moral decision making. One thing of special note, though, is that the insight – which applies to actual judges as much as it does to anyone called upon to condemn or to forgive – is developed and expressed in quite explicitly legal language. For we have not merely the language of the *iudex*, but also other technical legal terms such as *formula*. In the context of advice to Nero, this is not surprising, but its broader implications are brought out by a consideration of similar ideas in *On Anger*.

For the relevance of such a personal history to the capacity of the sage to act as a moral judge had been of interest to Seneca for some time. In a familiar passage of the treatise *On Anger* (1.16.6–7) the same collocation

of ideas occurs. Here Seneca is arguing that the judgment on misdeeds
that is required should be carried out in a spirit of quasi-judicial calm
and control. Violent emotions are not needed to stimulate the judge to
take action. His interlocutor suggests, "A readiness to anger is needed for
punishment." But Seneca replies:

Tell me, does the law seem angry with men whom it has never known, whom it has
never seen, whom it hoped would never exist? That is the spirit to be adopted, a
spirit not of anger but of resolution. For if anger at bad deeds befits a good man,
so too will resentment at the prosperity of bad men. What is more scandalous
than the fact that some souls flourish and abuse the kindness of fortune, when
no fortune could be bad enough for them? Yet he will view their gains without
resentment and their crimes without anger. A good judge [*bonus iudex*] condemns
what is damnable; he does not hate it.

"Tell me then. When the wise man has to deal with something of this sort, will
his mind not be touched by some unwonted excitement?" It will, I admit it. He
will feel a slight, tiny throb. As Zeno says, the soul of the wise man too, even when
the wound is healed, shows the scar. He will feel a hint or shadow of them, but
will be without the affections themselves.

The good judge envisaged here is a wise man, for only such a person is
free of the passions relevant to his situation. And the wise man, in dealing
with provocations to anger, will be like that good judge; he will still feel
something in his soul, a reminder of the passionate and foolish past that
he, like the judge of the treatise *On Clemency*, has had. Like that judge,
he will act with an awareness of his former self and its failings. In judging
others without anger he will remember his own fallibility.

In fact, this whole section of the treatise *On Anger* (1.14–19) is built on
the model of the judge. Consider the description of the *aequus iudex* at
1.14.2–3:

What has he, in truth, to hate about wrong-doers? Error is what has driven them
to their sort of misdeeds. But there is no reason for a man of understanding
[*prudens*] to hate those who have gone astray. If there were, he would hate himself.
He should consider how often he himself has not behaved well, how often his own
actions have required forgiveness – his anger will extend to himself. No fair judge
[*aequus iudex*] will reach a different verdict on his own case than on another's.
No one, I say, will be found who can acquit himself; anyone who declares himself
innocent has his eyes on the witness-box, not on his own conscience. How much
humaner it is to show a mild, paternal spirit, not harrying those who do wrong
but calling them back! Those who stray in the fields, through ignorance of the
way, are better brought back to the right path than chased out altogether.

The *prudens* here may or may not be a sage yet; but he is certainly
someone in a position of authoritative judgment who acts under two

constraints: he must be fair, using the same considerations for his own case and others; and he must act in the light of his own fallibility and proven track record for moral error. Anyone who has ever been in need of forgiveness[7] must extend to the objects of his judgment the kind of well-rounded consideration that makes possible his own forgiveness. He will not act in light of what he can get away with (with an eye to the witness box, believing that no one can *prove* that he has erred) but on the basis of true self-knowledge, in honest realization of his fallible character. As Seneca says in 1.15.3, this judicious attitude is a key to making the educational purpose of punishment succeed. He does not say why this should be so, but it is not hard to see what he has in mind: if the person punished believes that the judge is evenhanded and fair-minded, he or she is more likely to avoid the kind of recalcitrance often provoked by the perception of a double standard. In the chapters that follow (1.17–19) reason's judgment is preferred to that of a passion like anger in large measure because the rational agent has the judicial quality of holding itself to the same standard as others, whereas anger is *in totum inaequalis*, grants itself special standing (*sibi enim indulget*), and impedes any correction of its own judgment (1.17.7).

Seneca returns to this important feature of fair judging in book 2 (2.28). The *aequi iudices* will be those who acknowledge that no one is without *culpa*. What provokes resentment (*indignatio*), he says, is the claim by a judge that he is free of error (*nihil peccavi, nihil feci*), and this resentment at hypocritical double standards makes punishment inefficacious. And in considering the unlikely claim that someone might be free of crime under statute law, Seneca gives yet another reason for preferring a broader standard for judgment than merely legal requirements. The *iuris regula* is narrow, the *officiorum regula* is a wider and more relevant standard (and these *officia* include the requirements for humane and generous treatment of our fellow men). The *innocentiae formula* is a narrow and legalistic requirement for evaluation, Seneca maintains, and we should take into account in our judgments our own moral self-awareness. If we bear in mind that our own behavior may have been only technically and accidentally proper – though still proper enough to make us unconvictable – then we will be more fair in our judgments of those who actually do wrong (2.28.3–4). Such a broad and inclusive judgment is again recommended at 3.26.3: if we consider the general state of human affairs we will be *aequi iudices*, but we will be unfair (*iniquus*) if we treat some general human failing as specific to the person we are judging.

Seneca is clearly self-conscious in his use of the figure of the judge to sketch a standard of rational fair-mindedness in moral dealings with other people. A central feature of that fair-mindedness lies in knowing oneself, that is, in coming to see that one's own moral behavior is and has been flawed (although we also have to admit that this is a *relevant* factor in our judgments of others). His systematic use of the model of a trial before a judge extends even to this process of self-knowledge; not only does he contrast working with an eye to the witness box to working with an eye to one's own *conscientia*, but even in *On Anger* 3.36, the famous passage recommending Sextius' practice of daily self-examination, the trial model is detectable: each day the mind is to be summoned to give an account of itself; Sextius used to interrogate his own mind – and quite aggressively too. Seneca clearly takes this as a trial: "[Y]our anger will cease or moderate if it knows that each day it must come before a judge." And when he applies this lesson to himself, Seneca again uses trial language: *cotidie apud me causam dico.*

So far we have seen Seneca working with the model of a judge to outline a moral norm, a conception of fair-minded interaction with other people based on certain important general principles. The *aequus iudex* is opposed to the *severus iudex* at least insofar as the latter is a narrow judge of legality, exercising a kind of judgment compatible with a form of moral blindness that undermines his own effectiveness. I want now to shift attention to a later stage in Seneca's career, to the time of the treatise *On Favors* (and one of the *Letters on Ethics* that reflects on the same theme). In *On Favors* Seneca carries forward several of the features of the *iudex* model from these earlier works. Thus in *On Favors* 2.26.2, when discussing the causes of ingratitude, he notes the prevalence of the sort of one-sided and unequal judgment we have noticed already: in the giving and receiving of favors, which is a matter of estimating meritorious service and the value of recompense for it, *nemo non benignus est sui iudex.*[8] We discount the value of what others give us in a way that we do not discount our own services. The *aequus iudex* Seneca has already established would not do that – a *benignus sui iudex* is an *iniquus iudex.* By contrast, in 4.11.5 he points out that even ordinary people can escape this kind of selfish favoritism when conditions are right:

And yet we never give more carefully nor do we ever give our judging faculties a tougher workout than when all considerations of utility are eliminated and only what is honourable stands before our eyes. We are bad judges of our responsibilities [*officiorum mali iudices*] as long as they are distorted by hope, fear, and pleasure (that most sluggish of vices). But when death eliminates all of that and sends an unbribed judge in to deliver sentence, then we seek out the most worthy recipient for our goods; we prepare nothing with greater care than the things which don't matter to us.

In matters of practical reason, we are thought of as judges weighing the merits of various courses of action, our *officia*. Selfish considerations are the bribes that corrupt our moral judgment and the only way an ordinary man can be counted on to set aside such selfishness in his choices is to wait until he is so close to death that he cannot count on benefiting from the choice.[9] At 3.12.2–3 Seneca refers to comparable limitations on the good judgment of a moral judge; the values placed on various kinds of benefits are variable, *prout fuerit iudex aut huc aut illo inclinatus animo*. (Cf. *Epistulae* 81.31.)

In a later book of the *On Favors* there is another echo of the *iudex* model developed so far. In 6.6.1–2 Seneca is emphasizing the freedom of judgment of the moral judge. Unlike legally defined offenses, favors are bound by no specific laws and the agent plays the role of an *arbiter*, free of the narrow constraints of interpreting specific bits of legislation. In those cases, "nothing is in our own power [*nostrae potestatis*], we must go where we are led. But in the case of favors I have full discretion [*tota potestas mea est*], I am the judge. And so I do not separate or distinguish favors and injuries, but I refer them to the same judge [*ad eundem iudicem mitto*]."

The difficult task of weighing benefit and injury must be done in a coordinated way and demands a judge with full power to decide on the relevance of all factors. The *formula* and *leges* that bind an ordinary judge would be unreasonable constraints in such cases; although he refers to himself as an *arbiter* in such cases, it is clear that the arbiter is thought of as a judge with particular latitude, but still as a judge.[10]

This contrast between the freedom of the moral judge and the constraints binding the ordinary judge is a disanalogy, and Seneca uses the contrast to give sharper definition to his model of moral judgment. In book 3, sections 6–8, Seneca considers the question of whether it should be possible to bring legal actions for ingratitude.[11] His reply, in brief, is no: this is a job for moral, not legal, judgment. But in setting out this reply, his use of the model of legal judgment gives clearer shape to the concept of moral judgment he has been developing.

It is not the case, Seneca argues, that ingratitude is not a very serious offense; yet the tradition at Rome as almost everywhere else is not to punish it (3.6). One explanation for this is that the assessments involved in such cases are so extremely difficult (*cum difficilis esset incertae rei aestimatio*) that we suspend our own judgments and refer the matter to divine *iudices*. Variable human inclinations cloud human assessments, just as they do the decisions of judges.

In 3.7 he outlines justifications for exempting ingratitude from actual legal judgment and reserving it for moral judgment. The first three do not bear closely on our theme of moral judgment, but at 3.7.5–8 the *iudex* model comes into play again.

Moreover, all the issues which are the basis for a legal action can be delimited and do not provide unbounded freedom for the judge. That is why a good case is in better shape if it is sent to a judge than to an arbitrator, because the *formula* constrains the judge and imposes fixed limits which he cannot violate; but an arbitrator has the freedom of his own integrity [*libera religio*] and is not restricted by any bounds. He can devalue one factor and play up another, regulating his verdict not by the arguments of law and justice but in accordance with the demands of humanity and pity [*misericordia*]. A trial for ingratitude would not bind the judge but would put him in a position of complete freedom of decision [*sed regno liberrimo positura*]. For there is no agreement on what a favor is, nor on how great it is. It makes a big difference how indulgently [*benigne*] the judge interprets it. No law shows us what an ungrateful man is: often even the man who returned what he received is ungrateful and the man who did not is grateful. There are some matters on which even an inexperienced judge can give a verdict, as when one must decide that someone did or did not do something, or when the dispute is eliminated by offering written commitments, or when reason dictates to the parties what is right. But when an assessment of someone's state of mind has to be made, when the only matter at issue is one on which only wisdom can decide, then you cannot pick a judge for these matters from the standard roster – some man whose wealth and equestrian inheritance put him on the list. So it is not the case that this matter is inappropriate for referral to a judge. It is just that no one has been discovered who is a fit judge for this issue. This won't surprise you if you consider the difficulty that anyone would have who is to take action against a man charged in such a matter.

After outlining the range of complicated assessments that would need to be made, Seneca continues:

Who will weigh up these factors? It is a hard verdict, and calls for investigation not into the thing itself but into its significance. For though the things be identical, they have different weight if they are given in different ways. This man gave me a favor, but not willingly; rather he *complained* that he had done so, or looked at me with more arrogance than he used to, or gave so slowly that he would have done me more service if he had said a rapid "no." How will a judge go about appraising these things, when one's words or hesitation or expression can destroy the gratitude in a service?

Ordinary human judges would not be capable of the fair-minded and complex assessments that a trial for ingratitude would demand. Yet these are matters on which an ideal judge, the sage, could decide,[12] and although Seneca rather hyperbolically contrasts the freedom from constraint of the *arbiter* from the restrictions imposed on a judge (even saying in 3.7.5 that he follows *humanitas* and *misericordia* rather than *lex* or *iustitia*), it emerges from the whole context that the moral judge is expected to weigh facts and assess merit by principles of fairness and justice. The various forms of fallibility that impair the rest of us lead, in such cases, not to more cautious judgments but to none at all. The question of whether a realization of one's personal limitations should induce us nonsages to temper or to avoid passing moral judgments returns in one of Seneca's *Letters*.

Letter 81 introduces one more kind of judge to deal with in outlining Seneca's model of moral judgment. Here he addresses a detailed problem about the assessment of favors. In sections 4–6, Seneca uses the model of judgment to discuss another difficult evaluation (which involves balancing prior good deeds against more recent injuries). But the way he sets out his approach to the decision is important for present purposes. He asks what the verdict of a *rigidus iudex* might be – and it turns out that such a judge would make the difficult assessments that are required to come to a firm assessment of the relative values of benefit and injury, including the detailed assessment of the state of mind of the agents involved. As he says in 81.6, "a good man [*vir bonus*] makes his calculation in such a way as to limit himself:[13] he adds to the benefit and subtracts from the injury. But that other *remissior iudex*, whom I prefer to be, will order the parties to forget the injury and remember the service."[14]

It is now, I think, clear what is going on in this case.[15] The sage (*vir bonus*) enters into the difficult business of making fine assessments of people's motivations and the values of their actions, while Seneca himself, as an ordinary moral agent, must be a looser sort of judge. He must handle the case in such a way that judgments that he cannot in fact make accurately are not called for. So he does not *reduce* the weighting assigned to the injury, he *eliminates* it, thus simplifying a moral dilemma in a manner with which many who have been faced with the challenge of weighing the imponderable can sympathize. The sage, and he alone, can properly form a *rigida sententia*, a verdict that is both exact and inflexible. It takes enormous self-confidence to formulate such a verdict; no wonder only the sage can do it.

I indulge in a slight digression at this point to bring in an interesting parallel to the sort of self-critical modesty in judgment that Seneca displays here in moral matters. In the *Natural Questions* – a somewhat neglected work with a strong epistemological subtext not advertised in its title[16] – Seneca shows the same sensitivity. In the fragmentary book 4b Seneca raises a curious Stoic theory about snow (5.1) and at the same apologizes for introducing a theory that is (shall we say) less than compelling (*infirma* is Seneca's word):

I dare neither to mention nor to omit a consideration adduced by my own school. For what harm is done by occasionally writing for an easy-going judge [*facilior iudex*]? Indeed, if we are going to start testing every argument by the standard of a gold assay, silence will be imposed. There are very few arguments without an opponent; the rest are contested even if they do win.

An easygoing judge is one, I think, who does not impose the highest standards on every theory, simply because he or she is aware that in a field like meteorology the demand for demonstrative proof cannot be met. Epistemic humility and pragmatism suggest the wisdom of being a *facilior iudex* where certainty is not attainable. As in the moral sphere, so here, Seneca works out this essentially liberal notion through the metaphor of judging.

If one wants a chilling picture of the results to which a *rigida sententia* can lead if it is formed by some lesser man, one need only to turn back to the treatise *On Anger*. In his discussion of the traits of the *aequus iudex* in book 1, Seneca tells the story of one Cn. Piso: he was free of many vices, but he was perversely stubborn and mistook *rigor* for *constantia* (1.18.3). *Constantia*, of course, is a virtue of the sage – Seneca wrote a short treatise on the *constantia* of the sage – and, as we see in the anecdote that follows, (1.18.3–6) *rigor* is the vice that corresponds to it:

I can remember Gnaeus Piso, a man free of many faults, but wrong-headed in taking obduracy [*rigor*] for firmness [*constantia*]. In a fit of anger, he had ordered the execution of a soldier who had returned from leave without his companion, on the grounds that if he could not produce him he must have killed him. The man requested time for an enquiry to be made. His request was refused. Condemned and led outside the rampart, he was already stretching out his neck for execution when suddenly there appeared the very companion who was thought to have been murdered. The centurion in charge of the execution told his subordinate to sheathe his sword, and led the condemned man back to Piso, intending to exonerate Piso of guilt – for fortune had already exonerated the soldier. A huge crowd accompanied the two soldiers locked in each others's embrace amid great rejoicing in the camp. In a fury Piso mounted the tribunal and ordered them both to be executed, the soldier who had not committed murder and the one who had not been murdered. What could be more scandalous? The vindication of the one meant the death of the two. And Piso added a third. He ordered the centurion who had brought the condemned man back to be himself executed. On the self-same spot, three were consigned to execution, all for the innocence of one! How skilful bad temper can be at devising pretexts for rage! "You," it says, "I command to be executed because you have been condemned; you, because you have been the cause of your companion's condemnation; and you, because you have disobeyed orders from your general to kill." It invented three charges, having discovered grounds for none.[17]

When we consider *Letter* 81 we realize how very risky a *rigida sententia* would be for anyone except a sage. Seneca holds the Stoic view that anyone except a sage is vicious and morally unreliable. So everyone except a sage needs to exercise his role as a moral *iudex* with a self-restraint that the sage would not need. Seneca's respect for the epistemic and moral limitations of ordinary human beings leads him to develop a model of moral judgment worked out in terms drawn from the practices and institutions of *iudices* in Roman society, a model that many of us might still find worth considering. Such judges seek fairness through self-knowledge; they find their way to clemency through reflection on the universality of human failings and the fact that they too share those faults; they work to rehabilitate others more effectively by not placing themselves on a moral pedestal; in unmanageably hard cases they refuse to judge and in others adopt a decision-making strategy designed to obviate the need for exact decisions about the motivations of others, which they are in no position to make. The ideal judge and the ordinary judge share one important trait: as moral judges they need to have latitude to consider the widest possible range of relevant factors (though, of course, they will use this latitude differently). Both kinds of judge make independent decisions guided but not constrained by detailed legislation and the praetor's *formula* for the case.

So far we have, I think, at least prima facie evidence that Seneca was self-consciously and creatively exploiting aspects of the (to him) familiar notion of a *iudex* as a guide to reflection on the kind of rationality appropriate to situations that call for moral decision making. This is an example of one of the ways Seneca's philosophical creativity emerges in his works. This project can also be observed in his exploitation of the corresponding notion of judgment itself, *iudicium*. Because I cannot range so widely over the corpus to illustrate this claim, I simply focus here on a small number of especially revealing texts.

I want to recall, first of all, a passage to which I have already alluded. In *On Anger* 3.36 Seneca recommends the practice of daily moral self-examination, and in so doing he presents the review as an internal trial. He brings his awareness of his daily behavior before an internal judge: *apud me causam dico*, he says (3.36.2). There is, in the life of this metaphor, an internal trial at which a verdict can be reached. We might compare here the end of *Letter* 28: "So, as far as you can, bring charges against yourself, conduct an enquiry against yourself. First, play the role of prosecutor, then of judge and only then, finally, plead for mitigation. Be tough on yourself at last" (*Epistulae* 28.10).

This internal judgment is described elsewhere as a *iudicium*. In *On the Private Life* 1.2–3, for example, Seneca laments the fact that our own *iudicia* are corrupt and fickle (*prava, levia*) and that in our weakness we remain dependent on *aliena iudicia* instead of on our own. There are, in fact, many places where Seneca contrasts this kind of internal judgment (whether of ourselves or of the morally significant factors we face in our life) to that of others, and these passages alone don't suffice to show that the legal model is alive and functioning. After all, *iudicium* is a common enough term in Latin for assessments, beliefs, and decisions of all kinds. Of slightly greater weight, perhaps, is *On Clemency* 2.2.2, where *iudicium* refers to the kind of settled and reflective judgment that confirms tendencies that are otherwise merely matters of *impetus* and *natura* (this is, I suspect, pretty much the sense that *iudicium* has in *On Anger* 2, where it used to demarcate passion from rational action and seems to have close ties (especially in chapters 1–4) to the earlier Stoic notion of assent).[18]

Another aspect of moral *iudicium*, its stability, appears clearly in the treatise *On the Happy Life*. Here Seneca articulates a contrast between judging and merely believing (1.4–5), in which judging is clearly an act of fully deliberate and self-conscious moral decision: "No one goes wrong only for himself, but he is also the cause and agent of someone else's mistake . . . and as long as each and every person prefers believing to judging he never makes a *judgment* about his life, merely forms *beliefs*, and the mistake passed from hand to hand overturns us and casts us down headlong."[19]

Here "judgment" in the strong sense is aligned with what is stable, internal, and our own. This is also apparent in section 5, allied with his claim that rationality is the indispensable key to happiness is his summary definition of the happy life: it is a life *in recto certoque iudicio stabilita et immutabilis*. That immobility and consistency yield a *pura mens, soluta omnibus malis.* As he says at 6.2, the happy man is exactly he who is *iudicii rectus.*[20] This remark comes in the midst of his discussion of the role of pleasure in the happy life, a discussion that culminates in section 9.2–3 with an apt statement of the normal Stoic view on pleasure:[21]

> It is not a cause or reward for virtue, but an adjunct [*accessio*] to it. The highest good is in *iudicium* itself and the condition of a mind in the best state, which, when it has filled up its own domain and fenced itself about at its boundaries is then the complete and highest good and wants for nothing further. For there is nothing beyond the whole, any more than there is anything beyond the boundary.

The location of happiness in judgment and the close connection of it to a mental disposition (rather than a transient act of mental decision) suggest that *iudicium* for Seneca plays much the same role that *prohairesis* plays in Epictetus, as a term signifying both a morally significant act of decision making, a form of assent, and a stable disposition that constitutes the locus of happiness.[22] As in *On Anger* 2.4.2 *iudicium* is connected closely to the idea of stable and irreversible moral decision. In this sense *iudicium* verges on becoming a faculty – as also at *On Favors* 4.11.5, where we are said to torment our *iudicia* when we work through a tough moral decision. We might say that such decisions are a test of "character"; for Seneca it is our judicial capacity that is being put to the test.

Throughout the *Letters on Ethics* Seneca uses the language of judgment for moral assessments of many kinds, and a close consideration of how his usage varies and grows would be interesting. But in *Letter* 71 (which deals extensively with moral decisions) Seneca strengthens this connection between a robust notion of judgment and the kind of ideal *prohairesis* that constitutes the stable character state of the sage. The passage of interest deals with the Stoic paradox that all goods are equal (*Epistulae* 71.17ff.). After some familiar argumentation on the topic, Seneca describes his notion of virtue in lofty terms (18–20). He compares it with the criterion (*regula*, i.e., the *kanōn*) for what is straight (*rectum*), which cannot vary without rendering the notion of straight meaningless. Similarly, virtue is *recta* (indeed, must be if it is to function as a standard of rightness) and so admits of no bending (*flexuram non recipit*). In the corrupt sentence that follows[23] there was clearly some reference to virtue being *rigida* as well – natural enough since it is also said to be unbending, and its unbending straightness could not be preserved if it were not rigid. Virtue, Seneca adds, makes judgments about all things, and nothing judges it. Like other standards, virtue is an unqualified instance of the property it measures in others.[24]

This rigidity of virtue, its inflexibility (so termed explicitly at *Epistulae* 95.62 also: *inflexibile iudicium*), is tied here to its status as an instrument of judgment. Let us move ahead to section 29, where Seneca affects to anticipate Lucilius' impatience, as he so often does: *venio nunc illo quo me vocat expectatio tua.* He concedes that the wise man will suffer a variety of physical pains but that these are not bad things unless the sage's mental reaction makes them so. At sections 32–33 he summarizes (my translation):

> This point can be stated quickly and quite succinctly: virtue is the only good and certainly there is no good without it; virtue itself is situated in the better part of us, the rational part. So what is this virtue? A true and immovable *iudicium*; this is the source of mental impulses, and by this we put to the test every presentation that stimulates impulse. It is appropriate for this *iudicium* to judge that all things touched by virtue are both good and equal to each other.

Here again our judgment is an unchangeable inner disposition, cognitive in its function and determinative in the process of regulating actions. It is, in the relevant sense, our perfected *hēgemonikon*, our *prohairesis*.

I want to conclude by emphasizing just two points. First, it really is remarkable that Seneca uses the language of legal judgment to express this idea. I concede happily that the noun *iudicium* does not always carry the full weight of a live legal metaphor. But in the context of the brief survey I have offered of Seneca's active and long-term interest in that metaphorical field, it seems implausible to suggest that it plays no role here – even if the nonlegal idea of *kanōn* is also prominently in play in this letter.

And, second, this is a good and effective metaphor with which to work. Consider only the key point of this letter, the notion that the *iudicium* of the sage is unbendable and rigid. Seneca had written elsewhere about rigidity of judgment – we think of the perverse and passionate *iudex* Cn. Piso from the *On Anger*. Yet here judgment in its normative sense is *supposed to be* rigid and unbending. The merely human judge on the bench, like the ordinary man exercising moral judgment, must not be a *severus* or *rigidus iudex*, for reasons we know about from his other discussions of moral judgment: human affairs call for the kind of fine evaluations and judgment calls that lead anyone with a grain of self-knowledge to refrain, to suspend, to wait. On matters so complex that it is wiser (as Seneca says in *On Favors* 3.6) to refer them to the gods, only the sage, Zeus' intellectual equal, can truly judge. The inflexibility suitable for gods and for the sage would be mad rigidity for us.[25] It is often said that Seneca, like all later Stoics, adopts a double code of ethics, one for the sage and one for miserable mankind. I have argued before that this is not so.[26] What Seneca accomplishes in this bold experiment of thinking by means of a living legal metaphor is to show that, despite all of the differences between sage and fool, there is still but one norm by which all humans should live. The inescapable fact that we are all moral judges, each according to his or her abilities, unites us in the shared humanity that Seneca urged so ineffectively on Nero in his address *On Clemency*.

Notes

1. As Janet Sisson reminds me (in correspondence), the judicial metaphor is also used in relatively straightforward epistemological contexts as well, as by Plato at *Theaetetus* 201. But the issues involved with moral judgment are markedly different, as we shall see.
2. In Plato too there are examples of such models. Socrates' account in the *Protagoras* of moral decision as a matter of measurement and calculation is an obvious example of such a philosophical redescription.
3. My thanks to Michael Dewar for this observation.
4. This nexus of ideas has not been fully explored in Seneca, although I am aware of three helpful discussions. First, Düll 1976, though jejune, nevertheless confirms the realism and legal accuracy of Seneca's handling of legal concepts. (Indeed, his discussion of the *exceptio*, pp. 377–80, would shed useful light on discussions of reservation in Seneca's works, although I do not pursue that issue here.) Second, Maurach 1965 makes some tantalizing but underdeveloped suggestions along the lines I pursue here (the pertinent remarks are on pp. 316ff. of the reprinted version). Closer to my argument is Maria Bellincioni's discussion of the judicial metaphor in connection with the theme of clemency (Bellincioni 1984a). In this paper, I think, her view of how Seneca uses the metaphor is somewhat one-sided: "The sense . . . is, then, always just one: it is an invitation to seek in human relations, such as they are, the sole authentic justice which is born from an attitude of love" (124 of the reprinted version); compare her remarks about *Ep.* 81 on p. 115, which opposes *clementia* to the rigidity of the *iudex* rather too starkly. I argue, first, that the judicial metaphor is more of a conceptual tool for thinking through a range of problems; and, second, that Seneca makes more positive use of the notion of a moral judge than Bellincioni allows for. Her thesis is (in outline) that *humanitas*, love, and forgiveness stand in opposition to the rigidity of "judging," whereas I think Seneca leaves considerable room for an idealized form of judging that is practicable only for a sage. I am grateful to Miriam Griffin for pointing out the importance of Bellincioni's work for my discussion. (See too her book, Bellincioni 1984b.)
5. *tamquam in alieno iudicio dicam* – I think that Procopé's translation is wrong here. I would prefer to translate "as though I were speaking at someone else's trial" – which he is not really doing, since this issue affects us all.

6. Bellincioni 1984b: 95 comments on the legal metaphor here: "*Liberum arbitrium* is in fact the freedom of judgment of the *arbiter*, who, in the Roman legal system is contrasted with the normal *iudex*, who, by contrast delivered his verdict for the case in question on the basis of the praetor's *formula* furnished to him on each occasion." See my later comments on the *arbiter*. Chapter 2 of this book ("La clemenza del giudice") is useful background for my treatment of the metaphor. See too Bellincioni 1984a: 120–22.

7. The term, *venia*, is used differently than in *On Clemency*.

8. See later on 3.7.5 on indulgent interpretation.

9. One might compare this with the myth in Plato's *Gorgias*, which tells how the judges of men's lives appointed by Zeus did a poor job as long as they exercised their judgments while still alive.

10. See Bellincioni 1984a:123–24, and my note 13.

11. See Bellincioni 1984a: 116–18.

12. Contrast the view of Bellincioni, who thinks that for Seneca judging per se is a bad model for moral behavior and assessment. At Bellincioni 1984a: 117, apropos of this passage, she overstates the opposition of the *arbiter* to that of the *iudex*, holding that the former is bound by "nessuno schema giuridico" (whereas there were in fact some procedural guidelines for *arbitri*, although they were, of course, free of the *formula* of a *praetor*). On p. 118 she envisages Seneca propounding as a norm a "judgment" free of *all* constraints, not just of procedure but also of fact. Rather, Seneca merely acknowledges in this text that nonsages cannot be counted on to assess the facts; he is far from urging the positive value of operating without constraint from the facts, guided only by *humanitas* and *misericordia*. Similarly on p. 119 she opposes the constraints of any judicial procedure to an unlimited "libertà di perdonare," and at pp. 120–21 she opposes the *arbiter* to the *iudex* in a similarly absolute manner. Two texts of which she needed to take more careful account are *On Favors* 3.8.1, cited earlier: "[I]t is not the case that this matter is inappropriate for referral to a judge. It is just that no one has been discovered who is a fit judge for this issue"; and *On Clemency* 2.7.3, cited earlier, does not oppose the activity of judging to that of the *arbiter*, but notes that mercy *judges* with *liberum arbitrium*. Hence the opposition of the *iudex* to the *arbiter* cannot be supported by this passage. It is safer, I think, to take the activity of the *arbiter* as a form of judging (one that has a freedom and sensitivity that the *formula* denies) rather than an activity opposed to the rational activity of judging per se.

13. This is the interpretation of *circumscribere* also arrived at by Bellincioni 1984a: 116. The rejected possibility is that *circumscribere* means "cheat."

14. Compare *rigidus* versus *remissus* in *Epistulae* 1.10.

15. Contrast the discussion in Bellincioni 1984a: 113–16. She treats the *rigidus iudex* too simplistically when she regards him solely (115) as a foil for what she sees as Seneca's preferred solution based on *humanitas*. See my note 13. I have also discussed this text in Inwood 1995, written before I was aware of Bellincioni's work.

16. See Inwood 1999a.

17. Cf. 3.29.2 on *pertinacia*.

18. Compare *On Favors* 2.14.1: *iudicium interpellat adfectus.* Also *Epistulae* 45.3–4 where *iudicium* is contrasted to externally motivated *indulgentia.* Tony Long pointed out that *sunkatathesis* (so important in Stoic analysis of the passions) is originally a legal term for casting a vote at a trial. I have discussed this passage of *On Anger* in Inwood 1993.

19. In 1.5 the term *iudicium* is used generically too – Seneca avoids technical precision and consistency. At *On Favors* 1.10.5 it is *iudicare* which is used for unstable opinion in contrast to *scire.*

20. Compare *Epistulae* 66.32: *sola ratio est immutabilis et iudicii tenax.*

21. See Diogenes Laertius 7.85–86, where pleasure is an *epigennēma.*

22. See *Epistulae* 108.21: *iudicium quidem tuum sustine.*

23. In the Oxford Classical Text: *rigidari quidem amplius quam intendi potest.*

24. The invariability of virtue forms the basis for the argument in support of the main proposition under discussion, that all goods are equal. Because the other goods are measured by virtue and (as goods) found to measure up to its standard, they must all be equal with regard to the trait measured by that absolute standard (in this case, straightness, *Epistulae* 71.20). See also *Epistulae* 66.32: *Ratio rationi par est, sicut rectum recto. Omnes virtutes rationes sunt; rationes sunt, si rectae sunt; si rectae sunt et pares sunt.*

25. I am grateful to Tony Long for directing my attention to what the Stoic Hierocles says about divine judgments in Stobaeus (1: 63, 6 W): they are unswerving and implacable in their *krimata.* The virtues on which this rigidity is based are epistemological, of course (*ametaptōsia* and *bebaiotēs*), and shared with the sage.

26. See Inwood 1999b.

5

Stoic First Movements in Christianity

Richard Sorabji

The great study on first movements in Christianity by O. Lottin ascribes the invention of the idea to the eleventh century.[1] But in fact the idea of first movements in emotion has its first extant record a thousand years earlier in Seneca's *On Anger*, book 2, chapters 2–4, and has a long history in Christianity after that.

2.2.1 To what, you ask, is this inquiry relevant? It is so that we can know what anger is. For if it comes to birth against our will [*invitis*], it will never succumb to reason. For all movements which are not brought about by our will [*voluntas*] are beyond control and inevitable, like shivering when sprinkled with cold water and the recoil from certain contacts. At bad news our hair stands on end, at improper words a blush suffuses us, and vertigo follows when we look at a steep drop.

2.2.2 Anger is put to flight by precepts [*praecepta*]. For it is a voluntary vice of the mind, not something that comes out of some circumstance of the human lot, so befalls even the wisest. Under that heading we must put that first shock [*ictus*] of the mind which moves us after we believe there is an injustice.

2.2.3 This creeps in even amid the theatrical sights of the stage or the recital of ancient deeds. Often we seem [*videmur*] to be angry with Clodius for exiling Cicero and with Antony for killing him. Who is not roused [*concitari*] against the weapons of Marius, or the proscription of Sulla? Who is not disturbed [*infestus*] at Theodotus and Achillas and that child who dared the unchildlike crime?

2.2.4 Singing and quick rhythms and the martial sound of trumpets incite [*instigare*] us. A grim painting or the sad spectacle of punishment, however just, moves [*movere*] the mind.

2.2.5 This is why we laugh with people who are laughing, while a crowd of mourners saddens [*contristare*] us too, and we seethe with excitement [*effervescere*] at contests between other people. This is not anger, any more than what furrows the brow at the sight of a simulated shipwreck is sadness, or what runs through the minds of readers at Hannibal besieging the walls after [the battle of] Cannae is fear. All those things are movements of minds unwilling to be moved, and not emotions [*adfectus*], but preliminary [*principia*] preludes to emotions.

2.2.6 It is in this way that the trumpet excites [*suscitare*] the ears of a military man who is now wearing his toga in the middle of peacetime and the clatter of weapons alerts [*erigere*] the camp horses. They say that Alexander put his hand to his weapons when Xenophantus sang.

2.3.1 None of these things which jolt the mind by chance ought to be called emotions [*adfectus*], but are things to which the mind is subject, so to speak, rather than being active. So emotion is not being moved at the appearances presented by things, but is giving oneself up to them and following up this chance movement.

2.3.2 For with pallor, and falling tears, and irritation from fluid in the private parts, or a deep sigh, and eyes suddenly flashing, or anything like these, if anyone thinks that they are a sign of emotion and a manifestation of the mind, he is mistaken and does not understand that these are jolts to the body.

2.3.3 So very often even the bravest man grows pale as he puts on his armor, and when the signal for battle is given, the knees of the fiercest soldier tremble a little, and before the battle lines ram each other, the heart of the great commander jumps, and the extremities of the most eloquent speaker stiffen as he gets ready to speak.

2.3.4 Anger must not merely be moved; it must rush out. For it is an impulse [*impetus*], but there is never impulse without assent of the mind [*adsensus mentis*]. For it is impossible that revenge and punishment should be at stake without the mind's knowledge. Someone thinks himself injured, he wills revenge, but he settles down at once when some consideration dissuades him. I do not call this anger, this movement of the mind obedient to reason. That is anger which leap-frogs reason and drags reason with it.

2.3.5 So that first agitation of the mind which the appearance of injustice [*species iniuriae*] inflicts [*incussit*] is no more anger than is the appearance of injustice itself. It is the subsequent impulse [*impetus*], which not only receives but approves [*adprobavit*] the appearance of injustice, that is anger: the rousing of a mind that prosecutes vengeance with will and judgment [*voluntas, iudicium*]. There is never any doubt that fear involves flight and anger impulse [*impetus*]. See if you think anything can be chosen or avoided without the assent of the mind [*adsensus mentis*].

2.4.1 In order that you may know how emotions [*adfectus*] (1) begin, or (2) grow, or (3) are carried away [*efferri*], (1) the first movement is involuntary [*non voluntarius*], like a preparation for emotion and a kind of threat. (2) The second movement is accompanied by will [*voluntas*], not an obstinate one, to the effect that it is appropriate [*oporteat*] for me to be avenged since I am injured, or it is appropriate for him to be punished since he has committed a crime. (3) The third movement is by now uncontrolled [*impotens*], and wills [*vult*] to be avenged, not if it is appropriate [*si oportet*], but come what may [*utique*], and it has overthrown [*evicit*] reason.

2.4.2 We cannot escape that first shock [*ictus*] of the mind by reason, just as we cannot escape those things we mentioned which befall the body either, so as to avoid another's yawn infecting us, or avoid our eyes blinking when fingers are suddenly poked toward us. Reason cannot control those things, though perhaps familiarity and constant attention may weaken them. The second movement, which is born of judgment, is removed by judgment.[2]

I think Seneca was defending the view of his Stoic predecessor Chrysippus that the emotions are judgments. Distress is the judgment that there is present harm and that it is appropriate to feel a sinking of the soul. Pleasure is the judgment that there is present benefit and that it is appropriate to feel an expansion of the soul. Fear is the judgment that there is future harm and that it is appropriate to avoid it. Appetite is the judgment that there is future good and that it is appropriate to reach for it. Sharply distinguished from these judgments are the mere appearances that there is benefit or harm in the offing. The mere appearance is not yet a judgment and not yet an emotion because a judgment – and, hence, an emotion – is the assent of reason to the appearance. Ordinary people not trained in Stoicism may give the assent of reason so automatically that they do not realize that assent is a separate operation of the mind from receiving an appearance. But Stoicism trains you to stand back from appearances and interrogate them without automatically giving them the assent of your reason.

This account of the emotions as judgments of reason is very intellectualistic. Seneca wants to distinguish sharply from the genuine emotion what he calls "first movements." The first movements are involuntary. They do not involve the voluntary assent of reason. Seneca wants to show, by contrast, that anger and other emotions can be eradicated by rational means and that is why he wants to distinguish so decisively between the emotion itself, which involves the voluntary assent of reason, and the mere first movements, which are admittedly involuntary but are not to be confused with voluntary emotions.

First movements are initial shocks that are caused (Seneca's verb in 2.3.5 is *incussit*) by the mere appearance of harm or benefit. Seneca distinguishes physical and mental first movements. His examples of physical first movements are shivering, recoiling, having one's hair stand on end, blushing, vertigo, pallor, tears, sexual irritation, sighing, the eyes flashing, the knees trembling, the heart jumping. Even in the most eloquent speaker, he adds, the fingers will stiffen. There has been controversy about what he means by mental first movements, but I think this is revealed by a passage in Cicero in the preceding century, *Tusculan Disputations* 3.82–83, where Cicero talks of bites and little contractions which are independent of judgment and, unlike judgment, are involuntary.[3] Cicero does not yet say that these bites and little contractions can precede the judgment, but he does at least make them independent of judgment. I have argued elsewhere that bites and little contractions are fully explained by Galen in *On the Doctrines of Hippocrates and Plato*, books 2–3, as being sharp contractions of the soul, and the soul, Chrysippus believed, was a physical entity located in the chest.[4] These contractions can be felt. We ourselves, and Galen like us, would reinterpret them as physiological rather than as movements of a physical soul. Thus reinterpreted, they are familiar to everyone. We have all experienced sinking feelings when distressed.

I believe that Seneca's first movements perform four important functions. First, we have seen by distinguishing them from emotions, Seneca hoped to dispel the impression that emotions are involuntary. Second, I think that first movements provide an answer to Posidonius' objections to the claim that emotions consist exclusively of judgments. Posidonius, as reported by Galen,[5] offers examples in which, he says, we have emotion without the relevant judgments. Sometimes we shed tears even though we disown the judgment that there is harm. People can have their emotions changed by music, which is wordless and therefore does nothing to change their judgments. Animals are not capable of the relevant judgments and yet they too, Posidonius urges, experience emotions. It is noteworthy that Seneca, without mentioning Posidonius, has a reply to all three of these alleged examples of emotion without the relevant judgments. In no case do we have here genuine emotion. We have only first movements. Seneca explicitly mentions tears and the effects of music as examples of first movements. Just before our passage, without actually mentioning first movements, at 1.3.8, he denies that animals experience genuine emotions. A further function of his discussion, then, is to rule out Posidonius' alleged examples of emotion not requiring judgment.

Third, it is noteworthy that Seneca speaks as if the arts do not arouse genuine emotion but only first movements. In 2.2.3–4 he considers the theater, historical narrative, singing, rhythm, trumpets, and painting, and he says that these arts arouse only first movements. This I think helps to explain what has proved something of a mystery. Why do not the Stoics, given their enormous interest in the theater, discuss the brilliant theory, provided by Aristotle in response to Plato, the theory of catharsis? According to Aristotle, there is no need to banish from the ideal society the writers of tragedy and comedy because the stirring up of emotions has, after all, a good effect, overlooked by Plato, of lightening us by some catharsis of the emotions. Whatever Aristotle means by catharsis, which is controversial, he gives the analogy of a medical laxative or emetic. We can now begin to guess why at least the later Stoics did not need to discuss Aristotle's theory further. Seneca had in effect ruled it out by his claim in our passage that the theater does not arouse emotions at all but only first movements. In that case, it could not perform the cathartic function that Aristotle postulated. No wonder, then, the later Stoics look for another justification for the theater in society.

Fourth, I think Seneca's distinction of first movements is useful in the treatment of unwanted emotions. William James said we do not cry because we are sad; we are sad because we cry.[6] This is not entirely true, but there is some truth in it. One can think, "I must have been unjustly treated. Look, I am even crying." Noticing the tears can intensify our emotion. Conversely, Seneca's advice should help us to calm our emotions. We need only say to ourselves, "these are just tears, in other words, first movements. So they are irrelevant. The only question that matters is whether I am really in a bad situation." The distinction of first movements can be genuinely calming.

The term "first movement" is explicitly used in 2.4.1, although the vaguer term "beginnings" (*principia*) is used in 2.2.5. Seneca's contemporary in the first century A.D., Philo of Alexandria, the Jewish philosopher, tells us of another name for Stoic first movements: prepassions.[7]

I want to turn now to the brilliant Christian thinker Origen two centuries later than Seneca in the third century A.D., or at least to the fourth-century Latin translation provided by Rufinus of Origen's *On First Principles*.[8] In *On First Principles* 3.2.2, Origen, in Rufinus' translation, explicitly uses the expression "first movements" but he completely transforms the Stoic idea of first movements by connecting them in 3.2.2 and 3.2.4 with the bad thoughts that are discussed in the Gospels of Mark 7:21 and Matthew 15:19. By identifying first movements with thoughts and suggestions, he blurs the sharp distinction between first movements and emotions on which the Stoics had insisted. For now first movements like emotions are thoughts. In his commentary on Matthew 26:36–39, Origen uses the same word as Seneca had used at 2.2.5 – that first movements are beginnings (*principia*). But now the word "beginnings" has become vague because it is no longer so clear whether a beginning of emotion is distinct from emotion or whether it is a little bit of emotion. Origen adds that these first movements are no more than incitements and that they may be aroused either naturally or, in some cases, by the devil.

After Philo and Origen, who both worked in Alexandria, the Stoic tradition about prepassion continued in that city. Didymus the Blind and his pupil Jerome, who were both in Alexandria, continue to talk of prepassion. It is no surprise, then, if Origen's idea of first movements was familiar to Evagrius, who came to live in the Egyptian desert in the fourth century A.D.

Evagrius had been ordained first by Basil of Caesarea and then by Gregory of Nazianzus. But in 382 he had an affair with a married woman and had to leave Constantinople. He was first sheltered in Jerusalem by Rufinus and Melania, who were the heads of monastic communities in Jerusalem for men and women, respectively. After staying with them he went to join the monks in the Egyptian desert and soon became a semi-anchorite. The semianchorites lived in solitude for six days of the week and met their fellow monks only on the seventh day. He had ample time to study the emotional states that afflict the hermit in the solitude of the desert. Coming to Evagrius from the Stoics is like moving from Aristotle's logic of individual terms to the Stoic logic of complete propositions, in that Evagrius studies not the individual types of emotions so much as the interrelations between emotions. In his *Practical Treatise*, Sentence 6, it is clear that he is talking about first movements, even though he does not use the name, for he says that it is not up to us whether bad thoughts affect us but it is up to us whether they linger or stir up emotions (*pathē*). There are eight bad thoughts, which, using a Stoic term, he calls generic. They are thoughts of gluttony, fornication, avarice, distress, anger, depression, vanity, and pride. Having the thoughts is not yet sin but only temptation. Sin, he says, is assent, assent to the pleasure of the thought. These last points are made in *Practical Treatise* 74–75.

The most generic thoughts, in which every thought is included, are eight in all. First the thought of gluttony, and after that the thought of fornication, third that of avarice, fourth that of distress, fifth that of anger, sixth that of depression [*akēdia*], seventh that of vanity, eighth that of pride. It is not up to us whether any of these afflict the soul or not, but it is up to us whether they linger or not, and whether they stir up emotions [*pathē*] or not.[9]

For a monk temptation [*peirasmos*] is a thought arising through the emotional part [*to pathētikon*] of the soul and darkening the intellect. For a monk sin [*hamartia*] is assent [*sunkathathesis*] to the forbidden pleasure of the thought.[10]

Evagrius says that thoughts of vanity play a special role. For if you have defeated the other seven bad thoughts, you are liable to be defeated in turn by thoughts of vanity. Even if you defeat thoughts of vanity themselves, you may be overcome by vanity at that achievement, so we learn in *Practical Treatise* 30–31. In 58, we learn that the only way of defeating vanity may be deliberately to arouse thoughts of fornication because those, at least to a desert monk, are very humiliating. However, 58 also tells us that this process of playing off one bad thought against another can only bring us near the frontiers of freedom from emotion, the Stoic ideal (*apatheia*). In order to reach true *apatheia* one must pray to God for His Grace.

Are we ourselves free from bad thoughts? I would at one time misguidedly have said so. But let us see whether we do not recognize ourselves, when we read Evagrius' descriptions of bad thoughts. The first description I shall give concerns the temptations that sometimes beset senior academics whose duties include the necessity of fund raising. Those of us who have had to do this may encounter the demon of avarice.

> The demon of avarice seems to me very versatile and ingenious at deception. Often when squeezed by [the monk's] extreme renunciation, he at once assumes the mask of provisioner and lover of the poor. Strangers not yet present he receives with much sincerity and to others left behind he sends ministrations. He visits the prisons of the city and of course ransoms those who are being sold. He sticks to wealthy ladies and indicates people who deserve to be well treated, and he advises others who have acquired a well-stuffed purse to renounce it. And so having deceived the soul little by little, he subjects it to thoughts of avarice and hands it over to the demon of vanity. So the demon introduces a crowd of people praising the Lord for those provisions and gradually projects [*proballei*] others chatting about our ordination, and prophesies the speedy death of the present incumbent.[11]

This description, worthy of Trollope, may nonetheless leave many people still feeling comfortable. But I wonder how many of us can feel comfortable after hearing the account of depression [*akēdia*] from *Eight Spirits of Wickedness* 14:

> The eyes of the depressed [monk] continually gaze at the windows and his mind imagines visitors. The door creaks, and he jumps up. He hears a voice and peeps through the window. He does not come away until numb with sitting. While reading, he yawns repeatedly and easily slides toward sleep. He rubs his eyes and stretches his hands; he takes his eyes off the book and gazes at the wall. Turning back, he reads a little. He takes a lot of trouble opening the ends of the sections. He counts the pages and calculates the quaternions. He complains of the handwriting and decoration. Then, folding the book, he puts in under his head, and sleeps but not very deeply, for hunger then rouses his consciousness and instills its own cares.[12]

Which of us has not counted how many pages are left in a boring book?

A third demon encourages uncomfortable memories of the home that the monk has left forever, sometimes, like Evagrius, after an affair, sometimes after a family quarrel. There are harrowing stories of mothers trekking through the desert at great danger to themselves, to see their sons, and being told, without their sons' knowledge, that their sons had no wish to see them. There is a demon who reminds monks of the emotions of their homes but does so subtly by leading them around adjacent countries – perhaps first to Persia, then Thrace, before descending to their homeland in Greece.

There is a demon called the one who leads astray. He approaches the brothers at dawn. He leads the mind of the anchorite round from city to city, from house to house, and from village to village, making the meetings simple at first, of course, then running into some acquaintances and chatting longer, doing away with the proper position in relation to encounters.... It is not at random or by chance that the demon works that long circuit, but he does it from a wish to do away with the anchorite's position, so that the mind may at once fall to the demons of fornication, or of anger, or of distress, which are especially harmful to the luster of his position.[13]

When we have read Evagrius' description of bad thoughts, I think we can see that we are subject to them all the time.

Evagrius died in A.D. 399. Fifteen years later, in 414–15, Jerome attacked Evagrius at least three times along with his sponsors, Jerome's former friends Melania and Rufinus. Rufinus had meanwhile translated into Latin the letters of advice that Evagrius had written to the monks and nuns of Melania's and Rufinus' monasteries. Jerome was preoccupied by a controversy that had sprung up since Evagrius' death, the Pelagian controversy. The followers of the British ascetic Pelagius denied the doctrine that we were all infected by the original sin transmitted from Adam our forefather. Jerome considered that it was Pelagian to aim, as Evagrius had, at self-perfection in the desert. This was rather unfair to Evagrius, who, we have seen, insisted that God's Grace was needed to reach the ideal of *apatheia*. Nonetheless Jerome makes a great play on words, exploiting the fact that Melania's name in Greek is connected with blackness and describing Rufinus as *grunnius*, the Grunter.[14] Augustine also, we shall see, opposed the Stoic ideal of *apatheia* as an ideal for human beings. But Evagrius' ideal lived on in the Christian Church, despite the opposition of the Latin-speaking fathers Jerome and Augustine. It survived in the Greek-speaking Eastern Church and was restored to the Western Church by Cassian who founded the monastery at Monte Cassino in 529 A.D. The ideal thus passed also into the Western Latin-speaking monastic tradition. In the seventh century, the eight bad thoughts of Evagrius were transformed by Pope Gregory the Great into the Seven Cardinal Sins (*principalia vitia*). Gregory reached the number seven by separating off pride as the root of all sin, by collapsing depression and distress, and by adding envy. A further transformation occurred, in that depression was itself transformed into what for Evagrius and Cassian been merely the effect of depression, mainly sloth. Evagrius' depressed monk is not doing the reading he was supposed to. But in Evagrius the term *akēdia* applied to the depression, not to its effect, the slothfulness in reading.

Augustine had surely read Evagrius. In an earlier treatise written in A.D. 394, *On the Sermon on the Mount*, he repeats the term from Rufinus' translation of Origen that we are subject to *suggestions*.[15] Augustine also explains that when Christ tells us that a man who looks at a woman to lust after her has already committed adultery with her in his heart, Christ was not condemning titillation. Titillation is involuntary. What is condemned is only looking at a woman in order deliberately to stir up lust. Jerome repeats this explanation four years later and adds that the titillation itself is only a prepassion.

Some twenty years later in A.D. 414, in *On the Trinity*, Augustine returns to the subject of bad thoughts.[16] He explains that we all have bad thoughts, but they become sins only if one is pleased by the thought, or retains it and willingly revolves it instead of spitting it out. These criteria for sin, of being pleased and retaining, are extraordinarily close to Evagrius. Augustine thinks that if we believe that we do not need forgiveness, we are in fact committing the sin of pride, and he is very critical of Pelagians for allegedly thinking this way. We can atone for our bad thoughts according to *On the Trinity* by saying the Lord's Prayer and asking for our sins to be forgiven. As we ask for forgiveness we must beat our breast, and we must add that we forgive others. Elsewhere, for example, in *On the Sermon on the Mount*, Augustine connects the request in the Lord's Prayer for our daily bread with the necessity of taking the bread of communion every day, every day because we are subject to temptation and sin every day.[17] Augustine also distinguishes different degrees of sin according to whether we assent merely to the pleasure of the thought or whether we actually act on it. New questions about first movements became possible once they were transformed into thoughts. One could also ask, "Did you put yourself in the way of the thought?" Thomas Aquinas later asks, "Did you take pleasure in the process of thinking or in the content of the thought?"[18]

Augustine has an agenda. In *City of God*, he defends Aristotle's idea of moderate emotion (*metriopatheia*) against the Stoic ideal of freedom from emotion (*apatheia*).[19] Saint Paul, Augustine points out, bids us rejoice with them who do rejoice, and Christ was really saddened. The insistence on

Christ's sadness is connected with the necessity of believing that he had a human nature as well as a divine one. Augustine here insists that in this life since the Fall of Man, we need even the painful emotions like grief and fear. And even in the next life we shall still need joy and love. The need for grief can be illustrated from the *Confessions* where Augustine's grief at the loss of an unnamed friend led him by a roundabout route to appreciate that God is the only friend who never leaves us.[20] Origen, Didymus the Blind, and Jerome had differed from Augustine in one respect. They considered Christ's beginning to be sad as only a first movement. The difference from Augustine, however, is not so great, because Jerome, like Augustine, says that Christ was really sad. This was made possible by the fact that first movements were now treated as not so clearly distinct from genuine emotion as they had been in the Stoics. Augustine ascribes prepassion to Abraham, but not to Christ himself.

In siding with Aristotle about the value of emotions, when exercised in moderation, Augustine makes some exceptions. In *City of God* 14.13 he makes an exception of pride, and in *City of God* 14.19 and surroundings, he makes an exception of lust. But by and large, Augustine favored the moderate exercise of emotions. Consequently he took the opposite view from Evagrius. Whereas Evagrius had agreed with the Stoic ideal of freedom from emotion, Augustine thought it was necessary to disarm the Stoics' advocacy of *apatheia*. He set about disarming them by trying to present them as really agreeing that emotion was acceptable after all. His attempt turns on a story told by the philosophical journalist Aulus Gellius, who wrote the *Attic Nights* in the second century A.D.

In *Attic Nights* 19.1 Gellius tells us of a Stoic sailor who grew pale in a storm at sea.[21] When the ship got safely to harbor, an Asiatic nouveau riche came up to the Stoic and said, "Tell me, how is it that you, a Stoic, who are supposed to have no emotions, grew pale in the storm?" The Stoic's first reply repeats a joke that is already adumbrated in Aristotle. "Of course a rascal like yourself had little reason to fear the loss of his life, but in the case of a life like mine, the case was different." However, the philosophical journalist Aulus Gellius came up to the Stoic and said, "No, please tell me really why you grew pale in the storm." The Stoic then drew out of his wallet a book by the Stoic Epictetus, who gives an orthodox and impeccable account of first movements. Epictetus says, in this precious fragment, which was otherwise lost, that is it alright for the Stoic sage to be moved, to grow pale, and to suffer contractions. So far the account of Stoic first movements is unexceptionable, but something very dangerous happens when Gellius explains his reasons for quoting from

Epictetus. Gellius then introduces a new word and says that it is alright for the Stoic sage to experience *pavor*. *Pavor* is a word ambiguous between real fear and mere trembling: we might translate it "having the jitters." Gellius uses the word *pavor* twice, the adjective *pavidus* once, and the verb *pavescere* once. This new word gives a distinct impression that real fear may be accepted for the Stoic sage. As a literary word, *pavor* is ideal, because it preserves the ambiguity of the situation. Was the Stoic sailor allowed only to tremble or to feel real fear? But as a philosophical word, *pavor* was a disaster because a philosopher needs to know exactly which of the two, fear or trembling, is what the Stoics allow. *Pallor* is what is allowed to the Stoic, but the alliteration was no doubt an added attraction for Gellius, when he moved to *pavor*.

It is a great pity that Augustine read Aulus Gellius, the philosophical journalist, instead of Seneca, who would have been absolutely clear. Augustine says in *City of God* 9.4, that he will tell Gellius' story a little more clearly (*planius*). He repeats the word *pavescere* but disambiguates it the wrong way. He says that it is alright for the Stoic sailor to have the jitters (*pavescere*) with real fear (*metu*) and to experience contractions (*contrahi*) with real sadness (*tristitia*). Augustine moreover uses the word passions (*passiones*) three times to describe what is allowed to the Stoic sage. He uses another word for genuine fear (*timor*), and he wrongly claims that the Stoic sailor failed to set his life at naught (*nihili pendere*). The two very different concepts of *pallor* and *pavor* would have been related in Augustine's mind because he tells us in *City of God* 6.10 that *pallor* and *pavor* were recognized as two gods. In fact, however, Gellius' easy slide between *pallor* and *pavor* was to prove disastrous in Augustine.

There is a further mistreatment of first movements by Augustine in *City of God* 14.19. Augustine is there discussing one of the exceptional emotions of which he disapproves, namely lust. He explains that lust is unlike anger because it is not under the control of the will, whereas anger is. Augustine fails to notice the point that is so clearly made in Seneca, *On Anger* 2.3.2, that angry flashing of eyes, sexual irritation, and pallor are all on the same footing. All three of them are mentioned by Seneca as involuntary first movements. It makes no difference that each of them can lead to voluntary behavior. In this regard anger is still no different from lust. All three involve first movements that are not under the control of the mind.

Why does Augustine misrepresent the Stoic theory of first movements? In *City of God* 9.4, his aim is to dismiss the Stoics. He was further writing in the tradition that came from Origen which blurred the distinction between first movements and real emotions by turning first movements into thoughts. It has also been put to me by Miriam Griffin that Augustine may be too much of a Platonist in his view of the soul to take in fully the Stoic doctrine according to which the Stoic will feel no emotion once his reason has judged that there is no harm at hand. On a Platonist view reason could still be opposed by emotional parts of the soul, not recognized by Chrysippus or Seneca, that oppose reason. However, one small factor in Augustine's misrepresentation of Stoic first movements is undoubtedly the linguistic change of one single letter of the alphabet by Aulus Gellius, the change of the double *l* to the *v* of *pavor*.

I have been seeking to explain how Christians, starting with Origen, shifted the Stoic concept of first movements 180 degrees, turning first movements into bad thoughts. If we were, misguidedly, to judge Origen simply in terms of historical scholarship, we should condemn the misuse of the Stoic term. But this would be a misconception on our part. What we have been witnessing is how fruitful it can be when one group of thinkers transforms the ideas of another group, in order to set them to new purposes. The original concept of first movements was ideally suited to the Stoic school, which analyzed emotion in order to show us how to combat it. The new concept of first movements bequeathed by Origen was ideally suited for the new Christian thinkers, who needed to develop a doctrine on how to resist temptation.[22]

Notes

1. Lottin 1942–60: 2:493–589.
2. Seneca, *De Ira* 2.2.1–2.4.2 (ed. Reynolds 1977).
3. Cicero, *Tusculanae Disputationes* 3.82–3.
4. Sorabji 2000: 37–41.
5. See Galen, *De Placitis Hippocratis et Platonis*, books 4–5.
6. See W. James 1890: 450.
7. Philo of Alexandria, new fragment, p. 78, Wendland (*Neu Entdeckte Fragmente*), from Procopius MS 394, f. 110r = *Philo Supplement*, vol. 2 (ed. Marcus 1953: 220).
8. Origen 1966.
9. Evagrius, *Practical Treatise* 6.
10. Ibid., 74–75.
11. Evagrius, *On Various Bad Thoughts* 22–23 = *On Discrimination in Respect of Passions and Thoughts* 21 (*PG* 79: 1200–34).
12. Pseudo-Nilus = Evagrius, *On the Eight Spirits of Wickedness*, ch. 14 (*PG* 79: 1160A–B).
13. Ibid.

14. See Jerome, *Letter* 133, to Ctesiphon (*CSEL* 56: 246); *Against the Pelagians*, Prologue (*PL* 23: 496A); *On Jeremiah* 4.1 (*CSEL* 59: 220–21).
15. Augustine, *De Sermone Domini in Monte* 1.12.33–34 (*PL* 34: 1246).
16. Augustine, *De Trinitate* 12.12 (*PL* 42).
17. Augustine, *De Sermone Domini in Monte* 2.7.25 (*PL* 34).
18. Thomas Aquinas, *Summa Theologiae* IaIIae, q. 74, a. 8.
19. Augustine, *De Civitate Dei* 14.9 (*PL* 41).
20. Augustine, *Confessiones* 4.4 (7) – 9 (14) (*PL* 32).
21. Aulus Gellius, *Noctes Atticae* 19.1.
22. For a more detailed account of this transformation, see Sorabji 2000.

6

Where Were the Stoics in the Late Middle Ages?

Sten Ebbesen

Where were the Stoics in the late Middle Ages? The short answer is: everywhere and nowhere.

Stoicism is not a sport for gentlemen; it requires far too much rigorous intellectual work. Most of Western history consists of gentlemen's centuries. But there were the couple of centuries, the fourth and the third B.C., in which the ancient philosophical schools were created, and there were the three centuries from A.D. 1100 to 1400, when medieval scholasticism flourished – centuries that produced a considerable number of tough men ready to chew their way through all the tedious logical stuff that disgusts a gentleman and to make all the nice distinctions that a gentleman can never understand but only ridicule, distinctions necessary to work out a coherent, and perhaps even consistent, picture of the structure of the world. In this respect, a good scholastic and a good Stoic are kindred spirits. As an attitude to doing philosophy, Stoicism is everywhere in the late Middle Ages.

Also, bits and snippets of Stoic doctrine were available in a large number of ancient writings and could inspire or be integrated in scholastic theory. Further, some works with a high concentration of Stoicism were widely known, notably Cicero's *Paradoxes of the Stoics, De Officiis*, and Seneca's *Letters to Lucilius*. Finally, Saint Paul was a crypto-Stoic ethicist,[1] and so were several of the church fathers.

In another way Stoicism is nowhere. After all, the philosophical authority par excellence was Aristotle, whose works were available, whereas the medievals were like us in not possessing a single work by one of the major Stoics, and they had not a Hans von Arnim to collect and organize the fragments from secondary sources. A well-educated man might know that the Stoics thought everything was governed by fate and that virtue is the highest good, and little else. He might have some general idea of the history of ancient philosophy, but it would be a rather different history from ours. To him Democritus and Leucippus might be Epicureans, and Socrates the founder of the Stoic school, while the leading Peripatetics would be Aristotle, Porphyry, and Avicenna.

Real knowledge of Stoicism had become extinct already by A.D. 500, the time, that is, of Boethius, the man who more than anyone else decided the direction scholastic philosophy was to take. Simplicius, who was a contemporary of Boethius, apparently had access to just about any piece of older Greek philosophical literature available anywhere in the empire, but he could find none or very few of the writings of the Stoics.[2]

It can make a scholar cry to read such remarks of Boethius as these in his larger commentary on Aristotle's *De Interpretatione*:

> Here Porphyry inserts much about the dialectic of the Stoics and the other schools, and he has done the same in his comments on several other parts of this work. We however, shall have to skip that, for superfluous explanation rather generates obscurity <than clarity>.[3]

> Porphyry, however, inserts some information about Stoic dialectic, but since that [i.e., Stoic dialectic] is unfamiliar to Latin ears ... we purposely omit it.[4]

Even when Boethius had access to an account of Stoic doctrine, he considered it irrelevant and decided not to hand it down to the Middle Ages.

Thus, no schoolman had a clear idea about what Stoicism had been all about, and very few Stoic tenets were known as such. In this sense Stoicism was nowhere.

In a fundamental sense all philosophy in the medieval West had been Aristotelian since its birth in the Carolingian age. Out of the study of Porphyry's *Isagoge*, Aristotle's *Categories* and *De Interpretatione*, Boethius' commentaries and monographs, and Priscian's grammar developed a peculiar sort of Aristotelianism with a strong emphasis on logic and linguistic analysis. In Abelard's youth, about the year 1100, this native Western philosophical tradition was already highly developed. Between 1130 and 1270 the whole *Corpus Aristotelicum* became available. The philosophical landscape changed, but the way philosophers worked remained true to the native tradition: *all scholastic work is marked by the analytical approach developed in its early phase.*

I see a connection between the scholastics' analytic approach and Stoicism. I also find Stoic inspiration in the development of some central pieces of doctrine relating to propositions, arguments, and intentional objects and in a radical trend in ethics that made liberty a key concept. I shall use some Stoic divisions to structure the main part of this essay.

THE THREE DEPARTMENTS OF PHILOSOPHY

The Stoic division of philosophy into dialectic, physics, and ethics was well known to the medievals,[5] but it did not fit the world of mature scholasticism because it had no slots for such sciences as that of the soul, or metaphysics. In the twelfth century, however, this was no impediment, and imaginative use was made of the tripartition in the theory of language of Gilbert of Poitiers (ca. 1085–1154) and his followers, the Porretans.

The Porretans started from the same assumption as old Porphyry, the assumption, that is, that the core of any language is a vocabulary that allows communication about the world of sensible nature. Once such a core exists, it is possible to add a second layer of words, so that we can speak about the language itself, saying "noun, verb, sentence" and the like. This much of the Porphyrian theory any medieval thinker would know from Boethius.[6] The pre-Porphyrian history of this notion of two "impositions" of words, one for an object language and one for a meta-language, is unknown. A Stoic origin has been plausibly suggested,[7] and if the suggestion is right, we here have a piece of Stoic theory that was to be immensely influential in the Middle Ages.

The Porretans, then, started from the assumption of a core language by means of which we speak about the nature that God created in the first six days. But besides the sphere of nature they operated with those of culture (*mores*) and of reason (*ratio*), each with a language of its own. The vocabulary of culture covers artifacts, social institutions, and all evaluation. The vocabulary of reason consists of logical terms and the like. The way the Porretans saw it, we are only capable of talking about cultural or rational matters by taking the language of nature, keeping its grammatical and logical syntax, but using its words in transferred senses, as when we use "higher" not only about mountains but also about prices and about genera.

Among other things, this theory required a triplication of the Aristotelian system of ten categories, which included a basic system for the language of nature and secondary systems for the languages of culture and reason.

The Porretans' real problem was how it is possible to speak sensibly about the incomprehensible God, and so their final point was that the language of theology must be related to the language of nature in fundamentally the same ways as those that took care of human rationality and its products. Hence, although we may not grasp what "God" or "is" means in the true proposition "God is God," we must assume that it obeys standard rules of inference, so that it is equivalent to "God is God by virtue of Godhood," while "God is Godhood" must be considered ill-formed and untrue. This conclusion nearly earned Gilbert a condemnation for denying the unity of God.[8]

Now, what has this to do with Stoicism? This: the Porretans' spheres of nature, culture, and reason were clearly inspired by the Stoic division into natural science, ethics, and dialectic, in Porretan language *facultas naturalis, moralis* or *ethica*, and *rationalis*. The Porretan understanding of *facultas moralis* as comprising not only human action and its evaluation but any sort of evaluation and any sort of human product was novel and did not have a long future. The addition of a *facultas theologica* was another novelty, for which a better future was in store. But, anyhow, Gilbert's was an original development of a Stoic piece of thinking.

The understanding of "nature" as the sensible world with the constituents mentioned in the biblical account of creation was not equally original. This equation provided a setting in which certain pieces of Stoic physical theory could be used. Several twelfth-century thinkers made it their aim to lay the foundations of a science of nature by sketching a cosmogony that required no direct divine intervention after the creation of the four elements. Once the elements had been created, the laws of nature had been established, and the world would gradually articulate itself until reaching its present state. Men like Thierry of Chartres (a contemporary of Gilbert's) read the biblical *Genesis* as a succinct account of such a cosmogony. One common feature of their theories was the assignment of a special role to fire as the active element in the cosmogonic process. To some extent, this was a revival of the Stoic *pur technikōn/ignis artifex*, and even the very expression was occasionally used. Thierry's type of natural philosophy disappeared or receded into the background after the twelfth century, and *ignis artifex* was not to become an important concept again until the Renaissance.[9]

SOMETHINGS AND NOTHINGS

The Stoics divided the total realm of thinkables into somethings and nothings. Universal concepts were considered nothings. Somethings comprised things-that-are and things-that-are-not, the former being corporeal, the latter incorporeal. The Stoics famously considered many more things corporeal than did most philosophers, whereas their list of incorporeals was short: time, place, the void, sayables.[10]

The Stoic division was used, but not explained, in a text every medieval philosopher knew. In the prologue to his *Isagoge*, Porphyry asks these famous questions about genera and species: (1) Do they subsist or do they repose in mere secondary conceptualizations? (2) If they subsist, are they corporeal or incorporeal? (3) Do they subsist in separation or in and about sensible things?[11]

The first two questions presuppose Stoic ontology. They ask: (1) Are *genera* and *species tina* or *outina* – somethings or nothings? (2) Supposing they are somethings, are they bodies or incorporeals? The third question reflects the perennial debate between Platonists and Aristotelians.

Although a sketchy account of the Stoic notion of somethings and nothings was in principle available in Seneca's *Letter* 58, this was largely unknown to the schoolmen, and no other source available to them carried the information. When, in the fourteenth century, John Buridan seriously considers whether "something" – *quid* or *aliquid* – might function as a *genus generalissimum*, he betrays no awareness of the Stoic theory.[12] Neither are those medieval theories directly linked to the Stoics which make universals and other objects of thought similar to Stoic *outina*; we even find people who call some *entia rationis* "nothing" (*nihil*).[13] But it seems that by using the Stoic division Porphyry had smuggled in a conceptual possibility that some people were to develop.

Moreover, at least after about 1140, the medievals knew Chrysippus' *outis*, that is, the "nobody" argument, which runs:

> If someone is in Megara, he is not in Athens.
> Man is in Megara, *ergo* man is not in Athens.

The argument shows the absurdity that a theory incurs if it allows there to be a universal man and treats him as a somebody. While never becoming immensely popular in the West, it did play a certain role in teaching people the dangers of hypostatizing universals. Commentaries on Aristotle's *Categories* and *Sophistical Refutations* seem to have been important vehicles in the argument's long travels from Chrysippus to the West.[14]

The distinction between real corporeal things and incorporeal quasi things was not very relevant in the Middle Ages when everybody accepted the existence of real incorporeal things. Already Boethius had a problem when a revered author used the distinction. Cicero, in his *Topics* 5.26–27, divides things into those which are, that is, corporeal things; and those which are not, that is, intelligible things. Boethius comments lengthily to show that, strictly speaking, it is false to say that incorporeal things are not and, to excuse Cicero, resorts to the expedient of claiming that Cicero does not in this place express his own opinion but just one commonly held by uneducated people.[15]

John Scotus Eriugena in the ninth century seems to have had the Ciceronian passage in mind when he divided nature into things that are and things that are not, the chief representative of the latter class being God.[16] The result, of course, is most un-Stoic.

We seem closer to Stoic thought when a text from the second half of the twelfth century text lists things that do not fall into any Aristotelian category: "Universals, then, are neither substances nor properties, but have a being of their own, as is also the case with enunciables, times, words [*voces*, possibly an error for *loca*, 'places'] and voids [*inania*, the manuscript has *fama*, 'rumor']."[17] Apart from universals, this text mentions four noncategorial quasi things, at least two, probably three, and possibly four of which also occur in the Stoic list of four incorporeals (sayable, time, place, void). An enunciable is something very much like a Stoic complete sayable *(lekton)*.

A longer list occurs in a *Categories* commentary from about 1200:

There are several noncompound terms that neither signify substance nor are contained in any category due to their meaning, such as (1) any name that contains everything, (2) any name of the second imposition, (3) any name imposed as a technical term, (4) any name that denotes an enunciable, "a truth," e.g., and (5) "time," (6) "space," (7) "place," (8) "void," and any other extracategorials.[18]

Elsewhere the same author tells us that the void *(inane)* has a being of its own *(suum esse per se)*,[19] and the same is said about enunciables in yet another near contemporary text.[20]

One might think that book 4 of Aristotle's *Physics* could have inspired twelfth-century speculation about the ontological status of place, the void, and time, but the book was virtually unknown at the time and the texts that speak about these quasi things having a being of their own contain no echos of the *Physics*. Anyhow, an Aristotelian connection is quite impossible as regards the enunciables; only the Stoics had a somewhat similar notion, namely, that of a sayable. Sadly, I have not succeeded in identifying any text available in twelfth-century Latin Europe that could have transmitted the Stoic list of not-being somethings. Hence we may be facing a case of parallel development, similar problems giving rise to similar ideas. But at least the development was encouraged by some genuine inheritance.

STOIC DIALECTIC AND SCHOLASTIC GRAMMAR AND LOGIC

To the Stoics the art of language – *logikē* – had only two species, rhetoric and dialectic, the latter consisting of a part dealing with things that signify and one dealing with things signified. Because treating of each of those correlative parts requires constant recourse to the other, there could be no real separation into disciplines.

Many scholastics, especially in the early period, followed the Stoics in operating with a class of linguistic disciplines – *artes sermocinales* – with the same field of study as the Stoic *logikē* but subdivided in a different way into three species on the same level: grammar, logic, and rhetoric. The different classification of the linguistic disciplines was not totally a surface phenomenon, and it was reflected in the structure of education. Nevertheless, while rhetoric remained on a sidetrack, the medieval disciplines of grammar and logic were almost as closely connected as the two parts of Stoic dialectic – and the Stoic binary of things signifying and things signified was ever present in both disciplines. Let me mention a few examples.

The eleventh and twelfth centuries knew a classification of philosophical sects into two main kinds: *reales* on one side and *vocales* or *nominales* on the other; there were thing-people and there were word- or name-people. When advertising their respective philosophical wares the former group would cry "A genus is a thing" and the latter "A genus is a word." Anyone who actually bought a course in a school would find that the differences between thing-theories and word-theories were subtler than the vendors' cries indicated. Yet there was a difference, and the whole matrix of thought was, of course, the old Stoic one: do we think this is primarily a matter of words that signify or of things that are signified?[21]

In this case the historical connection is rather clear. The distinction was well known from a number of ancient sources, and it had been applied when people began to comment on and attack Aristotle's *Categories* at the beginning of the Christian era.[22] The question "Is this a book about words that signify or about things that are signified?" continued to haunt the exegesis of the book for all time to come. Are the ten categories as many different sorts of words or as many different sorts of things? The medievals inherited the question via Boethius, and by 1100 a teacher might either *legere in re – legere in voce*, "expound a passage as dealing with a thing" or "expound it as a text about a word." Centrist philosophers might choose one alternative for one passage and the other for some other passage; or they might indicate that a passage could make sense on either reading.[23]

Radicals would try to make a consistent thing-reading of the whole book or a consistent word-reading. It did not take much imagination to apply the same alternative when reading Porphyry's *Isagoge*, also known as the book about the five universals. In fact, that must have happened early in the Greek tradition, for there it was commonly known as the book about the five words, *Peri tōn pente phōnōn*.

In short, the whole realist-nominalist debate was shaped in a Stoic mold, that of words that signify versus things that are signified.

Another example of use of the dichotomy is of a much less general character. Two important texts from the second half of the twelfth century, known respectively as *Compendium Logicae Porretanum* and *Ars Meliduna*, are structured by means of two dichotomies, term-proposition and signifying-signified, the result being four parts: on terms, on propositions, on the things signified by terms, on the things signified by propositions.[24] Whereas the term-proposition dichotomy has an Aristotelian background, crossing it with the Stoic division produces that most un-Aristotelian item, "thing-signified-by-a-proposition," alias "thing-said" (*dictum*) or enunciable.

UN-ARISTOTELIAN LOGIC

To most scholastics Aristotelian logic equaled logic. Any later additions, including their own products, were just extensions of Aristotle's work, nothing really new. A modern observer may find it hard to share the schoolmen's self-perception on this point.

Among the strikingly un-Aristotelian features of scholastic logic is the great attention paid to syncategorematic words. The class includes quantifiers, modal operators, exclusives like "only," exceptives like "besides," the verbs "is," "begins," "ceases," the conjunction "if" – and several other members.

Another strikingly un-Aristotelian feature is a strong interest in conditionals and a two-part analysis of arguments, eventually issuing in the genre of *consequentiae*, that is, special treatises about molecular propositions consisting each of two propositions joined by the particles "therefore" or "if-then" (*ergo, si*). The two parts of a consequence were called the antecedent and the consequent. Categorical syllogisms might be viewed as consequences with a molecular antecedent – the conjunction of the two premises – and an atomic consequent (the conclusion). A frequently cited criterion for validity of a consequence was this: "[I]f the opposite of the consequent is inconsistent with the antecedent, the consequence is valid."[25] This rule was commonly thought to derive from Aristotle's *Prior Analytics*, but one looks in vain for it there. It does, however, to a startling degree match one Stoic definition of a true conditional: "A true conditional is one in which the opposite of the consequent is inconsistent with the antecedent."[26] The scholastics used the terms *antecedens* and *consequens* for the parts of the consequence, and *repugnat* for "is inconsistent with." Of these, *antecedens* and *repugnat* almost certainly render the Stoic terms *hē goumenon* and *machetai* while *consequens* may render a non-Stoic replacement for the Stoic *lēgon*.[27]

The scholastic terms can be traced back to Boethius and, with a little bit of goodwill, to Cicero, and thus to a time when it would be natural for such bits of Stoic logic to have survived.

The terminology has a Stoic background, and we know the route by which it reached the West. The strange thing is that so far no route has been discovered by which the rule about how to check for validity can have traveled from the Stoics to the scholastics. Parallel development is a possibility. After all, Aristotle does teach how to check on a syllogism by seeing whether the negation of the conclusion together with one of the premises will yield the negation of the remaining one (*Prior Analytics* 2.8, *Topics* 8.14), and according to Apuleius the Peripatetics had a rule that

in any syllogism, if the conclusion is destroyed and one of the premises posited, the remaining one will be destroyed, which the Stoics made into their first thema and formulated thus: If from two [*axiomata*, presumably] a third is inferred, one of them together with its [contradictorily] opposite infers the opposite of the remaining one.[28]

Consideration of this rule for checking on three-piece syllogisms – whether Peripatetic or Stoic – could independently have inspired the ancient Stoics and the scholastics to formulate the rules for the truth of conditionals and the validity of consequences, respectively. So, perhaps parallel development, but even so, the medievals owed something to the Stoics, as I shall try to show.

As Sextus Empiricus indicates, accepting this definition of the conditional implies requiring some sort of natural cohesion (*sunartēsis*) between the antecedent and consequent of a true conditional. A similar requirement for a true argument is also reported: one way an argument could fail to be conclusive was to suffer from dis-hesion – *diartēsis* – between the constituent *axiomata*.[29]

A related requirement for the antecedent and consequent was for-mulated by the people whom Sextus characterizes as "those who judge by inclusion" (*emphasis*): "Those who judge by inclusion say that that conditional is true whose consequent is potentially contained in the antecedent."[30] Modern scholars have not been able to agree on who these inclusion-people were. Michael Frede in his book on Stoic logic comforted himself with the remark that, anyhow, this definition of a true conditional appeared to have been of little historical importance because nobody else mentions it.[31]

Personally, I feel tempted to ascribe it to Posidonius, because it may be seen as an attempt to flesh out what "cohesion" means, the answer being: semantic inclusion of consequent in antecedent – and Posidonius claimed that (one class of) relational syllogisms hold *kata dunamin, axiōmatos* possibly because he viewed an argument such as $a:b = c:d$. $a:b = 2:1 \therefore c:d = 2:1$ as implicitly contained in the axiom *Those between which there is the same ratio universally, between those all the particular ratios are also the same.*[32]

Be that as it may, the "historically unimportant" cohesion definition of a true conditional turns up almost verbatim in the scholastic period, when very many adhered to the view that "it is a good consequence, when the consequent is included [or: understood] in the antecedent."[33] Once again, however, it has not been possible to demonstrate a direct historical connection between the ancient Greek and the medieval Latin formulation of the view. Parallel development, perhaps.

Special treatises on *consequentiae* only appeared about the year 1300, but the notion had been around for a long time, and so had the rules I discussed earlier. Already about 1100 there was a debate whether a syllogism is one molecular proposition, and if so, whether this meant that true instances of "p, q, therefore r" and true instances of "p, therefore q" could be treated alike as depending for their truth on a topical maxim.

Some Westerners saw every consequence, including syllogisms, as one molecular proposition. This was already proposed by Abelard's teacher, William of Champeaux.[34] Abelard disagreed. In his discussion of the opposing view, he tells us that its champions claim that subcontin-uative conjunctions glue sentences together just as well as continua-tive conjunctions.[35] Now, what is that? That's a recycled piece of Stoic dialectic! The Stoics had a healthy interest in conjunctions, and a classifi-cation allowing for primary and secondary types in some classes. Thus we find the synaptic conjunction "if" (*ei*) and the parasynaptic conjunction "as" (*epei*), the diazeuctic conjunction "or" (which expresses exclusive disjunction) and its paradiazeuctic twin, the nonexclusive "or." These in Latin became *continuativa, subcontinuativa, disiunctiva,* and *subdisiunctiva,* respectively.

The term *continuativa* seems to be of Peripatetic origin,[36] the Peripatetics using *sunecheia* rather than *sunaphē* for the link between antecedent and consequent. But the classification of the conjunctions is Stoic, and it was transmitted to the scholastics by Priscian. By the thirteenth century, the conjunction "if" had become one of the items standardly discussed in logical treatises on syncategoremata.

So, what we find in mature scholasticism is a branch of logic dealing with conditionals and associated arguments. Arguments tend to be seen as two-piece things consisting of an antecedent and a consequent. Although all the details in the medieval theories were genuinely new inventions, the impulse for that sort of interest was largely Stoic.

And this was not only a matter of importance to logicians. The fourteenth-century debate around Nicholas of Autrecourt could hardly have occurred if the participants had not had the conceptual apparatus of consequences with antecedents and consequents. In Autrecourt's case, the rule about inclusion of the consequent in the antecedent was of particular importance. He undermined the belief in substances by arguing that you cannot infer the existence of a substance from the existence of an accident unless you have built the notion of substance into that of accident, so that the consequent "there is a substance" is included in the antecedent "there is an accident."[37]

The subcontinuative conjunction was called *parasunaptikos sundesmos* in Greek. The term was part of a systematic terminology for couples of senior and junior brothers, a *para*-prefix characterizing the junior brother.

1.1	*sunēmmenon*	*parasunēmmenon*
1.2	*sunaptikos sundesmos*	*parasunaptikos sundesmos*
1.3	*diezeugmenon*	*paradiezeugmenon*
2.2	*diazeuktikos sundesmos*	*paradiazeutikos sundesmos*
3	*sumbama*	*parasumbama*

The system was not meant for more than two brothers, but in the case of *sumbama – parasumbama* there was a third one, and this littlest brother was called *elattone ē parasumbama* "less than by-companionship."

Careful distinctions accompanied by a systematic terminology were one of the hallmarks of Stoicism. Thus, the use of nominal suffixes had been regulated. An action understood as a state of someone's center

of command (*hēgemonikon*) and hence corporeal was *praxis*; one understood as the result of acting and hence incorporeal was a *pragma*. Similarly, other -*ma* words were used for incorporeal objects of wish and
the like. Now, careful distinctions and bold linguistic creativity with the
goal of having a systematic terminology were also characteristic traits of
much of scholasticism. Was there a historical connection? There probably was. The remains of Stoic terminology in grammar helped build a
tradition for being systematic. Boethius' *De Topicis Differentiis*, one of the
most widely read logic books in early scholasticism, provided another
link.

In the beginning of that work Boethius introduces a distinction between *argumentum* and *argumentatio*. An *argumentum* is the sense and force
of an *argumentatio*, which, in turn, is the expression of the *argumentum*.[38]
Wherever Boethius learned this distinction, I have little doubt that it is
based on the Stoic distinction between incorporeals with a -μα name and
corporeal entities with a -σις name.[39]

As I have already indicated, an *enuntiabile* – also called a *dictum* –
is a close relative of the Stoic sayable (*lekton*). It is that-which-a-
proposition-states, and it is a truth or a falsehood. It was the sort of mental
exercise they got when reading about arguments versus argumentations
that taught the medievals how to make a distinction between an enunci-
ation and its content, the enunciable.

Abelard, who may have been the inventor of the *dictum*, has *ea quae
propositionibus dicuntur* as one possible interpretation of the Boethian
argumentum.[40] It is just possible that he derived the term *dictum* from
Seneca's 117th letter to Lucilius,[41] which contains some important information about sayables and offers *dictum* as one possible Latin translation.
The rival term among the scholastics, *enuntiabile*, may be a creation of
Adam of Balsham, who belonged to the generation after Abelard,[42] and
it may owe something to Augustine's use of *dicibile*.[43]

The reinvention of something similar to a Stoic sayable was facilitated
by the presence in Boethius of a modified version of the Stoic definition
of an *axiōma*: "[A] proposition is an utterance that signifies a truth or a
falsehood."[44] This definition called for an answer to the question "what
sort of thing are those truths and falsehoods signified by propositions?"

The answer, we have already seen, was "They are not things" in any
ordinary sense; they do not really add to our ontological inventory. This
was a momentous decision, to introduce quasi things besides genuine
things. The move was repeated many times over for the next couple of
centuries. Universals could be considered quasi things, for instance; or

one could distinguish between things and modes – scholastic thinkers were to produce many variations of the theme.

The notion of propositional content, *dictum, enuntiabile,* or, as it was to be called in the fourteenth century, *complexe significabile,* offered a way to talk about the truth and falsity of propositions. Some twelfth-century philosophers identified a true enunciable with the event that made it true, thus making enunciables be untensed: as a result, the same truth will be expressed by three differently tensed propositions, one in the future before the event, another in the present during the event, and a third in the past after the event. This had the advantage that the patriarchs of the Old Testament and Christians could be said to believe in the same truth, although the patriarchs would express it in the future tense, "The Christ will be born," whereas Christians say, "The Christ has been born."[45] Others rejected this thesis. The price to be paid for having tensed enunciables was that they can change from being truths to being falsehoods and vice versa.

The problem of changing truth-value had been touched on by Aristotle in the *Categories,*[46] though not in terms of enunciables, of course, but just in terms of *logoi.* The Stoics had also dealt with it, and because they did not identify sayable and event either, a Stoic axiom could change its truth-value.[47] The Stoics said that such an axiom "falls over" – in Greek: *metapiptei.* The scholastics said that such an enunciable or proposition "falls over" – *transcadit.*[48] There is no attested use of *transcadere* in Latin except for this specific purpose, nor is the word known to have been used before the twelfth century. It so obviously looks like a calque of the Greek technical term, but it almost defies my imagination by which route the Stoic term may have traveled from Greek to Latin.[49]

The notion of enunciables or *dicta* was immediately put into use in modal logic, resulting in the well-known distinction between modality *de dicto* and modality *de re.* It further promised an answer to the question what sort of thing an object of knowing is.

In the thirteenth century there was a tendency to forget about propositional objects of knowledge and take essences to be the proper object of knowledge with a risk of hypostatizing essences. In the fourteenth century, however, the propositional view gained many adherents. Some would now take the significates of oral propositions to be mental events or mental propositions, and thus avoid positing special nonthings. While receding from Stoicism in this respect, they approached it in another way. To state the truth conditions of an affirmative proposition $x \, \Phi s$ they resorted to an analysis of the type *this is an x and this Φs.* This insistence on a deictic foundation for descriptive terms is one we know from the old Stoa. It does not go well with the Aristotelian notion of substance, but though few were willing to drop traditional substances, one may, I think, talk of a crisis for substances in the fourteenth century.

But we have not finished with the sayable-like entities and nonentities. John Buridan, in the fourteenth century, makes much of the difference between entertaining a proposition and accepting it. In his philosophy of knowledge and science this means that "knowledge is certain and evident assent supervening on a mental proposition, by which we assent to it with certitude and evidence."[50] Knowledge, then, is a propositional attitude, like opinion.[51] As in Stoicism, the basis is an assent, a *sunkatathesis* as the ancients said.[52] We need no more-or-less hypostatized essences to be the objects of our knowledge. For the object of knowledge to have the requisite immutability, all we need is to take the relevant propositions to be conditionals, or to take them as having an omni- or atemporal copula.[53]

The idea of separating assent to a proposition from understanding it is obviously transferable to ethics, and a move in that direction had been taken as early as the twelfth century.

In his *Ethics*, Peter Abelard tries to establish what is required for something to be morally wrong, what it takes to be a *peccatum*, or "error" as I shall call it. He considers various candidates for the criterion of whether an action is an error: vicious disposition, a desire (*voluntas*) to do the wrong thing, and wrong done, and eliminates each of them in turn. The primary bearer of moral predicates is the agent's intention, his conscious *acceptance* of acting in some way. Abelard's elimination of the other candidates for primary bearer of moral predicates culminates in his fantasy of a monk who is trussed up with rope and thrown into a soft bed containing a couple of attractive women. The monk experiences pleasant feelings. That is not a good thing for a monk, but it makes no sense to say: what is evil here is pleasant feelings, or: what is evil here is a man's natural inclination to experience such feelings in such circumstances, or: what is evil here is his desire – for we want to praise people who can resist desires to do wrong things. So, if the monk is to be blamed in this case, it can only be if he accepts having those pleasant feelings; if they occur against his internal protests, he is blameless.[54]

Abelard's word for "acceptance" is *consensus*. He may owe it to Augustine, or even to Saint Paul.[55] The similarity to the Stoic *sunkatathesis* is striking. To err or sin, then, is to consent to something that is not proper or allowed,[56] and "what is not proper" is acting in some way. Abelard does not discuss the ontological status of this object of consent, but later in the century, at least, some would say that the object must be a *dictum* – the content of a proposition, that is, for the monk "my having pleasant feelings."[57]

Two centuries later after Abelard, John Buridan makes it a central point of his ethics that man has the freedom to accept (*acceptare*), refuse, or postpone the decision about a certain course of action presented to the will by the intellect. He does not explicitly say that the object of acceptance refusal, or postponement is a mental proposition, but given his other philosophy it can hardly be anything but a proposition of the form, "This is to be done."[58]

CRAZY EXAMPLES AND PARADOXICAL THESES

The Stoics were famous for their crazy examples:

Dio and Theo are identical except for the fact that Theo misses his left leg. You amputate Dio's left leg. Identicals are the same, so we are left with one man. Which of the two disappears?[59]

Two sages are swimming in the sea after a shipwreck. Within reach there is one piece of timber from the wreck capable of keeping exactly one of them afloat. How do they avoid fighting over who is to survive?[60]

The scholastics were no less crazy:

Suppose that Socrates is in the second-to-last instant of his life. Is this proposition true: "Socrates ceases to be as he does not cease to be"?[61]

Take a chaste monk. Handcuff him, etc., as in Abelard's example.

Socrates vows to enter a monastery if the abbot will speak the truth to him. When he arrives for an interview with the abbot, he is met with the utterance, "You will not enter this monastery!" Is Socrates obliged to become a monk or not?[62]

The old Stoics and at least some scholastics also share a predilection for outrageous, paradoxical theses. The twelfth century shared with the Hellenistic age the trait of having competing philosophical sects, and each of them made a list of remarkably strange theses that they were willing to defend: "No noun is equivocal," "No animal is rational or irrational," and so on. Most of the twelfth-century theses have to do with logic.[63] The Stoic ones are ethical: "All errors (sins) are equal" and "Only the sage is a king."

The use of crazy examples and the flaunting of paradoxical theses are symptoms of an intellectual fanaticism common to the Stoa and the medieval schoolmen. They always try to carry the discussion to the extremes, hoping to construct a totally consistent philosophy, and they happily sacrifice a lot of commonsense views to achieve that goal.

STOIC PARADOXES, FOOLS AND SAGES, FREEDOM

The second of Cicero's *Stoic Paradoxes* is, "Virtue is all that is needed for happiness." This thesis famously clashes both with Aristotle's commonsense admission of a need for external goods so that one can actually exercise one's virtue, and with Christian religion. That did not prevent John Buridan from taking the thesis into serious consideration. In his discussion, he discards the Christian point of view as irrelevant in a philosophical context because it presupposes supernatural agency. That leaves him with the controversy between Peripatetics and Stoics. As might be expected, he ends up on the Peripatetic side, but only after having argued strongly for the Stoic view, drawing his ammunition mainly from Seneca's letters and dialogues, which (or, at least, some of which) he had read with some care. The Stoic view is not meant only as a foil for the Peripatetic one, for Buridan takes the unusual step of declaring that he finds it very attractive.[64] Now, Buridan was, above all, a great logician. Doubtless, it was the logical tidiness of the Stoic view that attracted him.

Cicero's fifth paradox is, "Only the sage is free, and every fool is a slave." The theme of freedom enters at a vital point in Buridan's *Ethics*, namely in the definition of the subject matter of ethics: "I hold that the proper subject in this branch of knowledge is man in respect of the things that are relevant to him insofar as he is free, or: man insofar as he is capable of being happy, that is, with regard to the things that are relevant to him for leading a happy life."[65] As Buridan makes clear later, he considers the two formulations almost equivalent. The "things" that are relevant are specified as *opera* – "works, functions." The reason for the clause, "insofar as he is free," is that being moral implies choosing and being master of one's acts.[66] In other words, ethics is about humans as free agents, humans in relation to what is in their own power – *ta eph' hēmin*.

In another place Buridan discusses whether happiness can consist in external goods, such as honors. The answer, supported by several references to Seneca, is a no, for that would mean that it was in other people's power to reduce a happy man to an unhappy one by removing honors.[67]

The Stoic sage was never quite forgotten; there was enough information about him in classical Latin texts to secure that. Until the end of the thirteenth century, however, his presence among scholars was discreet. But then he returned with his entourage of fools.

The most striking monument to the new faith in the sage is Boethius of Dacia's "On the Highest Good" (*De Summo Bono*) from about 1270. The sage can still be called a sage – *sapiens* – but mostly he is now called *philosophus*. Everything (with the exception of a little something about the first cause) is accessible to human reason and a man *can* reach a full understanding of everything. Once that is the case, he will not slip in his actions either; he will possess all the virtues and cannot fail to act rightly. He "never errs" or "sins" (*peccat*).

Boethius of Dacia left a little something about the first cause to be inscrutable to the human mind. Anyone who operates with a first cause ought to do just that, and the move also allowed Boethius to find a way to make it reasonable to believe in something unreasonable, namely Christian doctrine. This, of course, was important in the cultural context, but equally important was his forceful presentation of an ideal, the life of a philosopher, which is the highest good for a man and attainable without recourse to anything but man's natural resources: being observant and thinking hard.

Boethius does not make all errors equal, but there is much of the Stoic all-or-nothing atmosphere around his notion of the philosopher. Nonphilosophers are only quasi human, deficient humans, he says – *homines deminuti.* When one is operating under a rule,[68] any action that tends to realize the goal of the rule is right, and any action that does not do so is an error, a *peccatum.*

The happy man does not do any work except works of happiness or works by means of which he is made stronger or fitter to do the works of happiness. Therefore the happy man lives happily whether he is asleep or awake or is eating, as long as he does those things to become stronger with respect to the works of happiness. But all those of a man's actions that are not directed toward this highest good for a man..., whether they are opposed to it or indifferent, are an error [*peccatum*] on that man's part, albeit to a major or a minor degree, as is self-evident.[69]

Boethius ends his diatribe with speaking of the philosopher's love for and delight in the first principle, concluding:

This is the life of the philosopher, and whoever has not that life does not have a right life. By "philosopher" I mean any man who lives according to the right order of nature and who has acquired the best and ultimate end of human life.

The first principle, which I have spoken about, is God the glorious and most high, who is blessed for ever and ever.[70]

Boethius was perhaps the philosophically most sophisticated as well as the most eloquent proponent of the resurrected belief in the sage, but he was by far not the only believer. In the late thirteenth century, some variant of the belief in the sage-philosopher was shared by most masters of arts in Paris.

Boethius of Dacia and his like thought they found their philosopher-sage in Aristotle's *Ethics*, but their interpretation of that work was colored by a series of mediators – Averroes, Eustratius, Neoplatonists, Alexander of Aphrodisias – via whom the happy Aristotelian man had acquired traits from the Stoic sage. Latin sources such as Cicero and Seneca also played a role.

In the 1290s, a generation after Boethius and one before Buridan, Radulphus Brito would present his view about the highest good and his picture of the happy man, the sage, the philosopher, as a commentary on a passage from Seneca, starting a eulogy of philosophy as follows: "As Seneca says in his thirty-sixth letter to Lucilius: Come over to her – and he is speaking of philosophy – if you wish to be safe, unworried, happy, and – what is the greatest of all – if you wish to be free."[71] The freedom of the sage had deeply impressed the scholastics of the late thirteenth and early fourteenth centuries.

CONCLUSION

Although clad in Aristotelian garbs, all variants of scholastic philosophy differed markedly from Aristotle's. None was Stoic either. But there was a community of spirit with the Stoics, which made it possible for various Stoic *rationes seminales* preserved in ancient texts to develop into fresh organisms, themselves organic parts of different totalities of theory from that of the parent plants. Stoicism was nowhere and everywhere in the Middle Ages – but it was everywhere in a more important sense than the one in which it was nowhere.

Notes

1. Cf. Engberg-Pedersen 2000 and Chapter 3 in this volume.
2. Simplicius, *In Categorias Aristotelis* (ed. Kalbfleisch 1907 in *CAG* 8.334.2–3): *tois Stōikois, hōn eph' hēmōn kai hē didaskalia kai ta pleista tōn suggrammatōn ekleloipen.*

3. Boethius, *In Librum Peri Hermeneias* 2a (ed. Meiser 1880: 71): "Hoc loco Porphyrius de Stoicorum dialectica aliarumque scholarum multa permiscet et in aliis quoque huius libri partibus idem in expositionibus fecit, quod interdum nobis est neglegendum. Saepe enim superflua explanatione magis obscuritas comparatur."

4. Ibid. (201): "Porphyrius tamen quaedam de Stoica dialectica permiscet: quae cum Latinis auribus nota non sit, nec hoc ipsum quod in quaestionem venit agnoscitur atque ideo illa studio praetermittemus."

5. Among the sources transmitting the classification was Isidorus' much-used *Origines (Etymologiae)* 2.24.3–8. For early medieval divisions of philosophy, see Iwakuma 1999.

6. Boethius, *In Categorias Aristotelis*, PL 64: 159A–C.

7. Among other things, this might allow us to say that what unites the sciences they called *dialectic* is exactly that they speak the second-imposition language. See Pinborg 1962: 160.

8. The account given here represents my interpretation of the whole Porretan project. Documenting it is not possible within the space of this chapter. The main sources are Gilbert's commentary on Boethius' *Opuscula Sacra* (ed. Häring 1966), the *Compendium Logicae Porretanum* (ed. Ebbesen, Fredborg, and Nielsen 1983), and Evrard of Ypres' *Dialogus* (ed. Häring 1953). For secondary literature, see in particular Nielsen 1982, Jolivet and Libera 1987, and Jacobi 1987.

9. On Stoicism in twelfth-century physics, see Lapidge 1988. For Thierry's cosmogony, see Häring 1971. A brief version of the same cosmogony occurs in Andrew Sunesen's *Hexaemeron* (3.1468–1516) from about 1190 (ed. Ebbesen and Mortensen 1985–88).

10. Sextus Empiricus, *Adversus Mathematicos* 10.218 (= *SVF* 2:31: 117): *tōn de asōmatōn tessara eidē katarithmountai hōs lekton kai kenon kai topon kai chronon.*

11. Porphyrius, *Isagoge* (ed. Busse 1887) (= *CAG* 4.1: 1.10–12): *peri tōn genōn te kai eidōn to men <1> eite huphestēken eite kai en monais psilais epinoiais keitai <2> eite kai huphestēkota sōmata estin hē asōmata <3> kai poteron chōrista hē en tois aisthētois kai peri tauta huphestōta.* In Boethius' Latin rendition (*Aristoteles Latinus* 1.6–7; 5.10–14): "de generibus et speciebus illud quidem sive subsistunt sive in solis nudis purisque intellectibus posita sunt sive subsistentia corporalia sunt an incorporalia, et utrum separata an in sensibilibus et circa ea constantia."

12. Buridanus, *In Metaphysicen Quaestiones* 4.6 (ed. 1518: f. 17rb–va).

13. See, for example, Lambertini 1989.

14. Cf. Ebbesen 1981: 1:46–49, 203–204; 2:465, 471; 3:199. Variants of the argument continued to be used until the fourteenth century at least.

15. Boethius, *In Topica Ciceronis* (PL 64: 1092D–1093A): "Sed id sciendum est, M. Tullium ad hominum protulisse opinionem, non ad veritatem. Nam ut inter optime philosophantes constitit, illa maxime sunt quae longe a sensibus segregata sunt, illa minus, quae opiniones sensibus subministrant.... Sed, ut dictum est, corporea esse, et incorporea non esse, non ad veritatem sed ad communem quorumlibet hominum opinionem locutus est."

16. Eriugena, *Periphyseon* 1 (ed. Sheldon-Williams 1968: 36). This is the opening remark of the work: "Saepe mihi cogitanti diligentiusque quantum uires

suppetunt inquirenti rerum omnium quae uel animo percipi possunt uel intentionem eius superant primam summamque diuisionem esse in ea quae sunt et in ea quae non sunt horum omnium generale uocabulum occurrit quod graece, ΦΥCIC latine vero natura uocitatur."

17. *Ars Meliduna*, ch. 2 (ed. Iwakuma, forthcoming), f. 219rb: "Non sunt ergo universalia substantie nec proprietates sed habent suum esse per se, sicut enuntiabilia, tempora, et voces et fama." The proposed emendations are mine. I feel rather confident that *fama* is a scribal error for *inania*, whereas *voces* may be a correct reading, though it is tempting to change it into *loca* since *locus* and *inane* both appear in Anonymous D'Orvillensis' list of extracategorial words. In ch. 1, the *Ars Meliduna* has a long discussion of the ontological status of *voces*, and it seems possible that the author would claim that (in a certain sense) they have a sort of being of their own.

18. Anonymous D'Orvillensis, *In Categorias Aristotelis* (ed. Ebbesen 1999a: 273): "sunt enim plurimi [sc. termini incomplexi] qui nec significant substantiam nec continentur in aliquo praedicamento significatione, ut nomen omnia continens et nomen secundae impositionis et nomen ab artificio impositum et nomen appellans enuntiabile, ut 'verum,' et 'tempus' 'spatium' et 'locus' 'inane,' et omnia extrapraedicamentalia."

19. Ibid. (314): "Hoc nomen 'locus' tres habet acceptiones. Dicitur enim locus inane, ut: Socrates est in aliquo loco, movetur ab illo, locus ille a quo movetur intelligatur vacuus talem habens partium dispositionem qualem habet Socrates, ita quod ibi non subintret aer, licet hoc sit impossibile; et talis locus dicitur inane. Dicitur etiam locus aliquod superficiale cui aliquid superponitur, ut pratum. Dicitur etiam locus substantia ut domus, scyphus et alia huiusmodi concava quae infra sui concavitatem aliquid continent. In nulla harum significationum accipitur hic. Quia prout dicitur inane nec est substantia nec qualitas nec res praedicamentalis sed suum habens esse per se."

20. Anonymous, *Ars Burana* (ed. de Rijk 1962–67: 2:208): "dicendum est de enuntiabili, sicut de predicabili, quod nec est substantia nec accidens nec est de aliquo predicamentorum. Suum enim habet modum per se existendi. Et dicitur extrapredicamentale..."

21. On the twelfth-century schools, see Ebbesen 1992 and the other articles in *Vivarium* 30/1.

22. The main source for the ancient debate is Simplicius, *In Categorias Aristotelis* (ed. Kalbfleisch 1907 = *CAG* 8.9–13). It appears from his account that the question had already been raised by the time of Alexander of Aigai in the first century.

23. This is what the moderate nominalist, Anonymus D'Orvillensis, does about 1200 (ed. Ebbesen 1999a).

24. *Compendium Logicae Porretanum* (ed. Ebbesen et al. 1983): I. De terminis, II. De propositionibus, III. De significatis terminorum, IV. De significatis propositionum. *Ars Meliduna* (ed. Iwakuma, forthcoming): I. De terminis, II. De significatis terminorum, III. De propositionibus, IV. De dictis propositionum sive de enuntiabilibus.

25. *Auctoritates* (ed. Hamesse 1974: no. 34 [i.e., *Analytica Priora*] 7, p. 309): "Quando oppositum consequentis repugnat antecedenti, tunc consequentia fuit bona." Cf. ibid., no. 14: "Quandocumque ex opposito consequentis infertur oppositum antecedentis, tunc prima consequentia fuit bona." Cf. also *Incerti Auctores* (ed. Ebbesen 1977), qu. 90: "Dicendum ad hoc quod non sequitur, quia oppositum consequentis potest stare cum antecedente," and qu. 99: "Item oppositum consequentis non potest stare cum antecedente, ergo prima consequentia fuit bona per artem Aristotelis."

26. Diogenes Laertius, *Lives of Eminent Philosophers* 7.73 (ed. Hicks 1979–80: 180): *sunēmmenon oun alēthes estin hou to antikeimenon oui lēgontos machetai tōi hēgoumenōi.* Cf. Sextus Empiricus, *Outlines of Pyrrhonism* 2.111: *hoi de tēn sunartēsin eisagontes hugies einai phasin sunēmmenon hotan to antikeimenon tōi en autōi lēgonti machetai tōi en autōi hēgoumenōi,* "Those who introduce coherence, say that a conditional is sound when the opposite of its consequent is inconsistent with its antecedent."

27. *Akolouthoun* or *hepomenon* are likely Greek models. For *akolouthoun* speaks the fact that Boethius uses *consequentia* for *akolouthia/akolouthēsis* and that *akolouthei* is attested with the proper sense in Stoic logic. On the other hand, substantival use of *akolouthoun* is not attested. For *hepomenon* speaks the fact that this is used by others as a noun meaning "consequent." Alexander of Aphrodisias, *In Analytica Priora,* CAG 2.1: 178 (= FDS 994, p. 1268) uses the pair *hēgoumenon/hepomenon* in a passage relating Chrysippean doctrine. Boethius uses *consequi* and derivatives for the *akolouthein* family in his translations of *Categories, De Interpretatione,* and *Topics,* but for *hepesthai* in *Sophistici Elenchi* (and once in *Topics*); for references, see the relevant volumes of *Aristoteles Latinus.* Cicero uses *consequi* and *antecedere* in related senses. Boethius may have been inspired by the *locus ab antecedentibus et consequentibus* in Cicero's *Topics.* At one point in his career, Boethius used *praecedens/consequens* (*Hyp. Syll.* I, ed. Obertello 1969: 221 = PL 64: 835D–836A).

28. Apuleius, *Perihermeneias* (ed. Thomas 1938: 191): "est et altera probatio communius omnium etiam indemonstrabilium, quae dicitur per impossibile appellaturque a Stoicis prima constitutio vel primum expositum. quod sic definiunt: Si ex duobus terminum quid colligitur, alterum eorum cum contrario illationis colligit contrarium reliquo. veteres autem sic definierunt: Omnis conclusionis si sublata sit illatio, assumpta alterutra propositione tolli reliquam."

29. Ebbesen 1981: 1.26 (Sextus Empiricus, *Outlines of Pyrrhonism* 2.146–53, *Adversus mathematicos.* 8.429–37 [SVF 2:79, no. 240]).

30. Sextus Empiricus, *Outlines of Pyrrhonism* 2.112: *hoi de tēi emphasei krinontes phasin hoti alēthes esti sunēmmenon hou to lēgon en tō hēgoumenōi periechetai dunamei.*

31. Frede 1974: 90.

32. Galen, *Institutio Logica* 18 (ed. Kalbfleisch 1896: 46–47).

33. "Illa consequentia est bona in qua consequens includitur [or: intelligitur] in antecedente." See, for example, *Incerti Auctores, Quaestiones super Libro Elenchorum,* qu. 47 (ed. Ebbesen 1977: 98): "illa consequentia est bona

in qua consequens actu includitur in antecedente." Simon of Faversham, *Quaestiones super Libro Elenchorum* (ed. Ebbesen et al. 1984: 69–71) (where it is said that *includitur* is too weak a criterion; one must also require that *intelligendo antecedens necessario intelligatur consequens*) and QN 23 (pp. 159–61) (where the rule is accepted without qualifications, and with *includitur* and *intelligitur* used indifferently).

34. Anonymus, *Introductiones Montanae Maiores*, ms. Paris, BN 15141: 51ra–rb: "Potest concedi quia syllogismus est hypothetica propositio in hoc sensu, id est composita, sed non est hypothetica, id est condicionalis, quamvis magister Guillelmus Capellensis constituens in syllogismo quendam sensum diceret syllogismum omnem esse ratiocinativam propositionem." E. P. Bos of Leiden is preparing an edition of this text.

35. Abelard, *Super Topica Glossae* (ed. dal Pra 1969: 322–23).

36. Cf. Frede 1974: 80, n18.

37. For Autrecourt, see the edition by de Rijk 1994a.

38. Boethius, *De Topicis Differentiis* (ed. Nikitas 1990: 1.1.5–7: 3 = *PL* 64: 1174C). Notice the use of *vis* and *virtus* in the attempts to say "sense." Cf. Augustine, *De Dialectica*.

39. Cf. Ebbesen 1993. Boethius in his translation of Aristotle's *Topics* renders *epicheirēsis* (111b16, 139b10) by *argumentatio*, and prefers *argumentum* for *epicheirēma* but also twice uses *argumentatio*.

40. Abelard, *Dialectica* (ed. de Rijk 1970: 460).

41. Seneca, *Epistulae* 117. Cf. Nuchelmans 1973: 152. In spite of much later literature on *dicta*, Nuchelmans remains indispensible. Notice that even if Abelard knew *Letter* 117, he may not have met the term, but rather the variant *edictum* favored by one branch of the manuscript tradition.

42. So Nuchelmans 1973: 169.

43. Augustine, *Dialectica* 5 (ed. Pinborg 1975: 88–90).

44. Boethius, *De Topicis Differentiis* 1.1.2 (ed. Nikitas 1990: 2 = *PL* 64: 1174B): "propositio est oratio verum falsumve significans."

45. See, for example, Ebbesen 1997.

46. Aristotle, *Categoriae* 6.4a34–b13.

47. *FDS* 994, 1025, 1200; cf. Gourinat 1999: 147.

48. The first attestation of the verb may be in *Ars Meliduna*, quoted in de Rijk 1962–67: 1:371 and 385 (but with the thing that changes as subject). Walter Burley, much later, defines as follows: "Et est transcasus quando aliqua proposito mutatur a veritate in falsitatem vel econverso" (quoted in Spade 1982: 248, n22).

49. The only possible, though hardly plausible, route I have found so far is from Philoponus, *In Analytica Posteriora* (ed. Wallies 1909, *CAG* 13.3: 325.13–16): *phamen gar abebaion einai tēn doxan, dihoti ta hupokeimena autēi endechetai kai allōs echein. toutōn oun metapesontōn kai hē peri autōn doxa metapiptei ē ex alēthous pseudēs genomenē ē kai holōs metaballomenē* via James of Venice's lost translation of that passage.

50. Buridanus, *Summulae* 8.3.7: "scientia est assensus certus et evidens superveniens propositioni mentali, quo illi cum certitudine et evidentia assentimus." Cf. de Rijk 1994b.

51. In other places Buridan operates with a knowledge that has both things and a proposition for their object, that is, knowledge becomes a triadic relation between knower, thing known, and proposition known. Cf. Willing 1999.

52. For other propositional attitudes among the Stoics, one might think of the verbal moods. Cf. Ildefonse 1999: 169–70.

53. Conditionals: see William of Ockham. Omni- or atemporal: see Buridanus, *Summulae* 4.3.4 (ed. de Rijk 1998: 47). Cf. Buridan's discussion in his *Quaestiones super decem libros Ethicorum* VI.6. See also Ebbesen 1984: 109, n19.

54. Abelard, *Ethica* (ed. Luscombe 1971: 20).

55. Cf. Marenbon 1997: 260 n31. See also Romans 7:16.

56. Cf. Marenbon 1997: 260 with footnotes.

57. Cf. the discussion of "Deus vult Iudam furari" in Andrew Sunesen 8.4823–31 (ed. Ebbesen and Mortensen 1985–88: 230).

58. Buridan's *Quaestiones super decem libros Ethicorum* VI.6 is curiously ambiguous: "acceptare" and "assentire" both occur, but the object of "assentire" is "apparentiis."

59. *FDS* 845. Similar examples, using a donkey with or without one foot, occur in the *Sentences* commentary of Roger Rosetus (fourteenth century), of which an edition is being prepared by Olli Hallamaa of Helsinki.

60. Cicero, *De Officiis* 2.23.90 (from Hecaton).

61. See, for example, Peter of Auvergne, *Sophisma* VII, in Ebbesen 1989: 157. "Socrates desinit esse non desinendo esse etc. Ista oratio probatur facta positione sc. quod Socrates sit in paenultimo instanti vitae suae."

62. Ps.-Buridan = Nicholas of Vaudémont, *Quaestiones super Octo Libros Politicorum Aristotelis* VI.7 (Paris 1513; rpr., Frankfurt am Main: Minerva, 1969) f. 92ra. See emended text in *Cahiers de l'Institut du Moyen Age Grec et Latin* 56 (1988): 194–95.

63. *Nullum nomen est aequivocum* was a tenet of the Melun school; see Ebbesen 1992: 63. An anonymous list of tenets of the Albricani (discovered by Yukio Iwakuma), ms. Wien, ÖNB lat. 2237: 31ra has "Prima in categoricis est nostrae sententiae positio quod nullum animal est rationale vel irrationale."

64. Buridanus, *Quaestiones super decem libros Ethicorum* I.10: Utrum felicitas in virtute consistat an in operatione virtutis; I.16: Utrum ad felicitatem requiratur usus virtutis et delectatio et bonorum exteriorum abundantia et bona corporis dispositio.

65. Ibid., I.3, f. 4va (my orthography): "videtur mihi quod homo in ordine ad ea quae sibi conveniunt ut est liber, vel homo ut est felicitabilis, hoc est quantum ad ea quae sibi conveniunt ad ducendum felicem vitam, est subiectum proprium in hac scientia."

66. Ibid., I.3, f. 4vb: "mechanici non sunt proprie domini neque electivi suarum operationum, propter quod dicuntur. Morales autem nulli dicuntur nisi secundum quod sunt suorum actuum electivi et domini. Propter quod morales scientias dictum fuit non esse serviles sed liberas. Ideo addere oportuit quod homo esset huiusmodi subiectum sub ordine ad opera sibi debita non quocumque modo sed secundum quod est liber, vel secundum quod est felicitabilis, quod rationabilius sustineri potest, quia felicitas est consideratorum ultimus finis, et ultimus finis in operationibus est primum principium a quo

sumi debet originaliter ratio formalis considerandi. Et hi duo modi dicendi videntur esse satis propinqui."

67. Ibid., I.8, f. 8ra.
68. Boethius Dacus, *De Summo Bono* (ed. Green-Pedersen 1976, CPhD 6: 372). The word is *lex*. Notice that in Boethius' time *lex* was also commonly used for "religion."
69. Ibid. (372–73): "Unde homo felix nihil operatur nisi opera felicitatis vel opera per quae redditur fortior vel magis habilis ad opera felicitatis. Ideo felix sive dormiat sive vigilet sive comedat, feliciter vivit, dummodo illa facit, ut reddatur fortior ad opera felicitatis. Unde omnes actiones hominis, quae non diriguntur in hoc summum bonum hominis, quod iam dictum est, sive opponantur sibi, sive sint indifferentes, peccatum sunt in homine, secundum tamen magis et minus, ut patet ex se."
70. Ibid. (6.377): "Haec est vita philosophi, quam quicumque non habuerit non habet rectam vitam. Philosophum autem voco omnem hominem viventem secundum rectum ordinem naturae, et qui acquisivit optimum et ultimum finem vitae humanae. Primum autem principium, de quo sermo factus est, est deus gloriosus et sublimis, qui est benedictus in saecula saeculorum. Amen."
71. Radulphus Brito, *Quaestiones super Sophisticos Elenchos*, prooemium, edited in Ebbesen and Pinborg 1982. Cf. Ebbesen 1999.

7

Abelard's Stoicism and Its Consequences

Calvin Normore

As Sten Ebbesen has emphasized in his contribution to this volume, the influence of Stoicism in the Middle Ages is to be found everywhere and is yet felt subtly enough that one is often unsure whether it is Stoicism itself that is being encountered. Part of the reason for this is fairly simple: Stoicism was so very influential in the Roman Empire that it left its mark on most of the church fathers and on most of the philosophical schools of late antiquity. Because so little work by card-carrying Stoics has survived, Stoic ideas were transmitted into the Middle Ages largely through thinkers who, while influenced by Stoicism, were not themselves Stoics and who often made free with Stoic ideas. Not surprisingly, it is often hard to tell when a later thinker is in some important way a Stoic.

In this chapter I want to make one piece of what would have to be a much more complex argument to be complete. My larger thesis is that Peter Abelard is as close to Stoicism as a Christian could be and that in his case this is not some independent rediscovery of Stoic ideas but a self-conscious taking up of them with profound consequences for later medieval philosophy. I stake this claim as a claim about Abelard's positions in a variety of areas, including logic – hence my ambiguous title. Here and now I want to focus just on one theme in Abelard's ethics, to discuss Abelard's views on it, to argue that it is a Stoic theme in a Stoic context, and to trace part of its *fortuna* into the fourteenth century.

That there is some connection between Peter Abelard's ethical views and Stoicism is widely accepted. In his 1983 monograph, The *Presence of Stoicism in Medieval Thought,* Gerard Verbeke devotes a couple of pages to the comparison of Abelard's views with those of the Stoics. He finds that they agree on emphasizing the role of internal factors in moral responsibility and he finds that the Philosopher in Abelard's *Collationes* holds a largely Stoic brief, emphasizing the role of natural law, the view that virtue is happiness, and the strict unity of the virtues. Verbeke concludes, "Like so many other positions which he develops, these views show that the Philosopher's main inspiration is Stoic."[1] I want to take up Verbeke's claim and to make more precise the sense in which Abelard's ethics is Stoic by focusing on one central theme in it. First, then, one part of Abelard's ethics.

Abelard has two works explicitly devoted to ethics. One is a treatise variously titled *Ethica* or *Scito Te Ipsum*,[2] which has come down to us incomplete and seems in fact never to have been finished. The second is a pair of dialogues or *Collationes*, one between a Philosopher and a Jew, the other between a Philosopher and a Christian.[3] This work appears to be incomplete but seems to have been intended to so appear and to be, in fact, complete.

The central problem of the part of the *Ethics* that has come down to us is to find the locus of sin. When one sins, what exactly is it about what one has done that makes it a sin, that is, which makes it *morally blameworthy*? Abelard considers and rejects several proposals. The most obvious suggestion (and the one most favored in the history of ethics, I suspect) is that the moral character of an act is an intrinsic feature of the particular act itself – or even, perhaps, of the act type. But Abelard thinks that this suggestion fails because acts of precisely the same type, indeed even numerically the same act, can be both good and bad. An example that comes up both in the *Ethics* and in the *Dialogue* is of two men who collaborate in hanging a criminal. As Abelard puts it:

Often in fact the same thing is done by different people through the justice of one and the viciousness of the other. For example, if two people hang a criminal, one out of a zeal for justice and the other out of hatred springing from an old feud, then, although the hanging is the same action, and although they certainly do what is good to be done and what justice demands, nevertheless through the difference in their intention the same thing is done by different people, one badly and the other well.[4]

That a difference in the reason for which an act is done can affect its moral character shows that it is not merely intrinsic features of the act that matter but leaves open what extrinsic features might be relevant.

As preparation for his own positive view, Abelard insists that the moral significance of an act cannot derive solely from what he calls the *voluntas* from which it is done either. To show this, he borrows Augustine's example

of the slave who kills his master to avoid being beaten but who does it –
as Abelard, like Augustine, insists – without a *voluntas* for doing it: "[F]or
behold there is an innocent man whose cruel lord is so moved by rage
that he chases him with a drawn sword to kill him. Eventually, the man,
though he flees for a long time and avoids his own death as much as he
can, forced and unwilling kills the lord lest he be killed by him. Tell me,
whoever you are, what bad will he would have had in doing this."[5] After
considering several possible defenses for the view that there is some bad
voluntas involved, Abelard concludes: "[S]o it is evident that sometimes
sin is committed entirely without bad will; it is clear from this that it ought
not to be said that sin is will."[6] Abelard goes on to conclude that not every
sin is voluntary either because "There are those who are wholly ashamed
to be dragged into consent to concupiscence or into a bad *voluntas* and
are dragged by the infirmity of the flesh to *velle* this which they do not at
all *velle* to *velle*."[7] What then remains? In the *Ethics* Abelard insists that:

Vice is that by which we are made prone to sin, that is, are inclined to what is not
fitting so that we either do it or forsake it. Now this consent we properly call sin,
that is, the fault of the soul by which it earns damnation or is made guilty before
God. . . . And so our sin is contempt of the Creator and to sin is to hold the creator
in contempt, that is, not at all to do on his account what we believe we ought to
do on his account or to forsake on his account what we believe is to be forsaken.[8]

   Sin is *contemptus dei*. But how does one commit it? The passage just
quoted suggests that one sins by *not acting* in a certain way, but this is
elliptical. As Abelard goes on a few pages later:

We truly then consent to that which is not permitted when we do not at all draw
back from its accomplishment but are wholly ready, if given the chance, to do
it. Anyone who is found in this disposition [*proposito*] incurs the fullness of guilt;
nor does the addition of the carrying out of the deed add anything to increase
the sin. On the contrary, before God the one who strives to do it as much as he
can is as guilty as the one who does it as much as he can.[9]

So we sin by being in a certain state – the state of not acting in a certain
way. And this is the only way we sin, for Abelard insists that "the doing
of deeds has no bearing upon an increase of sin and nothing pollutes
the soul except what is of the soul."[10] The state of being "inwardly ready"
that Abelard talks about in the *Ethica* seems to be the same state that
he describes there and elsewhere as that of "having an intention" (*in-
tentio*). Thus one consents by having an intention and so we can speak
indifferently of the goodness or badness of an intention or of a consent.[11]

To drive the point home, Abelard adds: "So when we call a person's intention good and his deed good, we are distinguishing two things, the intention and the deed, but we are talking about *one* goodness – that of the intention."[12] Thus, intentions or consents are primarily good or bad. Deeds, Abelard claims, can be called good or bad but only derivatively – a good deed is one that is caused by a good intention, a bad deed one that is caused by a bad intention.[13]

As so far outlined, Abelard's position is both striking and tolerably clear, but it is both more problematic and more sophisticated than it first appears. First, there is an interesting asymmetry in his view: to sin, it is necessary and sufficient to have a bad intention; to merit, it is necessary and sufficient to have a good intention. But there are, it seems, intentions that are neither good nor bad. As we shall see, these arise because Abelard's account of bad intention is in a significant way *subjective*, but his account of good intention is *objective*.

We saw that we sin when we do not do (or avoid) what we believe we should do (or avoid) for God's sake. Hence, sin involves our beliefs about what should be done for God's sake. Thus no one sins properly speaking (i.e., sins *per culpam*) if she acts against her conscience, even if that conscience is in error. Thus consenting to or intending what one believes erroneously not to be what should be done for God's sake is bad, and so such an intention is a bad intention. But Abelard insists that it is not enough for a good intention that one intends what one believes ought to be done for God's sake. One has a good intention only if the belief is correct. As he puts it: "And so an intention should not be called good because it seems to be good but because in addition it is just as it is thought to be, that is, when, believing that one's objective is pleasing to God, one is in no way deceived in one's own estimation."[14]

Abelard explains that if this were not so, one would have to admit that unbelievers could act as well as believers. I would go further and suggest that, if it were not so, Abelard would have slipped into a thoroughgoing moral relativism according to which an act is good or bad if it follows from a good or bad intention and a good or bad intention is just one that the agent thinks is good or bad. But Abelard has not slipped into this morass. He insists that a good intention is one that intends what really is pleasing to God – one that really ought to be done for God's sake – so objectivity is preserved.

Still, matters are not so simple. On Abelard's view, it seems, the moral goodness or badness of an action derives from the intention with which it is performed. An intention is, typically, an intention to perform an action. If the moral value of an intention does not derive from the moral value of the act that it is an intention to perform, then from what does it derive? By making the moral value of acts derivative on the moral value of intentions to perform them, has not Abelard made it impossible to assign a value to acts at all?

Abelard's procedure appears to be *ungrounded.* In contrast, moral theories that first assign a moral value to acts and then use that to assign a value to intentions are typically grounded. For example, in *The Theory of Morality*, Alan Donagan first works out an account of which acts it is permissible to perform and then connects this to an account of intention through the principle: "It is impermissible to intend to do what it is impermissible to do."[15] Donagan's account of the permissibility of actions makes no reference whatever to intentions and so avoids circularity. Abelard can, it is true, accept the principle that it is permissible to intend just what it is permissible to do, but, because the permissibility of acts is, for him, derivative upon the permissibility of intentions, it cannot provide the basis from which we compute the permissibility of an intention. An independent specification of the permissibility of an intention is needed.

One might seek a beginning for such an independent specification in Abelard's remark that for an intention to be good, what one intends must be in fact pleasing to God. This would do, provided there was a specification of what was pleasing to God that did not depend on specifying what is good. But is there?

Abelard was infamous for the claim that God was not able to do anything other than what God did do. Abelard's argument was simple. Because God acted for the best, this was the best. Because this was the best, anything else would be less good. But God cannot do the less good; therefore God cannot do anything other than what God does do.[16] If we take this at face value, we see at once that if we suppose that the best is just whatever most pleases God, then Abelard's argument reduces to the claim that whatever most pleases God necessarily most pleases God. This may be defensible but it cannot be defended on the grounds that Abelard himself invokes. For example, it cannot be reconciled with this passage from the *Dialogue*:

So since plainly nothing is done except with God's permitting it – indeed nothing can be done if he is unwilling or resists – and since in addition it's certain that God never permits anything without a cause and does nothing whatever except reasonably, so that both his permission and his action are reasonable, surely therefore, since he sees why he permits the individual things that are done to be done, he isn't ignorant why they should be done, even if they're evil or are evilly done. For it wouldn't be good for them to be permitted unless it were good for them to be done. And he wouldn't be perfectly good who would not interfere, even though he could, with what wouldn't be good to be done. Rather, by agreeing that something be done that isn't good to be done, he would obviously be to blame.

So obviously whatever happens to be done or happens not to be done has a reasonable cause why it's done or not done.[17]

Here the Christian of the *Dialogue* (who seems to be Abelard's spokesman at this point) goes out of his way to insist on the need for a reason why God permits what he does. So, unless we suppose that Abelard just never brought the various bits of his philosophy together, we cannot suppose that Abelard just identifies the good as what pleases God. Abelard is not Euthyphro.

But this then revives our problem. What can ground intentions? Our deeds are good if they proceed from good intentions. Our intentions are good if they are intentions to do what we believe to be and what is pleasing to God. But something is pleasing to God only if it is good. We seem to have a short and vicious circle.

This circle could be broken in at least two ways, which can, but need not, exclude one another. On the one hand there could be a structural constraint on intentions, the satisfaction of which would make them good (or at least not bad) intentions. For example (and very roughly), Kant's Categorical Imperative requires that the intention with which you act be such that acting on the intention is compatible with everyone else acting on (relevantly) similar intentions. If your intention passes this test, then acting on it is *permissible*. One might go on to suggest that intending a permissible act is good just in case one intends it conditional on its being a permissible act.

This procedure will break the circle, but it is not obvious that it does justice to Abelard's view that God can only do what he does. There may well be more than one maximal set of intentions that could be jointly realized. If there is, then any intention in any such set which is conditional on it being in such a set would be a good intention by this procedure and so might well be pleasing to God. Yet Abelard seems to think that there is a single possible history of the world that could be pleasing to God – the one the world actually has.

To resolve this problem I think, following suggestions both Marilyn Adams and Peter King have made, that we must distinguish two very different uses of "good." For the moment I call them the moral and the metaphysical sense. Our solution, then, is to suggest that morally good acts depend on morally good intentions that are grounded in states of affairs that have no moral value but are metaphysically good. These metaphysically good states can, the proposal goes, be identified without any recourse to morality at all.

Can we find the distinction this proposal needs in Abelard?

Abelard is very sensitive to the logic of the word *bonum*. At the end of the first book of the *Dialogue* where the Christian and the Philosopher seem to have just about arrived at a consensus, he has the Christian say that when it is used adjectively (as in "good horse" or "good thief"), the word *bonum* has its signification affected by the noun to which it is attached. Thus to be a good man is not the same thing as to be a good worker even if the same thing is man and a worker. The Christian points out that we apply the term *bonum* both to things (*res*) and to *dicta* and rather differently. We could say for example that it is bad that there exists a good thief.

At this point, Abelard's moral theory intersects with his ontology and his logic. In his ontology Abelard has individual *res* and individual forms – there is nothing else. But Abelard is happy to speak about two other items, which he usually calls *statuses* and *dicta*. "Being a human" is a status, and we are all humans because we agree in this status. But a status is not a thing, and there is no*thing* in which we agree. "That we are all human" is a dictum but it too is not a thing. I don't really know exactly how to fit actions into Abelard's metaphysics (despite the discussion of *facere* and *pati* in the *Dialectica*), but I am reasonably certain that these too are nonthings. My evidence for this is that, when Abelard gives examples of causation (which he expressly claims is a relation among nonthings), the examples he gives are of actions – thus, committing a murder is a cause of being hanged, he says. So whether or not actions just are statuses, they are like them in many ways.

The primary adjectival uses of the word *bonum* are to things under a *status* and to *dicta*. We speak of good people, good horses, and good thieves, and we say that it is good *that freon levels in the atmosphere have stopped rising so quickly*. Especially important for our purposes is the status of being human.

"We say a man is good for his morals," Abelard has the Christian say,[18] and his morals are a matter of the man's intentions. Hence to be a good man is to have good intentions or, as the Christian sometimes puts it, to act well (as contrasted with doing good).

This brings us back to an earlier worry: what is it to have a good intention or to act well?

Near the end of the *Dialogue*, the Christian says:

> I think that is called "good" simply – that is a "good thing" – which, while it is fit for some use, of nothing is it necessary that it impede the advantage or worthiness. Contrariwise, I believe a thing is called "evil" that necessarily carries one of these features with it. The "indifferent" on the other hand – that is, a thing that's neither good nor evil – I think is one such that no good is necessarily delayed or impeded by its existence. For example, the casual movement of a finger or any actions like that. For actions aren't judged good or evil except according to their root, the intention. Rather, by themselves they're all indifferent.[19]

In this passage, Abelard apparently assumes what I will call the Principle of the Concomitance of All Goods (PCG) – the view that real goods never conflict.

Now Abelard expressly accepts the PCG. In his *Dialectica*, for example, he writes: "However, truth is not opposed to truth. For it is not the case that as a falsehood can be found to be contrary to a falsehood or an evil to an evil so can a truth be opposed to a truth or a good to a good; rather to it [the good] all things good are *consona et convenientia*."[20] PCG is a principle of which various corollaries figure prominently in Abelard's logic and metaphysics. For example, Abelard is distinctive among twelfth-century logicians for rejecting the so-called *locus ab oppositis*, that is, the topical rule that enables one to infer from the presence of one feature to the absence of its contrary. The consequences of this for ethics emerge in another passage very late in the *Dialogue* where the Christian says:

> As was said, we call a thing good that, while it's fit for some use, mustn't impede the advantage or worthiness of anything. Now a thing's being impeded or lessened would indeed be necessary if through its contrary or lack the worthiness or advantage would necessarily not remain. For example, life, immortality, joy, health, knowledge, and chastity are such that although they have some worthiness or advantage, it plainly doesn't remain when their contraries overtake them. So too any substances whatever are plainly to be called good things because, while they're able to impart some usefulness, no worthiness or advantage is necessarily hampered through them. For even a perverse man whose life is corrupt or even *causes* corruption, could be such that he were not perverse, and so nothing's being made worse would be necessary through him.[21]

The upshot of this passage, as I read it in conjunction with the endorsement of PCG in the *Dialectica*, is that we have a test for telling metaphysical goods from nongoods. Metaphysical goods are elements that necessarily can coexist together. Evils on the other hand may coexist, but do not necessarily coexist.

God, the Supreme Good, always and necessarily acts for the best on Abelard's view. The best for which he acts is not a *moral* best but a metaphysical best; he creates the maximal collection of necessarily compatible things and forms – the metaphysically best world.[22] Moreover, he makes this collection in such a way that each item in it has a "reasonable cause" of its coming to be in it.

For a human being to intend well is to intend to do what is pleasing to God, that is, to intend to bring about a situation (an *eventus rei* in Abelard's terminology) which you believe to be part of the metaphysically best world *and* which is, in fact, part of the metaphysically best world, *and* to intend to do this in a way which you believe to be and which in fact is reasonable. For a human being to act badly is to intend to bring about a situation that you believe to be inconsistent with the metaphysically perfect world, either because you believe the intended effect to not have a place in such a world or because you believe the way you intend to bring it about not to be a reasonable one. An intention is neither good nor bad if it is an intention to bring about something that you believe to be part of the metaphysically best world and to be reasonably brought about as you intend but which in fact is not. On this account, metaphysical perfection is specifiable independently of intentions, and so the circle that threatened Abelard's account is broken.

I will now try to suggest that the ethical picture attributed to Abelard so far is Stoic, both in content and inspiration.

If I guess correctly, much of the account just related will seem familiar to those interested in Stoicism. The division of items into goods, evils, and indifferents, and the Principle of the Concomitance of All Goods are well-known Stoic themes. But I want to make a stronger claim – that the central feature of Abelard's ethics, his view that the locus of sin is consent or intention – is a Stoic view. Since this feature of Abelard's ethics also becomes a central feature of fourteenth-century Franciscan ethical theory, it is, I suggest, plausible to think that through Abelard an interesting aspect of Stoic ethical theory is transmitted. The first hurdle my claim must clear is the suggestion that by Abelard's time, at least, there is nothing distinctively Stoic about the suggestion that sin is a matter of consent and intention. After all, does not Abelard himself quote Augustine in support of his doctrine?

Like Abelard, the Stoics face the problem of accounting for moral responsibility within the best of all possible worlds. Let me stress the importance of this. Stoic determinism is also a providentialism: on the

Stoic view this is not only the only possible world, but also the best possible world. There is a wealth of evidence for the Zenonian equation of Fate, Providence, and Nature, and for the Chrysippean equation of Fate, Providence, and Zeus.[23] In such a setting, to live in accordance with nature is to accept Fate. It is to identify with what must (and so will) happen.

Such a stance raises very peculiar problems for moral responsibility. Dio will kill Theo if and only if that is for the best. Thus, if Dio kills Theo it is good, even best, that Theo be killed by Dio. How then can we blame Dio? Both Abelard and the Stoics have this problem and both respond in the same way – by making moral praise and blame not a matter of what is done but of the description under which it is done. In Abelard's example of the two men who cooperate to hang a criminal, the hanging of the criminal justly is a good; what is bad is the revenging of oneself. The executioner and the vengeful man both hang the criminal, and both consent to hang the criminal, but only the vengeful man consents to revenging himself and only he is blameworthy.

Abelard's solution to this common problem is to make consent or intention the locus of moral responsibility. The ancient Stoic solution is to locate moral responsibility in *sunkatathesis* – which Cicero translated as *adsensio* and English writers translate as "assent."

First, then, let me try to make plausible the identification of Abelardian consent and intention with Stoic assent so as to defend the claim that it would be reasonable for Abelard to think his consent a Stoic notion. Here I appeal to Brad Inwood's authority:

[I]f one wants to know what someone's intentions are, one simply checks to see what hormetic propositions receive assent. If there is a quarrel about what an agent was intending to do, the dispute is in principle soluble. Did Dion intend to wound Theon when he threw the javelin across the playing field? We need only ask what proposition he assented to in performing that action.[24]

A little later Inwood adds:

On this theory intentions are always followed by actions unless external obstacles intervene. It is never possible for a man to be sure that his intentions will succeed. Since, however, we would not hold a man responsible for such hindrances to his actions, it follows that intentions are the correct locus of moral evaluation.[25]

Inwood admits that, although there is no ancient source for the claim that there are strictly hormetic propositions, there is plenty of theoretical justification for thinking the Stoics distinguished them. And what would such a hormetic proposition, assent to which leads directly to *hormē* (impulse), be like? Inwood's example is that of a man with a sweet tooth who in the presence of a piece of cake forms the hormetic proposition, "It is fitting for me to eat cake."[26]

What now of Abelard? Usually he speaks of consent not to *dicta* but to acts. X consents to take his sister in marriage, or to build a house for the poor, or to kill his master. But Abelard also insists that there is belief involved. "Thus an intention isn't to be called good because it *appears* good, but more than that, because it *is* such as it is considered to be – that is, when if one believes that what he is aiming at is pleasing to God, he is in addition not deceived in his evaluation."[27] And he sometimes describes sin to be scorn for God or consenting to what one believes shouldn't be consented to.

Because believing that your intention is one you should (or should not) have is a matter of accepting or assenting to a dictum, it seems clear that assent is involved in Abelardian consent.[28]

Grant me for a moment that Abelard's consent or intention is close enough to our best current understanding of Stoic theory on this matter that, if Abelard had had our sources, it would not be unreasonable for him to think that the view was Stoic. Still the question remains whether it is plausible to think that he thought of it as a Stoic doctrine.

In the *Ethics*, Abelard proposes the doctrine that the locus of sin is consent as his own, but in the *Collationes* and in particular in the *Dialogue of a Philosopher with a Christian*, Abelard introduces it first as the Philosopher's position. The Philosopher claims:

For certain things are called goods or evils properly and so to speak substantially. For instance the virtues and vices themselves. But certain things are so called by accident and through something else, like actions that are our deeds. Although they're indifferent in themselves, nevertheless they're called good or evil from the intention from which they proceed. Frequently, therefore, when the same thing is done by different people, or by the same person at different times, the same deed is nevertheless called both "good" and evil because of the difference in the intentions. On the other hand, things that are called goods or evils substantially and from their own nature remain so permanently unmixed that what is once good can never become evil, or conversely.[29]

This is the first occurrence in the *Dialogue* of the claim that intention is the locus of moral culpability, and it follows shortly a passage in which the Christian refuses to take a stand on the issue. It seems plain then that in the *Dialogue* Abelard is marking this as a distinctive position of the Philosopher.

Who then is this Philosopher? On this issue opinions have differed. Some commentators have suggested that he is modeled on an Arab philosopher.[30] Much more plausible is the suggestion that he is a figure who is to represent what Abelard thinks best in ancient philosophy. If so, that best turns out to be remarkably Stoic. Not only does the philosopher endorse the Stoic themes I have claimed Abelard himself to endorse; he also endorses the Stoic paradox that all evils and all goods are equal and cites Cicero for it.[31] Moreover, he accepts the Stoic view that virtue is the ultimate good – although he uses the authority of Seneca to argue that the Epicurean view that the ultimate good is pleasure is only verbally different.

I hope to have convinced you by now that Abelard is himself deeply influenced by Stoic doctrine and is self-consciously taking up Stoic themes in his ethics. There remains my claim that it is in virtue of Abelard's taking up these themes that they remain part of the philosophical landscape in the later Middle Ages.

The doctrine that the exterior act adds nothing to the sin (because the locus of sin is entirely interior) was identified with the *Nominales* in the early thirteenth century. In his *Summa*, written between 1212 and 1219, Godfrey of Poitiers attributes to the *Nominales* the view that "the will [*voluntas*] and the act are the same sin."[32] Exactly who the *Nominales* are is rather obscure, but there is fairly general agreement that, whoever they were, they were followers of Abelard. We can then find the doctrine that the sin is wholly exhausted in the interior act explicitly attributed to Abelard's school in the first quarter of the thirteenth century. Their way of putting the point is, however, rather different from Abelard's. Abelard had gone out of his way to distinguish *voluntas* and *consensum*, but his followers did not. It would take me too far afield to discuss this thoroughly here, but I doubt any substantive change of doctrine. Rather, *voluntas* is undergoing a change of sense in the twelfth century. In Abelard's time it can still mean something like a motive or even a desire (as it does in some of Anselm's uses), but by the end of the twelfth century this usage is dead and it means either a power in the soul or the exercise of that power. So I think the view attributed to the *Nominales* just reflects this new usage.

It seems that the *Nominales* disappear before the end of the twelfth century, and I know of no one in the first three-quarters of the thirteenth century who shares Abelard's view. But the view is kept alive (as so many ancient Stoic views are) by its attackers. In particular, the view is presented and criticized by Peter Lombard in his *Sententiae*. In book II, d. 35, the Lombard takes up the question of what a sin is and canvasses three opinions:

Because of the ambiguity occasioned by these words, widely divergent opinions on sin have been observed. For some say that the will alone is sinful, and not external acts; others, that both the will and acts are sinful; still others reject both, saying that all acts are good and from God and exist by divine authorship. Evil, however, is nothing, as Augustine says in his *Commentary on the Gospel of John* (16): "*All things are made through him, and without him nothing is made,*" that is, sin is nothing, and when men sin they are not producing anything."[33]

The first of these opinions is Abelard's (with the terminological shift just mentioned). Lombard returns to it in d. 40:

Next, regarding acts, it seems that we must also ask whether they should be considered good or evil in view of their ends, just like the will. For although some believe that all things are naturally good insofar as they exist, we should not call all things good or praiseworthy absolutely, but some are said to be absolutely evil, in the same way as others are called good. For those acts are absolutely and truly good which are accompanied by good reasons and intentions, that is, which are accompanied by a good will, and which tend to good ends. But those acts are said to be absolutely evil which are done for perverse reasons and intentions.[34]

Lombard does not endorse Abelard's view, but he does treat it with respect, and as commenting on his *Sententiae* became the standard way a theologian showed his mettle in the mid-thirteenth century, Abelard's view became one of those every theologian had to consider and discuss.

Finding thinkers who attack Abelard's view of this matter during the thirteenth century is easy, but finding thinkers who endorse it is much harder, and I have not been able to discover any of whom I am confident before Peter John Olivi. But the view does appear very explicitly in Ockham. Here is one of the first occurrences in Ockham in book 3 of his *Commentary on the Sentences*:

If you were to ask what the goodness or badness of the act adds beyond the substance of the act that is merely by an extrinsic denomination called "good" or "bad", such as an act of the sensitive part or, similarly, an act of the will, I say that it adds nothing that is positive, whether absolute or relative having being in the act through any cause, that is, distinct from the act. Rather, the goodness is only a connotative name or concept, principally signifying the act itself as neutral and connoting an act of will that is perfectly virtuous and the right reason in conformity with which it is elicited.[35]

In his biblical *Question on the Connection of the Virtues*, and in his *Quodlibeta*, Ockham adopts the same strategy. He argues that all exterior acts and many interior acts can be called "good" or "bad" only derivatively, in virtue of their relation to other acts. Because this process cannot go on to infinity, there must be acts that are essentially and intrinsically good or bad. Ockham identifies these with acts of loving or hating God.[36]

If we identify hating God with Abelard's "having contempt for God," and we identify that in turn with refusing to act on what you know to be God's law and identify loving God with willing what God wills, we have here a picture that Abelard and the Stoics could both accept. What is intrinsically good is willing in accord with God or nature. What is intrinsically bad is knowingly refusing to do this.

But although Ockham comes very close to Abelard and the Stoics here, he cannot follow them all the way. He cannot because while both Abelard and the Stoics accept that this world is in itself the best of all possible worlds, Ockham would have it that such a claim makes no sense. The Stoic Zeus and Abelard's God have criteria for the goodness of worlds that do not depend on their choices, but for Ockham God is the intrinsically best thing there could be, doing God's bidding is the best thing one could do, and there are no nonsemantic constraints on what God could bid us do. In his *Sentences Commentary* Ockham even considers whether God could bid us to hate him.[37] Ockham's conclusion is that God could command it but that we could not obey the command.[38] In that bizarre situation there would be no intrinsically good act – and so no good or bad acts at all.

This conclusion, of course, neither Abelard nor the Stoics would embrace; that Ockham reaches it shows that by the early fourteenth century the internalism about immutability and the providentialism that had come together in Abelard and the Stoics had come very far apart. Ockham is not a Stoic. He is, however, heir to one important strand in Stoic ethics, and through him and his followers that strand was kept on the philosophical stage until new editions and new discussions of Stoic views provided a context in which it could again be seen as a Stoic theme.

Notes

1. Verbeke 1983: 53.
2. Ed. Luscombe 1971.
3. Ed. Marenbon and Orlandi in Abelard 2001.
4. Abelard, *Ethica* I (tr. Spade 1995: 12–13).
5. Abelard, *Ethica* I (ed. Luscombe 1971: 6). Cf. Augustine, *De Libero Arbitrio* I.
6. Abelard, *Ethica* I (ed. Luscombe 1971: 10–11).
7. Ibid. (16–17).
8. Ibid. (4, 6).

9. Ibid. (14).
10. Ibid. (22).
11. That said, it must be admitted that, as Blomme (1958: 128–44) and Luscombe (1971: 42–43, n2) have pointed out, Abelard usually speaks of consent when he talks of sin and of intention when he talks of merit. I do not think that this is philosophically significant since he is quite explicit that "When the same thing is done by the same man at different times, his action is said to be now good and now bad on account of the diversity of his intention" (*Ethica* I; ed. Luscombe 1971: 52), which pretty clearly suggests that intentions account for bad actions as well as for good.
12. Abelard, *Ethica* I (tr. Spade 1995: 20).
13. Abelard, *Ethica* I (ed. Luscombe 1971: 54).
14. Ibid.
15. See Donagan 1977: 127.
16. Abelard himself attributes the argument to Plato in the *Timaeus* (28a; see *Timaeus a Calcidio translatus*, ed. Waszink 1962: 20, lines 20–22) in the second *Dialogue*, between the Philosopher and the Christian (tr. Spade 1995: 145).
17. Abelard, *Dialogus* II (tr. Spade 1995: 145; ed. Marenbon and Orlandi 2001: 216–17).
18. Abelard, *Dialogus* II (ed. Marenbon and Orlando 2001: 204).
19. Ibid. (204–6): "Quantum tamen michi nunc occurrit, bonum simpliciter idest bonam rem dici arbitror, que cum alicui usui sit apta, nullius rei commodum uel dignitatem per eam impediri necesse est. E contrario malam rem uocari credo, per quam alterum horum conferri [conferri//impediri] necesse est. Indifferens uero, idest rem que neque bona est neque mala, illam arbitror per cuius existentiam nec ulla bona [ulla bona//illa] deferri [deferri//conferri] neque impediri necesse est, sicut est fortuita motio digiti uel quecunque actiones huiusmodi. Non enim actiones bone uel male nisi secundum intentionis radicem iudicantur, sed omnes ex se indifferentes sunt et, si diligenter inspiciamus, nichil ad meritum conferunt, que nequaquam ex se bone sunt aut male, cum ipse uidelicet tam reprobis quam electis eque conueniant." Square brackets indicate adoption of a variant reading. The translation in the text is mine, although it is based on Spade 1995: 141. I have treated the scope of some modal expressions differently from the way Professor Spade's translation does.
20. Abelard, *Dialectica* IV.1 (ed. de Rijk 1970: 469, l.17–20): "veritas autem veritati non est adversa. Non enim sicut falsum falso vel malum malo contrarium potest reperiri, ita verum vero vel bonum bono potest adversari, sed omnia sibi bona consona sunt et convenientia."
21. Abelard, *Dialogus* II (tr. Spade 1995: 147).
22. See ibid.; Abelard, *Dialogus* II (ed. Marenbon and Orlando 2001: 140–42): "For since nothing happens without a cause, because God arranges all things for the best, what is it that occurs that makes a just person have to grieve or be sad, and insofar as he can to go against God's arrangement for the best, as if he thinks it has to be corrected?" (Cum enim nichil sine causa, Deo cuncta optime disponente, fiat, quid accidit, unde iustum tristari uel dolere

oporteat et sic optime dispositioni Dei, quantum in se est, contrarie, quasi eam censeat corrigendam esse?).

23. See Bobzien 1998: 45–47.

24. Inwood 1995: 95–96.

25. Inwood 1995: 96.

26. Inwood 1995: 62.

27. Abelard, *Ethica* I (tr. Spade 1995: 109).

28. I cannot deny that there *may be* more to Abelardian consent than to Stoic assent, however. To determine whether there is would take us into a detailed discussion of both Abelard's theory of action and that of his main Stoic source, Seneca. I hope to be forgiven for not undertaking either here.

29. Abelard, *Dialogus* II (tr. Spade 1995: 112). The Latin text reads as follows (ed. Marenbon and Orlando 2001: 130–32): "Quedam etenim bona uel mala ex se ipsis proprie et quasi substantialiter dicuntur, utpote uirtutes ipse uel uitia, quedam uero per accidens et per aliud, velut operum nostrorum actiones, cum in se sint indifferentes, ex intentione tamen ex qua procedunt bone dicuntur aut male. Unde et sepe, cum idem a diuersis agitur uel ab eodem in diuersis temporibus, pro diuersitate tamen intentionum idem opus bonum dicitur atque malum. Quae uero substantialiter et ex propria natura bona dicuntur aut mala ita impermixta perenniter manent, ut quod semel bonum est nunquam malum fieri possit uel e conuerso."

30. See Jolivet 1963, but also Jolivet 1980.

31. Abelard, *Dialogus* II (tr. Spade 1995: 105–6).

32. Cf. number 48 in the list of sources compiled in Iwakuma and Ebbesen 1992.

33. Peter Lombard, II *Sententiae*, d. 35, cap. 2 (ed. Grottaferrata 1971–81, vol. 1: 530.13–19): "Quocirca diversitatis hujus verborum occasione, de peccato plurimi diversa senserunt. Alii enim dicunt voluntatem malam tantum esse peccatum, et non actus exteriores; alii, voluntatem et actus; alii neutrum dicentes, omnes actus esse bonos et a Deo et ex Deo auctore esse, malum autem nihil esse, ut ait August. *Super Joan.* (16): Omnia per ipsum facta sunt, et sine ipso factum est nihil, id est, peccatum quod nihil est, et nihil fiunt homines, cum peccant."

34. Ibid., d. 40, cap. un. (ed. Grottaferrata 1971–81, vol. 1: 556.24–557.5): "Post haec de actibus adjiciendum videtur utrum et ipsi ex fine, sicut voluntas, pensari debeant boni vel mali. Licet enim secundum quosdam omnes boni sint, in quantum naturaliter sunt; non tamen absolute dicendi sunt omnes boni, nec omnes remunerabiles, sed quidam simpliciter mali dicuntur, sicut et alii boni. Nam simpliciter ac vere sunt boni illi actus, qui bonam causam et intentionem, id est, qui voluntatem bonam comitantur, et ad bonum finem tendunt; mali vero simpliciter dici debent qui perversam habent causam et intentionem."

35. William of Ockham, III *Sententiae*, d. 11 (*Opera Theologica* 7:388–89); the translation is based on King 1999: 230.

36. For discussion, see King 1999.

37. William of Ockham, IV *Sententiae*, d. 16 (*Opera Theologica* 7:352).

38. William of Ockham, *Quodlibeta Septem* III.14 (*Opera Theologica* 9). For discussion, see McGrade 1999: 279–86.

8

Constancy and Coherence

Jacqueline Lagrée

In the French language, to call someone a Stoic is to recognize the virtue of standing firm in adversity, of enduring misfortune with courage and tenacity, without being driven from the path one has chosen. The characteristic Stoic attitude thus appears to be constancy. The image of the sage as a rock, immovable in a storm, was a standard trope in French moral literature during the seventeenth century. On the mark of the publisher Plantin we read the motto, *labore et constantia* (by labor and constancy). This illustrates the extent to which this virtue seems characteristic of the rebirth of the Stoic movement at the end of the Renaissance. The restoration began with the philological work of the humanists, but it is also tied to a definite political context, marked by the renewed outbreak of religious troubles and civil war.[1] Treatises on the subject of constancy flourished at the end of the sixteenth and beginning of the seventeenth centuries and had impressive publishing histories.[2] But treating constancy as a cardinal virtue was not merely a compromise choice: Charron had preferred prudence, Descartes generosity, Pascal charity.[3] Constancy is the virtue of someone who relies first and foremost on his own strengths and not on God or others. As Lipsius says,[4] a man writes a treatise on constancy primarily for himself and his own benefit, and not because he seeks fame. Moreover, if it is a matter of appealing to philosophy here rather than to its rival, religion, the difference is that religion instills hope and fear in connection with a future end, eternal life, whereas philosophy calms such affections in the present. Lipsius is well aware of the novelty of his approach: "Solatia malis publicis quaesivi, quis ante me?"[5]

Translated by Jack Zupko.

In Greek Stoicism, constancy is paradoxical and even inconceivable unless it is placed in the context of the physical account of the sage's soul, which is hot and dry, having acquired the firmness of the system of kataleptic impressions Zeno compared to a closed fist with its fingers clenched tightly together.[6] Nearly twenty centuries later, Stoic physics had become obsolete, even if traces of it could still be found in alchemy.[7] So it was necessary to ask, What is the proper basis for this firmness of soul, so rare and paradoxical? By examining the philosophical presuppositions of the Neostoic conception of constancy and comparing them with Christian treatises sympathetic to Stoicism,[8] I will consider what specific effects Neostoicism had in the moral sphere, how it was articulated in support of Christianity, and how both Stoicism and Christianity influenced moral philosophy in the age of Louis XIV.

To do this, I rely primarily – after a brief overview of the ancient account – on texts from the close of the sixteenth century: Montaigne's chapter, "De la constance," from the *Essais* I.12 (1580),[9] Justus Lipsius' *De Constantia* (1584), and Guillaume du Vair's *De la constance et de la consolation* (1590). I then situate them in relation to treatises written a little later that were clearly aimed at redressing the balance on behalf of Christianity, namely, those of Joseph Hall, Simon Goulart, and Jean-François Senault, all of whom belong to the period that was "the height of infatuation for the Stoa."[10]

THE ANCIENT SOURCES

Why did the Stoics privilege the virtue of constancy over others they insisted upon just as strongly (and in such a paradoxical fashion as well), such as detachment from material goods or the pretense of absolute knowledge? Why prefer constancy to courage? Because it is an appropriate response in periods of public crisis and private misfortune. Ancient Stoicism teaches constancy for oneself and consolation for others.[11] But in an age where philosophy must adapt to the rule of Christianity, choosing to defend constancy rather than seeking refuge in prayer or in a cry for help shows that a thinker wishes to rely only on himself and not primarily on God or others. This is not how it was in antiquity. The Stoics had a flair for conceptual distinctions and definitions, distinguishing constancy from temperance as well as indifference. Constancy (*constantia* being the Latin translation of *kartēria*) is "knowledge (or a stable disposition of the soul) relative to what one must endure or not [endure], or neither [endure or not endure]."[12] It is a virtue subordinated to courage, which is exhibited in torture, grave illness, and physical suffering.

The passions are in our power, since they depend on belief and therefore assent. To control the passions, it suffices to learn how, by sheer force of exercise and discipline,[13] to detach the impression affecting the soul from its act of assent and thus from the judgment made about the object sensed. If suffering is not something bad but a nonpreferred indifferent, someone who is subject to suffering can learn how to anticipate it and not fear it, to avoid it as much as possible, and, when it is present, to endure it with firmness of character, knowing full well that he is capable of enduring it or at least that it will end either by vanishing on its own or through death.[14] In this sense of firmness, order, endurance, equilibrium, and permanence, constancy is less a particular virtue than something that colors all of the virtues, driving the *hexis* quality of the sage's soul – a firm and stable disposition that results from its agreement with nature, or reason, and from the systematic quality of representations bound together as knowledge. Because the sage soul is wise, strengthened and tempered by fire,[15] it can endure what is disagreeable without dissolution or loss of the self.

Of all the works that inspired Neostoic treatises during the Renaissance, the most significant is clearly Seneca's treatise *De Constantia*, to which one should add his treatise, *De Tranquillitate Animi*. In these works, Seneca provides numerous rules and pieces of practical advice permitting the reader to confront adversity serenely by preparing for reversals of fortune, by anticipating obstacles, and by not becoming attached to goods of fortune, that is, to wealth, honor, and pleasure. Constancy is presented as a manly virtue, belonging to the sage alone as a man equal to the gods, situated above the blows the impious try to rain upon him. It is worth noting that there is a movement here from the field of personal or private relations to that of political action, because the blows that strike the sage without wounding him are no longer illnesses, or sorrow for those who are close to him, as in the *Consolations*, but war, banishment, and the loss of power or political influence. Nevertheless, the sage is not insensible, as the Megarians wanted him to be,[16] but impassible, first because the blows do not reach the inner citadel of his soul, but also because he cannot lose what is constitutive of his identity – knowledge of his own virtue. The sage is thus the only man at peace in the midst of war or public disorder because he has learned to separate his identity from his fortunes and to disassociate himself from what is not properly his. He can therefore reply to the tyrant, "It is not you who defeat me, but your fortune that defeats my fortune."[17] Even so, the goods of fortune are not truly goods because there is no good except honor; they are all, at most, preferred indifferents. They are also unpredictable advantages, destined by their very nature to change whomever they favor frequently and in unforeseeable ways. The sage therefore learns to separate himself from fortune in order to take refuge in his "inner citadel."

To summarize Seneca's main points:

1. Constancy is a virtue proper to the sage alone. To be sure, this is true of every virtue, but it is especially true in this case because constancy is virtue par excellence. It exhibits the specific quality of the wisdom that is the coherent life lived in accordance with nature and reason (*homologoumenōs zēn/convenienter vivere*). In this sense, constancy is identified with wisdom. It testifies to the particular excellence of the sage, to his divine status, beyond the reach of the blows of fortune. This firmness of character is what corresponds externally to the solidity and internal coherence of the representations in his soul.

2. Constancy is the virtue that responds to the onslaughts of fortune. It represents the stability of the sage's soul when faced with the absolute exteriority of fortune, which signifies the changeability of events outside us, their never-ending vacillation from favorable to unfavorable and back again. No compromise is possible between the sage and fortune: *vincit nos fortuna nisi tota vincitur* (fortune vanquishes us unless it is utterly vanquished). To defeat fortune is to demystify it: to show that it is only a mistaken personification of temporal change, which has the least reality. The door to the sage's home is wide open, but fortune cannot enter there because it can only take up residence where something is attributed to it,[18] and fortune is nothing. On the other hand, as soon as we confuse what is disagreeable with what is evil (*incommodum* with *malum*),[19] that is, as soon as we attribute any reality to this phantom, it besieges our soul and fills it with troubles – joy and sorrow, desire and fear – all of which stem from our inability to live truly in the present.

3. The true name of fortune in the Stoic system is destiny. But although Seneca thoroughly examines providence and destiny in *De Providentia*, *Naturales Quaestiones*, and *De Beneficiis*, he utters not a word about them in *De Constantia*. That is because constancy is not considered there in relation to freedom but in the context of

negative interpersonal relations (injury and offense), especially in the struggle for political power.[20] This emerges in the powerful bond between constancy, providence, and destiny in Neostoicism.

NEOSTOIC CONSTANCY

The flowering of treatises on constancy at the end of the Renaissance can be attributed to a frightening political landscape of religious war, pestilence, and famine. Here one needs not only personal consolation – as when one is bereaved, in exile, or faced with impending death[21] – but well-being [*salut*] in both the political and philosophical senses of the term.[22] How does one keep one's peace of mind when one's only salvation appears to be a flight that is for all intents and purposes impossible?

For so many years now we have been tossed about by the tempest of civil war; we are buffeted by winds of trouble and sedition from every direction, as on a stormy sea. If I seek quietude and peace of mind, I am deafened by the sound of trumpets and armed conflict. If I take refuge in the gardens and countryside, soldiers and assassins drive me back into the town. It is for this reason that I have decided to flee.[23]

But where to go? What part of Europe is peaceful today?[24] And how does one flee passions of the soul? Can one flee from oneself?[25] "Strengthen your spirit and fortify it," replies Langius, "that is the true way of finding inner calm in the midst of troubles, peace in the midst of armed conflict."[26]

To better understand the force and originality of Lipsius' treatment of constancy, we should compare it with that of Montaigne, who a number of years before (1573–75) had written a short lecture on constancy in the context of his reflections on military life.[27] The appeal to Stoicism is here a matter of circumstance. What does Montaigne say? "The game of constancy is played principally to tolerate inconveniences patiently when they have no remedy."[28] Constancy is the virtue of a soldier faced with the enemy, not at all characteristic of everyday life.[29] Alluding to the impassibility attributed to the Stoic sage, Montaigne remarks that his feeling fear and suffering is not out of the question, "provided that his judgment remains safe and intact, and that the foundation of his discourse does not suffer injury or any alteration, and that he gives no consent to his terror and suffering."[30] In short, constancy is a virtue of brave and military men, not of private individuals. But the situation becomes quite different after the publication of Lipsius' treatise and its revival by Guillaume du Vair.

Lipsius' Discovery

I do not dwell on Lipsius' philological writings, which are vast and well known.[31] Lipsius not only gave to his contemporaries scholarly editions of Seneca, which were made more authoritative through references, in their notes, to his two treatises on Stoic doxography, the *Guide to Stoic Philosophy* (*Manuductio ad Stoicam Philosophiam*) and the *Natural Philosophy of the Stoics* (*Physiologia Stoicorum*) (Anvers 1604); he also provided them with a newer and more modern version of the Stoic system. In these two works, which are filled with long quotations, Lipsius tries to explain the Stoic system thoroughly and show that for the most part, it is not incompatible with Christianity while also offering a sure path to wisdom. To be sure, it should be said that this is possible only by a certain amount of borrowing from Neoplatonism, but it should also be recognized that the ancient Stoic school was always borrowing ideas that originated in other schools, and that this practice – quite normal in the life of a philosophical school – did not necessarily water down its teachings. In the *Manuductio* and *Physiologia*, Lipsius proposes a Stoicism close to that of the church fathers,[32] that is, as acceptable with some reservations,[33] whereas in the treatise *De Constantia* he advocates a Stoicized Christianity. Because I wish to analyze the points of convergence and divergence between Stoicism and Christianity at the end of the Renaissance, it is certainly a good idea to focus on the latter work and its impact.

Lipsius' *De Constantia*

In point of fact, Lipsius' properly philosophical output comes down to the treatise *De Constantia*, since the *Politics*, despite its historical importance, is only a well-organized cento of quotations. *De Constantia* contains only a few quotations and a structured discussion linked by a central theme. Above all, it is a work written for himself – for a man who has suffered loss in the midst of public calamity[34] – and a work to which anyone should be able to return for encouragement. Still, why look to the Stoics for a lesson in virtue rather than the Bible? Lipsius gives a number of different reasons: (1) in *De Constantia*, he rejects the help of religion in a century rife with controversy and quarrels but lacking in true piety;[35] (2) he offers three arguments in the *Manuductio*:[36] (a) philosophy in the service of theology prepares the way for Christianity; (b) the ancient philosophers (*prisci philosophi*) are capable of transmitting to us something of the wisdom of antiquity (*prisca theologia*), since they were closer in their origins to God; (c) at night and when the sun is no longer shining, we

must navigate by the stars – it being conceded that the night of faith is the result of these controversies.[37]

Let us now turn to the nature of constancy: what it is distinct from, as well as what it presupposes, what it requires, and what it produces.

DEFINITION AND PRESUPPOSITIONS

Lipsius' definition of constancy – the "rectitude and unchanging resistance of the soul, which is neither lifted up nor beaten down by external or fortuitous things"[38] – insists on the vocabulary of firmness and rectitude of judgment founded on right reason and not on mere opinion; it clearly distinguishes constancy from obstinacy (*pervicacia*) and stubbornness (*pertinacia*).[39] This power is rooted in patience or "voluntary and uncomplaining submission to all external circumstances and events that unexpectedly befall a man."[40] Founded on reason, the portion of the divine spirit that dwells within us, constancy is directly associated with the grasp of truth and is opposed to opinion,[41] which is always unstable and inevitably causes regret and feelings of repentance. Truth, on the other hand, is always stable, and leads to balance, constancy, and *ataraxia*.[42]

Constancy cannot be acquired without spiritual and intellectual exercises aimed at sweeping away false virtues and acquiring a clear understanding of what is influencing us from the outside. But first it must be understood that what we mistakenly take to be evil arrives at our doorstep not by chance or misfortune but through a God who is all-powerful, wise, and good. God and Reason coincide. Divine providence is identified with the supreme law of the universe.[43] In this law our individual destiny unfolds via eternal decrees connecting the sequence of events and the different moments in a man's life in a causal series all the way back to God, the first cause. Our destiny is absolutely certain, though unknowable in detail. But even though we cannot know the destiny of any particular person, we can know a priori that he has a destiny and that it comes from a source that is unique, wise, and good. Providence is one and absolutely simple. Destiny, which concerns to the details, should be seen as "the manifestation and expression of this general providence acting in a determinate and particular fashion."[44]

A SPIRITUAL AND INTELLECTUAL EXERCISE

To acquire constancy, a thoroughgoing discipline of judgment is needed as well as a capacity for discernment concerned in particular with a person's emotions, which lie hidden under the appearance of virtue.

The first exercise of clear thinking in relation to oneself is to take off one's mask and reject the pretense (*simulatio*) involved in the claim that one is affected by public disasters only when one weeps, like the comedian Polus,[45] at private misfortune.[46] The second consists in distinguishing one's sense of duty (*pietas*) from patriotism; the latter confuses the place of the soul with that of the body and mistakes cultural ties established and upheld by custom with the natural affection one feels for one's country.[47] Without being abstract,[48] this cosmopolitanism involves distancing oneself from both one's country and one's everyday affairs. From this perspective, the difference in the way patriotism is regarded – devalued in Lipsius but partially rehabilitated in du Vair[49] – in the first instance expresses the difference in status between the intellectual, Professor Lipsius, whose country is wherever his library is located, and the public man, the Minister of Justice du Vair, who is concerned with the welfare of his country and his fellow citizens, and who reacts to public disasters as a public man. The third exercise involves eliminating pity (*miseratio*) – a passive, narcissistic, exhibitionist affection[50] – in order to make room for mercy (*misericordia*), "an inclination of the soul to answer a call of distress or to see to the comfort of others,"[51] which is an active, impassible, silent, and efficacious virtue that brings with it reserve, restraint, and the refusal to submit to emotional contagion.

CULTIVATION OF JUDGMENT

If everything begins with judgment, then emotion is merely weak opinion, as Cicero says.[52] To guide his young friend and restore the equilibrium of his soul, Languis proposes a fourfold remedy:[53] public evils are (a) sent by God; (b) necessary, because they have been fated to happen; (c) useful; and (d) less serious than one might at first imagine.[54] Corresponding to these are four requirements: knowledge, discernment, perspective, and comparison.

Knowledge

To the age-old question, "Whence evil?" (*unde malum?*), Lipsius gives the traditional answer: "From God" (*a deo*). How? Necessarily. "On the ocean of life, the man who refuses to sail with the winds of the universe refuses in vain because he must either do so or be dragged along."[55] When a man knows that the ultimate source of what he sees as evil is both good and rational, he can admit that "freedom is obedience to God," the formula of Seneca that emerges as a leitmotif in Lipsius' writings.[56] But to attain true *ataraxia*, he must also begin to practice this discipline of assent, to use the felicitous expression of Hadot.[57]

Discernment

The first false opinion to be uprooted is the confusion between goods and preferred indifferents, or again, between evils and dispreferred indifferents. False goods and false evils (*falsa bona et falsa mala*) are external, fortuitous things affecting our well-being that do not properly concern our soul and its good, that is, virtue or honor.[58] Among these, public evils (war, pestilence, famine, tyranny, etc.) are without a doubt more serious than private evils (suffering, poverty, infamy, death, etc.) because they have grievous effects on a greater number of people and cause greater turmoil, but especially because they elicit passionate, virulent, and pernicious responses that masquerade as virtue.

Perspective

The third discipline of judgment involves putting what happens to us into perspective and ascribing particular misfortunes to global political upheaval, a vision of history that insists upon the rise and fall of empires and, at a higher level, that involves a cosmological vision revealing a world that totters everywhere. In nature, as in history, everything eventually wears out. Everything changes, even what is thought to be unchangeable, such as in the celestial order, because new stars and new lands have been observed.[59] All the elements are invoked, one after another: the transformation of stars (fire), atmospheric changes (air), the movement of the ocean and the flooding of rivers (water), earthquakes and the swallowing up of islands (earth). War between men is written into the immense cosmic framework of war between elements. So, too, it goes with the rise and fall of empires: "Nations, like men, have their youth, their maturity, and their old age."[60] To judge correctly, you must vary your point of view and change your perspective. Lipsius revives Machiavelli's distinction between top-down and bottom-up perspectives:[61] viewed from the bottom, there is much in the vanity of human affairs to make one weep; viewed from the top, that is, from the perspective of God and Providence, one will recognize "that everything is governed in a planned and unchangeable order."[62] Guillaume du Vair uses another image, that of the Great Pyramid of Egypt, which travelers approach from different directions.[63]

Each one sees only the side facing him and, without walking around it and thereby realizing that its three faces form one body, resumes his journey convinced that he alone has seen it as it really is.

When these people came to reflect on this sovereign power directing and governing the universe, which they had hitherto considered in its effects, each was content to view it from afar and conceive of it in whatever way it first appeared to him. The one who perceived order and a regulated sequence of causes pushing themselves into existence one after another called it *Nature* and believed that it is responsible for everything that happens. The one who saw a number of things happen that were foreseen and predicted that they could in no way be avoided called the power that produced them *Destiny* and "fatal necessity" and judged everything to be subordinate to it. Another still, who saw infinitely many events that he could not make sense of and that seemed to happen without cause called the power from which they originated *Fortune* and reckoned that all things are governed in this way.[64]

Nature, destiny, and fortune are only imperfect names, representing one-sided views of a unique divine Providence that is, as it were, the geometric projection of these perspectives. In the final analysis, fortune and necessity are no more than two faces of an omnipotent deity, the one inscrutable, the other capable of being foreseen by men.[65]

Comparison

We can see a thing without its disguises by putting it into its proper perspective. Once we have learned not to see our misfortunes as evils, their proper perspective will show that they are less serious than we first imagined and that they have beneficial effects not apparent at first glance. Change is the law of the universe;[66] discord is necessary for harmony;[67] what frightens us, like the masks that terrify children, is the false image of things we make for ourselves.[68] When we compare actual evils to ancient calamities, we find that they are neither so great nor so serious.[69] Consequently, we will be able to move on to the other, more positive, aspect of this recovery of the self, that is, to the cultivation of the will.

CULTIVATION OF WILL

The will belongs to us. As an expression of our freedom, it participates in secondary causes inscribed in the providential system of cosmic order: "God carries along all that is human by the force of destiny, without taking anything away from its particular power or movement."[70] True freedom lies not in pointless rebellion against God – which nevertheless remains possible for us[71] – but in obedience to God, like the man who ties his boat to a rock and uses the rope to pull himself to shore rather than to bring the rock to himself.[72]

In the end, one must concede that the finality of evil has a certain purposefulness for man and the world at the same time.[73] For man, this utility is captured in three words: practice, correction, and punishment.[74] Calamities serve to restrict our access to the goods we seek: they lash, restrain, and strengthen the weak, as well as punishing the wicked directly or through their acquaintances and descendants.[75] For the world, they keep the population under control.[76] However, these bitter remedies are less effective than the shock treatment one feels once one becomes aware of their necessity. It is no use to protest, since one cannot rebel but only consent to an outcome that is inescapable.[77] Faced with the search for the ultimate cause of the evils that afflict us, Lipsius reaches for the remedy of learned ignorance: "[W]here divine and transcendent things are concerned there is only one kind of knowledge – that of knowing nothing" (*in divinis superisque, una scientia, nihil scire*).[78]

THE FRUITS OF CONSTANCY

Once this twofold discipline of judgment and will is put into practice, one can enjoy the fruits of constancy, which reveal themselves in an understanding of how all things are connected, as well as in *ataraxia* and contentment. There is, in effect, a link between constancy and *ataraxia* on the one hand, and security, tranquillity, and faith in God on the other.[79] Constancy is a virtue that reflects a threefold sequence, order, or *akolouthia*. The first step is destiny, symbolized by the Homeric golden chain, which joins the heavens to the earth and symbolizes the sequence of causes and reasons that anchor events in divine providence and the universal law.[80] The second is the coherence of representations and the logical consequence (*sequela*) that holds between principles and precepts.[81] The third is the connection of the virtues, founded on the unity of judgment.[82] The courage that accompanies constancy does not lack prudence, that is, discernment. This is what scandalized Guez de Balzac: "It is impossible to have one virtue without having all the others, to be just without being courageous, to be generous without being chaste. They mix what must be kept distinct. They forcibly connect qualities that do not belong together. This erases the boundaries reason has placed there to indicate the uniqueness of each thing."[83]

The fruits of constancy are likewise threefold. First of all, there is *ataraxia*, which must not be confused with apathy. The *Manuductio* follows

Diogenes Laertius in distinguishing between two kinds of apathy: that of the sage and that of the fool. The latter is pure insensitivity;[84] the former is the stability of the soul founded on immutable reason. The tranquil soul is like a walled garden, protected from the noise of the city.[85] Next, there is courage, steadfast and upright, "always equal to whatever fortune may bring."[86] Courage gives effective force to one's struggles against public misfortune, causing the movement from pity (*miseratio*) to compassion (*misericordia*). Finally, there is – if not contentment in the sense that term came to have in Descartes – at least one's acceptance of the situation, with a focus on the present and recognition of what is hidden and underappreciated in human history.[87] No longer susceptible to regret, the sage experiences neither hope nor fear.

To sum up: Lipsius's account of constancy is absolutely faithful to Stoic principles. Steadfast conduct bespeaks order to the outside world, of the immutability of the system of truths that is the sage soul, guided by right reason and leaving no place for opinion. Its benefit is that it forces one to look at things in a deeper and more reflective way than the ordinary person, namely, by bringing historical and political change and the rise and fall of empires together in the ebb and flow of a universe ruled by immutable and necessary law. This law is the act of thinking about God most high, who is "fixed, determined, immutable, always one and identical to himself."[88] From this height, this firmness will be based on recognizing the necessity that is itself based on the rational idea of universal providence or the intelligent governance of the world by God. Constancy is an unbroken link to a continuous present, ignoring the fleeting, affective relationships that constitute regret, fear, and hope. Its primary characteristics fit perfectly Leibniz's description of Stoic morality as "patience without hope":

One has only to glance at the admirable manual of Epictetus and the Epicureanism in Diogenes Laertius [i.e., in his "Life of Epicurus"] to see that Descartes has not advanced the practical side of morality. But it seems that the art of patience in which the art of living must consist is not the whole story. Patience without hope does not last and offers hardly any consolation. It is in this regard that Plato, in my view, surpasses the other philosophers because he gives us good reason to hope for a better life, and because he comes closest to Christianity.[89]

AN AMBIVALENT VIEW OF STOICISM

Following Tertullian's *Seneca saepe noster,* there was a tendency at the end of the Renaissance to read Seneca in an ambivalent fashion. Take, for example, Simon Goulart, an eminent pastor from Geneva, who was sympathetic enough to Stoicism to translate Lipsius and write his *Ample discours sur la morale des stoïques,* but with the warning, "If you read Seneca as a pagan, he seems to have written as a Christian, but if you read him as a Christian, you feel that it is really a pagan who is speaking."[90]

Especially important here were the reformers,[91] who seized upon Stoicism to give their moral system a reference point in antiquity, because they were interested in an austere morality in keeping with their desire to reform human life. In addition, because it was founded on a conception of universal reason (the Logos, the Universal Law identified with Zeus), Stoic morality fit their rigorous and rational conception of religion. Some examples taken from England, Switzerland, and France will help us construct a typology of the various links that were forged between Stoicism and Christianity at the dawn of the modern era, so that we may better distinguish the Christian discourse – which, instead of citing Aristotle, makes reference to the Stoics, especially Seneca – from the Neostoic discourse that strictly upheld Stoic doctrine, striving only to make it compatible with Christianity.[92] This work is all the more necessary seeing that these authors all borrow from each other freely.[93] Thus, du Vair reprises the structure and topics of Lipsius; Urbain Chevreau plagiarizes Joseph Hall in the first book of *L'escole du sage.*

The Subtle Shift to Christianity: Guillaume du Vair (1556–1621)

Of all the imitators of Lipsius, Guillaume du Vair was surely the greatest. He follows *De Constantia* very closely in its structure, topics, and particular examples. But there are subtle shifts from constancy to consolation and from patience to hope, which are interesting because they reveal his aim of reinterpreting Stoicism in a more religious fashion. Book I of the *Traité de la constance et de la consolation* follows this pattern very closely: the description of public calamities; the concern to limit suffering to its proper place rather than permitting it to invade and destroy our souls; the criticism of beliefs that augment imaginary evils and fears; the praise of the faculty of judgment that cuts them down to size; the criticism of mindless patriotism in order to focus attention on our true homeland (which for du Vair is heaven and no longer the world);[94] the qualification and attenuation of our needs down to those that are truly necessary; the moral character that is able to endure suffering:[95] "[N]o evil is so great that reason and philosophical conversation cannot overcome it."[96] Here, constancy refers to the firmness of spirit that enables us to deal with suffering; it is patience or endurance.[97]

In book II, du Vair connects this virtue to the account of providence:

> The greatest truth and most certain *consolation* that men can grasp onto and take in during public or private disasters is to *persuade* themselves that whatever happens to them has been preordained by this eternal power and distributed by this infinite wisdom, which governs the world with the same goodness and justice that went into creating it.[98]

Here we notice immediately that *consolation* has been substituted for *constancy*, and that men *persuade* themselves of something instead of actually *knowing* it. Nature, Destiny, and Fortune are but three faces covering the summit of the pyramid named Providence.[99] Finally, a more moral vision replaces the cosmic vision of the fall of empires:

> Consider, if you will, the fall of any empire and of all the great cities; compare its rise to its fall; you will see that its worthy ascendance was helped along by its virtue and that it was also assisted in its endeavors by this holy Providence; on the other hand, you will concede that its fall was just and that its vices made its ruin by divine justice virtually inevitable.[100]

God made man an active participant in creation when he inserted human free will into the order of causes that constitute his destiny.[101] Human failings, then, explain public calamity. From this vantage point, the traditional arguments of Stoic and Christian theodicy can be linked: evils have a point of origin (God) and a good end (the testing of good people and the punishment of the wicked); there are very useful remedies, like theriac, containing dangerous poisons.[102] These rational considerations are exhortations to patience and noble action. Already by the end of book II, however, constancy, a virtue of the present, can blossom into contentment only by means of *an opening into the future*, which causes "the hidden feeling of the true place of the soul": "up there, in the heavens, in an unchanging city that is the true and natural domicile of the soul – the gate through which it must rise to rest eternally after the flux and the torment of its earthly existence, filled with the kind of joy and contentment that can only be supplied to it by the object of its happiness, the sacred consummation of every kind of beauty and goodness in the world drawn from its pure and original source."[103]

In book III, constancy is finally transformed from a pagan to a Christian virtue when it is tied to the three theological virtues of faith, hope, and charity. But if the only justification for constancy is our acknowledgment of destiny and necessity, there is the twofold problem of the lazy argument and the temptation to despair. However, the refutation of the lazy argument through the analysis of action allows us to steer clear of

despair and hope alike:[104] "So then, since we are so doubtful about things
in the future and misled by our hopes and fears, what steps can we take
to resolve our fear of the future that will cause us to abandon our present
duty?"[105] True constancy is nourished by the three theological virtues of
faith in a good and provident God and belief in the immortality of the
soul[106] – a common notion,[107] central to philosophy,[108] which is specified
and reinforced by religion; *hope*, indeed, "assurance" in eternal life after
death;[109] and finally, *charity*, because beyond compassion, there is a duty
to relieve the suffering of those who are close to us.[110] Constancy is a moral
position taken by and for oneself; consolation is concerned with others.

Finally, the exhortation to virtue in du Vair opens into eschatological
time because future history will inevitably know the same vicissitudes of
fortune and the return of the same public disasters. The examination of
all the perfections a man seeks – goodness, wisdom, power and authority,
truth, eternal being, creative power (children, works, discoveries), justice,
perseverence in achieving one's goals, affluence in life, contemplation,
joy in oneself[111] – shows that they are but human reflections of the divine
perfections.

The Christian reading of Stoicism expressed in du Vair can be sum-
marized as follows: the sage and God are no longer identical, but
analogous;[112] constancy is determined not only by the recognition of
order in the world but by the hope of eternal life; and, therefore, constancy becomes a virtue with regard to weak theoretical determinations.
In fact, in the final analysis, the ultimate basis of du Vair's exhortation to
patience is no longer philosophical but theological, and the treatise concludes with pages invoking the incarnation, resurrection, redemption,
and eternal life.

AN EFFECTIVE BUT DANGEROUS THERAPY

Du Vair used the metaphor of theriac in the context of public evils. Among
the moralist reformers who were readers of Seneca, however, the "school
of nature" that is Stoicism represented a risky self-medication that needs
to be used with caution.

Against Religious Inconstancy: Joseph Hall (1574–1656)

Joseph Hall, a disciple of Lipsius and bishop of Exeter, was described
as the "English Seneca." He published various works inspired by the
Stoics.[113] Looking at these a little more closely, however, we see that his

Christian Seneca does not include any reference to Seneca and seems a rather traditional, pious discussion.[114] Hall simply praises the pagans for having done a better job of repudiating Fortune than Christians who were "so illuminated by the light of the Gospel that a casual observer would be unable to tell what is pagan in our practice."[115] He uses Stoic exhortations to constancy as a means of combating religious inconstancy caused by the desire for novelty,[116] which leads the superstitious person from Rome to Münster, before finally turning Anabaptist.[117] But even if the Stoics really knew how to combat the fear of death or misfortune, they were like "greyhounds, quick but lacking a good nose."[118] That is because they did not know the true source of peace: Jesus Christ, the mediator between God and man. They found tranquillity in themselves but not in "the sweet and pleasurable enjoyment of their God." Thus, their constancy borders on obstinacy and pride, and among "those great examples of contentment outside the church,"[119] Zeno and Cleanthes are but two examples among others (e.g., Diogenes, Socrates, the gymnosophists) of what philosophical medicine can do.

The Danger of Passive Indifference: Yves of Paris (1590–1678)

Stoic constancy, praised as a power of the soul, is also dangerous in that it can tempt one to passive indifference. This is how Father Yves of Paris describes it in his treatise, *De l'indifférence*,[120] presenting a hierarchy of three forms of indifference: the sacriligious indifference of the free thinkers who, "being slaves to fortune, try to make themselves free from anything pertaining to religion and unleash themselves from its yoke in order to be exempted more generally from any duty it imposes on them";[121] then, the indifference of the philosophers – of the Stoic philosophers, in fact[122] – who certainly knew how to control their judgments and passions in order to reach the port of wisdom, but fell short of the perfection of indifference that is Christian indifference. This third, perfect, indifference is not a matter of being resigned to one's fate or simply being aware of the relativity and inconsistency of the goods of fortune. It is a loving acquiesence in the divine will, which desires only what is good for us. It blossoms into charity and inner peace.[123]

Christian indifference perfects the happiness reason begins to acquire and grants us a perfect peace because as soon as we abandon ourselves to divine providence and no longer desire to will other than what it wills, our successes and desires entirely match: when we want everything that happens, nothing that happens fails to satisfy us. This is an ability that disarms fortune, an antidote that neutralizes all poisons, a catalyst that turns all metals into gold,[124] a wisdom that expresses the hidden aspects of self-love, a general maxim that is applicable to everything that happens.[125]

Suffering, Constancy, and Self-Knowledge:
Urbain Chevreau (1613–1701)

With Urbain Chevreau, as with his master Joseph Hall, the problem of constancy – though it is always understood in the context of universal misfortune[126] – gets reinstated through the traditional philosophical demand for self-knowledge. The man who lacks constancy is "a stranger in his own house and a fool everywhere else, and would rather be anything other than himself."[127] Shifting fortunes are what really make this loss of self stand out in someone who lacks wisdom.[128] By contrast, the sage is no more blinded by good fortune than terrified by bad.[129] Indifferent to goods sought by the ordinary run of humanity[130] – for example, to riches, honors, pleasures: these "golden chains" – he is more indifferent in the conduct of his life than any sage ever was in his conviction.[131] Book III of *L'escole du sage* follows rather closely the pattern of book III of the *Manuductio* of Lipsius, though with two significant changes: Chevreau does not seek to justify all the paradoxes of the sage[132] but focuses in particular on indifference, strength, constancy, prudence, and spiritual tranquillity;[133] and he adds to these considerations such as fear of God, study, charity, and conversation, which appear to have nothing to do with the Stoic ideal.[134] More than the mastery of events, what characterizes his wisdom is his own coherence or self-identification: "It is the sage alone who stands firm above the rest and who can preserve his self in the universal confusion. He is not surprised either by the chaos of nature or the whims of fortune. He is always equal to the challenge, always in the same frame of mind, and always the same in the different circumstances he faces."[135] Only someone who has suffered and been able to stand firm and maintain his composure in the storm can be said to be truly happy. And, paradoxically, it is Job who wins out over Solomon, who was "perhaps unhappy never to have suffered."[136]

An Excess of Pride: Simon Goulart (1543–1628)

Simon Goulart, who was born in Senlis and became a reformed minister in Geneva,[137] was a humanist and popularizer who translated Seneca and Lipsius into French.[138] He defends himself in a letter of dedication, expressing his "desire to make known . . . [Seneca's] terse but edifying teachings, which, given the level to which conditions in the world have sunk, can offer much help to less confident souls."[139] But at the same time as he praises Seneca for providing remedies for the causes of bad living,[140] Goulart reproaches the Stoics for being unaware of grace and sin and for raising their wise man above even the gods.[141] In short, the Stoics sin through pride. "As long as man glorifies himself and is unaware of the infinite extent of his own misery and the benefit of his Savior, everything he says about God, providence, justice, kindness, and the good life will be but empty and vain prattle."[142] Goulart returns in various contexts to this excessive praise of the sage,[143] the error of seeking contentment in oneself rather than God,[144] and the question of suicide. In addition, one can know merely by reflecting on the contents of the Epistles of Paul and the letters of Seneca, without having to turn to philological and stylistic considerations, that any supposed correspondence between them is a forgery.[145]

Speaking about his perfect sage, Seneca presents us with a man who, left to his own devices, is ignorant of God, possessed of an understanding shrouded in a terrifying darkness that places him in the grip of idolatry, superstition, and strange beliefs; his will fixed on human glory, he is defiant in his virtue and looks for all his sources of happiness within himself; in other words, he paints castles in the air and looks for life in death.[146]

Actually, Goulart remains faithful to the scholastic model, which sees philosophy as the maidservant of theology. Thus, when philosophical reason claims to liberate itself from theological and ecclesiastical authority, it is like a "roughly educated maidservant who speaks more aristocratically than the wise mistress of the house,"[147] a situation that "would not be tolerated in any well-ordered family." It is because everything is going badly and because men lack fear that they must read Seneca, in order to subject themselves to reason – although this must still be ordered to divine wisdom. For otherwise, "it is no longer reason but a wild animal unceasingly and senselessly fighting against its mistress, wanting to deprive her of her authority."[148]

A Philosophy of Hyperbole: Jean-François Senault (1599–1672)

The orator Jean François Senault, who wrote somewhat later, seems to me typical of the shift that occurred in the middle of the seventeenth century from the acceptance of Stoicism (perhaps with some Christian

modifications) as a philosophy of moral fortitude, a valuable resource for
dangerous and troubled times, to its criticism as a philosophy of pride – a
pride that can reach the point of extravagance. The latter point is much
discussed in Pascal, Francis of Sales, and Malebranche.[149] For Senault,
Seneca is the "worldly philosopher" par excellence.[150] He criticizes the
Stoics first for their ignorance of how useful the passions can be for man's
affective and moral life and, subsequently, for their dangerous wish to
eradicate them.[151] Properly directed passions are the seeds of virtue:[152]
fear is the natural source of prudence, anger is the shadow of justice,
desire the image of charity, hatred sets the stage for righteous indigna-
tion, and flight is useful to preserve chastity.[153] Constancy, as the Stoics
describe it, is illusory and idolatrous because wanting men to lose their
sensitivity is like wanting them to be either angels or beasts.[154] But Stoic
constancy is also useless because patience of this sort necessarily lacks real
disciples, unlike patience with hope, which is the mark of Christianity. It
has produced many martyrs:

> Vanity is not strong enough to inspire us to be contemptuous of suffering, and
> the Stoic sect, proud that it is, could make only a small number of philosophers
> able to suffer easily the violence of torture and the cruelty of torturers. But the
> Christian religion produced swarms of martyrs who withstood flames, overcame
> wild beasts, and defeated infidel emperors.[155]

The impassive sage, relying only on himself and not on God, has made
himself a prisoner in his own inner fortress. In the final analysis, Stoicism
looks to be a philosophy of hyperbole that can have admirers but no
disciples. "Furthermore, when these philosophers utter these lofty words,
they are in my opinion imitating orators who, using hyperbole, lead us to
the truth by lying to us and persuade us to do what is difficult by making us
think we can do the impossible."[156] Must this kind of Stoicism be entirely
condemned? Certainly not more than tropes of orators. It is valuable to
the extent that it persuades us to do what is difficult:

> All their pompous speeches managed only to prop up the spirit in its domain, lest
> it succumb to bodily weakness; they authorized its power in words more eloquent
> than true, thinking that in order to bring us to the rational point of view, they
> had to lift us higher, and that, in order not to assign any superfluous function to
> our senses, they had to deny them what they needed.[157]

So Senault makes good use of Stoicism and in particular of the constancy
of the sage. This constancy is good so long as it is taken as an ideal showing
what we must aim for; but if we rely solely on our own powers to reach
it and are contemptuous of divine assistance, if we put the sage above

Jupiter, then everything is turned on its head.[158] The angels become beasts, our power becomes the insensibility of a brute animal, the sage's maxims cause us despair instead of instructing us, "and these haughty waves, after having made so much noise, dissolve into foam."[159] Lipsius did not defend suicide or the paradox of the equality of needs but he did explain them. As Guez de Balzac remarked: "Since the deaths of Justus Lipsius and Mr. Minister of Justice du Vair, we can speak freely of Zeno and Chrysippus and say that the opinions of these enemies of common sense were sometimes more bizarre than the strangest tales of the poets."[160]

THE STOIC LEGACY

As it happened, although after 1621 (the date of Guillaume du Vair's death) Christianity could sometimes be expressed in Stoic fashion, Stoicism did not become a philosophy to take the place of Aristotelianism, as Lipius had hoped. It was possible to find some virtue in it and not find fault with it – and even make use of it for encouragement – but without actually subscribing to it.[161]

For all that, the moral and religious legacy of Stoicism is hardly meager. We could list treatises on self-knowledge and on the tranquillity of the soul inspired by the Stoics,[162] Stoic discourses,[163] the theater of Corneille, and, with some reservations, Cartesian moral philosophy.[164] But rather than presenting a tedious catalog of works in morality and religion claiming Stoic influence,[165] I would like to close with a comment on Descartes.

We often emphasize the Cartesian tone of the provisional rules of morality in the *Discourse on Method*. In a stimulating article, Vincent Carraud showed that these rules also owe much to the work of moral philosophers of the second scholasticism on the relation between speculative probability and practical or moral certainty, which obviously moves us some distance from the metaphysical certainty asserted by Stoic moral philosophy.[166] On the other hand, one cannot avoid being struck, both in the rules of the *Discourse* and in his reformulation of this moral philosophy for Princess Elisabeth,[167] by the way the vocabulary of constancy is repeated in adverbial form: "The first 'maxim' was to obey the laws and customs of my country, adhering to religion without fail [*constamment*]";[168] "My second maxim was to be as firm and resolute in my actions as I could, and not follow less often [*moins constamment*] the most doubtful opinions . . .";[169] and to Elisabeth, "the second [rule] is to have a firm and constant [*ferme et constante*] resolution to do whatever that reason advises one to do . . . and it is the firmness of this resolution that I believe must be understood to be virtuous";[170] "It is not necessary merely that our reason be free from error; it is sufficient if our conscience tells us that we never lacked the resolve and virtue [*manqué de résolution et de vertu*] to do what we have judged to be the best."[171] "Without fail" *constamment* or "constant" (*constant*) does not mean "always" (*toujours*) but rather "continuously" (*continûment*) and "with constancy" (*avec constance*). The proper use of reason and constancy of resolution are sufficient to reach the natural happiness taught by Seneca, which, although not supreme and perfect, never fails to be pleasant and agreeable. Beginning with Descartes, "the secret of those philosophers who once were able to escape from fortune's bonds and, despite their poverty and suffering, dispute with their gods about the nature of happiness"[172] – one can see that he is talking about the Stoics here – is no longer in their physics or even in the rules of their moral philosophy, but in this spiritual attitude, this coherence of resolution that offsets the external uncertainty of moral choice. After the death of Lipsius and especially with the advent of the new and influential philosophical system of Descartes, modern stoicism ceases to be a true philosophy and becomes instead an ethical and then legal *attitude*.

Notes

1. This is what Spanneut suggests (1973: 387): "Stoicism – a philosophy for times of misfortune? Certainly."
2. The *De Constantia* of Lipsius appeared in some eighty editions and translations.
3. See Charron, *De la sagesse* II, ch. 3; Descartes, *Traité des passions de l'âme* (1649), art. 153.
4. "I have written many other works for other people; this book I have written primarily for myself. The former were for my reputation, the latter for my own well-being" (*De Constantia*, preface to the first edition, tr. Du Bois, 1873: 117).
5. "I have sought consolation for public evils; who has done so before me?" (*De Constantia*, preface to the first edition, p. 116).
6. Cicero, *Academica* 2.47.145.
7. Cf. Bernard Joly, *Rationalité de l'alchemie au XVIIè siècle*, Collection Mathesis (Paris: Vrin, 1992).
8. In contrast to the conception of a Pascal or Malebranche, for example.
9. This very brief treatise was written between 1572 and 1578.
10. Eymard d'Angers 1964.
11. Notice in Seneca the difference in tone between the *Ad Marciam de Consolatione* or *Ad Helviam* and the *De Constantia Sapientis*.
12. Andronicus, *Peri pathōn*, *SVF* 3:270. See also Diogenes Laertius, *Lives of Eminent Philosophers* 7.93, in *SVF* 3:265. Goulet translates this as "endurance."

13. Pierre Hadot translates the Latin *dogma* as "discipline," a term designating a principle based on a rule of life. See his analysis of the three disciplines of assent, desire, and impulse in Hadot 1992: esp. 59–62.

14. Seneca thoroughly explores this Epicurean theme with specific examples in *De Tranquillitate Animi.*

15. Diogenes Laertius, *Lives of Eminent Philosophers* 7.157; Plutarch, *De Communibus Notitiis contra Stoicos* 46.

16. Seneca is more insistent about this in *De Beata Vita.*

17. "Teneo, habeo quicquid mei habui. . . . vicit fortuna tua fortunam meam" (Seneca, *De Constantia* 7.5–6).

18. Ibid., 15.5.

19. These two notions are carefully distinguished by Cicero in *De Finibus* 3.21. 69.

20. Whence the insistence on the fact that constancy is a manly virtue: "Defend the post you have been assigned by nature. Which post, you ask? That of a man [*viri*]" (Seneca, *De Constantia* 19.4).

21. This can be seen in the three consolations of Seneca or even in Boethius' *Consolation of Philosophy,* which also plays a very important role as a source of the treatises discussed later.

22. Recall that well-being [*salut*] – a term the Pythagoreans used in closing their letters – above all signifies health and equilibrium in mind and body.

23. "Iactamur jam tot annos ut vides, bellorum civilium aestu: et, ut in undoso mari, non uno vento agitamur turbarum seditionumque. Otium mihi cordi et quies? tubae interpellant et strepitus armorum. Horti et rura? miles et sicarius compellit in urbem" (Lipsius, *De Constantia* I, 1: 133).

24. Ibid., I, 1: 135.

25. "So you are going to flee your country. But tell me seriously, in fleeing, are you not fleeing yourself? Make sure that adversity does not arrive at your doorstep and that you do not bring with you, in your heart, the source and cause of your grief" (ibid., I, 2: 137).

26. "Et firmandus ita formandusque hic animus ut quies nobis in turba sit et pax inter media arma" (ibid., I, 2: 134–35).

27. The first eighteen essays of book I of Montaigne's *Essais* pertain to military questions.

28. Montaigne, *Essais* I.12: 45.

29. This explains the choice of the examples referred to: the Lacedaemonians, the Scythians (i.e., warrior peoples), and the case of the siege of towns (of Arles by Charles Quint; of Mondolphe by Lorenzo di Medici).

30. Montaigne, *Essais* I.12: 46.

31. For discussion, see Lagrée 1994.

32. Actually, he refers to this explicitly as a guarantee in the preface to *De Constantia.*

33. Included here, of course, would be the prohibition against suicide and the rehabilitation of repentance.

34. In this dialogue, Lipsius makes no mention of any loss that affected him personally, although he suffered terribly from the loss of his library.

35. *De Constantia,* preface to the second edition, p. 127.

36. *Manuductio* I, 3.
37. The comparison of God (or the Supreme Good or First Being) to the sun was standard since the Platonists. Lipsius extends the metaphor, comparing the teaching of the philosophical schools to the glimmering of the stars. Cf. his introduction to the *Physiologia*: "Only when set apart from our religion will these stars be able to shine" (*Sole religionis nostrae seposito, et hae stellae poterant lucere*).
38. "Constantiam hic appello rectum et immotum animi robur non elati externis aut fortuitis non depressi" (*De Constantia* I, 4: 148).
39. The Latin term robur signifies the oak tree and by extension its firmness, or the firmness of iron. Lipsius makes this clear in what follows: "I said 'oak,' and by that I mean the soul's innate firmness" (*robur dixi et intelligo firmitudinem insitam animo*)."
40. "rerum quaecunque homini aliunde accidunt aut incidunt voluntariam et sine querela perpessionem" (*De Constantia* I, 4: 150).
41. Ibid., I, 5: 157. On this point Lipsius is closer to Marcus Aurelius than to Seneca.
42. Ibid., I, 6: 159–61.
43. Providence is defined as "the everlasting and vigilant care by which God sees, knows, and is present to all things, directing and governing them in an unchangeable order that pays no heed to our concerns" (*pervigil illa et perpes cura qua res omnes inspicit, adit, cognoscit et cognitas immota quadam et ignota nobis serie dirigit et gubernat*) (ibid., I, 13: 210).
44. "digestio et explicatio communis illius Providentiae distinctae et per partes" (ibid., I, 19: 251).
45. Ibid., I, 8: 175. The comedian Polus had perfected a role in which he played a grief-stricken man who brings an urn containing the ashes of his dead son on stage and fills the theater with his tears and wailing.
46. Ibid., I, 9: 177 and ff.
47. Ibid., I, 9: 179.
48. Think of the different cities that successively figured in Lipsius' university career: Louvain, Jena, Leiden, and Louvain again.
49. Du Vair, *Philosophie morale des Stoïques*: 93; *Traité de la constance et de la consolation*, pp. 34–36.
50. *De Constantia* I, 12: 201.
51. "inclinationem animi ad alienam inopiam aut luctum sublevandum" (ibid., I, 12: 203).
52. Cicero, *Tusculan Disputations* 4.6.
53. This is probably reminiscent of the Epicurean *tetrapharmakon* for freeing the soul from fear.
54. *De Constantia* I, 13.
55. "Aut sequere, aut trahere" (ibid., I, 14: 217). This is clearly an allusion to Seneca: "Fate leads the willing, and drags along the unwilling" (*ducunt volentem fata, nolentem trahunt*) (*Epistulae* 107.10).
56. Seneca, *De Vita Beata* 15.7; cited in Lipsius, *De Constantia* I, 14: 217.
57. See Hadot 1992.
58. *De Constantia* I, 7: 165.

59. "In that very year [1572], a star arose whose brightening and dimming could clearly be observed. And, although it is difficult to believe, we could see with our own eyes that something could be born and die even in the heavens" (ibid., I, 16: 225).

60. Ibid., I, 16: 227, a passage reminiscent of Lucretius.

61. See the dedication of *The Prince* to Lorenzo di Medici: "As those who draw maps stand low on the plain in order to view the mountains and high places, and perch themselves on the latter in order to take in the low places."

62. *De Constantia* I, 17: 233.

63. It is conceivable that Leibniz had this example in mind when he compared the point of view of the monads with that of travelers approaching the same village from opposite directions.

64. Du Vair, *Traité de la constance et de la consolation*, p. 91.

65. "[I]n this Nature, in this Destiny, in this Fortune, taken together, there shines through in contrast to human ignorance, this wise and unsurpassed divine Providence, even though our acquaintance with it is more in keeping with our feeble understanding than with its incomprehensible grandeur and majesty" (ibid., p. 92).

66. *De Constantia* I, 16.

67. "I do not conceive of any ornament in this immense machine without the variety and vicissitudes of things. . . . Satiety and boredom always accompany uniformity" (*De Constantia* II, 11: 343).

68. Ibid., II, 19: 401.

69. Ibid., II, 20: 405. In order to minimize the present troubles, Lipsius offers a numerical comparison of human losses during various ancient and modern wars.

70. "Sic Deus fati impetus humana omnia trahit sed pecularium cujusque vim aut motionem non tollit" (ibid., I, 20: 261).

71. "Quia arbitrium saltem relictum homini quo reluctari et obniti deo libeat: non vis etiam qua possit" (Because at least man is left with choice, by which he is able to try to resist and struggle against God, even though he does not have the power to succeed) (ibid., I, 20: 265).

72. Ibid., I, 14: 217.

73. Ibid., II, 6: 309.

74. See ibid., II, chs. 8–9 and 10.

75. Lipsius returns at this point to a theme from the Bible and from Plutarch's *On the Delay of Divine Justice*: the joint responsibility of mankind in the midst of evil and punishment.

76. *De Constantia* II, 11: 341.

77. Ibid., I, 21: 269.

78. Ibid., II, 13: 354.

79. *Manuductio* III, 5: the wise man is always joyful (a chapter that concerns the three types of Ciceronian constancy).

80. Homer, *Iliad* 8.19; see also *De Constantia* I, 14.

81. "It is characteristic of the Stoics to join everything up and connect them like links in a chain, so that there is not only an order but a coherent, orderly sequence of things" (*Manuductio* III, 1; cf. Lagrée 1994: 98).

82. This is according to Seneca, *Epistulae* 67.10, as cited in the *Manuductio*, in the chapter entitled, "All Virtues Are Equal." Courage has endurance, patience, and toleration as its species; prudence is connected to constancy.

83. De Balzac, *Socrate Chrétien*, Discours III: 265.

84. According to Diogenes Laertius (*Lives* 7.117), the apathy of the Megarians is viewed as foolish or bad, that is, a hard and implacable sensitivity.

85. "Closed-off from the rest of the world and sheltered from external affairs, I am wholly preoccupied with the single aim of subjecting my subdued spirit to right reason and to God, and all human affairs to my spirit" (*De Constantia* II, 3: 297).

86. Lipsius, *Monita et exempla politica* I, 7.

87. Cf. Seneca, *De Brevitate Vitae* 9.1; *De Vita Beata* 6.2; Marcus Aurelius, *Meditations* 2.14; 3.10; 4.47.

88. *De Constantia* I, 17; Lagrée 1994: 138.

89. Letters from Leibniz regarding Descartes in *Philosophische Schriften* (ed. Gerhardt), 4:298–99.

90. Simon Goulart, *Œuvres morales et mêlées*, 12.

91. Recall that in 1532 Calvin published an edition, with commentary, of Seneca's *De Clementia*.

92. I here distance myself somewhat from the typology of Spanneut and Eymard d'Angers, which I endorsed in my 1994 book (pp. 16–17) in order to distinguish (1) the Christian Neostoicism of Lipsius; (2) the Christianized Stoicism of Hall and Grotius; (3) the Stoicizing Christianity of Cherbury; (4) humanism in the Stoic references of Descartes or Francis of Sales; (5) the freethinking movement; and (6) the anti-Stoicism of Pascal and Malbranche.

93. Cf. also Pierre Charron's systematic reworking of the doctrinal content of Montaigne's *Essais* in *De la sagesse* (1604).

94. "The whole earth is home to the wise man, or, as Pompey said, he must at the very least think that his home is wherever his freedom is" (*Traité de la constance et de la consolation*, p. 36). See also: "Who taught us that we were born to stay in one place? ... The whole earth is home to the wise man, or rather, his home is no place on earth. The home to which he aspires is in heaven. He is only passing through here below, as if on a pilgrimage, staying in cities and provinces as if they were rooms in an inn" (*Philosophie morale des Stoïques*, p. 93).

95. This was a common Epicurean and Stoic theme. Cf. Seneca: "There is in extreme suffering this consolation: as a rule, one ceases to sense when the sensation becomes too intense" (*Epistulae* 18.10).

96. *Traité de la constance et de la consolation*, p. 50.

97. Ibid.

98. Ibid., p. 88 (emphasis added).

99. "[I]n this Nature, this Fortune, this Destiny taken together, and shining through human ignorance, is this wise and excellent divine Providence, which is in any case acknowledged more in keeping with our feeble understanding than according to its incomprehensible grandeur and majesty" (ibid., p. 92).

100. Ibid., p. 109.
101. "This destiny which has preordained all things has also ordained that our wills be free, so much so that there is no necessity in them other than the fact that they are necessarily free. And with respect to our free choices being foreseen to be as they are, they were foreseen for what they are, and it is false that they must be as they are because they were foreseen" (ibid., p. 101).
102. An antidote for snake venom discovered in the time of Nero, theriac was supposed to contain, among its many ingredients, the extract of viper's venom.
103. *Traité de la constance et de la consolation*, p. 152.
104. On the Chrysippean model, action implies dependent causes that form part of my will.
105. *Traité de la constance et de la consolation*, p. 161.
106. "Of all the things in the world about whose cognition we can be mistaken, there is no ignorance more pernicious and detrimental than that which concerns the state of our soul after this frail and mortal life, because flowing from there is a current of anxiety and contemptible worry, which makes it so that men find no happiness in this life and anticipate nothing for certain after it, thinking themselves sent here below as if to a fatal torment, where they must live and die in misery" (ibid., p. 188).
107. "This belief has different effects on different people, though it has been present in everyone ... This makes it clear that it is innate, and therefore natural, right, and true, because a nature that is universal and uncorrupted by our particular vices makes us think only of healthy and pure beliefs" (ibid., p. 191).
108. Ibid., p. 192.
109. "God was not content with what we could learn about the immortality of our souls from the everyday book of nature via our fallible capacity to reason, but wanted to confirm this evidence for us himself by his own word and to ignite the first sparks of this natural hope in a clear light" (ibid., pp. 208–9).
110. Compare the *Exhortation à la vie civile* (in *Oeuvres*), which was for the most part published after the *Traité de la constance et de la consolation*, where du Vair seeks to convince a man tempted to flee the world by joining a monastery that it is part of his duty to remain in public life and *to practice constancy there in the service of charity*: "What then? While so many people work to establish principles only to be ruined by them and their countries, do you – you who have always taken charge and whose position obliges you to work for the public good – wish to remain in solitude, standing on one side to watch in safety the fire that has set your country ablaze, saving yourself so that you might contemplate its ashes? Wouldn't you regret not having helped when you could, or at least not having tried to help?"
111. For the enumeration and analysis of these desires for perfection, see *Traité de la constance et de la consolation*, pp. 202–4).
112. On this topic of the equality and then of the superiority of the sage with respect to God, see my "Le sage et le dieu," in *Ainsi parlaient les Anciens* (Lille, 1994): 205–16.
113. Spanneut 1973: 273.

114. *Sénèque chrétien* (1605), translated by T. Jaquemot (Geneva, 1628).

115. Ibid., p. 276.

116. "In minor things, novelty is the higher form of recommendation. If a book is good, no one asks about it, but only if it is new; and the newest way, though inconvenient, is always the easiest" (*Les caractères des virtues et des vices*, p. 66).

117. Ibid., p. 65. Paraphrasing this chapter in his *Escole du sage*, Chevreau elaborates: "He goes from Rome to Münster to become an Anabaptist or Lutheran; he will go as far as Geneva to become a Calvinist, and, if necessary, he will make use of the Koran in Constantinople. His condition is so uncertain that he does not know what he will do from one moment to the next. He changes everything that occurs in his soul" (book I, ch. 15, p. 48).

118. *Le ciel sur la terre*, introduction.

119. *Remède contre les mécontentements*, ch. 16.

120. *De l'indifférence* (Paris, 1638).

121. Ibid., ch. 1, p. 14.

122. "The Stoics found the right place for human sovereignty in the watchful custody of our two principal faculties. They believed that if judgment is properly informed of the truth and the will is not carried away by passion, that only then – in this clear and tranquil state of the soul, this straight path that forges ahead through all kinds of extremes, this peace where the heart is a treasure trove of consolations – can a man be said to be happy" (ibid., ch. 2, p. 18).

123. This theme is developed in ibid., ch. 5.

124. In chapter 8 (p. 54) of *De l'indifférence*, Yves of Paris says that "charity is a marvelous alchemy that produces a sun from the earth."

125. Ibid., ch. 10, pp. 59–60.

126. That is, earthquakes, floods, hurricanes, eclipses, and the rise and fall of empires, all of which are mentioned in book III, ch. 6, pp. 229–30.

127. *L'escole du sage* I, 15, p. 49.

128. Ibid., II, 8, p. 171.

129. Ibid., II, 8, p. 179.

130. This is the topic, traditional since Cicero, of "apparent goods" qualified by false goods, which Spinoza more reservedly refers to as "these three" (*haec tria*) in the prologue to his *Tractatus de Intellectus Emendatione*.

131. *L'escole du sage* III, 4 (on the indifference of the wise man), p. 214.

132. And, notably, not the equality of the vices.

133. Chs. 4–7 and 9, respectively.

134. Chs. 1–3 and 8, respectively.

135. *L'escole du sage* III, 6, p. 231.

136. Ibid., III, 6, p. 235. This is reminiscent of a verse from A. de Musset: "No one knows himself as much as one who suffers."

137. An unflinching moralist, he attacked Henry IV for his affair with Gabrielle d'Estrées. He was also president of the Council of Geneva in 1607, and head of the association of the pastors in Geneva from 1608 to 1628.

138. He translated the *Politiques* of Lipsius in 1594.

139. Dedicatory letter to Nicolas de Harlay, lord of Sancy.

140. The four causes of bad living are the apprehension of death, bodily pains, heartache, and pleasure (*Vie de Sénèque* §11).

141. "What I approve least of all in him, or, rather, what I am not able to approve, is the excessive praise he gives to his sage, raising him above even the gods. Then, on several occasions further on, he indicates that this sage should also be able to give himself over to death and free himself from the bonds of life on his own authority, without the permission of the sovereign ruler and accompanied by an uncharacteristic fear and mistrust of the doctrine of eternal providence, which has it that we should keep our hopes high even when things seem desperate" (ibid., ii, iiii).

142. "Ample discours sur la doctrine des Stoïques" *Œuvres morales et mêlées* (Geneva, 1606), t. III, p. 317.

143. *Vie de Sénèque*, ii, iii.

144. Ibid., §12 (The criticisms are addressed to Seneca).

145. Like Casaubon, who first showed that the alleged correspondence between Seneca and Saint Paul was a poorly executed forgery. See the preface to Goulart's 1606 edition of Seneca.

146. A summary of his translation of *De la tranquillité de l'âme* (1595), p. 225 (rpr. in *Œuvres morales et mêlées*). The remedy proposed by Seneca is harshly characterized as "a band-aid for a paralytic."

147. Ibid., p. 226 b.

148. Ibid.

149. Pascal, *Entretien avec M. de Sacy*; Francis of Sales, *Traité de l'amour de Dieu*, I, 5; Malebranche, *Traité de morale* I, 1 and 8; also *La recherche de la vérité*, IXè éclaircissement. See also Guez de Balzac: "It is possible to resolve the Stoic paradox and make their *proud philosophy* more human. But when all is said and done, I choose not to become involved in the affairs of Zeno or Chrysippus. I do not feel obliged to defend all of the foolish things they have said about their sage. I remain a Stoic only as long as Stoicism is reasonable. But *I take leave of it when it begins to talk nonsense*" (*Socrate chrétien*, Discours II) (emphasis added).

150. Senault, *De l'usage des passions*, II.ii.2, p. 216.

151. Ibid., I.iii.5, p. 113 and ff. The former criticism was also voiced by Spinoza in the preface to *Ethics* IV.

152. "Stoic philosophy has conspired to cause the death of our passions. But this proud sect did not consider that by destroying them it also brought about the death of all the virtues because the passions are the seeds of virtue, and for the little trouble it takes to cultivate them, they yield pleasant fruits" (*De l'usage des passions* I.iv.1, p. 118).

153. Ibid., I.iv.1, p. 119.

154. "In their desire to produce gods they have only raised idols" (ibid., I.i.1, p. 45). "Thus our proud Stoics, having raised their sage up to the heavens and granted him titles to which not even the fallen angels pretended during their rebellion, reduce him to the level of animals, and, unable to make him impassible, they try instead to make him stupid. They blame reason for being the cause of our disorders. They complain about the advantages nature has produced for us and would like to lose memory and prudence so that they

never have to envisage future evils or think about past ones" (ibid., I.ii.5, p. 93).

155. Ibid., II.iii.3, p. 245.
156. Ibid., II.vi.6, p. 346.
157. Ibid., II.vi.6, p. 346.
158. "The Stoic philosophy, which does not consider an undertaking glorious unless it is impossible, wanted to prohibit any commerce between the mind and body, and with uncharacteristic passion tried to separate the two parts that make a single whole. It forbid to its disciples the use of tears, and, breaking up the holiest of all friendships, it wanted the mind to be insensitive to bodily pain. . . . *This barbarian philosophy had some admirers but never any true disciples*; its advice mires them in despair; all those who wanted to follow its maxims were misled into vanity and were unable to protect themselves against pain" (ibid., II.vi.4, p. 334; emphasis added).
159. Ibid., II.ii.3, p. 219, and I.iv.1, p. 117, respectively.
160. *Socrate chrétien*, Discours III, p. 265.
161. "These philosophers are austere only because they are too virtuous: they condemn penitence only because they love fidelity and if they find fault with the repentance, it is because they presuppose the crime. . . . Their zeal deserves some pardon" (Senault, *De l'usage des passions* II.vi.6, p. 347).
162. On self-knowledge, see Jean Abbadie, *L'art de se connaître soi-même ou la recherche des sources de la morale* (Rotterdam, 1693); on the tranquillity of the soul: Claude Cardinal Bona, *Manuductio ad coelum medullam continens Sanctorum patrum et veterum philosophum* (Cologne, 1658), and Alfonse Antoine de Sarasa, *Ars semper gaudiendi ex principiis divinae providentiae et rectae conscientiae deducta* (Anvers, 1664).
163. Daniel Heinsius, *De stoica philosophia oratio* (1626); Georges MacKenzie, *Religio stoici, with a friendly address to the Phanaticks of all sects and sorts* (Edinburgh: 1665); and Jacob Thomasius Lipsius, *Exercitatio de stoico mundi exustione* (1676).
164. On this subject, see Olivo 1999 and Mehl 1999.
165. See the classic studies of Eymard d'Angers (1951–52 and 1964), Michel Spanneut (1957, 1964, and 1973), or, more recently, Taranto (1990).
166. Carraud 1997.
167. Descartes to Elisabeth, 4 August 1645; AT IV 265–66 (AT = Descartes 1964–74).
168. AT VII 22, 30–23, 1.
169. AT VII 24, 18–20, and a little further on: "And this was consequently able to deliver me from all the repentance and remorse that has usually agitated the conscience of these weak and vacillating spirits, who sometimes [*inconstamment*] allow themselves to treat as good what they later judge to be evil."
170. AT IV 265, 16–20.
171. AT IV 266, 24–29.
172. *Discourse on Method* III, AT VII 26, 19–22.

9

On the Happy Life

Descartes vis-à-vis Seneca

Donald Rutherford

Descartes wrote little in the way of moral philosophy, but he regarded the topic as of the utmost importance. As he describes it in the preface to the French edition of his *Principles of Philosophy*, the uppermost branch of the tree of philosophy is occupied by *la morale*, "the highest and most perfect moral system, which presupposes a complete knowledge of the other sciences and is the ultimate level of wisdom" (AT IXB 14/CSM I 186).[1] This moral system would be more than just the final element of Descartes' philosophy; it also defines the end, or *telos*, of his ordered reconstruction of knowledge. In an important sense, the prior, theoretical parts of his philosophy are established for the sake of the practical benefits that follow from them. To those skeptical about what philosophy has to offer, Descartes confidently replies that the difference between his principles and those of other philosophers, "as well as the long chain of truths that can be deduced from them, will finally make them realize how important it is to continue in the search for these truths, and to what a high level of wisdom, and to what perfection and felicity of life, these truths can bring us" (AT IXB 20/CSM I 190).

Descartes is usually seen as the quintessential modern philosopher, yet in his broader conception of philosophy's goal we find repeated a central ancient theme: philosophical knowledge is valued not only for its own sake, but as the basis of the best sort of human life – one in which we realize the greatest perfection and happiness. Here, as elsewhere in Descartes' writings, we hear echoes of the Stoics.[2] The influence of Stoicism on the ethical outlook of early modern philosophy is pervasive and takes a variety of forms. In the sixteenth century, Justus Lipsius and Guillaume du Vair self-consciously promoted the revival of

Stoicism in a form compatible with Christianity.[3] With later philosophers, such as Descartes, Spinoza, or Leibniz, a more complicated story needs to be told.[4] In contrast to Lipsius and du Vair, the seventeenth-century rationalists neither saw themselves as contributing to a revival of Stoicism nor desired to have their own views labeled as Stoic ones. All were familiar with the works of Seneca and Cicero, bastions of Latin literature in the seventeenth century, and with Epictetus. Yet for the most part there is little evidence of careful study of Stoic texts or attention to the principal doctrines of Stoic ethics.

A notable exception to this is found in the case of Descartes, whose correspondence with Princess Elisabeth offers a rare example of a direct engagement between a major figure of early modern philosophy and a central Stoic text, Seneca's *De Vita Beata*. Descartes' discussion of Seneca's dialogue comes late in his career (1645), at a time when his main ethical commitments were already in place. Nevertheless, the encounter is significant, since it spurs Descartes to a fuller elaboration of the foundations of his moral system – the system he refers to in the French edition of the *Principles* (1647) and refines in the *Passions of the Soul* (1649). Descartes' reaction to Seneca takes the form of a complex yes and no: at some points, he acknowledges the essential correctness of Seneca's views; at others, he finds grounds for disagreeing strongly with him. In analyzing Descartes' seeming ambivalence to Seneca's position, we can learn much about the fate of Stoic ethics in the early modern period. Furthermore, although Descartes divides himself from Seneca on a number of key issues, I argue that the comparison with Stoicism is invaluable for understanding the larger structure and ambition of Descartes' own philosophy.

HAPPINESS AND THE HIGHEST GOOD

The first detailed statement of Descartes' ethical theory appears in a series of letters composed for Princess Elisabeth of Bohemia in the summer and fall of 1645.[5] Elisabeth, suffering from an array of ills that left her in a persistent state of melancholy, had indicated to Descartes how much she valued his letters and the counsel they contained.[6] Descartes, in reply, promised to try to raise her spirits by writing about "the means which philosophy provides for acquiring that supreme felicity which common souls vainly expect from fortune, but which can be acquired only from ourselves" (AT IV 252/CSMK 256). To this end, he proposed that they examine what the ancients had written on the topic, and he suggested as a starting point Seneca's *De Vita Beata*.

From Descartes' perspective, the exercise was not a success. No sooner had he begun to study Seneca's work than he decided it was "not sufficiently rigorous to deserve to be followed." Consequently, he tells Elisabeth, he will try to explain how he thinks the topic "should have been treated by such a philosopher, unenlightened by faith, with only natural reason to guide him" (AT IV 263/CSMK 257). Descartes begins with an explanation of what he agrees is the chief desire of all men, to live happily (*vivere beate*). By this, he claims, we should understand not the ordinary happiness that depends on the favor of fortune (*l'heur*) but rather blessedness (*la béatitude*), which he defines as "a perfect contentment of mind and inner satisfaction . . . which is acquired by the wise without fortune's favor. So *vivere beate*, to live happily, is just to have a perfectly content and satisfied mind" (AT IV 264/CSMK 257).[7]

The crucial question is how to acquire such happiness. Perfect contentment of mind, Descartes argues, can be achieved by the person "least blest by nature and fortune," provided he respects three conditions, related to the three rules of provisional morality outlined in *Discourse on the Method*: first, that "he should always try to employ his mind as well as he can to discover what he should or should not do in all the circumstances of life"; second, that "he should have a firm and constant resolution to carry out whatever reason recommends without being diverted by his passions or appetites"; third, "that he should bear in mind that while he thus guides himself as far as he can, by reason, all the good things which he does not possess are one and all entirely outside his power" (AT IV 265–66/CSMK 257–58).[8] The second of these conditions, Descartes' formula for virtue, constitutes the core of his position. Virtue, he maintains, consists precisely in the "firmness" (*fermeté*) of our resolution to do whatever reason recommends; and "virtue by itself is sufficient to make us content in this life" (AT IV 265–66/CSMK 258).[9] Descartes insists that it is impossible to practice virtue without "the right use of reason," since reason "prevents virtue from being false" (ibid.). Nevertheless, he identifies virtue – the firmness of our resolution to do what reason recommends – as the basis of the mind's contentment. To achieve this happiness, he writes, it is "not necessary that our reason should be free from error; it is sufficient if our conscience testifies that we have never lacked resolution and virtue to carry out whatever we have judged the best course" (AT IV 266/CSMK 258). Provided we have reasoned to the best of our ability and recognize that we can do no more than this, we shall be content.

The account Descartes sketches for Elisabeth has two important points of contact with Seneca's Stoicism. In agreement with the eudaimonistic tradition, Descartes organizes his ethical theory around what he claims is "the chief desire of all men, to live happily"; and by "happiness" he means not simply the ordinary happiness that depends on fortune, but blessedness, "which is acquired by the wise without fortune's favor." Consistent with the Stoics, Descartes also maintains that the crucial factor in achieving this goal is virtue, which by itself is sufficient for happiness. It would be a mistake, however, to read too much into these points of verbal agreement. When Descartes goes on to compare Seneca's position with his own, he singles out for criticism Seneca's failure to have furnished "all the principal truths whose knowledge is necessary to facilitate the practice of virtue and to regulate our desires and passions, and thus to enjoy natural happiness" (AT IV 267/CSMK 258). This significant point, to which I return, directs us toward the knowledge of nature that Descartes believes is essential for the practice of virtue. Nevertheless, in stressing this point, Descartes appears to overlook a deeper difference between his ethics and that of Seneca.

Like Descartes, Seneca places considerable emphasis on the psychological benefits – the positive affects – that attend the practice of virtue. "A man thus grounded," he writes in *De Vita Beata*, "whether he wills it or not, is necessarily attended by a constant cheerfulness [*hilaritas*] and a deep joy [*laetitia*] coming from deep within, since he delights [*gaudeat*] in his own resources and desires nothing beyond his own possessions" (4.4).[10] Counseling Lucilius much as Descartes does Elisabeth, Seneca advises that the "remedy" for "melancholy and depression" (*tristitiam gravitatemque mentis*) is the enduring good that "the mind discovers for itself within itself. Only virtue keeps lasting joy [*gaudium*] secure" (*Epistulae* 27.9, 28.1, 27.3).[11] Yet for all the attention Seneca gives to the preservation of the mind's joy or tranquillity, he consistently denies that such affects have any role to play in defining the happy life. Instead, he begins from the principle that the happy life is to be identified with the attainment of our supreme good, which he characterizes as:

A mind free, upright, fearless and unshakeable, untouched by fear or desire; which considers honor [*honestas*] the only good and baseness the only evil, and everything else but a worthless mass of things, which come and go without increasing or diminishing the highest good, and neither subtract anything from the happy life nor add anything to it. (4.3)

Seneca is less definite about whether the positive affects that attend the exercise of virtue can be considered goods at all. In the preceding passage he appears to deny it; elsewhere in *De Vita Beata* he is more accommodating. But even if such affects are regarded as goods, Seneca is adamant that they form no part of the highest good, and hence contribute nothing to the happy life:

Not even that joy [*gaudium*] that arises from virtue, though a good, is part of the absolute good [*absoluti boni*], any more than delight [*laetitia*] and peace of mind [*tranquillitas*], even if they arise from the finest causes: for though these are goods, they are the sort which attend the highest good but do not bring it to perfection. (15.2)

Descartes' description of happiness as a "perfect contentment of mind and inner satisfaction" has suggested to some that his ethics is more closely allied with Epicureanism than with Stoicism. Descartes' understanding of happiness as a specific affective state – a kind of pleasure – seems to capture at least part of Epicurus' account of the happy life as one consisting of the best sort of pleasure, that derived from bodily health and the soul's freedom from disturbance (*ataraxia*) (LS 21B).[12] Thus, it might be argued that Descartes, like Epicurus, assigns no more than an instrumental value to virtue. Virtue is necessary and sufficient for the production of the most desirable mental state, and this is why we should pursue virtue.[13]

In subsequent letters to Elisabeth, Descartes makes it clear that this is not his position. Responding to Seneca's arguments against the inclusion of pleasure as part of the happy life, Descartes insists that it is necessary to distinguish three concepts: happiness, the supreme good, and the final end or goal toward which our actions ought to tend (AT IV 275/CSMK 261). Happiness, he argues, is "not the supreme good, but presupposes it, being the contentment or satisfaction of mind which results from possessing it." The supreme good itself "consists solely in virtue, because this is the only good, among all those we can possess, which depends entirely on our free will."[14] And the final end, Descartes claims, can be understood to be either of these, "for the supreme good is undoubtedly the thing we ought to set ourselves as the goal of all our actions, and the resulting contentment of mind is also rightly called our end, since it is the attraction which makes us seek the supreme good." The last point is illustrated with Descartes' version of the ancients' target metaphor: if there is a prize for hitting a bull's-eye, one can make people want to hit the bull's-eye by showing them the prize, but they cannot win the prize unless they see the bull's-eye; conversely, those who see the bull's-eye will not be motivated to fire at it unless they know there is a prize to be won.

So, Descartes concludes, "virtue, which is the bull's-eye, does not come
to be strongly desired when it is seen all on its own; and contentment,
like the prize, cannot be gained unless it is pursued" (AT IV 276/CSMK
262).

The position Descartes outlines for Elisabeth breaks decisively with a
key assumption of ancient eudaimonism. In the same letter, Descartes
maintains that on his account the positions of Zeno and Epicurus can
both "be accepted as true and as consistent with each other, provided
they are interpreted favourably" (AT IV 276/CSMK 261).[15] Zeno and
the Stoics have correctly identified the supreme good as virtue. Epicurus,
on the other hand, was right to think that happiness consists in "pleasure in general – that is to say, contentment of the mind" (ibid.). Yet
in bringing Stoicism and Epicureanism together in this way, Descartes
effectively abandons the framework within which both theories are developed. For both Stoics and Epicureans, the aim of ethical inquiry is
to articulate the content of happiness (*eudaimonia*), which is identified
as our supreme good and final end: that for the sake of which all else
is sought, which itself is not sought for the sake of anything else.[16] For
Epicureans, the supreme good is freedom from bodily pain and mental
disturbance (Diogenes Laertius 10.136); for the Stoics, it is living in accordance with virtue or, equivalently, "living in agreement with nature"
(Diogenes Laertius 7.87–89). By disengaging the notion of happiness
from that of the supreme good, Descartes lays the foundations of a theory that is distinct from both these ancient views. The difference can be
expressed in terms of a distinction between the intension and extension
of the word "happiness." Stoics and Epicureans operate with the same
concept of happiness: it is the supreme good, and final end, of action.
Where they differ is over the type of life in which happiness is realized –
whether a life of virtue or a life of pleasure. By contrast, Descartes begins
with a different understanding of happiness. For him, "happiness" means
a kind of pleasure. "[A]lthough the mere knowledge of our duty might
oblige us to do good actions," he writes, "yet this would not cause us to enjoy any happiness if we got no pleasure from it" (AT IV 276/CSMK 261).
Although this may make Descartes sound like a follower of Epicurus, he
undercuts this inference by identifying the supreme good in a way that
more closely resembles the Stoics' understanding of it. Yet he does not
embrace the Stoics' account of happiness.

Where does this leave Descartes? By identifying virtue as the supreme
good and maintaining that it is our final end in the sense of "what
we ought to set ourselves as the goal of all our actions" (AT IV 275/

CSMK 261), Descartes develops a theory that tracks an important dimension of Stoic ethics. Descartes agrees with the Stoics that a virtuous character is what reason commands us to pursue; and that, if it is achieved, our life will be complete from an ethical point of view. Furthermore, although he relies on a different conception of happiness, Descartes agrees, at least nominally, with the Stoics that virtue is necessary and sufficient for happiness. That virtue is necessary for happiness is explained by the fact that only it can supply us with a contentment that is "solid" (AT IV 280/CSMK 262), that is, one that lacks the instability of bodily pleasure and is independent of fortune. Only if our contentment derives from a source that is within us and within our power, namely virtue, can we rely on it never to be destroyed. The case for the sufficiency of virtue rests on the premise that virtue is naturally productive of contentment. According to Descartes, "we cannot ever practice any virtue – that is to say, do what our reason tells us we should do – without receiving satisfaction and pleasure from doing so" (AT IV 284/CSMK 263).[17] If, as Descartes assumes, the activity of virtue is naturally productive of "intellectual joy" (pleasure that depends only on the soul), and if this joy is (as he believes) strong enough to outweigh negative affects such as pain and sadness, then we have only to continue acting virtuously in order to be happy. "In order that our soul should have the means of happinesss," he writes in the *Passions of the Soul*,

it need only pursue virtue diligently. For if anyone lives in such a way that his conscience cannot reproach him for ever failing to do something he judges to be the best (which is what I here call "pursuing virtue"), he will receive from this a satisfaction which has such power to make him happy that the most violent assaults of the passions will never have sufficient power to disturb the tranquility of his soul. (art. 148; AT XI 442/CSM I 382)

Setting aide Descartes' use of the word "happiness," a Stoic could accept much of the preceding argument. As we have seen, for Seneca the activity of virtue is naturally linked to positive affective states. What Seneca denies is that these states contribute anything to our happiness, since, for him, happiness is identified with the *summum bonum*, and pleasure forms no part of that. This way of putting it may make it seem that Descartes and Seneca in the end disagree only about the meaning of a word. More than this, though, is at stake. The Stoics refuse to include any kind of pleasure as part of happiness, for that, they believe, would undermine the claim of virtue to be desirable for its sake alone and, hence, to be our highest good. "The highest good consists in judgment itself," Seneca writes, "and

in the disposition of the best type of mind, and when the mind has perfected itself and restrained itself within its own limits, the highest good
has been completed, and nothing further is desired; for there is nothing
outside the whole, any more than there is something beyond the end"
(9.3–4). To allow pleasure to be a part of happiness would imply that
virtue was not unqualifiedly complete as an end: it would be desired not
only for its own sake but also for the sake of the pleasure it produces.
Descartes' failure to be moved by this conclusion is an indication of his
distance from classical eudaimonism. In his view, as the supreme good,
virtue is what we ought to pursue in preference to any other good, and
what we have greatest reason to pursue, but not necessarily what we pursue for its sake alone. That the practice of virtue is naturally productive
of contentment only makes virtue that much more desirable. In no way
does it compromise the claim of virtue to be the supreme good.

VIRTUE AS PERFECTION

Descartes' account of the relation between virtue and happiness relies on
his particular understanding of virtue as a perfection. Descartes explains
the matter to Elisabeth in this way:

> [A]ll the actions of our soul that enable us to acquire some perfection are virtuous,
> and all our contentment consists simply in our inner awareness of possessing some
> perfection. Thus we cannot ever practice any virtue – that is to say, do what our
> reason tells us we should do – without receiving satisfaction and pleasure from
> doing so. (AT IV 283–84/CSMK 263)

Descartes accepts the traditional view that perfection is the intrinsic goodness of a being, that perfection or goodness comes in degrees, and that
the ranking of degrees of perfection is determined by their proximity to
the limiting case of God, the supremely perfect being. Descartes takes
it for granted that the perfection of the soul is greater than that of the
body, and that consequently the soul is a source of pleasure that is not only
more reliable but also intrinsically more desirable than that derived from
the body, since it is based on an object of greater perfection. Descartes
ascribes the ability to make such discriminations to reason, whose use is
thus essential to the practice of virtue.[18] The soul possesses greater perfection than the body because it comes closer to realizing the perfection
of God. Why this is so has crucial consequences for Descartes' account
of virtue. As he maintains in the *Fourth Meditation*, we are in no way more
like God – that is, more perfect – than in our possession of a free will.[19]

Hence the correct use of this will is our greatest virtue and the source of our greatest happiness:

[F]ree will [*le libre arbitre*] is in itself the noblest thing we can have, since it makes us in a way equal to God and seems to exempt us from being his subjects; and so its correct use [*son bon usage*] is the greatest of all the goods we possess; indeed there is nothing that is more our own or that matters more to us. From all this it follows that nothing but it can produce our greatest contentment. (AT V 85/CSMK 326)[20]

To Elisabeth, Descartes originally claimed that virtue consists in the firmness of our resolution to carry out whatever reason recommends without being diverted by the passions (AT IV 265/CSMK 257–58). It is now evident that this "firmness of resolution" is nothing other than the correct use of our free will, employing it to choose whatever reason represents as the greatest good. If allowed to function unimpeded, reason will show us that the greatest good within our power is the perfection of the will itself, since in this way we come closest to God's perfection. Thus, the supreme good for a human being, and the source of our greatest contentment, is the practice of virtue or the correct use of free will. In any choice we make, the value of particular goods is always less than that of the will itself; hence, provided we act virtuously, our happiness will be complete, whether or not we succeed in obtaining those goods.

Once again, we find broad similarities between Descartes' position and that of the Stoics – particularly the idea that virtue, or the will's governance by reason, is the only thing of absolute value, a value that is independent of the external goods (or "preferred indifferents") that are the objects of virtuous action. At the same time, though, this similarity masks a fundamental disagreement. For the Stoics, virtue is simply the perfection of reason, the only thing to which they ascribe intrinsic goodness.[21] By contrast, although Descartes interprets the will as acting virtuously to the extent that it acts in accordance with reason, he is clear that the value of this activity lies not in the fact that we are thereby acting *rationally* – according to a reason we share with God – but, rather, that we are thereby making proper use of our *freedom*, the perfection that brings us closest to God.[22]

The emphasis Descartes places on freedom of the will as an essential attribute of both God and human beings sharply divides his position from that of the Stoics. The magnitude of the gulf is apparent when we attempt to reconstruct Descartes's attitude toward the Stoic formula of the end. In *De Vita Beata* 3.3, Seneca maintains that the happy life is one that is "in agreement with its own nature" (*conveniens naturae suae*) and that among all Stoics it is agreed that such a life requires "assenting to nature itself [*rerum naturae*]." "Wisdom," he writes, "consists in not straying from nature, and in being directed by its law and pattern [*legem examplumque*]."[23] Responding to this passage, Descartes claims that he finds Seneca's statements "very obscure." To suggest that "wisdom is acquiescence in the order of things," or, as a Christian would have it, submission to the will of God, "explains almost nothing." The best interpretation he can put on Seneca's words is that "to live according to nature" means "to live in accordance with true reason" (AT IV 273–74/CSMK 260). But then, he believes, Seneca still owes us an account of the knowledge that reason must supply in order for us to be able to act virtuously.

In a subsequent letter to Elisabeth, Descartes summarizes the knowledge he thinks we require for this purpose. It consists of a surprisingly small class of truths, the most important of which are: the existence of an omnipotent and supremely perfect God, on which the existence of everything else depends; the immateriality of the soul; that we are but a small part of a vast universe; that we have duties to larger social wholes of which we are parts; that passions often distort the goodness of their objects; that pleasures of the body are more ephemeral and less reliable than pleasures of the soul (AT IV 291–95/CSMK 265–67). The propositions Descartes advances do not provide specific directives for action; they do not dictate what we ought to do in any particular circumstance. Instead, they are best seen simply as facilitating right action, by removing impediments to it (anxiety about the future, fear of death) or saving us from obvious errors (ignoring the good of others, giving priority to bodily goods). That the content of morality is underdetermined by the knowledge on which it depends is made clear by Descartes' final proposition, which instructs us to defer to the laws and customs of the land when it is not obvious how we ought to act: "Though we cannot have certain demonstrations of everything, still we must take sides, and in matters of custom embrace the opinions that seem the most probable, so that we may never be irresolute when we need to act. For nothing causes regret and remorse except irresolution" (AT IV 295/CSMK 267).[24]

The last remark reflects an abiding feature of Descartes' ethics. The truths that compose the contents of Cartesian wisdom lay down a set of general guidelines for how to use our freedom correctly. They do not guarantee that, when faced with a choice, we will know with certainty what we ought to do. As Descartes writes in his next letter to Elisabeth, "it is true that we lack the infinite knowledge which would be necessary for a

perfect acquaintance with all the goods between which we have to choose
in the various situations of our lives. We must, I think, be contented with
a modest knowledge of the most necessary truths such as those I listed in
my last letter" (AT IV 308/CSMK 269). The crucial thing is that we do
whatever we can to ascertain the best course of action, appealing if necessary to law or custom, and that we then will decisively. This creates an
important disanalogy for Descartes between the theoretical and the practical. In both cases, we have a responsibility to correct our understanding
before committing our will. Only in the case of theoretical judgment,
however, is it reasonable to suspend the will if we lack the knowledge
needed to be fully confident of our decision.[25]

In the *Fourth Meditation*, Descartes advances this as a rule for avoiding
error: if we lack the clear and distinct ideas needed to be certain of
the truth of a proposition, we should withhold assent from it. In the
case of action, he denies that this is possible: "As far as the conduct
of life is concerned, I am very far from thinking that we should assent
only to what is clearly perceived. On the contrary, I do not think we
should always expect even probable truths" (AT VII 149/CSM II 106).
In acting, the essential thing is that we will in the right manner, allowing
wisdom to guide our action so far as it can. "It is not necessary that our
reason should be free from error," he tells Elizabeth; "it is sufficient if
our conscience testifies that we have never lacked resolution and virtue to
carry out whatever we have judged the best course" (AT IV 266–67/CSMK
258). Resolution, or firmness of judgment, is critical, for it is the lack of
this above all that poses a threat to our tranquillity, or contentment of
mind.[26]

In this, again, we hear an echo of Stoic views, for example, Seneca's
description of the happy life in *Letter* 92: "What is the happy life? Peacefulness and uninterrupted tranquillity. Greatness of mind will bestow this,
and constancy [*constantia*] which holds fast to good judgment" (*Epistulae* 92.3). Absent from Descartes' position, however, is the Stoics' understanding of happiness as "living in agreement with nature." From
Cleanthes on, the Stoics advance the view that to live virtuously is for
there to be an agreement, or "conformity" (*homologia, convenientia*), between the rational principle that governs the will of an individual and the
"universal law" – or divine will – that governs nature as a whole (Diogenes
Laertius 7.86–88). To achieve happiness, the Stoics argue, it is not enough
simply that one's actions exemplify the traditional virtues of moderation,
courage, and justice. In addition, those actions must be chosen for the
right reason; and this requires wisdom, wherein one understands that

virtuous actions have value because they alone of all human things embody the divine reason immanent within nature.[27] The basic message of Stoicism is that by regulating our actions according to the universal law that governs nature as a whole, and finding value only in what conforms to that law, we are able to avoid the suffering that afflicts the lives of those driven by desire and passion.[28] In this way, we can through our own efforts become happy after the manner of a god: self-sufficient, independent of fortune, and perfectly tranquil.[29]

Descartes promises almost exactly the same benefits from his ethics as do the Stoics; however, he denies that these depend on our acknowledging a conformity between our reason and that of God. Nothing we learn by reason entitles us to say that we have understood the world as God understands it;[30] and virtue, as the perfection of our will, does not require this. Descartes flatly denies that we have any insight into the principles that govern God's will or furnish reasons for God's acting.[31] Lacking such knowledge, virtuous action cannot be identified with acting in agreement with nature, or with the universal law that is God's will. This does not mean, of course, that we should not act under the guidance of reason. Although we are limited in our knowledge, we are obliged to rely on reason as the basis for the correct use of our free will.[32] In this, for Descartes, consists our virtue, our greatest perfection, and our happiness.

DESCARTES AND THE STOICS RECONSIDERED

Descartes' ethical theory is divided from that of the Stoics on two fundamental points. By rejecting the claim of happiness to be the highest good, Descartes abandons the eudaimonistic framework within which the Stoics develop their ethics. Descartes agrees with the Stoics in identifying the supreme good with a life of virtue, but he refuses to equate such activity with happiness. Happiness instead is a certain affective state – contentment of mind – that accompanies virtue and motivates us to practice virtue. For Descartes, living virtuously is necessary and sufficient for a happy life but the two are not identical. The second point on which Descartes distinguishes his position involves the nature of virtue itself. While stressing that virtue requires the will's regulation by reason, Descartes, in contrast to the Stoics, neither identifies a virtuous will with a purely rational will nor seeks to ground virtue in the will's conformity with universal law (or divine reason). For Descartes, virtue consists in the will's perfection by reason, but this depends essentially on our learning how properly to use our freedom, the attribute by which we most closely approximate God's perfection.

Given the intellectual gulf that separates Descartes and the Stoics, one might conclude that they have very different conceptions of moral philosophy: Descartes is a modern thinker who transforms received views about mind and world, and as such we should expect from him an ethical theory that is fundamentally unlike that of the Stoics.[33] In this final section, I argue for a different way of approaching Descartes' position. Of course, Descartes is a modern thinker, whose philosophical and theological views divide him from the Stoics. Nevertheless, if we are interested in understanding the kind of comprehensive philosophical system Descartes envisioned, I believe we are helped by thinking about that system in relation to the Stoics. Although Descartes disagrees with the Stoics on key points of doctrine, his broader understanding of the structure of ethical theory and its relation to metaphysics and natural philosophy mirrors that of the Stoics.

To see this, consider the following set of five propositions, which collectively define Descartes' perfectionism:

1. True happiness, or blessedness, can in principle be achieved within this life through the exercise of the natural powers of a human being.
2. Such happiness can be fully explained in terms of the activity of virtue, which presupposes the ordering of the will by wisdom.
3. Wisdom sufficient for happiness requires the acquisition of specific intellectual knowledge, particularly knowledge of God and nature.
4. Virtue is a good that is always within our power and independent of fortune.
5. As a consequence of the exercise of virtue, we enjoy the most desirable affective states – lasting joy or contentment – and do so independently of fortune.

These five propositions establish a close connection between Descartes's ethical theory and the Stoics' eudaimonism. Although Descartes rejects the eudaimonist principle that happiness is the highest good, he retains the Stoics' assumption that happiness is what all human beings chiefly desire, and he regards the main task of ethics as the instruction (and disciplining) of the will in how best to achieve happiness. For Descartes, the basis of this happiness is, as it is for the Stoics, the activity of virtue, and virtue itself is perfected through the acquisition of wisdom, or what Seneca describes as "scientific knowledge [*scientia*] of the divine and the human" (*Epistulae* 89.4–5).[34] Finally, like the Stoics, Descartes links the unconditional goodness of virtue, and its relation to happiness, to the fact that it is always within our power and independent of fortune; and he associates the exercise of virtue with the enjoyment of a pleasing affective state, which he (but not the Stoics) equates with happiness.

The propositions most central to Descartes' perfectionism are propositions 2 and 3. Although Descartes emphasizes that virtue is a perfection of the will, it is a perfection that can be realized only when the will is used in conjunction with reason. Virtue is a "firm and constant resolution to carry out whatever reason recommends" (AT IV 265/CSMK 257). Furthermore, Descartes leaves no doubt that while native reason, or "the good sense" (*le bon sens*) with which all human beings are born, is the appropriate starting point for the attainment of happiness, such happiness can be guaranteed only if reason itself has been perfected through the acquisition and proper ordering of intellectual knowledge. As he argues in the preface to the French edition of the *Principles*, we are brought to the highest "perfection and felicity of life" by his principles and the "long chain of truths that can be deduced from them" (AT IXB 20/CSM I 190); the ethical theory that tops the tree of philosophy "presupposes a complete knowledge of all the other sciences and is the ultimate level of wisdom" (AT IXB 14/CSM I 186).

Here we see the deepest affinity between the aspirations of Descartes' philosophy and Stoicism. Setting aside the points on which I have distinguished them, Descartes propounds an ethical theory in which the perfection of reason (and hence of the will) through the acquisition of knowledge is critical to the attainment of happiness. Like the Stoics, he believes that only the person who has acquired wisdom can enjoy the full fruits of happiness. It goes without saying that Descartes' understanding of the content of this wisdom is different from that of the Stoics. Still, it is significant that Descartes' initial criticism of Seneca focuses not on the main theses of his ethical theory (e.g., the sufficiency of virtue for happiness), but on the requisite intellectual knowledge that he believes Seneca has failed to provide: "all the principal truths whose knowledge is necessary to facilitate the practice of virtue and to regulate our desires and passions, and thus to enjoy natural happiness" (AT IV 267/CSMK 258).

In his letter to Elisabeth of 15 September 1645, Descartes documents these principal truths whose knowledge is essential for happiness. In their scope the propositions correspond closely to Seneca's description of wisdom as "scientific knowledge of the divine and the human." They affirm the existence of God and the extent of his power, the place of human beings in the universe, and the content of human nature. On all of these points, we find obvious differences with the Stoics, but the thrust of Descartes' project matches that of the Stoics in seeking a body of knowledge in metaphysics and natural philosophy that is necessary for the perfection of virtue and, hence, happiness.

For Descartes, this knowledge includes what he takes to be the demonstrated truth of mind-body dualism. This is a fundamental point on which the Cartesian system is at odds with Stoicism. Descartes' explanation of virtue as the proper use of our freedom presupposes that the will is a power of mind distinct from the body – a power in which we come closest to divine perfection. With respect to the Stoics, an even more important contrast is found in what Descartes says about the passions. While it is common to note Descartes' commitment to mind-body dualism – the thesis that, metaphysically, mind and body are distinct substances – his theory of human nature assumes that these two substances are closely united and dependent upon each others' states. On this basis, Descartes constructs his theory of the passions as effects felt in the soul, which are caused by changes in the body.[35] In contrast to the Stoics, then, Descartes does not explain the passions as failures of reason: they arise from an entirely separate source, the body, and form an integral part of a normal human life. Given Descartes' explanation of the origin of the passions, the Stoics' strongest argument against them (that they are errors of judgment) collapses. At the same time, Descartes' own positive account of happiness prepares the ground for a fuller embrace of the emotional life of human beings. Because happiness as such is an affective state for Descartes, the passions are not, by their nature, opposed to happiness. Like the ancients, he stresses the need for the passions to be regulated because of the way in which they distort the goodness or badness of their objects (AT IV 295/CSMK 267). Yet, in opposition to the Stoics, he does not argue for the elimination of the passions. Provided that they are enjoyed in a way that is consistent with the maintenance of contentment of mind, they enrich our happiness and allow us to participate more fully in the world, particularly through relations with other human beings.[36]

In his last book, *The Passions of the Soul*, Descartes argues that the passions "are all by nature good, and that we have nothing to avoid but their misuse or their excess" (AT XI 485–86/CSM I 403). Their goodness consists in part in the pleasure they bring us. The pleasures common to the soul and the body "depend entirely on the passions, so that persons whom the passions can move most deeply are capable of enjoying the sweetest pleasures of this life" (AT XI 488/CSM I 404). But Descartes also makes an appeal for the goodness of the passions on teleological grounds: "[T]hey are all ordained by nature to relate to the body, and to belong to the soul only in so far as it is joined with the body. Hence, their natural function is to move the soul to consent and contribute to actions which may serve to preserve the body or render it in some way more perfect" (AT XI 430/CSM I 376). In a final irony, then, Descartes reclaims the idea of a purposiveness internal to nature, and associates it with the passions, whose sole function is to "dispose the soul to want the things which nature deems useful for us, and to persist in this volition" (AT XI 372/CSM I 349).[37]

In upholding against the Stoics the goodness of the passions, Descartes inadvertently gives a new meaning to the Stoic formula of the end. A life in which we allow ourselves to be guided by the passions, properly regulated, will be for Descartes (though not for the Stoics) a life "according to nature." We can make sense of this idea only if we see Descartes as operating with a fundamentally different conception of nature; however, in this case his disagreement with the Stoics cannot be framed in terms of a simple contrast between ancient and modern views. For Descartes, as against the Stoics, the relevant sense of "nature" is not the immanent rationality of the universe but "what God has bestowed on me as a combination of mind and body" (AT VII 82/CSM II 57). Thus, rather than being grounded in the eternal law that is divine reason, nature and purpose (and hence the goodness of the passions) are explained as particular products of God's will, whose ends are beyond human reason. It is a fact about human nature that the passions serve a beneficial function, but there is no deeper explanation for this than that God chose to make it so. The case of the passions highlights the danger in casting the opposition between Descartes and the Stoics in overly simple terms. Although Descartes is one of the architects of the new science of the seventeenth century, his differences with the Stoics are often as much a reflection of his voluntarist theology as they are of distinctively modern views in natural philosophy.

My primary concern, however, has been to stress a deeper bond between Descartes' ethics and that of the Stoics. When we consider their philosophies from the point of view of their principal goal, the attainment of happiness, we find a striking commonality of purpose. Philosophy teaches us how to live happily, to attain contentment, and it does so by ordering the will through wisdom, or scientific knowledge of the divine and the human. "No one can live happily, or even tolerably, without the study of wisdom," Seneca writes to Lucilius (*Epistulae* 16.1). Philosophy "molds and constructs the soul . . . it sits at the helm and directs our course as we waver amid uncertainties. Without it, no one can live fearlessly and with peace of mind" (16.3). A millenium and a half later, Descartes has much the same message for Elisabeth: "True philosophy . . . teaches that even amid the saddest disasters and most bitter pains we can always be content, provided that we know how to use our reason" (AT IV 315/CSMK 272).

Notes

1. Descartes' works are cited according to the following abbreviations: AT = Descartes 1964–74; CSM(K) = Descartes 1984–91.

2. A point noted by many commentators. See, inter alia, Rodis-Lewis 1962, Sorell 1993, and Marshall 1998.

3. On the reception of Stoic ethics in the sixteenth century, see Levi 1964, Lagrée 1994, and Schneewind 1998: ch. 9.

4. On Spinoza, see S. James 1993, Pereboom 1994, and Matheron 1999. On Leibniz, Rutherford 2001 and Rutherford 2003.

5. Descartes repeats the main points in his letter to Queen Christina of 20 November 1647 (AT V 81–86/CSMK 324–26). In an accompanying letter to the French ambassador Chanut, he included copies of his letters to Elisabeth, which were to be shared with the queen if she showed sufficient interest. In the same letter to Chanut, he offers the following excuse for why he has been reluctant to write about ethical matters: "It is true that normally I refuse to write down my thoughts concerning morality. I have two reasons for this. One is that there is no other subject in which malicious people can so readily find pretexts for vilifying me; and the other is that I believe only sovereigns, or those authorized by them, have the right to concern themselves with regulating the morals of other people" (AT V 86–87/CSMK 326). See also his letter to Chanut of 1 November 1646 (AT IV 536–37/CSMK 299–300).

6. See Elisabeth's letters of 24 May 1645 (AT IV 207–10) and 22 June 1645: "Your letters serve always as an antidote against melancholy, even when they do not instruct me, turning my mind away from disagreeable objects that impose themselves upon it every day, so as to make it contemplate the happiness that I possess in the friendship of a person of your merit, to whose counsel I can entrust the conduct of my life" (AT IV 233).

7. Significantly, Descartes here appears to break with the Christian eudaimonism of Augustine and Aquinas in allowing that true happiness, or blessedness, can be achieved within this life through the exercise of the natural powers of a human being. Cf. Thomas Aquinas, *Summa Theologiae* IaIIae, q. 3, a. 8, and q. 5, a. 3: "Some partial happiness can be achieved in this life, but true perfect happiness cannot."

8. While Descartes himself directs Elisabeth to the "provisional morality" elaborated in part 3 of the *Discourse*, there are important differences between the two sets of rules that reflect his different goals in the two works. The rules of the *Discourse* were framed, Descartes writes, so that he might live as happily as possible, while remaining indecisive in his theoretical judgments about nature. To this end, he proposed "a provisional moral code consisting of just three or four maxims. . . . The first was to obey the laws and customs of my country, holding constantly to the religion in which by God's grace I had been instructed from my childhood. . . . The second maxim was to be as firm and decisive in my actions as I could, and to follow even the most doubtful opinions, once I had adopted them, with no less constancy than if they had been quite certain. . . . My third maxim was to try always to master myself rather than fortune, and to change my desires rather than the order of the world. . . . Finally, to conclude this moral code . . . I thought I could do no better than to continue with the [occupation] I was engaged in, and to devote my whole life to cultivating my reason and advancing as far as I could in the knowledge of the truth, following the method I had prescribed for myself" (AT VII 22–27/CSM I 122–24). The crucial difference between the two sets of rules comes in the formulation of the second rule. The rule presented to Elisabeth repeats the injunction to act with "a firm and constant resolution"; however, this is now linked to the recommendations of reason, which furnishes the positive knowledge of metaphysics and natural philosophy that Descartes believes himself to have established. Also noteworthy is the absence of the provisional morality's first rule, prescribing deference to the laws and customs of one's country. As I discuss later, this feature of Descartes' position does not vanish completely, but it does acquire less prominence given the newfound authority of reason. Cf. Sorell 1993: 286–88.

9. Cf. AT IV 277/CSMK 262; AT V 82–83/CSMK 324–25.

10. In quoting from *De Vita Beata*, I have relied on the translations in Seneca 1963–65 and Seneca 1994, which I have sometimes modified.

11. See also *De Tranquillitate Animi* 2.4. Gisela Striker suggests that Seneca goes beyond other Stoics in stressing the pleasing character of the positive affects (*eupatheiai*) that attend a virtuous character. See Striker 1996:188. I am inclined to read loosely the statement at *De Vita Beata* 4.2 that, for the virtuous person, "true pleasure [*vera voluptas*] will be the disdain of pleasures." In *Epistulae* 23 and 59.1–4, Seneca reaffirms the orthodox Stoic distinction between *voluptas* and *gaudium*.

12. Descartes does not reject the importance of bodily health, or freedom from pain [*aponia*], but, consistent with his dualism, reinterprets its significance from the perspective of the mind: "I can conclude that happiness consists solely in contentment of mind – that is to say, in contentment in general. For although some contentment depends on the body, and some does not, there is none anywhere but in the mind" (AT IV 277/CSMK 262).

13. Cf. Gueroult 1985: 2:184–186.

14. See also his letter to Elisabeth of 6 October 1645: "If I thought joy the supreme good, I should not doubt that one ought to try to make oneself joyful at any price. . . . But I make a distinction between the supreme

good – which consists in the exercise of virtue, or, what comes to the same, the possession of all those goods whose acquisition depends upon our free will – and the satisfaction of mind which results from that acquisition" (AT IV 305/CSMK 268). A less careful formulation appears in a later letter to Queen Christina: "[T]he supreme good of each individual... consists only in a firm will to do well and the contentment which this produces" (AT V 82/CSMK 324).

15. See also his letter to Queen Christina of 20 November 1647 (AT V 83/CSMK 325). In his letter to Elisabeth, Descartes extends this judgment to a third main view about "the supreme good and the end of our actions," that of Aristotle, who, he says, "made it consist of all the perfections, as much of the body as of the mind." However, Descartes immediately sets this view aside, on the grounds that it "does not serve our purpose" (AT IV 275–76/CSMK 261).

16. Stoics and Epicureans both accept Aristotle's claim in the *Nicomachean Ethics* 1.7 that the highest good is an end "complete without qualification," that is, "what is always desirable in itself and never because of something else" (1097a30–b5); and they identify this end with happiness. For the Stoics, see Arius Didymus in Stobaeus 2.77.16–17 (LS 63A); for the Epicureans, Cicero in *De Finibus* 1.29 (LS 21A), 1.42.

17. Cf. *Passions of the Soul*, arts. 91, 190.

18. "The true function of reason... in the conduct of life is to examine and consider without passion the value of all the perfections, both of the body and of the soul, which can be acquired by our conduct, so that since we are commonly obliged to deprive ourselves of some goods in order to acquire others, we shall always choose the better" (AT IV 286–87/CSMK 265).

19. See also *Principles of Philosophy* I.37; *Passions of the Soul*, art. 152.

20. In the original, the final sentence reads: "... d'où il suit que ce n'est que de luy que nos plus grands contentmens peuvent proceder." CSMK translates *luy* as "free will." In my view the passage makes better sense if we interpret the pronoun as referring not to *le libre arbitre* but to *son bon usage*.

21. See, for example, Seneca, *Epistulae* 124.11–12, 23–24.

22. In the *Passions of the Soul*, Descartes identifies the recognition and proper use of our free will with the virtue of *générosité* (art. 153), which he describes as "the key to all the other virtues and a general remedy for every disorder of the passions" (art. 161; AT XI 454/CSM I 388).

23. Elsewhere Seneca describes wisdom (*sapientia*) as "the human mind's good brought to perfection" (*Epistulae* 89.4). Thus there is established an equivalence between the perfection of the human mind and its assent to the universal law (or "right reason") of nature.

24. In this qualified way, deference to custom remains part of Descartes' mature ethical theory. See note 3.

25. Descartes alerts us to this point in the *First Meditation* when feigning the hypothesis of a malicious demon: "I know that no danger or error will result from my plan, and that I cannot possibly go too far in my distrustful attitude. This is because the task now in hand does not involve action but merely the acquisition of knowledge" (AT VII 22/CSM II 15).

26. Cf. *Passions of the Soul*, art. 170.

27. In practical terms, living in agreement with nature presupposes both knowledge of how nature operates (i.e., what is "according to nature" [*secundam naturam*]), and the adoption of "living in agreement" as an end, with the result that one no longer merely acts according to nature but chooses to act in this way because to do so is to live in agreement with nature (*De Finibus* 3.20–21). As Cicero summarizes in *De Finibus* 3.31, "The supreme good is to live employing the knowledge of those things which happen in nature, selecting those which are according to nature and rejecting those which are against nature; that is, it is to live in agreement and conformity with nature."

28. According to the Stoics, those who suffer from the loss of external goods, or the frustration of desire, are precisely those whose wills are at odds with "right reason" or nature's universal law. As Cleanthes declares in his *Hymn to Zeus*: "You have so welded into one all things good and bad that they all share in a single everlasting reason. It is shunned and neglected by the bad among mortal men, the wretched, who ever yearn for the possession of goods yet neither see nor hear god's universal law, by obeying which they could lead a good life in partnership with intelligence. Instead, devoid of intelligence, they rush into this evil or that, some in their belligerent quest for fame, others with an unbridled bent for acquisition, others for leisure and the pleasurable acts of the body" (LS 54I).

29. Cf. again Seneca's *Letter* 92: "What is the happy life? Peacefulness and uninterrupted tranquility. Greatness of mind will bestow this, and constancy which holds fast to good judgment. How are these things attained? If all of truth has been seen, if order, moderation, and seemliness are preserved in actions, and a will which is guiltless and kindly, focused upon reason and never departing from it, as lovable as it is admirable. To put it in a nutshell for you, the wise man's mind should be such as befits god" (*Epistulae* 92.3).

30. "[B]ecause nobody except God knows everything perfectly," Descartes tells Elisabeth, "we have to content ourselves with knowing the truths most useful to us" (AT IV 291/CSMK 265). Cf. AT IV 608/CSMK 309.

31. "We will not stop to examine the ends which God adopted in creating the world, and we will reject entirely from our philosophy the search for final causes: for we ought not to be so presumptuous as to believe that God wanted to inform us of his purposes" (*Principles* I.28; AT IXB 37). See also *Principles* III.2; *Meditation* IV (AT VII 55/CSM II 39); *Conversation with Burman* (AT V 158/CSMK 341).

32. This is suggested by Descartes' remark to Henry More: "Our mind is not the measure of reality or of truth; but certainly it should be the measure of what we assert or deny" (AT V 274/CSMK 364).

33. Numerous authors have claimed to find in Descartes' philosophy the basis of a distinctively modern ethics. See, for example, Taylor 1989, and Susan James' critical response: James 1994. Sorell 1993 adopts a measured stance, recognizing Descartes' debt to Stoic ethics but arguing for his modernity based on the body of scientific knowledge with which he aims to support those views. Although she does not discuss Descartes, Julia Annas notes that it is characteristic of modern ethical theories that they reject the ancients'

concern with *eudaimonia* as a final end that is complete and self-sufficient, and instead treat happiness as a goal "independently specifiable as a state of pleasure or satisfaction" (Annas 1993: 431). In this sense, Descartes is rightly seen as a modern, though, as I argued earlier, he continues to insist on a necessary connection between virtue and happiness.

34. Cf. the fuller statement of this idea in Cicero, *De Finibus* 3.73.

35. *Passions of the Soul*, art. 27.

36. See, for example, the letters to Elisabeth of 1 September 1645 (AT IV 287/CSMK 265), and to Chanut of 1 February 1647 (AT IV 611–12/CSMK 311).

37. For a general defense of the place of teleology in Descartes' natural philosophy, see Simmons 2001.

10

Psychotherapy and Moral Perfection

Spinoza and the Stoics on the Prospect of Happiness

Firmin DeBrabander

Expressing the inimitable tranquillity of the Stoic sage, Seneca declares that

> it is impossible . . . for anyone either to injure or to benefit the wise man, since that which is divine does not need to be helped, and cannot be hurt; and the wise man is next-door neighbour to the gods and like a god in all save his mortality. . . . The man who, relying on reason, marches through mortal vicissitudes with the spirit of a god, has no vulnerable spot where he can receive injury.[1]

Perhaps one of Stoicism's greatest points of appeal, prominent in its resurgence in the early modern period, is its assertion that happiness is attainable by any rational individual. Moreover, this happiness is, as Seneca depicts it, a this-worldly salvation: the rational individual can aspire to a perfect happiness, a tranquillity impervious to any and all assaults of Fortune. Such is the virtue of Stoic ethics famously celebrated in the sixteenth century by Justus Lipsius, who, exasperated by the conflicts raging within the Christian tradition and the horrific wars accompanying them, looked to Stoicism for an alternate source of moral sustenance and the prospect of genuine respite from public tumult – to be sure, nothing less than an enduring peace of mind.[2] According to the Stoic model, such eminent tranquillity, which entails perfecting one's intellect, is founded on a specific collection of doctrines: an immanentist theology whereby God and the universe are rational in nature and can be perfectly apprehended by the human mind; virtue that is readily indicated in natural impulse; a diagnosis of the passions, the primary obstacle to virtue, in terms that immediately invoke their susceptibility to remedy; and, finally, psychotherapy as the means to happiness, a means that is subject to individual agency and responsibility.

"Of all the great classical philosophers," Alexandre Matheron remarks, "Spinoza is the one whose teaching best lends itself to a point-by-point comparison with Stoicism."[3] Indeed, Spinoza emulates the structure of Stoic moral perfectionism, notoriously asserting that God is the immanent cause of nature – God just *is* nature, in fact – and subject to human apprehension as a result. He also maintains that a being's *conatus* or natural striving for self-preservation is the basis of virtue, and attributes a cognitive element to the passions that so disturb the lives of men, making psychotherapy the centerpiece of his ethics. And yet, despite these striking similarities, Spinoza ultimately defies Matheron's assertion by diverging definitively from the Stoic project when he rejects the possibility of absolute control of the passions, that is, moral perfection. Spinoza's only explicit reference to the Stoics in the whole of the *Ethics* consists in a criticism of them on precisely this point. In fact, the rejection of perfection is central to psychotherapy, as Spinoza understands it. Animating the whole of the *Ethics* is Spinoza's intense desire to remind us all that we are part of nature, and that vain hopes to the contrary are responsible for a large part of human suffering. Thus, the spirit of his philosophy is directly opposed to Seneca's account of the wise man whose "virtue has placed him in another region of the universe" and who "has nothing in common with you."[4]

Why does Spinoza appeal to the Stoic model of ethics if he rejects its ultimate conclusion? What leads to this remarkable end? To explain their divergence, I survey the parallel foundations of psychotherapy in Spinoza and the Stoics,[5] examining the seeds of difference already planted in them, and paying close attention to how Spinoza's rejection of perfectionism is borne out by the very principle of his psychotherapy, and the therapeutic role played by this rejection.

According to the Stoic model, perfectionism is founded first of all on the intelligibility of God and the universe. Thanks to their essentially rational nature, God and the universe are intellectually accessible and, in fact, can be made wholly transparent to the human mind. God just is the inner workings of nature, according to the Stoics, the *logos* that pervades nature and internally directs the manner in which it unfolds.[6] God is intellectually accessible by virtue of his immanence in the world. Because he pervades nature, God is inseparable from nature, and only conceptually distinct from it.[7] The immanentism of Stoic theology is but

a small step from monism, and the words of Diogenes Laertius suggest
this when he reports that Zeno declared the substance of God to be the
whole world and the heavens.[8] According to the Stoic formula, insofar as
it grounds the intelligibility of God and the universe, divine immanence
in and identification with nature is a condition of moral perfectionism.
With his infamous monism, Spinoza posits this primary element of perfectionism. "Whatever is, is in God," Spinoza affirms, "and nothing can be
or be conceived without God" (Pr.15, I: 40).[9] Because he is nothing less
than the whole of Nature that surrounds us and motivates us, Spinoza's
God is likewise eminently accessible to human understanding.

Furthermore, the nature of God or the nature of Nature is intelligible
thanks to its internal logic. Nature is intelligible because it operates in a
determined manner, according to the Stoics. "One set of things follows
on and succeeds another," Chrysippus explains, "and the interconnex-
ion is inviolable."[10] For Spinoza, too, the interconnection among natural
events is inviolable, and infinite in extent. No finite individual thing can
exist or be determined to act, Spinoza says, unless it is determined to
exist or act by another cause that is a finite individual thing, which in
turn is determined by another finite individual thing, and so on ad in-
finitum (Pr.28, I: 50). Such inviolability is the basis for the intelligibility
of the universe – and God; any single event can be understood within
the logical order of which it is a part, and that event in itself provides
intellectual access to the same order. Spinoza and the Stoics disagree,
however, about the nature of this logical order. The Stoics maintain that
the universe is providentially ordered, whereas Spinoza rejects teleology
and insists rather that all things are connected in the order of efficient
causality. "Nature has no fixed goal," he declares, and "all final causes
are but figments of the human imagination" (App., I: 59) – especially
dangerous figments, in Spinoza's view, suggestive of the superstition that
incites anxiety and conflict.

Every single event and thing is purposive, according to Stoic doctrine.
If we were to perfect our intellects, we would discern that such purposiveness is familiar to ordinary human wishes and aspirations. In fact, the
Stoics go so far as to assert that human beings occupy an exalted place
in the universe and that things and events are fashioned especially for
their benefit. According to Chrysippus, "bed-bugs are useful for waking
us . . . mice encourage us not to be untidy."[11] Accordingly, understanding delivers tranquillity insofar as it includes a vision of ourselves as the
object of divine solicitude.[12] The Stoic sage can endure the assaults of
fortune because he discerns the purposiveness hidden in such assaults

and sees that they are ultimately to his advantage. Spinoza agrees with the basic idea that anxiety is eased by meditation upon the universe as absolutely determined, but he must insist that it rests upon a different dynamic. After all, Spinoza's universe is indifferent to particular human concerns. The universe offers no comfort to the teleological tendencies of the human mind. The Stoics might well wonder how Spinoza's uncompromising antianthropocentric view of things can produce joy, as Spinoza will insist that it does.[13]

Because nature is infused with providential *logos*, the Stoics trust that natural impulse (*hormē*) informs us of the proper human end and that the path to happiness is readily disclosed as a result. Specifically, they identify the impulse for self-preservation as the basis of virtue.[14] That virtue is readily indicated in natural impulse constitutes a further fundamental premise of moral perfectionism, since virtue is readily discernible by this account. If we would agree with nature, as is our *telos*, according to Zeno, we must heed our natural impulse for self-preservation, according to our proper nature.[15] Humans agree with nature when they pursue self-preservation rationally. Thus, agreement with nature involves understanding, an apprehension of the cosmic *logos* that affords harmony with that *logos*, that is, *homologia*.[16] I agree with nature when, after discerning nature's providential plan, I pursue reasonable ends – that is, ends appropriate to my nature – and I desire what actually occurs. In this manner, virtue conquers anxiety and disappointment.[17]

Spinoza agrees with the Stoics that virtue is grounded in the natural impulse or *conatus* to preserve one's being, which he identifies as nothing less than the very essence of a living thing (Pr.7, III: 108). Specifically, the virtuous life involves an intellectually illuminated *conatus*, for "to act in absolute conformity with virtue is nothing else in us but to act, to live, to preserve one's own being (these three mean the same) under the guidance of reason" (Pr.24, IV: 166–67). And furthermore, at one point in the *Ethics* – a passage Matheron calls "le moment Stoïcien de l'*Éthique*" – Spinoza invokes the Stoic agreement with nature, suggesting that understanding nature occasions acquiescence in its plan. Once we understand, he says, "we can desire nothing but that which must be," whereupon "the endeavor of the better part of us is in harmony with the order of the whole of Nature" (App.32, IV: 200).

Spinoza and the Stoics hold that the passions constitute the primary obstacle to the *telos*, or agreement with nature. Furthermore, they define passions in terms of irrational cognition, which suggests at once how the passions are susceptible to remedy – a remedy to be administered by the individual himself. The Stoics define passions (*pathê*) as excessive impulses to seek or avoid something, but according to their psychology, one must first assent to an impression, which then gives rise to a particular impulse. Though the vast majority remains ignorant of this fact, we invite passions to take root in us through a purely intelligible exchange, as it were, for impressions are propositional in nature, and assenting to them amounts to assenting to a proposition.[18] Just as an impulse is a judgment concerning the value of certain objects as they are deemed worthy of pursuit or avoidance, so a passion is also a judgment – an irrational one. A passion is irrational, according to Chrysippus, insofar as it attributes excessive value to things.[19] Because the passions are a case of "turning aside from reason,"[20] that is, from a person's rational essence, which he shares with God and the very order of the universe, passions are symptomatic of heteronomy.

The motivating question of Stoic morality is, in the face of a deter-mined universe, What is in our power? What means remain for us to secure our own happiness? Luckily, Epictetus explains, the gods have placed one thing in our power: the correct use of impressions.[21] Stoic therapy, then, rests on our ability to assent to or withhold assent from impressions freely. If I discern that an impression proposes something that does not agree with my nature, I may simply refrain from assenting to it and thereby preclude the passion it would invite.[22] Accordingly, ther-apy presupposes considerable understanding – of nature and my place in nature – in order to judge impressions appropriately. To understand nature and my place therein is to understand what nature demands of me, that is, what my duties are.[23] The wise man recognizes his duty in any given situation and assents accordingly. In fact, the Stoics assign utmost importance to such assent alone, as opposed to actually fulfilling one's duty, which, Cicero explains, amounts to a mere "afterbirth" that is ir-relevant to moral goodness.[24] Everything other than virtue is indifferent to happiness, the Stoics assert, virtue consisting in rational selection.[25] Hence the formidable impassivity of the Stoic sage, who, as Michael Frede puts it, "will be inclined towards natural things, not because he regards them as goods, but because he realizes that they are the rational things to pursue," and if he "doesn't obtain what he is impelled towards, this will be a minor loss."[26]

Stoic psychotherapy is directed at extirpating the passions. The fact that passions are irrational judgments means not only that they are sus-ceptible of treatment but also that they admit of complete and utter remedy. To treat a passion is just to clarify the poor cognition inherent in it and thereby to render its inherent judgment rational. Thus, Stoic therapy effectively involves transforming the passions, making them give way to *eupatheiai*, or rational emotions.[27] Accordingly, rational emotions are defined by reasonable or prudent judgments of the true value of things. The Stoic teaching that there are four root passions underlying all passions is a further indication that the passions lend themselves to extirpation: eradicate the basic constituent passions and you eradicate their derivatives as well.[28] Stoic psychotherapy is a process of replacing basic passions with basic rational emotions, which give rise to derivatives in their own right.

Like the Stoics, Spinoza attributes a cognitive component to the passions, which signifies that they are susceptible of treatment. He defines a passion – or, as he calls it, a passive affect – as "a confused idea whereby the mind affirms a greater or lesser force of existence of its body, or part of its body, than was previously the case" (General Definition of the Emotions, III: 150). Spinoza adds a new twist to his account of the passions in directly relating them to the body: they are confused ideas of the augmentation or diminution of bodily power. He formulates this definition otherwise by distinguishing passivity from activity: we are active insofar as "something takes place, in us or externally to us, of which we are the adequate cause; that is, . . . when from our nature there follows in us or externally something which can be clearly and distinctly understood through our nature alone," and we are passive "when something takes place in us, or follows from our nature, of which we are only the partial cause" (Def.2, III: 103). In the spirit of Stoicism, Spinoza associates the passions with a lack of self-determination, and yet he too is faced with the question of how any causality can rightfully be attributed to individual persons in light of this determinism. What does it mean for an individual to be an "adequate cause"? The Stoics invoke self-determination in our freedom to give or withhold assent from impressions, but Spinoza denies such a possibility, and thus, self-determination, the cure for the passions, must take a different form.

Spinoza prefaces his exposition of psychotherapy with a criticism of the Stoics, his only reference to them in the *Ethics*. The Stoics hold the view, he says, that "the emotions depend absolutely on our will, and that we can have absolute command over them" (Pref., V: 201). Experience rebels against this view, Spinoza declares. He immediately attributes it to Descartes, whom he proceeds to make the focus of his ridicule. Spinoza seems to credit the Stoics with the notion of a distinct faculty of free will – that he identifies their position with Descartes underscores this. The Stoic

view, so interpreted, is certainly repugnant to Spinoza since he enthusi-
astically rejects a faculty of free will (Pr.48, II: 95). However, a distinct
faculty of free will is alien to orthodox Stoic doctrine, which maintains
that the soul is unitary in character and nature. In this respect, Spinoza's
critique is slightly misguided, perhaps guilty of reconstructing the Stoic
position through Descartes. While the Stoics insist only upon freedom
of judgment as opposed to freedom of the will, this principle of their
psychotherapy, which affords "absolute command over the emotions," is
equally repugnant to Spinoza. For Spinoza maintains that the *conatus*, or
natural desire, internally informs and motivates our judgments – indeed,
he argues that desire is already implicit in any cognition (Pr.49, II: 96).
"We do not endeavor, will, seek after or desire anything because we judge
a thing to be good," Spinoza explains, but "we judge a thing to be good
because we endeavor, will, seek after and desire it" (Sch.Pr.9, III: 109).
Contrary to the Stoics, we are not free to manipulate our judgment. As
for the possibility of psychotherapy, Spinoza announces that "since the
power of the mind is defined solely by the understanding, . . . we shall
determine solely by the knowledge of the mind the remedies for the
emotions" (Pref., V: 203).

   In and of itself, knowledge does not preclude the emergence of passion, since "nothing positive contained in a false idea can be annulled by
the presence of what is true, insofar as it is true" (Pr.1, IV: 155). Spinoza
illustrates this claim by pointing out that although we may learn the true
distance of the sun from us, this knowledge does not dispel our impression that it is only two hundred feet away. "Imaginings do not disappear
at the presence of what is true insofar as it is true," he contends, "but
because other imaginings that are stronger supervene to exclude the
present existence of the things we imagine" (Sch.Pr.1, IV: 155–56). This
logic applies to passions as well, since they amount to ideas, albeit confused ones. Thus, "an emotion cannot be checked or destroyed except
by a contrary emotion which is stronger than the emotion which is to be
checked" (Pr.7, IV: 158). An emotion founded on something we imagine to be present, for example, is stronger than an emotion founded on
something absent (Pr.9, IV: 159), and an emotion referring to something
that is merely possible is eclipsed in power by an emotion referring to
something inevitable (Pr.11, IV: 160). Accordingly, "no emotion can be
checked by the true knowledge of good and evil insofar as it is true, but
only insofar as it is considered as an emotion" (Pr.14, IV: 161). Knowledge
can treat the passions only insofar as it exerts emotive force in its own
right.

Indeed, Spinoza holds that the mind "feels pleasure...insofar as it conceives adequate ideas, i.e., insofar as it is active" (Pr.58, III: 139). Conceived under the attribute of thought, to put it in terms of Spinoza's metaphysical vocabulary, an individual's *conatus* aims at understanding; this is the power inherent to the mind. When the mind achieves knowledge, therefore, its power is augmented, and it experiences pleasure. Reason has the power to check the passions because its operations are joyful, and produce active desire or striving rooted in human power.[29] In this respect, I am active so long as I understand because I exercise a power that is unique to me, or, as Spinoza puts it, because I bring about "something which can be clearly and distinctly understood through our nature alone" (Def.2, III: 103). Spinoza emulates the Stoics once again in distinguishing between passions and rational emotions as well as their root components of each. I wrest self-control from the passions, according to Spinoza, insofar as the pleasure of understanding checks the power. Thus, the principle of Spinozistic psychotherapy is the ability of reason to produce more powerful emotions than the passions, to combat and countervail the latter. Unlike the Stoic model, this principle of Spinozistic therapy precludes the possibility of eradicating the passions, as is evident in the concrete remedies Spinoza describes.

Spinoza distinguishes between three kinds of knowledge, the latter two of which lend themselves to therapy: imagination or sense perception; reason, which consists in "common notions and adequate ideas of the properties of things"; and intuitive knowledge, which proceeds from "an adequate idea of the formal essence of certain attributes of God to adequate knowledge of the essence of things" (Sch.2Pr.40, II: 90). Regarding the therapeutic force of reason, the second kind of knowledge, Spinoza says that the power of the mind consists in: the knowledge of emotions, the detachment of emotions from the thought of their external cause, the matter of time of the object to which an emotion is directed, the number of causes to which an emotion is directed, and the order according to which the mind can arrange its emotions (Sch.Pr.20, V: 211–13). Jonathan Bennett maintains that this list provides for three distinct therapeutic techniques: separating an emotion from one idea and joining it to another idea; turning passions into actions; and reflecting upon determinism.[30] However, these do not seem to be distinct techniques as much as elements of a general approach afforded by reason. Furthermore, Spinozistic therapy is not a matter of turning passions into actions, as Bennett has it, for that suggests the method of Stoic therapy. Passions are fundamentally irreducible, according to Spinoza, since the false ideas upon which they are founded are likewise irreducible. Spinozistic therapy is a matter of transforming a *mind* that is predominantly passive into one that is predominantly active, detaching the mind's focus from inadequate ideas and attaching it instead to adequate ideas derived from reflection upon determinism.

Spinoza states, "a passive emotion ceases to be a passive emotion as soon as we form a clear and distinct idea of it" (Pr.3, V: 204). Admittedly, this sounds as if therapy will involve transforming the passions, but Spinoza quickly adds that "the more an emotion is known to us, the *more* it is within our control, and the mind is less passive in respect of it" (Cor.Pr.3, V: 204) (emphasis added). Transforming a passion would mean eradicating it, as the Stoics have it, but Spinoza only suggests that we can subject it to a degree of control and, in turn, reduce the degree to which it has a hold on our mind. The very act of understanding a given passion produces a rational emotion that subdues that passion, an emotion that can be understood through my nature alone and which may be counted active in this respect. The mind becomes less passive and more active by the method of separating and joining. "If we remove an agitation of the mind, or emotion, from the thought of its external cause, and join it to other thoughts," Spinoza explains, "then love or hatred towards the external cause, and also the vacillations that arise from these emotions will be destroyed" (Pr.2, V: 203). I can subdue a passive affect by detaching it from the idea of the external cause upon which it is founded, and joining it to ideas of other causes.

Apprehending the necessity of things provides those ideas that fashion the mind with greater power over the passions, such as common notions or "things that are common to all things" (Pr.38, II: 87). Emotions founded on common notions are, "if we take account of time, more powerful than those that are related to particular things which we regard as absent" (Pr.7, V: 206) because ideas of the common properties of things are ideas of things "we regard as being *always present*" (Pr.7, V: 206) (emphasis added). In other words, common notions produce emotions of superior endurance. Conceiving things as necessary, that is, as determined, also aids the power of the mind by providing the idea of a greater number of causes for the occurrence of some perceived thing. I see them as part of a vast network of causes, and, as Spinoza explains, "an emotion that is related to several different causes ... is less harmful, and we suffer less from it ... than if we were affected by another equally great emotion which is related to only one or to a few causes" (Pr.9, V: 207). On the one hand, if we detach the mind from the image of something as being related to one or few causes – that is, something erroneously imagined to be free – and attach to it instead the idea of necessity, this will diminish the urgency of my affective state because the emotion is "deflected or diffused through a multiplicity of determining causes."[31] Thus, reason defeats the passions in a twofold manner: the idea of necessity loosens the grip of the passions on the mind, producing emotions that ultimately outlast those passions.

As for the final power the mind wields by virtue of rational knowledge, Spinoza states, "as long as we are not assailed by emotions that are contrary to our nature, we have the power to arrange and associate affections of the body according to the order of the intellect" (Pr.10, V: 207). He specifies this power as the ability to deduce clear and distinct ideas from one another, that is, the power to produce a self-generating sequence of logically connected ideas that is the distinctive mark of an active mind.[32] I may be counted active because I arrange ideas by virtue of my native rational activity and according to the order of reason, wherein every idea is ascribed a definite cause. As this sequence of ideas is produced by rational activity, it likewise gives rise to a sequence of rational emotions. Thus, I may also be counted autonomous insofar as I am the cause of my larger emotional state. And yet Spinoza reveals that the possibility of such autonomy rests on the precarious condition that we are not assailed by emotions contrary to our nature, which he specifies as emotions "that hinder the mind from understanding" (Pr.10, V: 207). Paradoxically, Spinozistic wisdom entails – indeed, essentially amounts to – the full vision of what may so impede the mind.

Intuitive knowledge, the third kind of knowledge, provides the most powerful idea at the mind's disposal: the idea of God. "As a mental image is related to more things," Spinoza maintains, "the more frequently does it occur – and the more it engages the mind" (Pr.11, V: 209).[33] He goes on to say that "images are more readily associated with those images that are related to things which we clearly and distinctly understand" (Pr.12, V: 209), such as common notions and the deductions made from them. The idea of God best satisfies these criteria since God – or Nature – is the collection of all common properties, and therefore, images are most easily associated with God and spring to life more often in respect of this association. Those images at the root of rational affects enjoy perpetual sustenance in the idea of God, that sustenance necessary for the mind's battle with the passions. But what is more, the idea of God produces a powerful emotion in its own right, namely, *amor dei intellectualis*. Spinoza asserts that "he who clearly and distinctly

understands himself and his emotions feels pleasure accompanied by
the idea of God" (Pr.15, V: 210), which, by definition, is to love God.[34]
Because "this love towards God is bound to hold chief place in the mind"
(Pr.16, V: 210) by virtue of the eternal and ubiquitous presence of its object, Harry Wolfson calls it "the sovereign remedy for the ailments of the
soul."[35]

And yet the intellectual content of this love of God that proves so em-
powering is the truth of my metaphysical status, the truth that I am just a
part of nature. If we possess intuitive knowledge and fully apprehend the
metaphysical truth of God and our relationship to God, Spinoza says that
"we see quite clearly how and in what way our mind, in respect of essence
and existence, follows from the divine nature and is continuously dependent on God" (Sch.Pr.36, V: 219). I am just one finite mode of infinite
substance among many finite modes, according to Spinoza's metaphysics,
and rely upon God for all sustenance. I am part of the vast interconnection of bodies that constitutes the universe, and it is the very condition of
my existence to be acted on by those bodies. Spinoza defines the mind as
the idea of the body and states that "the human mind has no knowledge
of the body, nor does it know it to exist, except through ideas of the affections by which the body is affected" (Pr.19, II: 80), that is, through ideas
of its relations with other bodies. Self-reflection immediately brings me
beyond the borders of myself, which borders are ultimately revealed to
be illusory. If I would define myself in proper Spinozistic fashion, Gilles
Deleuze maintains, it would be in terms of longitude and latitude: I am
merely a location on the face of God.[36]

Underlying the Stoic view that the passions may be subject to complete remedy is the controversial doctrine that the soul is wholly rational
in character. The Platonic and Aristotelian soul harbors irrational elements that are, at best, subject to training by the rational part of the soul.
Such a view accounts for temptation or moral incontinence in terms of
a struggle between different parts of the soul, whereas the Stoics find
themselves in the peculiar position of understanding temptation as a
movement of the entire unitary soul, fluttering between rational and
irrational judgments.[37] Why do the Stoics insist on this odd doctrine,
debated even within their own ranks?[38] Cicero explains that the Stoics
uphold the notion of a wholly rational soul in order "to indicate just
how much [the soul] is under our control."[39] One's soul may be rendered transparent to itself and devoid of passions because it is rational
in nature: there is no part of it that eludes my intellectual grasp.[40] The
Stoics are committed by their psychology to insist that virtue amounts to

perfection. As Anthony Long and David Sedley explain, the doctrine of the rational soul is the basis for the Stoic view that there are no degrees of virtue, since "a person's reasoning faculty is conceived as being either consistent or inconsistent."[41] Once I know, I destroy any given passion as well as all of its derivative passions. The sage is one whose intellect has been transformed in this way, as a result of which he enjoys a tranquillity that is complete and unassailable. The wise man can be happy even on the rack, the Stoics were fond of saying, because he is detached from natural forces and relations, which he deems indifferent to happiness, and finds himself completely self-sufficient in happiness.

In contrast, Spinozistic selfhood, the vision of which is central to therapeutic wisdom, rules out the prospect of self-control: to understand my modal nature is to understand that I am ultimately powerless in the face of other cosmic forces, that I am simultaneously vulnerable to and dependent upon such forces. I am defined by my relations to other bodies, and these relations occasionally prove treacherous. "There is in Nature no individual thing that is not surpassed in strength and power by some other thing," Spinoza tells us (Ax., IV: 155). Because I am one mode in a vast sea of modes, it is inevitable that I will encounter modifications or external influences that overwhelm me and surpass my intellect. "It is impossible for a man not to be part of nature and not to undergo changes other than those which can be understood solely through his own nature and of which he is the adequate cause," Spinoza explains, for if he could, "it would follow that he cannot perish but would always necessarily exist" (Pr.4, IV: 156–57).

If I would be happy, I must cease to cling to the prospect of controlling nature and self, or to the illusion that I am a privileged entity in the universe. On the contrary, I must come to terms with my relative insignificance and impotence. Spinozistic therapy concludes with such paradoxes as the notion that individual power is augmented by the recognition of impotence, and that freedom is attained in the acceptance of necessity. In this respect, Spinoza's differences with the Stoics constitute the beginnings of a transition within modern philosophy. Spinoza is ultimately critical of the notion of freedom Stoic psychotherapy presupposes, which he detects in the Cartesian tradition. The freedom of judgment Stoic therapy presupposes is freedom conceived as mere contingency and is thus symptomatic of a vision of humanity as extranatural, beyond the reach of nature's influence – a "kingdom within a kingdom," as Spinoza puts it (Pref., III: 102). The vast majority of men refuse to view themselves as natural phenomena, Spinoza believes, but if they would hope to augment their native power intellectually and physically, as their *conatus* desires, that is, as they are naturally disposed, then they must reckon with their natural situation and the true nature of power, both of which are governed by laws. Consequently, Spinoza strikes a distinctly Kantian chord in maintaining that freedom and the rational life entail a recognition of and even reverence for lawfulness. "Liberty . . . does not take away the necessity of acting," Spinoza states in his political writings, "but supposes it."[42]

The prospect of complete self-control is a harmful illusion that must be banished on the path to happiness, a happiness that consists only in degrees, since one's passivity can only be diminished to a degree.[43] Accordingly, Stoicism is ultimately a further casualty of the Spinozistic project, falling alongside the Judeo-Christian metaphysic Spinoza so excoriates in the opening books of the *Ethics*. In other words, central to Spinozistic therapy is a transcendence of the Stoic ethical ideal. In this respect, Spinoza anticipates another development of late modern thought, namely, Freudian psychotherapy.

Like Spinoza, Freud is pessimistic about the possibility of attaining complete happiness and, in fact, holds that the psychoanalytic cure for neurotic misery requires the dispersal of such a vain hope.[44] Whereas Stoic therapy is fatally optimistic, trumpeting the wise man's victory over fortune, Spinozistic and Freudian models of therapy call for resignation regarding our existential condition. Freud observes that his patients often object in frustration that psychoanalysis only reveals how their sufferings are due in large part to their own "relation and destinies," which can never be changed. Freud always replies in the same way: "I do not doubt at all that it would be easier for fate than for me to remove your sufferings, but you will be convinced that much will be gained if we succeed in transforming your hysterical misery into everyday unhappiness, against which you will be better able to defend yourself with a restored nervous system."[45] Whereas Spinozistic therapy purports to deliver salvation, Freud would surely eschew such an exalted goal, since psychoanalysis aims only to deliver normalcy.[46] Nevertheless, both thinkers identify the same means to these divergent ends, and, in any case, Spinoza might add that because the wise man is only "saved" insofar as he recognizes his normalcy, he is not terribly different from the common run of humanity. Indeed, Spinoza's philosopher is only separated from the unhappiness of the common people by a few degrees of intellectual clarity, and he is certainly no stranger to their sufferings. He only stands apart from the masses in resolutely facing up to his modal existence and the ramifications thereof.

Spinoza emulates the basis of Stoic perfectionism, it seems, in order to depict a moral life that is feasible for any rational individual who is sufficiently resolved, courageous, and insightful to carry through with it on his or her own. Following the Stoics, Spinoza aims to show that happiness is possible in this present life, although we realize it only once we recognize its truly modest form. If happiness is always a matter of degrees, according to Spinoza, and involves perpetual combat against the assault of the passions, the pursuit of happiness is a never-ending affair. The philosopher's life is defined by the constant endeavor to render all of his ideas adequate, that is, in a sense, to approach the status of the mind of God. And yet he can only achieve this status and adequately reflect the whole of nature once he unites with God and is subsumed by infinite substance – once he perishes. This is the recurring paradox of the Spinozistic self, as Genevieve Lloyd puts it, that it is "an idea whose very being consists in the struggle for a clarity the full attaining of which would involve the self's own destruction."[47] Ethics – and the therapy constituting its method – is the attempt to articulate myself, to express my identity and fulfill my native power in its intellectual and physical aspects amid forces that constantly overpower me. Thus, there is in the end a tragic element to Spinozistic ethics, since I am necessarily driven to pursue an end that is futile, and whose futility ought to become all the more clear as the content of my mind becomes more adequate. This project is impossible, but it leads to glimpses of God so glorious that they drive me on regardless – not as if it were some death drive motivating me toward self-destruction, but deeper, into more intimate familiarity with my own modal status, and in turn with the very fabric of God and Nature.

Notes

1. Seneca, *De Constantia* 8.2–3 (tr. Basore in Seneca 1963–65, vol. 1).
2. See Lipsius' *De Constantia.* In her essay in this volume, Jacqueline Lagrée notes that Lipsius' *De Constantia* was very widely read, as suggested by the more than eighty reprintings it received during this period.
3. Matheron 1999: 147: "Il est certain que, de tous les grands philosophes classiques, Spinoza est celui dont la doctrine se prête le mieux à une confrontation terme à terme avec le stoïcisme...."
4. Seneca, *De Constantia* 15.3.
5. By the term "psychotherapy," I understand the Socratic therapy of the soul characteristic of Hellenistic approaches to ethics, in distinction from Freudian psychoanalysis. See Nussbaum 1994.
6. Diogenes Laertius, *Lives of Eminent Philosophers* 7.134 (tr. Hicks 1979–80).
7. S. James 1993: 302.

8. Diogenes Laertius, *Lives of Eminent Philosophers* 7.148.
9. Spinoza, *Ethics* I, Pr. 15 (tr. Shirley 1992: 40). All further references to Spinoza's *Ethics* will be to Shirley's translation, by section, part, and page number.
10. Aulus Gellius, *Noctes Atticae* 7.2.3 (LS 55K).
11. Plutarch, *De Stoicorum Repugnantiis* 1044D (LS 54O).
12. Carnois 1980: 270.
13. DeDijn 1993: 253.
14. Diogenes Laertius, *Lives of Eminent Philosophers* 7.85.
15. Ibid., 7.87.
16. Ibid., 7.88.
17. See Epictetus, *Enchiridion* 8 (ed. Gill 1995). See also Carnois 1980: 260, 270.
18. Frede 1974: 106.
19. Galen, *De Placitis Hippocratis et Platonis* 4.5.21–5 (LS 65L).
20. Stobaeus 2.88.8–90.6 (LS 65A).
21. Epictetus, *Discourses* 1.1.7.
22. Aulus Gellius, *Noctes Atticae* 19.1.17–18.
23. Diogenes Laertius, *Lives of Eminent Philosophers* 7.108.
24. Cicero, *De Finibus* 3.9.
25. Ibid., 3.9. Cicero calls rational selection the "summum bonum."
26. Frede 1984: 109–10.
27. Diogenes Laertius, *Lives of Eminent Philosophers* 7.116.
28. See ibid., 7.111. See also Stobaeus 2.88.8–90.6.
29. Lloyd 1996: 86.
30. Bennett 1984: 333–42.
31. Lloyd 1996: 105.
32. Hampshire 1956: 103.
33. By "image," Spinoza does not seem to mean – at least not exclusively – the erroneous products of the imagination or sense perception but, rather, any conception conjured up by the mind that gives rise to an emotion. For, in the same breath, Spinoza speaks of "an image or emotion," which, he says, as it "is related to more things, the more causes there are by which it can be aroused and fostered" (Pr.11, V: 209).
34. By Definitions of the Emotions 6, III: 142.
35. Wolfson 1934: 273.
36. Deleuze 1981: 171.
37. Plutarch, *De Virtute Morali* 446F (LS 65G).
38. See Galen, *De Placitis Hippocratis et Platonis* 5.6.34–37. Posidonius is one Stoic who famously disagreed with the doctrine of the unitary soul and posited irrational parts of the soul. According to Galen, Posidonius claims Zeno and Cleanthes as forbears in his conviction.
39. Cicero, *Tusculanae Disputationes* 4.7.14 (tr. King 1966).
40. See Nussbaum 1994: 389. As she puts it, the passions are susceptible of extirpation because they are beliefs, and "not organic parts of our innate constitution."
41. Long and Sedley 1987: 383.
42. Spinoza, *Tractatus Politicus* II.11 (tr. Elwes 1951: 295–96).

43. Spinoza employs a language of degrees in describing beatitude at the end of *Ethics* V. For example, he writes that the love of God occupies only the greatest *part* of the mind, as a result of which the greatest *part* of the mind is rendered eternal (Pr.39, V: 220–21).
44. E. Becker 1973: 57.
45. Freud 1952: 81.
46. Yovel 1989: 155.
47. Lloyd 1996: 136.

11

Duties of Justice, Duties of Material Aid

Cicero's Problematic Legacy

Martha Nussbaum

THE STATESMEN'S BIBLE

A child born this year in the United States has a life expectancy of 76.4 years.[1] A child born in Sierra Leone can expect to live 34.7 years. Most adults in the United States and Europe are literate, although illiteracy remains a disturbing problem, correlated with poverty. Some developing countries attain nearly our overall rate of literacy: Sri Lanka, for example, has 90 percent adult literacy, the Philippines 94.6 percent, Jordan 86.6 percent. In many nations, however, a person's chance of learning to read (and, hence, to qualify for most well-paying jobs) is far lower. In India, only 37 percent of women and 65 percent of men are literate, in Bangladesh 26 percent of women and 49 percent of men, in Niger 6 percent of women and 20 percent of men. Clean water, health services, sanitation, maternal health and safety, adequate nutrition – all these basic human goods are distributed very unevenly around the world. The accident of being born in one country rather than another pervasively shapes the life chances of every child who is born. Being female, being lower-class, living in a rural area, and membership in an ethnic or racial or religious minority also affect life chances within every nation. But, on the whole, differences of wealth and opportunity among nations eclipse these differences. Thus, although females do worse than males in every nation on the United Nations Development Program's complex measure of human life quality, a woman born in Japan can expect to live 82 years and to enjoy many, at least, of the basic goods of a human life; a

This essay was previously published in the *Journal of Political Philosophy* 8 (2000). Reprinted by permission of Blackwell Publishing Ltd.

man born in Haiti can expect to live only 53 years, with correspondingly diminished expectation of other central human goods.

What do our theories of international law and morality have to say about this situation? By and large, very little. Although we have quite a few accounts of personal duties of aid at a distance,[2] and although in recent years theorists such as Charles Beitz and Thomas Pogge have begun to work out the foundations for a theory of material transfers between nations as part of a theory of global justice,[3] we have virtually no consensus on this question, and some of our major theories of justice are virtually silent about it, simply starting from the nation-state as their basic unit.[4] Nor has international law progressed far in this direction. Although many international documents by now do concern themselves with what are known as second-generation rights (economic and social rights) in addition to the standard political and civil rights, they typically do so in a nation-state-based way, portraying certain material entitlements as what all citizens have a right to demand from the state in which they live. Most of us, if pressed, would admit that we are members of a larger world community and bear some type of obligation to give material aid to poorer members of that community. But we have no clear picture of what those obligations are or what entity (the person, the state) is the bearer of them.

The primitive state of our thinking about this issue cannot be explained by saying that we have not thought at all about transnational obligations. For we have thought quite a lot about some of them, and we have by now sophisticated theories in some areas of this topic that command a wide consensus. Theories of the proper conduct of war and of proper conduct to the enemy during war; theories about torture and cruelty to persons; theories even about the rape of women and other transnational atrocities; theories about aggressive acts of various other sorts toward foreign nationals, whether on our soil or abroad – all these things we have seen fit to work out in some detail, and our theories of international law and justice have been dealing with them at least from the first century B.C., when Cicero described the "duties of justice" in his work *De Officiis*, perhaps the most influential book in the Western tradition of political philosophy. Cicero's ideas were further developed in the Middle Ages by thinkers such as Aquinas, Suarez, and Gentili; they were the basis for Grotius' account of just and unjust war, for many aspects of the thought of Wolff and Pufendorf, and for Kant's thinking about cosmopolitan obligation in *Perpetual Peace*.[5] By now we understand many nuances of this topic and have a rich array of subtly different views – for example, on such

questions as whether it is permissible to lie to the enemy in wartime, a
subject concerning which Cicero and Kant are the rigorists, and Grotius
takes a more indulgent line.

I argue here that not only our insights into the "duties of justice" but
also our primitive thinking about the duties of material aid can be laid
at the door of Cicero. In *De Officiis* he elaborates a distinction between
these two types of duties that, like everything he said in that book, has had
enormous influence on the course of political thought since. The general
line he takes is that duties of justice are very strict and require high moral
standards of all actors in their conduct across national boundaries. Duties
of material aid, however, allow much elasticity and give us a lot of room to
prefer the near and dear. Indeed, Cicero thinks that we positively ought to
prefer the near and dear, giving material aid to those outside our borders
only when that can be done without any sacrifice to ourselves. He cites a
famous poem of Ennius to make this point:

> A man who graciously shows the way to a someone who is lost
> kindles, so to speak, a light from his own light.
> For his own shines no less because he has lit another's. (1.51)[6]

That is how Cicero wants us to think about duties of material aid across
national boundaries: we undertake them only when it really is like giving
directions on the road or lighting someone's torch from our own: that is,
when no significant material loss ensues. And, as we all know, that is how
many of us have come to think of such duties.

It is important to understand just how central Cicero's work was to
the education of both philosophers and statesmen for many centuries.
For both Grotius and Pufendorf, who quote Cicero with enormous
regularity,[7] it was the obvious starting point, because its arguments could
be expected to be known to the audience for whom they were writing.
The same is true of Kant in the political writings: he shows his familiarity
with Cicero in many ways. Adam Smith, who usually footnotes with care
the Greek and Roman philosophical texts he cites, simply assumes his audience's familiarity with Cicero's *De Officiis*, feeling that he doesn't even
need to tell them when he is quoting huge chunks verbatim. Thus, in
A Theory of Moral Sentiments, we find a sizable chunk of book 3 simply introduced into Smith's own prose without any mention of the author, the
way we might do with Shakespeare or the Bible, feeling that to mention
the source would be to insult the learning of the audience.[8] English gentlemen typically had "Tully's *Offices*" on their desks to get them through
a difficult situation, or at least to display their rectitude. And they took

Cicero with them when they went "visiting" (as Kant notes, a favorite euphemism for colonial conquest).[9] African philosopher Kwame Anthony Appiah records that his father Joe Appiah, one of the founding political leaders of the Ghanaian nation, kept two books on his bedside table: the Bible and Cicero's *De Officiis*.[10] The book really was a kind of biblical text for the makers of public policy round the world. What I argue here is that in one important respect this bible was more like the serpent in the garden.

I believe that Cicero was a pernicious influence on this topic. But I also think that his arguments are of considerable interest – worth studying not only to discover how we went wrong but also in order to think better about what we want to say. We usually take on Cicero's conclusions without remembering, hence without criticizing, the arguments that led to them, and so we lack self-understanding about a very fundamental part of our own current situation. I propose to begin here to supply such a critical account; and I suggest that Cicero himself provides us with some of the most important resources for such critical argument. He also gives us, along with many inadequate arguments for his distinction, some much more plausible arguments that we might use to defend a moderate asymmetry between the two types of duties – but not one that has the strong anticosmopolitan consequences that he believes he has defended.

I begin by outlining Cicero's distinction between the two types of duties, and asking what explicit arguments Cicero uses to support the distinction. Then I suggest that the resulting position is regarded as acceptable by Cicero and his audience in large part because of a shared view that derives from Stoicism, concerning the irrelevance of material goods for human flourishing. I then argue that the distinction does not cohere internally, even if one should accept this Stoic doctrine; and, second, that we ought not to accept it. We then have to ask which Ciceronian arguments remain standing, and whether they give us any good ways of defending the distinction between the two types of duties.

There is one more reason for focusing on what Cicero says about this question. Cicero, more than any other philosopher who discussed this question, was immersed in it in a practical way. The *De Officiis* was written in 44 B.C., while Cicero was hiding out in the country, trying to escape assassination at the hands of the henchmen of Antony and the other triumvirs – who succeeded several months after the completion of the work. The work, dedicated to his son who is studying philosophy at Athens, argues that philosophy is essential for public life and also that philosophers have a duty to serve the public good. It is extremely moving to read the tribute this republican statesman pays to philosophy and its role in the guidance of the state, while remembering that he was in the midst of a desperate last-ditch attempt to save republican institutions at Rome through the composition of the *Second Philippic,* his major attack on Antony's tyrannical aims. Whatever one may think of Cicero as a personality, one cannot help feeling respect for this statesman who was struggling to write philosophical advice while fighting for his life, and for this philosopher who was putting his life on the line for the republic.

One important note, before we begin the argument. I focus here on duties we or our institutions may have to people who live in other nations. This single-minded emphasis produces distortion. It suggests that there is a "we" that is powerful and rich, and a "they" who are needy. But, of course, in reality the "we" in each nation is composed of privileged and oppressed groups. Distinctions of class, race and ethnicity, and, perhaps most fundamentally, sex, influence pervasively the life chances of every person in every nation. Being born in a certain region is one determinant of one's rights and opportunities; being born female is another, and these two dimensions (if we focus only on these two) interact in complicated ways. Thus any really good attempt to think about international obligation will need to take other differences, and associated injustices, into account, asking, for example, what duties we may have to address hierarchies of sex or race or religion in other nations (as well as our own), and whether there may be particularly urgent duties to use our resources in that way. I neglect all of these complexities here.

THE DUTIES OF JUSTICE

We must begin with some summarizing, to get the relevant pieces of Cicero's argument onto the table for inspection. Cicero opens his account by mentioning that justice and beneficence, *iustitia* and *beneficentia,* are two aspects of one and the same virtue (1.20). In fact, in his taxonomy of the four cardinal virtues they do figure as a single virtue, whose name is simply *iustitia* (the other three being wisdom, moderation, and courage). We are therefore led to expect that his account of the two parts of *iustitia* (the genus) will link them closely together. This expectation is disappointed.

Cicero's general account of the duties of *iustitia* (the species) has two parts. Justice requires, first, not doing any harm to anyone, unless provoked by a wrongful act.[11] This is the most basic way in which Cicero thinks about justice and injustice, and it proves fundamental to everything he says in what follows.

Second, justice requires "using common things as common, private possessions as one's own." The idea that it is a fundamental violation of justice to take property that is owned by someone else goes very deep in Cicero's thought, in a way that is explained by, but also explains, his fierce opposition to Julius Caesar's policies of redistribution of land. Here he says that any taking of property "violates the law of human fellowship" (21). The account of the relevant property rights and their origin is remarkable for its obscurity and arbitrariness:

Nothing is private by nature, but either by long-standing occupation (as when some people at some point came into an empty place), or by conquest (as when people acquired something through war), or by law or treaty or by agreement or by lot. Hence it comes about that the Arpine land is called that "of the Arpinates," the land of Tusculanum "that of the Tusculans." The account of private property is of a similar kind. Hence, because, among the things that were common by nature, each one has become someone's, therefore let each person hold onto what falls to his lot [*quod cuique obtigit, id quisque teneat*]. If someone tries to get something away for himself,[12] he violates the law of human fellowship. (21)

Cicero clearly thinks that a taking of private property is a serious injustice, analogous to an assault. But nothing in this passage explains why he should think this, or why he should think that there is any close relation between existing distributions and the property rights that justice would assign. The argument distinguishes several different ways in which nature's common stock could be appropriated. They look morally different, and yet Cicero makes no moral distinction among them. It seems as if he is saying, because they are all rather arbitrary anyhow, then each person may as well start with his own share, and we shall define property rights from that point, rather than looking back to the mode of acquisition. But once he has distinguished between agreement and conquest in war, between law and mere chance or lot, he invites us to notice that he has not said nearly enough to explain his strong preference for existing distributions. I return to this issue in the chapter's final section.

Having introduced the two types of injustice, Cicero now observes that the failure to prevent an injustice is itself a type of injustice; this important passage concerns us later in the chapter. Describing the causes of both types of injustice, he remarks that people are frequently led into immoral aggression by fear (24), by greed (25), and by the desire for glory and empire (26). The last, he notes, is the most disturbing, since it frequently coexists with great talent and force of character; he gives Julius Caesar as a case in point.

Cicero is very clear that justice requires us to use our adversaries with respect and honesty. Trickery of any sort is to be avoided (33). Furthermore, even those who have wronged you must be treated morally, for there is a limit to vengeance and punishment (34). Punishment seems to Cicero sufficient if the wrongdoer is brought to repentance and other potential wrongdoers are deterred. Anything that goes beyond this is excessive.

Cicero now turns from these general observations to the conduct of warfare. From now on he does not distinguish assault from property crime: and, of course, war standardly mingles the two subcategories of injustice. About the waging of war, he insists first that negotiated settlement is always preferable to war, since the former involves behaving humanly (and treating the other party as human), whereas the latter belongs to beasts (34). So war should be a last resort when all negotiation has failed. Cicero offers as a good example the ancient Roman fetial law, which insists that all warfare be preceded by a formal demand for restitution (37). And, of course, war is justified, in his view, only when one has been grievously wronged by the other party first. In general, war should always be limited to what will make it possible to live in peace without wrongful acts (35). After conflict has ended the vanquished should be given fair treatment, and even received into citizenship in one's own nation where that is possible (35).

During conflict, the foe is to be treated mercifully: for example, Cicero would permit an army to surrender unharmed even after the battering ram has touched their walls (35); in this he is more lenient than traditional Roman practice. Promises made to the enemy must be faithfully kept: Cicero cites with honor the example of Regulus, who returned to a terrible punishment because he had promised the Carthaginians he would return (39).[13] Even a powerful and egregiously unjust enemy leader should not be murdered by stealth (40). Cicero ends this section by reminding his readers that the duties of justice are to be observed even to slaves (41).

In general we might say that Ciceronian duties of justice involve an idea of respect for humanity, of treating a human being like an end rather than a means. (That is the reason that Kant was so deeply influenced by this account.) To assault one's enemies aggressively is to treat them as a tool of one's desire for wealth or power or pleasure. To take their property is, in Cicero's eyes, to treat them, again, as simply tools of one's own convenience. This underlying idea explains why Cicero prefers the injustice of force (*vis*) to the injustice of deception (*fraus*). The former is the act of a lion, the latter of a fox (41): "[B]oth are most foreign to the human being, but deception is more worthy of hatred" – presumably because it more designedly exploits and uses people.

In book 3 Cicero returns to the duties of justice, elaborating on his claim that they are the basis for a truly transnational law of humanity. Since the useful frequently conflicts with the honorable, he writes, we need a rule (*formula*) to follow. The rule is that of never using violence or theft against any other human being for our own advantage. This passage, more rhetorical than the book 1 account, is the text that most deeply influenced Grotius, Smith, and Kant:

> Then for someone to take anything away from another and for a human being to augment his own advantage at the cost of a human being's disadvantage, is more contrary to nature than death, than poverty, than pain, than all the other things that can happen to his body or his external possessions.[14] For to begin with it removes human fellowship and social life. For if we are so disposed to one another that anyone will plunder or assault another for the sake of his own profit, it is necessary that the fellowship of the human kind, which is most of all in accordance with nature, will be torn apart. Just as, if each limb had the idea that it could be strong if it took the strength of the adjacent limb away for itself, the whole body would necessarily weaken and perish, so too, if each one of us should take the advantages of others and should snatch away whatever he could for the sake of his own profit, the fellowship and common life of human beings must necessarily be overturned. (21–22)

The point is, presumably, that the universal law condemns any violation that, should it be general, would undermine human fellowship. Klaus Reich has found in this passage the origins of Kant's formula of universal law.[15] Whether this is right or wrong, we certainly should see a strong similarity between Cicero's argument and Kant's idea.

Cicero now calls this principle a part of "nature, that is the law of peoples," and also "nature's reason, which is divine and human law." He notes that it is also widely recognized in the laws of individual states. We should all devote ourselves to the upholding of this principle – as Hercules did, protecting the weak from assault, a humanitarian act for which he was made into a god. In general:

> If nature prescribes that a human being should consider the interests of a human being, no matter who he is, just because he is human, it is necessary that according to nature what is useful for all is something in common. And if this is so, then we

are all embraced by one and the same law of nature, and if that is so, then it is clear that the law of nature forbids us to do violence to [*violare*] anyone else. But the first claim is true, so the last is true also. (3.27)

Cicero remarks that it is absurd for us to hold to this principle when our family or friends are concerned, but to deny that it holds of all relations among citizens. But, then, it is equally absurd to hold to it for citizens and deny it to foreigners. People who make such a distinction "tear apart the common fellowship of the human kind" (28). (Hercules, his salient example of nature's law, was a cosmopolitan in his aid to the weak.)[16]

This section makes it very clear that Cicero's duties of justice are fully cosmopolitan. National boundaries are morally irrelevant, and Cicero sternly reproves those who think them relevant. At the core of Cicero's argument is an idea of not doing violence to the human person – and, when we add in the distinction from book 1 (and the Hercules example) of not allowing people to be violated when you can help them. *Violare* includes physical assault, sexual assault, cruel punishments, tortures, and also takings of property. Cicero now links to that idea of humanity as an end the idea of a universal law of nature: conduct is to be tested by asking whether it could be made into such a law. Cicero clearly wants the world citizen to be Hercules-like in his determination to create a world where such violations of humanity do not occur, a world that accords with nature's moral law. The law of nature is not actual positive law, but it is morally binding on our actions, even when we are outside the realm of positive law.

This is the material in Cicero that became the foundation for modern international law. Grotius' *De Lege Belli atque Pacis* is, we might say, a commentary on these passages. Kant's *Perpetual Peace* also follows them very closely.[17] Particularly influential was Cicero's moral rigor, his insistence that all promises be preserved; in the form of the Grotian maxim *pacta sunt servanda*, this is the basis for modern conceptions of treaty obligation – although of modern thinkers only Kant follows Cicero all the way to his praise of Regulus.

THE DUTIES OF MATERIAL AID

Duties of justice are fully universal, and impose strict, exceptionless obligations. Regulus had to return to his death; it is wrong to poison even the foulest of tyrants. Very different is Cicero's next group of duties, the duties involved in giving material aid to others. Cicero begins by saying that these duties, too, are basic to human nature, but there are many constraints. We have to make sure our gifts do not do harm; we have to make sure we do not impoverish ourselves; and we have to make sure the gift suits the status of the recipient. Distinctions that we may legitimately take into account under the last rubric include the recipient's character, his attitude toward us, benefits previously given to us, and the degree of our association and fellowship (1.45). Duties are strongest when all of these intersect; but throughout there is a role for judgment as to what seems weightier (45). If other things are equal, we should help the most needy (49).

As if introducing an independent consideration – which he never clearly ranks against the preceding – Cicero now says that human fellowship will be best served if the people to whom one has the closest ties (*ut quisque erit coniunctissimus*) should get the most benefit. He now enumerates the various degrees of association, beginning with the species as a whole, and the ties of reason and speech that link us all together. This all-embracing tie, he now says, citing Ennius, justifies only a type of material aid that can be given without personal diminution (*sine detrimento*). Examples are allowing a foreigner to have access to running water and fire; giving advice to anyone who asks. But, he says, because there's an infinite number of people in the world (*infinita multitudo*) who might possibly ask us for something, we have to draw the line at the point Ennius mentions.

Cicero then discusses other bonds that do, in his view, justify some substantial giving: the bond of nation and language; of the same state; of one's relatives; various degrees of familial propinquity; and, finally, one's own home. In no case, it is important to note, does his argument for the closeness of the connection rest simply on biology or heredity; at least one relevant feature, and usually the central one, is some aspect of shared human practices. Citizens are said to share "a forum, temples, porticoes, roads, laws, rights, courts, elections." Families are held together by blood, but also by the shared task of producing citizens, and by "goodwill and love: for it is a great thing to have the same tombs of ancestors, to use the same religious rites, to have common burial places" (54–55). (It is of considerable practical importance to Cicero to show that family ties are not merely blood ties, because adoption, remarriage, and other common features of Roman life had made family lines look quite different from bloodlines.) Cicero does not make it clear whether our duties are greater to those who are closer to us in these various shared observances.

Cicero now praises friendship as an especially powerful source of duties
of aid: for friendships are more likely to be cemented by the bonds of
virtue and shared aspiration than are family relations. But his highest
praise is reserved for shared political institutions:

> But when you look at everything with your reason and mind, of all the forms of
> fellowship none is weightier, none more dear, than that which each of us has with
> the republic. Parents are dear, children, relatives, acquaintances are dear; but
> the republic embraces all these loves of all of us together, and what good person
> would hesitate to die for her if it would help her? How much more detestable,
> then, is the monstrosity of those men who have cut up their country with every
> type of crime, and have been, and are still, engaged in her utter destruction! (57)

Although we cannot be certain, and the hasty character of the writing
in this passage makes the whole course of the argument rather unclear,
Cicero here appears to distinguish our affiliation with the republic from
the shared association he previously mentioned, that of fellow citizens
who share a forum, temples, and so forth. The affiliation praised here is
with the republican institutions themselves, which make it possible for us
to live a fully human life.

Cicero now turns to the question of the ranking of duties. First, he
says, are duties to the republic and our parents, because we are obligated
to both by strong duties of gratitude for their benefits to us in the past
(58). Next are our children and our household, because they "look to us
alone, and have no other available refuge." Next are our relatives, who
are congenial to us, and with whom we generally share our fortunes. But
at the same time, we must look to need as well, and to what anyone would
or would not be able to attain without our help. Different circumstances
suggest different orderings: for example, one should aid a neighbor in
preference to a brother in gathering the harvest; but in a lawsuit you
should defend your relative or friend rather than your neighbor.

In short, then, Cicero proposes a flexible account that recognizes many
criteria as pertinent to duties of aid: gratitude, need and dependency,
thick association – but which also preserves a role for flexible judgment
in adjudicating the claims when they might conflict. We have a great
deal of latitude in considering the cases.[18] What is clear, however, is that
people outside our own nation always lose out. They are just that *infinita
multitudo* who would drain off all our resources if we let their demand
be heard at all. Fire and water for the alien are not nothing: they can be
refused. But they are exemplary, for Cicero, of that which can be granted
without diminution of our own stock.

A LURKING VIEW ABOUT THE GOOD

Why is it at all acceptable to Cicero that this asymmetry should hold? He thinks it so terrible to contemplate a human being assaulting or stealing from another human being. Even a lie to the enemy seems to him the gravest desecration of the very concept of human fellowship. And yet if the same people are starving and my nation has a surplus, it seems to him just fine. There are many things that help explain these attitudes, including (as we shall see further in what follows) Cicero's strong and utterly unjustified account of property rights. But we must now mention another piece of the picture.

In the *De Officiis*, Cicero's view lies closer to orthodox Stoicism than in most of his other works. Perhaps because he is writing at such speed, basing his work on several Stoic texts, perhaps because these are topics on which he has in any case fewer disagreements than usual with the Stoics, he tends to sympathize with the Stoic doctrine about the badness of the passions and the beliefs about external goods that are their ground. Both here and in the *Tusculan Disputations* he takes the Stoic line that one should never have grief, or fear, or anger – and he goes even further, denying in *Tusculans* book 4 that one should even have the approved variety of Stoic *erōs*.[19] In *De Officiis*, the same view is evident. Right after the passage on justice and material aid, we find courage defined as a lofty attitude of mind that rises above the passions, and is able to look down serenely on the vicissitudes of fortune (1.61–68).

But of course the Stoic thesis about the passions is inseparable from their view that external things, the gifts of chance, are irrelevant for the truly well-lived life. The wise person scorns all such things and considers them small. He does not get upset at the loss of a fortune, or health, or reputation and honor, because all that is trivial stuff anyway.

This view Cicero accordingly endorses: the courageous person is "great and lofty in soul, despising human things" (61). Again, "a brave and great mind" is revealed "in the despising of external things, given that he is persuaded that a human being should wonder at and wish for and seek nothing but what is morally good and appropriate, nor should he yield to any human being or any disturbance of mind or any fortune" (66). In short then: we can afford not to worry about the evenhandedness of our benevolence, because the really strong person – and that is any of us at our best – does not need these things.

This Stoic thesis typically makes it very difficult for any Stoic to motivate and defend beneficence. The Greek Stoics seem to have turned

at this point to their view of providence: Zeus asks us to concern ourselves with the distribution of material goods, even though, strictly speaking, such things have no real importance. In general, these things are
"preferred," their opposites "dispreferred"; it is therefore appropriate to
pursue them, though not to grieve when one cannot attain them. Marcus
Aurelius says that the Stoic wise person will view people who weep over
lost externals as similar to children who weep over a lost toy: he will help
the child regain the toy (the needed externals), but he will know all the
while that it is only their own foolish immaturity that makes them care
about such things. Cicero, unable to take up Stoic teleology because of
his own epistemic skepticism, takes a line more like Marcus': if people
are really good they don't mind the loss of externals, so, by implication,
if they do mind them that shows they are morally defective.[20] That does
not mean that we should not aid them – but it does color our sense of
why that aid is needed, and what its limits might be.

DOES THE DISTINCTION STAND UP?

It is now time to ask some questions. First, we need to try to understand
whether Cicero's distinction of duties is coherent, even to one who accepts
the Stoic doctrine. Three arguments suggest that it is not.

Justice and Respectful Treatment Are External Goods

The first objection we might make is that if we are really thoroughgoing
Stoics, we should not care about just or respectful treatment any more
than about material aid. All these things are externals, in the hands of
chance. To a person who is truly free within, slavery, torture, and rape
are no worse than poverty. Stoics were quite explicit on this point. The
wise person is free, even though he may be a slave. The sage on the rack
is happy. The person who sees things aright will not care about the contempt and abuse of society: Seneca tells a story of Cato's undisturbed
demeanor when someone spat at him in the forum (*De Ira* 3.38). Even
political freedom, a goal dear to many Stoic statesmen both before and
after Cicero, is not, strictly speaking, important for true well-being. (At
one point Seneca, describing Cato's struggles for political freedom, feels
it necessary to remind his readers that Cato did not really think it important for himself but only for his followers – who, presumably, were still
too dependent on the gifts of fortune.)

If this is so, then one rationale for the distinction between the two types of duties disappears. If humanity is owed certain types of treatment from the world, it would seem it is owed good material treatment as well as respect and noncruelty. If the world's treatment *does not* matter to humanity, then it would seem that torture, rape, and disrespect are no more damaging, no more important, than poverty. It is incoherent to salve one's conscience on the duties of material aid by thinking about their nonnecessity for true flourishing and, at the same time, to insist so strictly on the absolute inviolability of the duties of justice, which are just other ways of supplying human beings with the external things they need.

To see how fascinating this Stoic incoherence can be, let me digress to consider Seneca's letter on slavery,[21] which is rightly regarded as one of the formative progressive documents on this topic. Its general argument is that slaves have human worth and dignity and therefore are due certain sorts of treatment suited to that human worth and dignity. Seneca's imaginary interlocutor keeps saying, "He is a slave" (*Servus est*). Seneca keeps on replying, "No, he is a human being" (*Immo homo est*). But to what, precisely, does Seneca think humanity entitles this human being? Both a lot and a little. A lot, in the sense that Seneca is prepared to make quite radical changes in customs of the use of slaves. Slaves are to be reasoned with and made partners in the planning of the household. They are to sit at our table and eat with us. All cruelty and physical abuse is absolutely banned. Especially radical is an equally absolute ban on using the slave as a sexual object: for intercourse with slaves was such an accepted part of the conduct of life, where male owners were concerned, that it was not defined as adultery under law,[22] and the only other person we know who objected to it was the Stoic philosopher Musonius Rufus.[23]

What, however, about the material conditions of the slave – his lack of self-ownership, his inability to own material goods, in short the institution of slavery? This, it seems, Seneca never thinks to question. And his rationale for this quietism is what we might by now expect: slavery does no harm, because the only important goods are the goods of the soul. The interlocutor utters his scornful "He is a slave" one last time, toward the end of the letter. But this time Seneca does not reply that the person is human and had therefore to be treated thus and so: "'He is a slave.' But maybe he has a free soul. 'He is a slave.' Will this do him any harm? [*hoc illi nocebit?*] Show me anyone who is not a slave: one person is a slave to lust, another to greed, another to ambition, all to hope, all to fear" (47.17).

But this tack confounds the person who had just been thinking that the treatment of people *does* matter, who had just been agreeing with Seneca that it is entirely wrong to use a human being the way one uses a beast of burden (47.5). For how can it be wrong to neglect or fondle or terrorize or even beat a slave, if all that matters is the free soul within and that cannot be touched by any contingency? How can it be wrong to treat a slave like a beast, if it is a matter of indifference whether one is a slave or a freeman? Seneca would like to say that humanity requires respectful treatment, and yet that it does not: for obviously enough, the entire institution is an insult to humanity, because it treats a free soul as an unfree possession. This was well known to Seneca and to his contemporaries. There was no coherent Stoic defense of the institution available to him, although in fact most Stoic philosophers did support it.[24] Seneca therefore falls back, at this point, on the familiar point about the external goods, and the familiar paradox that only virtue makes one truly free. But that maneuver does too much work if it does any at all, for it negates the importance of everything that has been argued up to this point. If it is really true that the only important form of slavery is internal slavery to passion, and if we accept the Stoic thesis that these passions are always in our control, then there is no reason to think that the lot of the abused and insulted slave is any worse than the lot of the slave who sits down with Seneca at the dinner table.

I believe that much modern thought about duties suffers from this same incoherence.[25] We allow that there are certain things that are so bad, so deforming of humanity, that we must go to great lengths to prevent them. Thus, with Cicero and Seneca, we hold that torture is an insult to humanity; and we now go further, rejecting slavery itself. But to deny people material aid seems to us not in the same category at all. We do not feel that we are torturing or raping people when we deny them the things that they need in order to live – presumably because we do not think that these goods are in the same class. Humanity can shine out in a poor dwelling, and we tell ourselves that human dignity has not been offended by the poverty itself. Poverty is just an external: it does not cut to the core of humanity. But, of course, it does. The human being is not like a block or a rock, but a body of flesh and blood that is made each day by its living conditions. Hope, desire, expectation, will, all these things are shaped by material surroundings. People can wonderfully rise above their conditions, but that does not mean that the conditions themselves are not important, shaping what they are able to do and to be. I believe that the Stoic idea of the invulnerability of the will to contingencies – and related Christian ideas about the soul – lie behind these judgments. At least the Christian version is consistent, holding that no sort of ill treatment in this life affects one's salvation. (Interestingly, many thinkers are inclined to draw the line at rape, feeling that it sullies the soul despite its unwilling character. Dante, for example, puts Piccarda Donati in the lowest rung of paradise simply for having been raped.) The Stoic version lies closer to the ordinary thought of many of us, when we express horror at "crimes against humanity" but never consider that failures of material aid might be such crimes.

Interdependence and Interweaving

Even if we should convince ourselves that the presence of humanity imposes duties of justice but no duties of material aid, we would still have a problem on our hands: for the duties of justice cost money. To promote justice requires material aid. Any political and legal order that is going to protect people against torture, rape, and cruelty will need material support. There will need to be lawyers, courts, police, other administrative officers, and these will need to be supported, presumably, by a system of taxation. Where internal budgetary discussions are concerned, Americans very often miss this point, thinking that money spent on welfare and relief of poverty is money spent, but that somehow the police, the courts, the fire department, everything that is required to maintain a system of contract, property rights, and personal safety, are all free of cost.[26] Similarly, political liberty is not free: once again, tax money supports the institutional structures that make liberties more than words on paper. Such issues become vivid when one visits a nation that has a weak tax structure. In India, for example, the national government is impoverished, since relatively few citizens pay taxes. This means that the infrastructure is in disarray, jeopardizing freedom of travel and public safety; that the legal system has huge multiyear delays, jeopardizing other rights and liberties; that personal security is not protected by effective law enforcement; and so on. In short, people are not free to do as they wish in matters touched on by the duties of justice, unless material resources have been distributed – and, in most cases, redistributed – to deal with the problem.

Such problems internal to each nation already put the Ciceronian project in trouble: for we are not going to be able to protect the rights of all world citizens in many areas of basic liberty without redistribution from richer to poorer nations. Humanity is being violated daily, not only because of evildoers, but also because of the sheer inability of nations to maintain public order and public safety. If we really care about the duties of justice, in short, this already requires us to think about material aid. But the problem is magnified when we think about what an effective system of international law requires. Maintaining a system of global justice that would be at all effective in dealing with torture, cruelty, unjust war, and the like involves massive expenses; meeting these expenses requires redistribution of resources from richer to poorer nations. In that sense the United States is at best muddled and at worst hypocritical when it sounds off about human rights around the world and yet opposes any attempt to create expensive institutions – or even to pay UN dues. Caring about basic human rights means spending money, not just talking fine talk.

But then the difference between the two types of duties becomes a matter of degree only. It looks like we would not have to spend very much to pay our dues to the United Nations, or support an international court. If we were really going to make a significant difference to poverty in Africa and Asia, it seems that we would have to spend a lot more money than that. To this we reply that now the whole terrain of argument has shifted: we are no longer making a point of principle, we are just haggling about the price.[27] And once we get off the high horse of false Ciceronian principle, we can notice that much of the aid we give to other nations actually goes to securing their citizens from violations of humanity covered under duties of justice, through expenditures on law enforcement and the legal system. We should also count at least a part of the military budget in this category, since being prepared to defend one's citizens against an unjust attack is a very important part of the duties of justice. In fact, when we look into the matter seriously, we will probably find that the enormous price of protecting citizens from torture, securing effective police protection, and protecting basic security of the person and of property is quite comparable with the cost of providing basic material necessities.[28] So we should conclude that if people say they are for the duties of justice and yet are unwilling to redistribute money across national borders, they are actually halfhearted about the duties of justice.

Positive and Negative

The duties of justice look different from the duties of material aid because they do not involve doing anything, or not very much. They mainly involve refraining from certain acts: aggressive war, torture, rape, and the like. Duties of material aid, by contrast, look like they require us to do a great deal for others. That intuitive idea is very central in our thinking when we suppose that the recognition of duties of material aid would impose a great burden on our nation, while the recognition of duties of justice would not. I have already cast doubt on the positive-negative distinction by pointing out that real protection of people against violations of justice is very expensive: so if we really are serious about protecting people in other parts of the world against wrongdoing, we will have to spend a lot of money on the institutions that do the protecting. But someone may now say, if we decide not to spend this money, violations may occur, but at least the violators won't be us. We can consistently draw a line, if not precisely where the old line between justice and material aid went, at least between acting and refraining. If we refrain from cruelty, torture, and the like, then we are doing no wrong, even if we are unwilling to spend our money on people at a distance, even where justice issues themselves are in play.

To this argument the best reply was given by Cicero himself. In this very section of book 1 of the *De Officiis*, he wrote:

There are two types of injustice: one committed by people who inflict a wrong, another by those who fail to ward it off from those on whom it is being inflicted, although it is in their power to do so. For a person who unjustly attacks another under the influence of anger or some other disturbance seems to be laying hands, so to speak, upon a colleague; but the person who does not provide a defense or oppose the injustice, if he can, is just as blameworthy as if he had deserted his parents or his friends or his country.

The more active sort of injustice, he continues, is usually motivated by fear, or greed, or the love of honor and glory. (Julius Caesar is, as elsewhere, his salient example of the last-named bad motive.) Cicero now turns to the second type, considering his own profession in the process:

As for neglecting the defense of others and deserting one's duty, there are many causes of that. Sometimes people are reluctant to incur enmities or hard work or expenses. Sometimes they are impeded by lack of concern or laziness or inactivity or by some pursuits or business of their own, to such an extent that they allow those whom they should protect to be abandoned. We must therefore watch out lest Plato's statements about philosophers prove to be insufficient: that because they are occupied in the pursuit of truth, and because they scorn and despise the things that most people intensely seek and for which they are in the habit of murdering one another, therefore they are just. For they attain one type of justice, not wronging anyone by the infliction of a wrong, but they fall into the other type of injustice. For impeded by their zeal for learning, they desert those whom they ought to protect. Thus he thought they would not even help the republic unless compelled. But it would have been fairer that this be done willingly; for a right action is only just if it is done willingly. There are also some people who either because of keenness to protect their estates or through some hatred of human beings say that they mind their own business and don't seem to be doing anyone any harm. They are free from one type of injustice, but they run into the other; for they abandon the fellowship of life, inasmuch as they do not expend on it any zeal or effort or resources. (1.28–29)

Cicero makes an important contribution in this fascinating section. He grants that in a certain way the active-passive distinction makes sense. There is a morally relevant distinction between actively doing a wrong oneself and simply sitting by while a wrong takes place. But this distinction, while morally relevant, does not entail that no wrong is done by the person who sits by. Not making unjust war is one thing: but not protecting your fellows (and the reference to "so to speak, colleagues" seems to mean fellow human beings) when you have the resources to do so is another.[29] We readily see this when we think of families, he suggests: for Cicero knows that the average Roman will think that the failure to defend one's family members from attack is a paradigm of bad behavior.[30] But the same is true for larger groupings of our fellow human beings: standing by idle while they get attacked is itself a wrong. There are many reasons why people behave like this: they don't want hard work, they don't want to make enemies, they are simply lazy. But none of these excuses the bad behavior or makes it the blameless innocence it represents itself as being.

Cicero's argument is not wholly satisfactory, because it relies on an antecedent analysis of when a wrong has taken place, or what help from others people have a right to expect. Cicero does not make that background account explicit. And yet he clearly believes that any acceptable such account would entail that failing to prevent a grave harm when one can is itself a wrong, comparable with an active assault. As I have suggested, he relies on a moral tradition in which the failure to defend friends and family is a paradigmatic moral failing. What he does is to extend that account to areas in which people do not usually think such thoughts.

Especially fascinating is Cicero's attack on his own philosophical colleagues. They love what they are doing, and they dislike the idea of getting messed up in politics. So, as Plato imagines, they will have to be forced to take part in the affairs of state. Cicero replies that they do wrong if they do not take part of their own choice. Like misanthropes and obsessive moneymakers, they do harm to humanity by failing to aid it. This theme is of urgent significance to Cicero, who is about to be murdered for having made a different choice, and he returns to it later, saying that such a life of retirement has been chosen by "the noblest and most distinguished philosophers, and also certain strict and serious men who could not bear the conduct of the people or their leaders" (1.69). What they were after is clearly appealing: "They wanted the same thing kings do: to need nothing, to obey nobody, to enjoy their liberty, which is defined as doing as you like." Cicero is even prepared to concede that sometimes that choice may perhaps be blameless – if people have retired because of ill health or "some other very serious reason," and, he now adds, if they have extremely fine minds and are devoting themselves to learning. (Here he seems to go back on what he said about Platonic philosophers, albeit in an uncertain and halfhearted way.)[31] But anyone other than these is surely in the wrong to pursue a life that does not involve service to others through political action.

How does Cicero see the relevance of these observations to his own argument? Clearly he means to blame people who will not serve their own nation, and to defend the life of committed public service. In the earlier passage, he also pretty clearly says that nations (or their citizens) should not stand by when wrong is going on somewhere else. Not to help someone who is being attacked is like deserting your family or friends. Perhaps there is an implicit restriction to conationals and important allies, but I don't think so: the active sort of injustice is defined fully generally, as assault "against anyone" (*in quempiam*), and the ensuing account of the passive sort seems equally broad in its application: when that same anyone is getting attacked, it is unjust to stand by.

Cicero certainly does not elaborate on the duties imposed by the requirement to avoid passive injustice. To whom do these duties belong? In the first instance to nations? To their citizens? To both? How widely do they extend? What is meant by "if you can" (*si potest*)? Does it mean only "if you can without any sacrifice to yourself"? But this reading seems ruled out by his attack on the motives of people who refuse to help because they don't want to incur expense or hard work. Presumably, then, he thinks that people are in the wrong unless they are willing to incur enmity and expense and hard work in order to protect their fellow human beings.

By placing this discussion inside the section on the duties of justice, and by characterizing active injustice as some sort of assault or aggression, Cicero seems to limit the passive sort to warding off actual attacks or assaults. Clearly he does not think that hunger and poverty are the type of assault against which one has duties to protect one's fellows, or else he would have to rewrite completely the section on benevolence. But why not? It seems quite unconvincing to treat the two types of harm asymmetrically. Furthermore, even Cicero's limited point has implications for the topic of benevolence, which he does not notice. For even to protect our neighbors from assault will surely require, as I have argued, massive uses of our own material resources, of a type that he seems to oppose in that later section.

At this point, then, we must part company with Cicero, viewing the discussion of passive injustice as highly suggestive but underdeveloped. Clearly Cicero did not see its importance for his later discussion of benevolence. This is perhaps not surprising, given the speed at which he was writing, with death looming ahead of him, and given his intense focus on justifying the philosopher's choice to serve the public realm.

The important point is that Cicero is right. It is no good to say, "I have done no wrong," if, in fact, what one has done is to sit by when one might have saved fellow human beings. That is true of assault, and it is true of material aid. Failures to aid when one can deserve the same charges Cicero addresses to those who fail to defend: laziness, self-preoccupation, lack of concern. Cicero has let in a consideration that is fatal to his own argument and to its modern descendants.

One more rescue will now be attempted. Cicero, it will be said, is perfectly consistent when he applies his doctrine of passive injustice only to the sphere covered by the "duties of justice." This is so because passive injustice is a failure to ward off *an assault or aggression.* But lack of material goods is not an assault or aggression. Nothing Cicero has said commits him to the view that it is also passive injustice not to supply things that people need in order to live. And, indeed, it seems likely that some such intuitive idea lies behind Cicero's way of arguing here. Moreover, this same intuitive idea is in many modern people's minds when they think of what justifies humanitarian intervention.

Of course, as we have already insisted, even to protect people against assaults takes money. So this distinction cannot really help us defend Cicero's original bifurcation of duties. But let us see whether there is even a limited coherence in Cicero's doctrine, so understood. We may think of assault or aggression in two ways. In one way, assault is something that hits people from outside, through no fault of their own. But in this way of thinking, many natural events look like assaults: floods, famines, depradations of many kinds from animals and the natural world.[32] Cicero lets himself in for this extension by his reliance on the example of

Hercules: for obviously enough, Hercules primarily helped people who were assailed by catastrophes of nonhuman origin: the Nemean lion, the Stymphalian birds, the Hydra, the boar. These are still monsters who commit humanlike assaults, but they remind us that many of the invasions of our well-being that we most fear have a nonhuman origin. And Hercules' monsters obviously have, as well, a mythic significance that makes them emblematic of the way in which ills such as disease and hunger stalk humanity: indeed, the Hydra is an apt metaphor for the ever renewing nature of bodily need.[33] Some of Hercules' labors, furthermore – for example, the descent to the Underworld – have this more general significance directly: Heracles faced death itself, for humanity's sake. In short, Cicero's use of Hercules betrays the fact that he has no clear way of drawing the line between human and nonhuman assaults, or even between assaults by animals and assaults by other malign aspects of the natural world.

We can add that Cicero himself is aware of this larger significance of the figure of Hercules. Indeed, he seems quite fascinated with this character, who, having endured risk to save humanity from various dangers, then found his body devoured by unendurable pain. In the *Tusculan Disputations* (2.20–22), discussing the question whether pain is the greatest of evils (a question on which he ultimately defends the Stoic line that pain is not an evil), Cicero takes time to translate into elegant Latin verse of his own the passage of Sophocles' *Trachiniai* in which Hercules depicts the assaults of the fatal poison upon his organs. This is among the most graphic passages in all of Greek literature in its depiction of bodily pain; the pain is seen as an invasion, akin to an assault. The poison "clinging bites and tears my vital organs and, pressing heavily, drains the breath from my lungs; now it has drunk up all my discolored blood. My body, used up by this terrible conflict, dwindles away."[34] The passage makes it clear that the assaults of monsters were nothing compared with this one. It seems fair for us to remind Cicero of this passage, given his evident fascination with it.

Suppose, however, we think of assault as *iniuria*, another person's wrongful act. The text suggests this, clearly. Then we may be able to let Cicero off the hook concerning animals and natural catastrophes – though it is still not terribly clear why, from the victim's viewpoint, such a line should be considered salient. Have we now given him a consistent way of maintaining that there is no passive injustice when people are hungry and impoverished, and so on? I believe not. For obviously enough, we cannot assume that their hunger and poverty is not caused

by another person or persons' wrongful act. Given that hunger is typically caused not so much by food shortage as by lack of entitlement to
food, it is a thoroughly human business, in which the arrangements of
society are profoundly implicated.[35] With poverty, this is even clearer. Just
because it is difficult to decide whom to blame, that does not mean that
no wrongful act has occurred and that no response need be made. Most
nations have the capacity to feed all their people, if they had a just system
of entitlements. Where war is concerned, we sometimes understand that
we can judge a wrong has taken place without being exactly clear on who
did it: we don't always require that there be an easily recognizable "bad
guy" such as Hitler or Saddam Hussein or Milosevic, before we undertake an act of humanitarian intervention, or declare war on a nation that
has wronged another (though clearly the presence of such a "bad guy"
gets Americans going more easily – witness the failure to intervene in the
genocide in Rwanda).

Moreover, we should at least consider that some of the wrongdoers
may be ourselves. Through aid, we can feed all the world's people; we
just don't. Of course, in the context of the present argument it would
be question begging to assert that the failure to give material aid across
national borders is *iniuria*. So too, however, would be the assertion that
our failure to aid involves no *iniuria*. At the very least, we should concede
that the question of our own moral rectitude has not been resolved.

On any understanding of the distinction between aggression and
nonaggression, then, Cicero's refusal to extend his analysis of "passive
injustice" to failures to give material aid looks unconvincing. If aggression is catastrophe, there are many natural and social catastrophes that
have no clear "bad guy"; if aggression is wrongful action, there is almost
certain to be wrongful action afoot, when people are starving and in
deep poverty, even though we cannot easily say whose wrongful action it
is. And, yet, most of us do continue to think in something like Cicero's
way, feeling that it is incumbent on us (maybe) to save people from thugs
and bad guys but not incumbent on us to save them from the equally
aggressive depradations of hunger, poverty, and disease. Hercules knew
better.

I have argued that Cicero's distinction is not fully coherent, even to
one who accepts the Stoic doctrine. And yet it also gets a lot of mileage
from that doctrine, because Stoic moral theory permits us to salve our
conscience about our failure to aid our distant fellows, telling ourselves
that no serious harm has befallen them. Let us, therefore, turn our attention to that doctrine.

The Falsity of the Stoic Doctrine

The Stoic view about external goods has been lurking around, providing a motivation for some of Cicero's arguments, a consolation in connection with others. But insofar as Cicero, or his modern descendants, would be disposed to reply by appealing to the Stoic doctrine that external goods are unnecessary for the good human life, we must now say that this doctrine is false. People do indeed have amazing powers of resistance and a dignity that can frequently surmount the blows of fortune. But this does not mean that these blows are unimportant. Moreover, they profoundly affect the very parts of the person that are of greatest interest to the Stoics: mentality, moral power, the power to form confirming associations with other human beings. The Stoic position seems to be: either these things are external blows, in which case they don't touch what really matters, or they are the result of some moral weakness in the person, in which case they do matter but the person herself is to blame. But this is a false dichotomy: the fact that moral character can sometimes survive the blows of fortune unaffected does not show that the blows of fortune do not deeply affect it, or that any such effect is the result of weak or bad character. The surmounter of fortune is an exception that does not show the moral culpability of those who yield to depression and hopelessness. Moreover, such a surmounter is very likely to have had the goods of fortune in at least some measure at some time: a good enough home in childhood, parents who nourished self-regard, and good enough nutrition when crucial faculties are developing.

Do we need to say this? Is there any danger that our modern Ciceronians will avail themselves of such a self-evidently false doctrine? I fear that there is. On another occasion I would be prepared to argue that Adam Smith's account of the operations of the market, in *The Wealth of Nations*, is deeply in the grip of the false doctrine: he is prepared to let the market do its worst with little constraint, partly because he believes that the poor don't suffer at their very core and retain a dignity that life's blows cannot remove. And, more important, many modern defenders of the market have a similar belief: that poverty does not really affect the will, and that, when we see the will affected, it must consequently be the result of personal weakness or failure. This is the Stoics' false dichotomy: either unimportant or in the control of will. Thus, as we know too well, poverty is often treated as a moral failing, even by people who would not so treat the damages done to a person by rape or torture or even racial discrimination. In the area of the duties of material aid, Stoicism lives on.

When differences between nations are at issue, differences that really do seem too large to be a matter of indifference, such modern Stoics can't quite bring themselves to blame each and every individual citizen of those nations for being shiftless and lazy. But then a substitute is quickly found: blame of the nation, or the people, for sluggishness or bad planning, or stupid management of their economy. Thus, for example, one frequently hears India's poverty blamed on its socialist government, instead of the despoiliation of resources and the damage to self-rule inflicted by years of empire. Of course it is not precisely false that India has made some foolish moves in the management of its economy. These include excessive reliance on a socialist bureaucracy in general economic matters; but they also include failures to take strong government action in matters of health and education, and basic protections of liberty and safety.[36] What even the toughest critics of the Indian state should grant, however, is that other nations are to blame in many ways for the current miserable situation. Insisting on the falsity of Stoic doctrine is a first necessary step to placing these important issues on the table.

The Stoic false dichotomy has deep roots and is not so easy to evade. For we do not want to treat human beings as simply the passive recipients of whatever nature dishes out. We want to say, with Kant and the Stoics, that there is a dignity that shines out even when nature has done its worst. Indeed, if we do not say this, we are in danger of losing the very basis for claims of aid: for if there is no longer a human being there, but simply a substance that has been pushed around in various ways by life, we no longer know why we have stringent duties to support that substance. Thus we need to be able to say that there is something about human beings that persists throughout the blows of chance, supplying us with a basis for our moral duties – and that this something is equal, providing a basis for attitudes of equal respect and concern – and yet, also, that the things that matter to human life can be deeply affected. I believe that the Stoics get into difficulty on this point precisely because they are so determined to insist that the basis for moral duties is never effaced by life's contingencies and hierarchies. Like their predecessors the Cynics, they want to say that wealth, rank, birth, freeborn status, ethnicity, nationality, and even sex are all morally irrelevant, in the sense that they do not create differences in fundamental human worth. But, like the Cynics, they think that maintaining this requires maintaining, as well, that free status, citizenship, wealth, and the like matter not at all for the things that are most important in life. They seem to be afraid that, if they did admit the importance of external goods, they would be in danger, once again, of creating plural races of human beings, with different degrees of dignity.[37] Because they are determined to insist that all humanity is equal, they refuse to acknowledge the depth at which humanity can be deformed by circumstances.

There is no easy solution to this dilemma, and it affects us every time we want to talk about poverty or social injustice. For we want to portray the claim of human dignity, and yet to insist that human dignity can itself be defiled by life. We should not solve this problem by the Stoic device of saying that the damages of luck do not affect the part of a human being that is the source of human worth. But then how should we proceed, if we also don't want to say that luck has turned these humans into mere animals? Here, I believe, we need to operate with a flexible multileveled notion of human capability. We should say that the innate power to de- velop higher-level human capacities is the source of our moral duties to others but that this power can be thwarted in development, so that the more developed forms (of reasoning, moral character, sociability, and so forth) never fully mature, or are blocked in expression.[38] To give a turtle a merely animal level of life is morally permissible; to give a human be- ing (someone with those basic powers) a merely animal level of living, in which characteristic human powers of choice and sociability are starved, is immoral and impermissible. Much more can be said about this central issue, but we can see that the Stoic view is no easily dismissed absurdity; nor has modern moral thought come to a satisfactory consensus on how to handle the issue.

WHAT IS LEFT?

We have removed some of the main props for Cicero's distinction of duties into two kinds, one strict and one less strict. Let us now consider his remaining arguments.

A great advantage of Cicero's discussion is that it does not simply as- sume that national boundaries are of obvious moral relevance; nor does he rely on mysterious ideas of blood and belonging that frequently sub- stitute for argument in these matters. Instead, he believes that we need to point to some feature or features of our fellow citizens that justify dif- ferential treatment. Indeed, even in the case of family he does not fall back on an allegedly obvious relevance of consanguinity: perhaps the prevalence of adoption of heirs in the Roman middle and upper classes helps him avoid a pitfall of some modern discussions. So although I am critical of some of his specific arguments, I think we should applaud their general direction: nationality in and of itself supplies no sufficient moral argument for a difference of duties. Nation, and indeed family, are proxies for other morally significant characteristics.[39] But once we make this step, the door is wide open to asking whether these features really do coincide with conationality or with shared family membership; other people situated elsewhere may possibly share with our conationals the relevant features. Thus most of my criticisms of Cicero in this section take advantage of an avenue of debate opened up by Cicero himself.

Property Rights

Cicero will insist that there is a fundamental part of justice itself that has implications for material redistribution. For, as we recall, he defined justice partly in terms of respect for property rights, understood as justified by the luck of existing distributions. He argued that once property is appropriated, no matter how, taking it away is the gravest kind of violation. Clearly it is his purpose to use that argument to oppose any state-mandated redistributive policies, such as Caesar's attempts at land reform. But this argument has implications for the entire issue of benevolence: for if I have a right to something, and it is egregiously bad for someone to take it away from me, then it would seem peculiar to say that I even have a strict *moral* duty to give it away to someone else.

Thus modern Ciceronians might grant everything I have said about the unfortunate problems in Cicero's distinction of duties and yet hold that property rights are so extremely important that by themselves they justify making the duties of benevolence at best imperfect duties. I believe that both Richard Epstein and Robert Nozick would take this line.

On the other hand, any such thinker who starts off from Cicero is bound to notice the thinness and arbitrariness of his account of these rights. Why should it actually be the case that "each should hold what falls to the share of each, and if anyone takes anything from this, he violates the law of human association"? Why not say, instead, that such claims to ownership are always provisional, to be adjudicated along with claims of need? By emphasizing need himself, as a legitimate source of moral claims, Cicero has left himself wide open to this objection.

Here we should say that Cicero's highly partisan politicking distorts his philosophy. His Stoic forebears, as he well knows, thought all property should be held in common;[40] he himself has staked his entire career on an opposition to any redistributive takings. That he skates rather rapidly over the whole issue of how property rights come into being, neglecting to consider alternative accounts, is no accident. But the modern reader needs to pause. By now in the history of philosophy we have too many different competing accounts of property rights to be at all satisfied by the thin account that Cicero (and Nozick 1974) hand us, unless some compelling argument is given as to why we should prefer that account to other available accounts.[41]

Gratitude for Nurture

A stronger and more interesting argument is Cicero's contention that citizens owe gratitude for their nurture to parents, relatives, and especially the republic. This gives them reasons to give their resources to those who have expended resources on them. This argument offers a good justification for at least some asymmetry in our duties of material aid. It seems unlikely, however, that it justifies Cicero's conclusion that we only have duties to people at a distance when it costs us absolutely nothing – a conclusion that modern Ciceronians eagerly embrace.

Need and Dependency

Another good argument Cicero makes is that some people depend on us in a very personal way. Our own children, for example, have needs that only we are likely to be able to meet well. In addition to those intimate needs, I think he is saying, they also have expectations of material aid that only we are likely to meet, and in that way, if we let them down, they are likely to suffer greatly.

Several things in this argument seem right. It seems right that some duties to children can be met only in a context of intimacy; something similar probably holds for fellow citizens, whose knowledge of one another's history and goals helps them relate well in political life. But it seems questionable whether the duties of material aid are like this. Of course, giving money is often done obtusely, and money, to be wisely used, needs to be used with knowledge of local circumstances. But that is a different point. The *need* for money can in principle be met by getting resources from abroad, so long as the actual user is intelligent about the local scene. Perhaps parents should give love and attention to their own children, but a lot of their money to international welfare agencies, and similarly for fellow citizens.

As to Cicero's point that the children rely on our material aid and would be bereft without it, we can say that this is an artifact of current arrangements and can hardly be used to justify current arrangements. It seems likely that a good way of organizing the care of children will involve a certain measure of parental responsibility and parental control over resources; similarly, a good way of organizing citizenship will almost surely involve various forms of local responsibility and local control. But as to how much, and whether this is at all incompatible with strong duties of transnational redistribution, Cicero has said nothing.

We might even grant to Cicero that families are usually the best performers of duties to children, and that nations, similarly, are the best protectors of various interests of citizens – without treating these duties as special duties in any deep or fundamental way. That is, we may see the so-called special duties as good ways of channeling the general duties we have to other humans worldwide. This seems to have been the position of the original Greek Stoics; it is also Adam Smith's position in at least some very important passages.[42] Whether this is the correct position about either nations or families requires further argument. My point is that Cicero has said nothing here to rule it out.

Thick Fellowship

Cicero's most interesting claim for the republic is that our participation in it makes claims on our human faculties that other more distant associations do not. We share in speech and reason in a variety of ways when we associate with our fellow citizens, thus confirming and developing our humanity in relation to them. This is not the case with the foreign national, unless that person is a guest on our soil. For this reason, Cicero thinks, we owe the republic more material aid than we do to foreign nations and nationals. The idea is presumably that we have reasons to make sure that the institutions that support and confirm our humanity prosper.

One might complain, first, that Cicero's point was already of dubious validity in his own time, because already Rome had complex civic and political ties with many parts of the world, and non-Italians were not yet, though some of them later became, Roman citizens. His son was off studying philosophy in Greece; his philosophical descendant Seneca was soon to be born in Spain. North Africa, Gaul, and Germany, though often crudely caricatured in imperialist writings,[43] were known to be the homes of people with whom Romans had many forms of cultural and human exchange. So citizenship and fellowship were not coextensive even then.

In our day, when we develop and exercise our human powers, we are increasingly associating with people elsewhere. Networks such as the international women's movement may supply people with some of their most fundamental confirming associations. So even if Cicero had made a good argument for the restriction of our duties, it would be less weighty today than formerly.

But thinking about international networks today shows us some reasons why we should doubt Cicero's argument. That is, why should it be the case that only those people who have already managed to join an international network have duties of material aid to people in other nations? Ignorance and neglect are, it would appear, their own justification. If, like all too many Americans, I manage my life in such a way that I have minimal knowledge of and contact with any other part of the world, I am thereby absolved of any duties to that world. This cannot be right.

Nor does the argument seem persuasive in any case as an argument about material resources. It might be that the networks I am in claim a larger proportion of my time, or my attention, or my work. But my money? Why should the fact that I share forms of life with my fellow citizens mean that I should deprive some child in India of a chance to live? The connections are too undeveloped for Cicero's argument to persuade.

Accountability

We might read Cicero's previous argument to make, as well, the following point. Our own republic is ours. One of the forms of association that we share, in that fine institution of the republic that Cicero is struggling to preserve, is mutual accountability, as well as accountability of public policy to citizens. This might be said to give us some reasons to use our money on a form of government that had this desirable feature. Does it give us reasons to support republican government all over the world, or does it give us special reasons to focus our material aid on our own? Here we might combine the accountability point with the points about need, dependency, and gratitude, and say that our own has an especially strong claim on our resources.

I think that there is something in this argument. But it also suggests that at least some of our resources might be well used in supporting other instances of republican government. Its main point is that institutions of a certain type are good protectors of people, because of their responsiveness to people's voices: this makes them good ways of channeling duties of aid. But once again, this is compatible with the duties themselves being fully general.[44] Certainly the argument does not get us anywhere near to Cicero's strong conclusion that no aid outside the nation is morally required if that will be even minimally costly.

In short, Cicero has some decent arguments that justify a partial asymmetry in our material duties: the arguments from gratitude, need, association, and accountability all do at least some work. But none justifies his radical confinement of duties to the interior of the republic. Another consideration, both in his day and now, is surely playing a part.

The Difficulty of Assigning the Duties

Implicit in Cicero's argument is a consideration he never fully develops: it is just too difficult to assign the relevant duties, once we get beyond the boundaries of the republic. Within the compass of the republic, we have a pretty good understanding of who owes what to whom. But once we start thinking internationally, it all seems quite bewildering and even hopeless. There are too many needy recipients, and there are all the many different levels of both giver and receiver: persons, groups, nongovernmental organizations, governments. As Cicero remarks: "[T]he resources of individuals are limited, and the needy are an unlimited horde [*infinita multitudo*]." How can we possibly say to whom we owe the finite resources we have, unless we do draw the line at our friends and fellow nationals?

This problem is not recognized for the duties of justice because we imagine we can can give respect and truthfulness and nonrape and nontorture and nonaggression to everyone, and there is no difficult distributional problem (until we start thinking of really supporting these policies with money!). Justice looks as if it can be universally distributed without cash; material aid obviously cannot. I've argued that this is a false asymmetry, but if we attack the asymmetry we are then left with the problem of assigning the relevant duties for all transnational duties, and thus we have made things harder and not easier.

I have no answers to these tough questions here. To answer them well will require working out theories of institutional versus individual responsibility,[45] and theories of just transfer between nations.[46] We don't yet have such theories, although we have good accounts of many aspects of them. We also will need to get clearer about what those duties require: equality, a Rawlsian difference principle, a substantial threshold level of basic goods? Again, we have refined alternatives before us in the domestic case, but only sketches at the transnational level. What is clear, however, is that the difficulty of these problems does not mean that we should fall back on the Ciceronian doctrine, with its multiple evasions. It means that we should continue our work.

Notes

1. All data in this paragraph are from United Nations Development Program 1998.
2. Most such theories take their start from the classical utilitarian tradition; an influential recent statement is Singer 1972; see also Kagan 1989 and Murphy 1993. Murphy has pursued these issues further in Murphy 2000. Another effort in this tradition – less successful, I believe – is Unger 1996. On limits to these personal duties of benevolence, see Nagel 1991 and Scheffler 1982.
3. Beitz 1979; Pogge 1989. For promising combinations of institutional and personal duties, see Goodin 1988; Shue 1988; Nagel 1991; see also Shue 1980; Goodin 1985.
4. A salient example, much discussed, is Rawls 1993.
5. On Kant's debt to Cicero, see Nussbaum 1997.
6. I translate the Latin of the *De Officiis* myself throughout, starting from Michael Winterbottom's excellent Oxford Classical Text (Cicero 1994). The best translation is in the excellent annotated version of the work by Miriam Griffin and Eileen Atkins (Cicero 1991). See also the commentary on the work by Andrew R. Dyck (1996).
7. By count of my research assistant Chad Flanders, ninety citations or close paraphrases of *De Officiis* in Grotius' *De Iure Belli atque Pacis*, eighty in Pufendorf's *De Iure Naturae et Gentium* (1688); most of these citations are to the portions of the work I am about to discuss. Both authors are also extremely fond of Seneca. (*Caveat lector*: some English translations, especially of Grotius, omit many of the citations, feeling that the text is top-heavy with them.) For Grotius' tremendous influence on the foundations of modern international law, see Lauterpacht 1946; on Kant's influence, see Tesón 1992: 53, 55. Grotius, and the closely related arguments of Vattel and Bynkershoek, all had a major influence on eighteenth- and nineteenth-century jurisprudence in the United States. A LEXIS search shows 74 U.S. Supreme Court cases that refer to Grotius, 176 that refer to Vattel, and 39 that refer to Bynkershoek, all before 1900; the reliance on these texts seems to be genuiine. (Search of LEXIS, Genfed Library, US File, January 1998: I owe this information to my colleague Jack Goldsmith, who informs me that a similar reliance is evident in diplomatic correspondence and political argument.)
8. Adam Smith, *The Theory of Moral Sentiments* (Smith 1982: first edition 1759, sixth edition 1790), III.3.6: "[A]nd who does not inwardly feel the truth of that great stoical maxim, that for one man to deprive another unjustly of any thing, or unjustly to promote his own advantage by the loss or disadvantage of another, is more contrary to nature, than death, than poverty, than pain, than all the misfortunes which can affect him, either in his body, or in his external circumstances." This, as will be seen, is a verbatim citation of III.21.

9. See *Perpetual Peace*, "Third Definitive Article of a Perpetual Peace: Cosmopolitan Right Shall Be Limited to Conditions of Universal Hospitality," p. 106 in Kant 1991:

> If we compare with this ultimate end the *inhospitable* conduct of the civilised states of our continent, especially the commercial states, the injustice which they display in *visiting* foreign countries and peoples (which in their case is the same as *conquering* them) seems appallingly great. America, the negro countries, the Spice Islands, the Cape, etc. were looked upon at the time of their discovery as ownerless territories; for the native inhabitants were counted as nothing. In East India (Hindustan), foreign troops were brought in under the pretext of merely setting up trading posts. This led to oppression of the natives, incitement of the various Indian states to widespread wars, famine, insurrection, treachery, and the whole litany of evils which can afflict the human race. . . . And all this is the work of powers who make endless ado about their piety, and who wish to be considered as chosen believers while they live on the fruits of iniquity.

10. Appiah 1996:23. Appiah actually says "Cicero and the Bible," but in this context there is only one text of Cicero that is likely to have had this privileged place.

11. I so translate *iniuria*; one should avoid saying "injustice," so that the definition does not seem circular, but also avoid saying something morally neutral, like "provocation," since *iniuria* clearly means something morally inappropriate.

12. There is a textual problem here, and Winterbottom obelizes the first half of this sentence; but the sense – not the argument! – seems clear.

13. The example of Regulus is very important to Cicero in *De Officiis*: he discusses it at greater length at 3.99–111, arguing against various people who would try to reconcile the conflict between virtue and expediency, or to urge that Regulus ought to have followed expediencey. Marcus Atilius Regulus, a prominent Roman politician and military leader, was captured by the Carthaginians in 255 B.C. Later he was sent to Rome to negotiate a peace (or, in some versions, the return of Carthaginian prisoners); he promised to return after executing his mission. When he arrived, he urged the Senate to decline the peace terms; but he kept his promise to return. The story goes that he was placed in the sunlight with his eyelids stapled open, dying an excruciating death by both starvation and enforced sleeplessness. (Sources characterize the torture in various ways, but all agree on the exceedingly painful character of the death, *exquisita supplicia*, as Cicero says [3.100] and compare the summary of the lost book 18 of Livy; for other references in Cicero and elsewhere, see Dyck 1996: 619–20.) Romans considered Regulus' story a salient example of honorable behavior, definitive of a national norm of virtue (see Horace *Odes* 3.5), although modern scholars note that the story may have been invented to defuse criticism of torture of Carthaginian prisoners at Rome (see Howard Hayes Scullard, "Regulus," *Oxford Classical Dictionary*, 2nd ed. [Oxford: Oxford University Press, 1970], 911, and the briefer article in the 3rd ed. [1966]: Andrew Drummond, "Atilius Regulus, Marcus," (207); they follow Polybius in holding that Regulus died in Carthaginian captivity and never went on an embassy to Rome (see Dyck 1996: 619). Horace's use of the story is exceedingly colonialistic and chauvinistic, with vilification

of the *barbarus tortor* and praise of the *virilis voltus* (manly face) of the hero, the chaste kisses of his proper Roman wife. (The context in which the story is introduced is anxiety about the dilution of warlike Roman blood by intermarriage with barbarian peoples.) Cicero standardly uses the story as an example of the victory of virtue over expediency: see also *De Finibus*, defending the Stoic ideal of virtue against Epicurean hedonism: "Virtue cries out that, even while tortured by sleeplessness and hunger, he was happier than Thorius getting drunk on his bed of roses" (2.65). In more recent times, the example, however extreme, still fascinates. Turner's painting *Regulus* is notorious for containing, it would appear, no representation of the central figure; the reason is that the viewer is placed in the position of Regulus, struck again and again by a hammering implacable sun.

14. It is quite unclear in what sense death and pain could be said to be contrary to nature; even to a Stoic, for whom the cosmos is thoroughly good, death itself will therefore have to be understood as a good, when it occurs. And Stoics energetically opposed the thesis that pain is intrinsically bad. Eric Brown suggests that the Stoics can defuse this problem by distinguishing two viewpoints: from the point of view of Providence, nothing is contrary to nature; from a local viewpoint, things like death are contrary to nature, in the sense that they mean the end of some natural organism. I am not sure: for the local perspective is not accurate, according to a strict Stoic account. Marcus and other writers insist again and again that we must meditate on the naturalness of our own death.

15. Reich 1939.

16. See Dyck 1996: 529: "The example of Hercules, a pan-Hellenic hero, breaks down the boundaries of individual states and emphasizes the common needs and interests of all human kind." He compares *Tusculan Disputations* 1.28 and *De Finibus* 3.65–66.

17. See Nussbaum 1997.

18. Probably Cicero does not allow quite as much latitude as does Kant: for the requirement that we become *boni ratiocinatores officiorum* suggests that we must learn to perform refined calculations, and that it is not simply up to us how they turn out. (I owe this observation to Eric Brown.)

19. See Nussbaum 1995.

20. Given that elsewhere Cicero prefers a position that ascribes a tiny bit of value to externals, though the preponderant amount to virtue, he may waver in this work between that position (which would make it easier to justify duties of material aid to our fellow citizens) and the stricter Stoic position.

21. Seneca, *Moral Epistle* 47.

22. See Treggiari 1991. The relevant law is the famous (or infamous) *Lex Iulia de Adulteriis*, passed by Augustus in the first century in an alleged attempt to restore the pristine mores of former times – although, as Treggiari persuasively argues, it is actually much more severe than either legal or social norms that prevailed during Cicero's lifetime. Even this severe law did not restrict sexual access of male owners to their slaves – and, as Musonius comments, public norms generally endorsed such conduct. Adultery was conceived of as a property offense against the husband or father of the woman in question.

23. See my "Musonius Rufus: Platonist, Stoic, and Roman," in Nussbaum and
    Sihvola 2002. I argue there that Musonius' position is actually more conser-
    vative than Seneca's: it does not claim that the slave has any right to respectful
    treatment; it treats the sex act as a problem of overindulgence for the free
    owner, rather than a problem of disrespect for the slave.
24. See Griffin 1992: ch. 8, 256–85.
25. A significant attempt to break down the distinction, in connection with think-
    ing about which duties to others are most urgent, is Shue 1980. See also
    Gewirth 1996 for argument that what should be considered in both cases is
    the prerequisites of human agency, and that both the "duties of justice" and
    the "duties of material aid" involve important prerequisites of agency. Also
    Gewirth 1985.
26. See Holmes and Sunstein 1999.
27. Recall George Bernard Shaw's similar remark to a rich society woman on the
    topic of prostitution. As legend has it, he asked her whether she would marry
    him if he had a million pounds: amused, she said yes. He then asked whether
    she would sleep with him for five pounds. She exclaimed, "Mr. Shaw, what
    kind of a woman do you think I am?" He replied, "We have already established
    that: now we're just haggling about the price."
28. See Shue 1980: 107–9, citing Wassily Leontief's claims about the relatively
    low cost of providing basic material support.
29. See the interesting discussion of this part of Cicero's view in Shklar 1990.
30. See Seneca, *De Ira* 1.12, where the interlocutor objects that the nonangry
    person will not be able to avenge the murder of a father or the rape of a
    mother, and Seneca hastens to reassure him that these central moral acts
    can all be done without anger.
31. Compare Seneca's *De Otio*, where he argues that the philosopher who does
    not enter public life may be able to serve the public better through philo-
    sophical insights: "We definitely hold that Zeno and Chrysippus did greater
    deeds than if they had led armies, won honors, and written laws: they wrote
    laws not for one nation but for the whole human race" (6). But Seneca's
    position is much more retirement-friendly than Cicero's.
32. See Landis 1998. Landis argues that Americans have always been reluctant to
    give relief unless they believe the person to have been the victim of something
    like a natural disaster, that comes on them from outside; in a dissertation in
    progress, she argues that Roosevelt understood this, and used the rhetoric
    of natural disaster to mobilize aid during the Depression. Even the term
    "The Depression" positioned an economic catastrophe as a quasi-flood or
    hurricane.
33. For a related myth used to exemplify this point about the bodily appetites,
    see Plato's account of the Danaids who had to carry water in a sieve, in *Gorgias*
    494.
34. O multa dictu gravia, perpessu aspera,
    Quae corpore exanclata atque animo pertuli....
    Haec me irretivit veste furiali inscium,
    Quae lateri inhaerens morsu lacerat viscera

Urguensque graviter pulmonum haurit spiritus:
Iam decolorem sanginem omnem exsorbuit.
Sic corpus clade horribili absumptum extabuit.

35. See Sen 1981.
36. See Sen and Drèze 1995.
37. Compare the closely related observations of Chomsky in Chomsky 1966, when he notes that empiricist theories that see the human being as a product of its circumstances have frequently been linked with racism and social hierarchy, while Cartesian rationalism insists that all human beings are fundamentally equal in worth.
38. See Nussbaum 2000, ch.1.
39. See Goodin 1998; Shue 1980: 135–37, 142–45.
40. For the relevant texts, see Schofield 1999.
41. Cicero, of course, is much worse than Nozick, because he doesn't even require a legitimate starting point and has no theory of just transfer.
42. See Smith 1982, VII.iii: "Of Universal Benevolence." For a related view, see Goodin 1988 and my lead essay in Nussbaum 2002.
43. On Horace's depiction of the Carthaginians, see note 14. Tacitus' *Germania* is a good example of the extremes of this tendency under the empire, but it was already afoot during the republic.
44. See, similarly, Shue 1980: 145–47. In Shue 1988, Shue notes that general duties of this sort will not be in the strict sense perfect duties, since they will take the form that I have a duty to aid either X or someone relevantly like X. But a duty of this type may nonetheless be highly stringent.
45. Unpublished work by Michael Green seems to me to get us going on this question in a more promising way than any other work I know.
46. Both Henry Shue and Thomas Pogge have made very promising outlines of such theories. Shue seems to me correct in his insistence that, although at a deep level, all duties are duties of persons to other persons, institutions play a crucial role of mediating those duties, both for reasons of efficiency and for reasons of respite; see also Nagel 1991.

12

Stoic Emotion

Lawrence C. Becker

A successful rehabilitation of Stoic ethics will have to defeat the idea that there is something deeply wrong, and perhaps even psychologically impossible, about the kind of emotional life that Stoics recommend. The image of the austere, dispassionate, detached, tranquil, and virtually affectless sage – an image destined to be self-refuting – has become a staple of anti-Stoic philosophy, literature, and popular culture. It has been constructed from incautious use of the ancient texts and is remarkably resistant to correction. Reminders that the ancient Stoics insisted that there are good emotions are typically brushed aside by asserting that the ancient catalog of such emotions is peculiar;[1] that the emotions in even that peculiar catalog are not accorded much significance by Stoics; and that the ruthless emotional therapy practiced by Epictetus is a reliable guide to the sort of emotional life Stoics want all of us to cultivate – namely, a life of desiccated affect and discardable attachments.

Both Stoics and anti-Stoics alike have developed an unwholesome fascination with a picture of the Stoic sage drawn for extreme circumstances. We persist, in high art and low journalism, in telling and retelling stories of good people who resolutely endure horrors – injustice, torture, disease, disability, and suffering. Those of us who are attracted to Stoicism

This is a revised version of a paper presented at the Second Leroy E. Loemker Conference, "Stoicism: Traditions and Transformations," 31 March–2 April 2000, at Emory University. I am grateful to the participants at the conference for their helpful discussion. Special acknowledgment goes to Tony Long, Brad Inwood, and Richard Sorabji. A much earlier version of the paper was presented at a Stoicism conference at the University of London, in May 1999. I am grateful to the justifiably more skeptical audience at that occasion, and particularly to my commentator, Anthony Price, as well as to Richard Sorabji and Gisela Striker.

often find such stories inspiring, and even anti-Stoics give them grudging admiration.[2] But our fascination with them can be seriously misleading. It can cause us to treat the emotional remoteness and austerity exhibited by their heroes as central to the Stoic *theory* of good emotion, as opposed to something central merely to its traditional therapies for people in extremis. This is a mistake.

Rather, as I argue here, Stoic ethical *theory* entails only that we make our emotions appropriate, by making sure that the beliefs implicit in them are true, and by making them good for, or at least consistent with, the development and exercise of virtue – that is, with the perfection of the activity of rational agency. At this very abstract level, a Stoic theory of emotion is similar to an Aristotelian one. But we should not be misled by this high-altitude similarity. Stoic theories of value and virtue are very different from their Aristotelian counterparts, so it will turn out that what counts as an appropriate Stoic emotion in a given case is often strikingly different from what counts as an appropriate Aristotelian one. But the central, high-altitude theoretical point is nonetheless important. Robust psychological health of the sort necessary for appropriate rational activity is a constitutive element of virtuoso rational agency – a constitutive element of Stoic virtue. It thus follows that, insofar as emotion is a necessary element of this aspect of psychological health, it is necessary for virtue.

It may be true that some ancient Stoics (notably Chrysippus) underestimated the extent to which emotion was a necessary component of psychological health and thus of virtue. But that is a matter of getting the facts straight, and surely all Stoics are committed to getting an adequate, accurate psychology as a basis for their normative account of good emotion. The things that Chrysippus said about the heart being the seat of consciousness – things ridiculed centuries later by Galen[3] – are surely errors that Chrysippus himself would have wanted corrected. Not ridiculed, but corrected. And if such errors informed his normative judgments, surely he would not only have corrected his errors about physiology but also have made the necessary adjustments in his normative views.

The obvious way to develop a contemporary version of Stoicism with respect to the emotions is therefore to fasten on what the theory requires – that is, on the conceptual relation between virtue and emotion in human beings – and on what the best contemporary psychology says about how such matters work out in practice. That is what I will do here, first by looking at some relevant features of empirical psychology, then by considering the value of emotions in human life, and finally by examining the nature of sagelike tranquillity and Stoic love.

THE NATURE OF EMOTION

Psychologists who study emotion have not yet developed a standard line of analysis of their subject, or even a standard nomenclature. I do not mean to suggest that the literature is chaotic; far from it. But it is difficult to summarize, because it is difficult to line up the accounts given by various writers. Much depends on the level of analysis – whether one is speaking of the neurophysiological substrate of emotion (i.e., the activity of certain discrete anatomical structures in the brain stem and limbic brain),[4] the more generalized physiology of emotional arousal (e.g., changes in blood chemistry and blood flow, pupillary dilation, galvanic skin response, muscle tension),[5] the interaction between these physiological states and cognitive responses to them,[6] or the phenomenology of emotional states as reported by human subjects during the treatment of their emotional disorders.[7] In order to stay in contact with both Stoic theory and the full range of contemporary psychological accounts, it seems wisest here to situate the discussion first within what might be called commonsense phenomenology and then to pay special attention to both the cognitive content and the physiology of the states that we ordinarily describe and experience as emotional ones.

Complexity: Affect, Sensation, Cognition, and Conation

As we commonly use the term, emotions have analytically distinct components, which may or may not be distinct phenomenologically. Unless we are simply going to construct a technical definition, then (e.g., by insisting, implausibly, that various emotions are *identical* to various constellations of beliefs, or gross somatic changes, or neurophysiological processes), we shall have to recognize the ways in which at least four elements configure emotional experience – elements we may call affect, sensation, cognition, and conation. To see this, consider the following bit of commonsense phenomenology.

There is a difference between emotional and nonemotional belief. For example, I can hold the beliefs ordinarily implicated in a given emotion without "feeling" one way or the other about the state of affairs those beliefs represent – that is, without being in a state we would ordinarily identify as emotional. I can believe that I am in mortal danger, for instance, and that things are going to turn out very badly for me, with no countervailing good results for anyone, and still have a "flat affect" about it. (Affect is difficult to define, but it may be enough for present purposes to think of it as varying levels of attention, alertness, readiness,

energized arousal, pro, con, or mixed valuational attitudes, and perhaps
a second-level awareness of that awareness.) This point about flat affect
seems true no matter how specific and value-laden one makes the beliefs:
in each case the believer may or may not be in a significant affective state
with respect to what the beliefs represent.[8] So whether or not beliefs are
necessary elements of all emotion, they are never sufficient for it. Affect
is a necessary element also, and it may come close to being a sufficient
element at the extremes of mood and passion.

Further, some affective experience is coupled with an awareness of
somatic phenomena – flushed face, racing heart, sweating, tightness in
the throat, tears, tumescence, and so forth. We can get, and be aware
of, such sensations without having the beliefs and affect requisite for a
full-fledged emotion. Whiskey can produce a flushed face; slicing onions
can produce tears. Moreover, we can have intense emotional experience
without the awareness of such somatic changes. Think of a person who
lacks sensation from the chin down, and thus literally cannot feel the hair
on the back of his neck stand up when it does, or his nipples go erect
when they do. So having the physical sensations characteristic of various
emotions is neither necessary nor sufficient for having the emotions. That
is why attempts to study emotion by studying facial expression, galvanic
skin response, vegal tone, pupillary dilation, and so forth seem indirect
at best.

Finally, we may make a similar point about conation – understood
as the orientation or urge to act that is often characteristic of emotion.
The point is that conation does not always track emotion. One may be
"paralyzed" by fear as well as set in motion by it. Diminished conation is as
characteristic of some emotional states (ranging from blissful tranquillity
to depression) as heightened conation is characteristic of some others.

It thus seems best to treat full-fledged emotion in adult human beings
as a complex phenomenon: affect, laden with beliefs, and sometimes
laden with sensation or conation. In part because we want to assess Stoic
claims about the way beliefs control emotion, it seems best to think of
emotions as special sorts of affective states rather than special sorts of
belief states.[9]

Moods, Feelings, Emotions, and Passions

Now suppose we distinguish four sorts of affective states, again considering them at first only in a commonsense, phenomenological way. Let us
call them moods, feelings, emotions, and passions. Although they differ

along several dimensions, we can for convenience imagine them as arranged along a line that forms a nearly closed circle, beginning and ending with more or less "pure" affect. At one end are "moods" or affective "tones" of various types (fleeting or prolonged, volatile or stable, discrete or diffuse, mild or intense), which begin at a point just discernibly different from no affect at all – a point at which, for example, a subject will report that consciousness is simply tinted or tinged with affect that does not seem to have a causal connection to either cognition or action, or to be related to any special physical sensation or somatic phenomena, or to be focused on anything in particular. Nonetheless, even the mildest, most fleeting moods can often be described in terms of quite complex subjective experience (anxious, secure, erotic, energized, serene, etc.), and neurological substrates for many of them can be identified and manipulated with drugs. Passions are at the other end of the line, ending in an extreme at which affect virtually obliterates cognition and agency – an extreme in which, for example, people are so overwhelmed with what began as anxiety or rage or fear or lust that they are "out of their minds," or "don't know the time of day," and, if they can make reports at all, can report only a one-dimensional, ferociously focused affect. Passions can be much milder than this, of course, but we will use the term to apply to affect that is focused enough and strong enough to interrupt (as opposed to color, focus, direct, or otherwise shape) deliberation and choice.

Between these extremes lie feelings and emotions. Feelings, we will say, are distinct from moods primarily by virtue of the subject's awareness of various sorts of physical sensations and somatic phenomena associated with the affect, as well as some causal implications for cognition and action – awareness that focuses and thus intensifies the affective experience, making it seem localized and often giving it an object. (Full-fledged sexual arousal is a feeling in this sense, whereas low-level erotic affect is a mood.) And let us then say that emotions are distinct from other affects primarily by virtue of the subject's awareness and appraisal of the cognitive components of an affect – the beliefs about the world that are implicated in the affect, awareness that complicates and further focuses, reinforces, or intensifies the feelings. Worry is an example; so is object-specific, manageable fear.

Contemporary Psychology and Stoic Theory

There is a fairly impressive convergence between Stoic positions and contemporary psychology – even psychotherapy[10] – on the general nature of moods, feelings, emotions, and passions. As far as I can tell, empirical psychology has so far settled one dispute within ancient Stoicism, has strengthened a few philosophical criticisms of the ancient Stoic account, has raised new problems about the unity of rational agency, but has also confirmed much of the ancient Stoic doctrine on these matters. Contemporary Stoics will have to make some adjustments to the ancient doctrines, but nothing, I think, that will undermine their claim to being Stoics.

The Persistence of Affective Impulse. The ancient dispute that modern psychology seems to have settled is one between Chrysippus and Posidonius, as reported by Galen.[11] If it is true that Chrysippus believed Stoic moral training could effectively remove excessive emotions at their source, by removing the erroneous beliefs involved in them, and that this training could be so effective and so thorough that excessive emotion would never arise in the sage, then Chrysippus was wrong. Instead, Posidonius had it right when he argued that primal affect was a permanent feature of human life that sages, like the rest of us, would always have to cope with.

The modern evidence for this comes from two sources: neurophysiology and pharmacology. Neurophysiologists have identified at least four anatomically distinct structures in the "ancient" or subcortical portion of the human brain that generate affective states – roughly fear, rage, panic, and goal-oriented desire.[12] These structures are directly responsive to both external stimuli and internal changes in brain chemistry prior to significant cognitive processing. There is, for example, a naturally occurring hormone called cholecystokinin, which regulates secretions of the pancreas and gallbladder. When this hormone is introduced directly into the bloodstream (a natural, but not normal occurrence in human physiology) it generates an anxiety response unconnected to any external or internal threat.[13] Similar stimulants exist for other affective structures in the amygdala, and there are blocking agents as well – pharmacological agents that cause those affective structures to quiet down temporarily, to cease generating affect. This does not mean that subsequent cognitive responses are ineffective in controlling such affect. It only means that this sort of affective *arousal* and its immediate emotional or passional consequences cannot be eliminated by cognitive (Stoic) training, any more than Stoic training can eliminate perspiration. Stoics with bad gallbladders will just have to cope with anxiety, whether they are sages or not; similarly for people who have brain injuries, or brain tumors, that excite affective structures. Modern medicine is clear that cognitive training is not always the treatment of first choice for such affective disturbances.

I assume that none of this causes fundamental or general problems for a Stoic account of the emotions, whatever it might mean for Chrysippus' particular theses. After all, other things being equal, if potable water is freely available to the thirsty sage, she will presumably drink it as a first remedy (reminding herself of its status as a preferred indifferent) rather than think away the thirst. So the fact that modern medicine sometimes recommends drugs or surgery as a first remedy should not, for that reason alone, make it inconsistent with Stoic theory. Moreover, the affects generated solely by subcortical structures in our brains correspond to the sort of primal impulses or excitation so often discussed by Stoics as leading more or less involuntarily to proto-emotions (*propatheiai*), and thence transformed by further cognitive processes into full-fledged emotions.[14] They thus fit comfortably into a contemporary Stoic account. The task for the Stoic is to recognize the source of affective agitation and proto-emotion, and to correct any false beliefs that may have arisen from it along with the affect. Done effectively, in accord with a Stoic account of the good, that process will eventually transform the *propatheiai* into *eupatheiai*. If anything is a fundamental or general aspect of a Stoic account of emotion, it is that. The reference to recognizing the etiology of the proto-emotion is a later amendment, but not one that is troublesome. More about that later.

Happily, there is settled agreement, in the modern psychology of emotion, that this fundamental aspect of the Stoic account is correct for a wide range of quite mild to quite strong affective states that are characteristic of psychological health. Leaving aside especially weak, strong, fleeting, or enduring emotional states for the moment, it looks as though there is no disagreement at all with even the ancient Stoic proposition that full-fledged emotions are distinguished from one another primarily by distinct (and constitutive) belief structures in the subject and are transformable by changes in the subject's beliefs.[15] The modern psychological amendment to this would simply be to insist that raw affect, generated in distinct neurological structures and having distinct behavioral consequences, often precedes the cognitive content that turns it into full-fledged emotion.

The only thing that is troubling for Stoic theory in this amendment is the reference to behavioral consequences. That reference is emblematic of the fact that modern empirical psychology is apparently much more comfortable with a modular conception of human agency than

Stoics would have expected it to be. In fact, it looks as though personality psychologists from Freud onward have generally worked with something more like a tripartite Platonic model of motivation and psychodynamics than a unified Stoic one. I think there is less to this than meets the eye, however.

The Stoic hypothesis is simply that rational agency in mature human beings is unified in the sense that it is a conative power in which the direct determinant of action is always the same one sort of thing – belief.[16] The idea is that in mature, healthy human beings, pure affect, as long as it does not initially overwhelm agency, is immediately subjected to cognitive appraisal and infused with cognitive content – beliefs that have consequences for the affect itself as well as for its translation to action. All affective states – or least all of those above the level of pure primal impulse – have at least implicit, controlling beliefs, and are ultimately subject to the agent's ability to control those beliefs. Thus Stoic psychotherapy is a form of cognitive therapy – an effort to focus on, and then to correct, the cognitive errors that underwrite pathology.[17]

It is clear that, in order to be consistent with modern psychology, we would now have to modify these references to belief by replacing them with references to cognitive states generally. Such states include both active and dispositional beliefs, but also include perceptual filters, information-processing routines, and so forth, some of which may be quite "modular" at the level of neurophysiology. The question is whether, even with this modification, the Stoic hypothesis about the unity and power of rational agency are consistent with modern empirical psychology.

It appears to me that the motivational part is consistent, almost by definition. If we distinguish between action and other sorts of behavior by using the former term to mark out the class of intentional or goal-directed behaviors, then it clearly follows that whatever the original motivating source of an action might be, that motivation will always be filtered through a cognitive state of some sort. And the evidence from psychology clearly supports the proposition that the content of the cognitive state determines the nature (if not always the timing) of the consequent action.[18] So that seems consistent with traditional Stoic doctrine.

Nonetheless, it does seem clear that modern empirical psychology would reject not only the idea that we can extirpate subcortical affective impulses but also the idea that rectifying our beliefs will always, ultimately, be effective in rectifying our affect. Modern Stoics will thus have to be more cautious than their ancient brethren in making claims for the general effectiveness of Stoic training. We will acknowledge a wide variety of cases in which the human body can be overwhelmed by unhealthy affect, just as it can be overwhelmed by unhealthy microbes or viruses. This is not, it seems to me, an admission that compromises anything fundamental in Stoicism. All sages are ultimately overcome by disease or injury. Their bodies are mortal. And because Stoics are materialists, we have always acknowledged that our minds and emotions too, like everything else about us, are physical entities subject to disease and injury. Ancient Stoics, confronted by the modern evidence, would surely have no difficulty adjusting their ideas about the root physical causes and appropriate physical remedies for such affective neuropsychological diseases and injuries, even for sages.

The necessity for such adjustment is an example of the way in which modern empirical psychology strengthens some of the traditional criticisms of the Stoic psychology of emotion. There are several others, most of which have to do with the relation between psychological health (which Stoics recognize as a necessary condition for the development of virtue) and the amount and variety of affect in one's life (which Stoics have perhaps traditionally underestimated). I deal with those matters in most of what follows. But I want to conclude this section by noting that contemporary Stoics will have to pay somewhat closer attention to moods and threshold affective states than the ancient texts do. Here is the problem.

The Etiology of Affect: Nonreferential or Liminal States

On the standard Stoic account, one assesses the appropriateness of affect by assessing the truth of the beliefs implicit in it – beliefs about the external events or states of affairs that elicit the affect, and beliefs about what attitudes we should take toward those external matters, given their value in Stoic terms. Appropriate emotion is necessarily emotion that is in accord with nature, that is, in accord with *true* beliefs about events and their value. The ancient Stoics were confident that cognition could drive affect and that rectifying our beliefs about the world could rectify our emotions in this sense.

Nonreferential Affect. Moods pose a problem for this traditional account for two reasons. One is that they often have peculiarly indeterminate cognitive content – content that is incorrigibly true (and thus not in need of correction) but that nonetheless can compromise rational agency in the following way.

Think of anxiety, of the sort induced as a side effect by a drug or hormone. Beliefs about the world that are implicit in such anxiety are often quite general, and quite probably true: "There are some things out there – things that I am missing right now – that might be difficult and unpleasant for me to cope with, and I can't be sure what they are, and therefore how to cope with them." That is certainly true, as a general proposition. And so, because this belief about the world is true, the standard Stoic response would be to focus on the evaluative beliefs implicit in the anxiety – beliefs about whether it matters, ultimately, how such things turn out, and how it is appropriate for us to feel and act.

The problem is that such a response will misdirect our attention. We will be focusing on the inappropriateness of some very general worry about the outer world, when the source of that general worry is not anything in the outer world, but rather a wholly internal feature of our body chemistry, or the operation of an unconscious emotional disposition. In serious cases we may make serious mistakes about our health in this way, repeatedly quieting the anxiety thrown up by a disease process by reminding ourselves again and again of what is of ultimate importance. In this way we ultimately end in a misdirected Stoic version of praying without ceasing, because the process becomes an ever tightening circle – waves of increasing anxiety followed by attempts at calm, followed by renewed anxiety from internal causes that become increasingly inaccessible to us as we focus ever more persistently on the value question, rather than on the physiology or psychodynamic that is repeatedly eliciting the anxiety.

The obvious solution to this problem is to make sure that we pay attention to the question of etiology. Is our affect being elicited by external events or internal ones? Is the anxiety prompted by something in the environment that we cannot quite identify? Or is it prompted by changes in our blood chemistry? In the case of emotions that have clear objects in the external world – fear of things that go bump in the night, for example – the standard Stoic analysis may indirectly suffice. After all, if we assess our beliefs about night noises and find that they are false because we were having auditory hallucinations, then when the fear persists we will presumably be led to think about internal causes for it. In the case of affect that has no specific object, however, and prompts only general, incorrigibly true beliefs about the world, we cannot rely on the assessment of their truth to lead us in the appropriate direction. So, especially in the case of what we might call "nonreferential" affect, we have to add something to the standard Stoic account. There are now three rather than two sorts of beliefs we must assess: beliefs about the etiology of the affect; beliefs about states of affairs; and beliefs about the appropriate response to those states of affairs.

Is this a significant change in Stoic theory? Probably not, but we should acknowledge that it makes the theory somewhat less tidy. We can no longer plausibly assert that the cognitive content implicit in the affect itself is all we need to address in order start down the right path toward assessing its appropriateness. We will have to include the question of its etiology as well.

Threshold Affect. There is a related problem about affect that hovers at the threshold of our awareness of it. Such liminal states are problematic for therapy because subjects have difficulty identifying the nature of their affect (putting an illuminating name to it), or difficulty in even identifying its existence as affect. There is no serious divergence between Stoicism and modern psychology about one extreme of the emotional continuum – namely the place where passions become so intense, so overwhelming, that they literally stop thought. Both agree that, at that threshold, maintaining or restoring self-control requires a reduction of the affect, and both agree that such self-control is necessary for health and a good life.

But consider affect at the other extreme of intensity – moods or feelings, for example, that are difficult for subjects to perceive or name. ("You are very angry today." – Angry? I am? – "Yes. Just think about what you've been doing.") Both Stoics and modern psychotherapists think that it is important for subjects to identify such states properly – to know themselves better. And just as we often need help in understanding that we are having difficulty seeing or hearing in threshold circumstances, we may need help identifying our affect. One obvious method for dealing with liminal auditory phenomena is to turn up the volume and keep it at a fully audible level. Doing something similar with our very mild affective states seems an obvious way of staying in cognitive contact with them. Even though deliberately dialing up the intensity of an affect sounds like a very un-Stoic thing to do,[19] I suppose there can be no serious Stoic objection to it as long as the resulting emotional state does not disturb one's tranquillity. It is hard to imagine, however, that this would not be disturbing, even for a sage, at the very least because it deliberately generates something that we then have to cope with.

This is at least a small puzzle for Stoics. Some of what I have to say here about the value of emotion and about the nature of tranquillity may indirectly help address it, but I am not confident I have solved the puzzle. Stoics would expect to solve it, of course, by noting that once such liminal emotion is raised to the point where it can be identified clearly, its cognitive content can be identified as well and dealt with in the usual way. The result of that, however, especially if the source of the original liminal emotion is neurophysiological, may simply be to reduce the deliberately heightened emotion back to its original liminal state, thus starting the cycle over again. Denial, or self-deception, or some form of sublimation – even if it is productive for psychological health – is not consistent with Stoic insistence on self-knowledge, so that option simply complicates things further. Again, we have reason to insist that the etiology of the affect be addressed.

THE GOOD OF EMOTION

I turn now to the question of the value of emotion in human life. Here Stoics resolutely diverge from common opinion, having enduring reasons for thinking that the value is not very great – or is, at any rate, not the sort of value most non-Stoics imagine. As far as I can tell, nothing in modern psychology (or modern philosophy, for that matter) undercuts this aspect of the traditional Stoic account of emotion.

Emotion as Natural

What good are human emotions? The answers one can get to that question are frustratingly circular. Ultimately, they amount to nothing more than this: human emotions, when they are good at all, are good for humans simply because humans are emotional creatures – creatures who are so constituted that they cannot stay healthy without certain sorts of emotional experience, or flourish without a rich and varied emotional life, or deliberate effectively about ends without giving those ends an emotional valence, or communicate adequately with each other without sympathy and emotional gestures, or form profound attachments to each other without empathy. But nothing in such answers suggests a transcendent value for emotions as such – something that would, for example, cause us to think that nonhuman beings would necessarily be deficient if they lacked emotion; something that would underwrite the temptation to think that if any unfortunate, emotionless creatures were intelligent enough to appreciate the difference between human lives and their own, they would be like the wistful androids of science fiction, superhuman in some respects but yearning to find love and laughter.

Now it is true, of course, that humans are not the only creatures who have affect. Many other forms of life on this planet, from reptiles to the great apes, have neurological structures that are homologous to some structures we have in subcortical areas of our brains – structures that are known to generate, in humans, raw primal affect such as fear, rage, separation anxiety, and desire (where that includes everything from pure curiosity to ferociously single-minded purposive behavior).[20] Moreover, we know that these subcortical structures operate initially, precognitively, in much the same way across all these species, and thus operate in human infants and very young children in much the same way as they do in some other species. But it is also clear that in adult human beings the firing of these primal, emotion-generating subcortical structures also lights up the neocortex – the information-processing apparatus associated with cognition and self-awareness – and that this cognitive activity dramatically reshapes our primal emotional responses. Adult human emotion is, as the ancient Stoics insisted, inescapably cognitive in ways that we cannot map onto the physiology of reptiles, the lower mammals, and even (in large part) those primates with whom we are most closely related physiologically. Their affective experience, whatever it is like, is apparently not much like adult human emotion. Consequently, the good of adult *human* emotion, whatever it is, is inescapably tied to *human* nature – to what constitutes (adult) human health, human flourishing, human deliberation, human communication, human relationships. And, of course, the obverse is true as well: the evils of human emotion lie in what constitutes ill health, failure to flourish, inability to deliberate effectively, inability to communicate fully, inability to form profound human relationships. This is circular, but instructive.

Emotion and Health

Consider health.[21] We are told, by the human sciences, that human infants literally wither – fail to thrive physically; fail to develop a healthy physiology – if their primal emotions ("seeking," fear, anxiety, desire, rage) are not appropriately responded to, where appropriate response means enabling their purposive activity, alleviating their fear and anxiety, satisfying or diverting their desire and rage, and in general holding, comforting, and caressing them. We are told that very young children develop pathological psychologies if they do not form healthy attachments to those humans nearest to them, where a healthy attachment means one characterized in part by reciprocal emotional interaction that creates a sense of security and possibility and enables learning and purposive activity. We are told that the way these early stages of our emotional lives go has a profound effect on our basic temperaments (whether anxious, distrustful, and pessimistic, for example, or secure, trustful, and optimistic), on the templates for human relationships we try to re-create and preserve throughout our whole lives (or perhaps cannot help but re-create and preserve, despite our best efforts to avoid them), and on the narrative expectations we have for the way our various endeavors will go (whether we think they will go well, for example, through our own efforts or only through magic; whether we think we deserve for them to go well only if we are beautiful, or please others, or have won success through struggle). We are told that these basic temperaments, templates, and expectations have "default" epistemic consequences – that they shape what we immediately perceive, and consequently what we initially believe about the world, in ways that are resistant to rational reassessment. We are told that these epistemic defaults, because they influence cognition generally,[22] influence the cognitive elements of mature human emotions as well, setting up the conditions under which we will continue to strive, or to give up; the conditions under which we will love or hate; the people with whom we will form profound relationships; and the general nature of those relationships, including how open, secure, and wholehearted, for example, or guarded, anxious, and tentative. All of this has consequences for our health, both physical and psychological, throughout our lives.

Emotion and a Good Life

Now consider *eudaimonia* – not just a healthy life but an abundantly good one, a flourishing life. Again we get circular arguments, but instructive ones. We say life without emotion (to the extent that is even possible, psychologically) would be unbearably bleak, dull, flat, boring, unmotivating, inert, depressing, *joyless*. But that is, of course, just another way of saying that emotion is good for emotional health; good emotion is emotionally good. And if circular arguments with a radius that short were generally available, philosophy would be remarkably easy.

Notice, though, what the circularity of this argument suggests: it suggests that adult human beings are so constituted that emotion is a necessary or basic good for us – something we must have in order to flourish in any form accessible to us, or at least to our imaginations, and hence to our choices as rational agents. If so, then if we want to flourish at all, we must follow our natures in this respect and get the affect we need. (*Homo sapiens* to be sure, but also *homo ludens*.)

There are similar things to be said about communication, and social and personal relationships among humans. Many people say (or, at least since the rise of romanticism, have obsessively said) that we cannot fully connect with other people without being able to read and respond to their emotional frame of mind – the feeling, or lack of it, that informs their actions, their choices, their dealings with us. We describe people whom we cannot read in this way as remote, or inaccessible; sometimes as arrogant, rude, or lacking in the emotional generosity needed to allow us to respond fully to them. We say that profound personal relationships are necessary to the best forms of life, are a constituent of the most complete forms of human happiness, and that such relationships require that people be emotionally accessible to each other. The fact that this sort of talk is a peculiarly modern obsession, though of course not unknown in antiquity, should not lessen our confidence in its truth. But again we should be aware of a sort of circle in the implicit argument. The truth is that we need emotion only to connect with, communicate with, form profound relationships with emotional beings like ourselves. Being emotionally generous with a sponge is pointless as far as we can tell. And just as we sense, intuitively, in love relationships that the degree and timing of emotional honesty and intimacy are delicate matters, so too we sense that what counts as appropriate behavior in this regard varies widely from one person to the next, and one situation to the next with the same person. Some people are psychologically damaged in ways that make emotional honesty or openness in others threatening – an obstacle to their regaining their health rather than a necessity for it.

Deliberation about Ends

There is a line of thought about the necessity of emotion in human life that goes roughly like this: means-end reasoning may be purely hypothetical or theoretical, aiming only at knowledge of causal relationships between an action and a goal in cases where neither is valued positively, or even thought to be permissible. That is to say, means-end reasoning may take this form: *if* one were to go for X, what would be the necessary (sufficient, the most efficient, best overall) means to take to get to that end? To turn such theoretical reasoning into genuinely practical reasoning, into deliberation, one must actually have an end, a goal, a purpose. Having a goal X is necessarily to value or prize X in a way that motivates one to go for X, and valuing or prizing something in that motivating way necessarily has an affective dimension – one that we typically sum up in the term desire. One may feel such desire as either a push from within (an impulse) or a pull from without (an attraction). But in either case one does *feel* this.[23] This is not to say that having an end is thoroughly or even dominantly a noncognitive business. It is merely to say that having an end is always partly a noncognitive business. It is to say that insofar as we lack desire with respect to X, insofar as we feel no impulse or attraction to it at all, X cannot be one of our ends. Thus, people who lack desire entirely (if that is psychologically possible) lack ends entirely and are entirely unable to deliberate – entirely unable to engage in practical reasoning that leads to decision, as opposed to mere theoretical reasoning about means to hypothetical ends.

In the hands of philosophers and philosophically inclined literary folk, this line of thought often appears to proceed in a priori terms, but this is clearly a mistake. One may, after all, have a motivating categorical commitment to some end – a commitment that operates without intermediate desire. The refugee knocks on the door and we find ourselves with the immediate, categorical thought that we must help in some way, whether we want to or not. In fact, such motivating commitment to an end often operates *despite our desire* for conflicting ends. So it cannot be the case that there is a purely conceptual connection between having an end and having a desire for it.

There is, however, some empirical evidence of a psychological connection that underwrites this line of thought about deliberation. People who are brain-damaged (or medicated) in ways that appear to dramatically reduce or perhaps even eliminate a broad range of motivating desires have great difficulty in making decisions – in deliberating. But notice now that this gives us only another tight circle of argument about the good of human emotion: human desire is good for human deliberation because human deliberation (as a matter of human psychology) requires human desire. So what moral shall we draw from this? Follow nature? A very Stoic moral, and none the worse for that.

VIRTUE AND TRANQUILLITY

The question we must now consider is whether the Stoic commitment to virtue demands a psychology that diverges significantly – especially with respect to emotion – from one that is recognizably healthy by the standards of modern psychology. As we have seen, it is relatively easy to make the case that there is a close connection between psychological health and the development of ordinary forms of rational agency along Stoic lines. The question that remains is about the sage, and about the fact that Stoicism requires one to strive to become a sage.

The question is this: is training someone to be a sage rather like training someone to become a very specialized athlete, whose specialized physique is, in the long run, quite unhealthy? (Think of a Sumo wrestler.) Our agency powers are one element of our human endowments. What is the cost to the rest of our human constitution of maximizing the development of agency? In particular, for present purposes, what is the cost to our emotions and feelings and to affect generally?

The abilities of the Stoic sage are extraordinary – at the apex of human agency. And it is not easy to describe in a positive way what those abilities would be like. The ancients were clear that while sages would have limited knowledge and power, by virtue of being finite creatures, and would therefore often fail in their endeavors (sometimes lethally fail), they would not be negligent in gathering and interpreting what information was accessible to them, and they would not make mistakes – in the sense of misinterpreting or misapplying their knowledge in humanly avoidable ways. Moreover, sages would be able to cope with all sorts of adversity, difficulty, suffering, and disappointment, to the utter limit of human endurance. That kind of perfection would require sages always to be free from psychological disturbances that would interfere with their optimal exercise of agency, and it would require that their optimal exercise of agency never be disturbed by their own failures (because these would not be due to avoidable errors) or by any other events beyond their control, such as the death of a loved one, enslavement, or losses of any kind.

What kind of psychology would such a sage have? Here it is easy to make a serious error, and answer that, in general, sages must have virtuosic abilities to cope with whatever befalls them. This is of course true, but only half the truth, and operating with that half-truth produces the following familiar but false picture of the sage:

Sages are poised – perfectly poised – to understand their circumstances and options and to move in whatever way reason dictates. They must be calm, alert, and not committed in advance to a particular course of action that would prevent them from responding adequately to unanticipated events. Attachments to externals – to people, relationships, wealth, health, anything not wholly within one's control – threaten to compromise their coping ability by restricting their options in advance, and must be modified accordingly. Passions and strong emotions

compromise coping ability as well because they generate momentum like running full tilt downhill – and render us incapable of certain responses we might
need to make (like stopping before we get to the cliff). So passions and strong
emotions must go. Similarly for any feelings and moods of a sort that disturb either perception, deliberation, or choice. What this leaves for the sage is a form of
tranquillity and detachment consistent with maximal alertness and readiness to
respond to anything that happens. It is as if we imagined the sage as a world-class
tennis player ready to receive serve – up on her toes, parallel to the baseline,
perfectly balanced for an instant move either to the right or the left, perfectly
positioned for a lunge, or a run, or a reflexive block of a shot hit directly at her
body, racquet loose in the hand, uncommitted as yet to a forehand or backhand
grip, eyes on the ball, but senses registering everything that is salient to making
an effective return of serve, and focused, calm, tranquil, detached in the sense
that she is not distracted by the crowd, her husband's infidelities, the injustice
of her pending prosecution for tax evasion, the recent death of her first child.
And, of course, we then imagine that this sort of tranquillity and detachment is
the sage's permanent (waking) psychological condition.

What is wrong with this picture is that it is constructed in terms of waiting
for things to happen – in terms of being ready to *receive* serve. But the
exercise of our agency is not just passive and reactive; it is also active,
intentional, inventive, provocative, determinative. We have to step up
and serve the ball and actually commit ourselves to making a particular
sort of return, as often as we wait to serve, or wait to receive serve. And
the picture of the sage in action is rather different than the picture of
the sage in waiting.

For one thing, inertia – getting going – is as big a problem for action
as getting stopped. So is commitment, and momentum. If you have to
jump from one rim of the narrow gorge to the other, you don't do it by
keeping your options open permanently. You need speed, and running
downhill (if you are lucky enough to have a hill nearby) is a good way to get
going and keep going, even if it means you reach the point of no return
sooner than you would if you tried to jump from a standing start. Focused,
energized, muscular affect (*tonos*)[24] of the sort American professional
football players work up before each game, and within the game before
each play, is not typically out of place either, because the momentum it
generates contributes to playing the game *under control* at the highest level.
It is, of course, possible to have an inappropriate type or amount of such
affect, as inexperienced players often do. And some players find it hard
to confine such energy to the game – to leave it on the field, as the saying
goes – or to work it up without repeating a litany of false propositions that
no Stoic could support. But no football coach thinks that such excesses

give him a reason to discourage players from "putting on a game face," because it is understood that this is something that belongs only to the game, and only when it is consistent with playing under control. The point is simply that once we are committed to acting in a particular way, such focused, energized affect and momentum are sometimes appropriate. And agents must always, ultimately, commit themselves to action.

So we must not be misled by the ancient analogy between passion and running full tilt. This cannot mean that extreme, energized affect and momentum are always inappropriate. After all, the ancient Stoics were certainly aware of the way in which sleep, especially deep sleep, could compromise rational agency precisely because it creates the opposite sort of difficulty to running. In the running case, it is hard for agents to get stopped; in the sleeping case it is hard for them to get started. I am not aware of any ancient Stoic arguments to the effect that because of the difficulty of getting started, sages should not sleep, or not sleep deeply. And I am unimpressed by the comparable argument that because of the difficulty of getting stopped, sages should not run. This makes no sense in terms of the sage's final end – the perfection of the exercise of rational agency. When running is appropriate, sages run. When momentum is appropriate, sages have it.

Notice, however, that this is not an Aristotelian point about the usefulness of passion (e.g., of anger) in *motivating* our actions, or even in sustaining the motivation. The ancient Stoics were right to insist that for the sage, the knowledge that a course of action is the appropriate one is always sufficient motivation to pursue it. The point here about momentum is rather a point about agent energy – about the physical and psychological resources an agent has to have to pursue an endeavor that is already motivated and already chosen. Sages who find themselves in close combat may find that they need ferocious energy, affect, and momentum as much as they need good blood gases – for fighting under control, to the limit of their abilities. And once we see that the intensity of the affect can be uncoupled from beliefs (recall that beliefs can be held with flat affect; ferociously intense affect can be generated precognitively, in the limbic system), we need not imagine that there is a necessary connection between achieving or sustaining such ferocity and holding false beliefs.

It is certainly true that Stoics will reject any passions, or other intense emotional states that involve false beliefs, and it may be true that passions and strong emotions are usually dependent on false beliefs in some way. But such dependence is neither a logical nor a psychological necessity. Because Stoics are committed to the perfection of the activity of rational agency, they are committed to cultivating the affective states needed for it. In the case of ferociously intense affective states, Stoics will reject those that invoke false beliefs and find other ways to cultivate intensity when it is needed.

The general point is that in any environment rich with possibilities, the sage's exercise of rational agency will be exceedingly complex and call for a comparably complex affective life. There will be extended periods of careful deliberation and reflex reactions; mundane routines and high-stakes risk taking; strength moves; moves requiring little strength but major amounts of fine muscle control; coping with success; coping with unexpected good fortune; coping with failure; inventing remedies for boredom; inventing remedies for the stress of overwork; solving conflict, coordination, and cooperation problems with benevolent people; with malevolent people; being a friend; being a competitor; being an adversary; being an enemy; making war; making peace; making love; on and on and on. And all repeated in a bewildering variety of situations calling for subtly and not so subtly different conduct. It seems highly implausible to hold that any single, well-defined affective state (such as tranquillity) could possibly be adequate for sages engaged in a reasonably wide range of endeavors in a reasonably rich set of circumstances. And no matter how limited the sages' circumstances and options might be at a given time, they must be prepared for an unexpected reversal – they must be capable of handling great *good* fortune and an abundance of opportunities.

Thus, whatever ground-down form of affect may be required of the slave of a drunken despot or the prisoner in a death camp, Stoic training must aim to produce a psychology that can also respond appropriately to safety, security, freedom, and affluence. Stoicism is for emperors as well as slaves, the rich and famous as well as the obscure, the strong and beautiful as well as the weak and ugly – in the full range of situations in which those people can find themselves. That much has never been in doubt. We simply add here that the appropriate affective dimension of such lives will be as varied as those people and their circumstances, and we think that, once this point is understood, concentrating on the perfection of agency will not move us away from psychological health.

LOVE, DETACHMENT, AND PURITY OF HEART

That leaves love. There are two problems with it. One concerns the sort of quick release mechanism recommended by Epictetus in some notorious passages about replacing lost wives and children, just as one replaces broken tea cups. Apparently the sage is supposed to be able to let go of externals so quickly that grief or suffering from a loss is not an issue. That persuades many people that there must be something phony about the way a sage loves in the first place. They suspect that the only way to achieve this sort of immediate release is to be more or less detached and unloving from the start. And, of course, Stoic insistence that virtue, rather than any external person or thing, is the only thing that is ultimately any good at all contributes to the impression that Stoics would resist becoming attached to externals – would resist, in that sense, a fundamental aspect of what we call love.

The second problem with fitting a Stoic account of emotion into our ordinary notion of love concerns the way in which Stoics must monitor their emotions intellectually, making sure that they do not involve any cognitive errors about what is ultimately valuable or about what affective responses are appropriate – that is, are psychologically healthy and otherwise consistent with the development of virtue. The result of such monitoring is undeniably a persistent sort of highly refined triple consciousness: first-order awareness within the emotional state itself, second-order awareness of being in the emotional state, and third-order awareness of the nature and value of being in that state. A Stoic is always going to be two parts observer and one part participant in emotional experience – something that will not only complicate the intentionality of Stoic loving but add a certain remoteness or distance to it as well. If purity of heart is to have simple intentions,[25] then it looks as though it is going to be difficult for a Stoic to be pure-hearted in love – or wholehearted either, for that matter. Recall the line from an exasperated E. E. Cummings: "since feeling is first / who pays any attention / to the syntax of things / will never wholly kiss you."[26]

Pure Love

Let me address this purity of heart problem first. Double consciousness – that is, awareness and awareness of being aware – is a necessary part of the kind of rational agency that develops in human beings as they mature. It is in that sense part of our nature as human beings. We can, of course, choose to regard it as a curse rather than a blessing and take steps to eliminate the self-consciousness part, leaving only first-order awareness. (I assume that people who valorize emotion would not want to go farther and eliminate first-order awareness.) But once we acquire language, self-consciousness is exceedingly difficult to strip away from first-order consciousness for more than short intervals, and it can be exceedingly dangerous to our health to do so in unfavorable circumstances. That suggests the importance of third-order assessments that address, among other things, when it is appropriate to lose ourselves in our experience and when it is not. ("Kiss me you fool." – Not now. The attic is on fire.) And the endorsement of the importance of those assessments is not anything unique to Stoicism. It is a matter of common sense, not to mention sound psychotherapy.

In the discussion of tranquillity I suggested that it was consistent with the notion of Stoic sagehood to recognize that the demands of virtuosic activity (as opposed to receptivity) sometimes include temporary, rationally controlled loss of self-consciousness. It seems reasonable to extend that point here to include the observation that third-order monitoring of one's emotions will thus sometimes be intermittent, controlled by sophisticated dispositions sensitive to changes in circumstance. A tennis player who is playing "in the zone," as they say, presumably still has a dispositional readiness to respond to things that are dramatically out of the ordinary (such as an earthquake or an attack by a spectator), as well as the dispositional readiness to come out of the zone when the match is over. In this respect there is little difference between Stoics and non-Stoics.

Where there is a striking difference on these matters between Stoics and at least some non-Stoics (call them romantics) is in how willingly they embrace the complexity of intention in actively monitored emotional states and the distancing it involves.[27] Stoics characteristically have no regrets about this at all, when it is the appropriate thing to do, and are unlikely to go out of their way to minimize the occasions when it is prudent to monitor their emotions. Romantics seem dismayed and regretful about the necessity of such monitoring and are likely to make persistent efforts to avoid it. The argument between them, however, is not properly construed as one about the availability of wholehearted Stoic kisses. It is rather about the value of emotion itself for the good life.

Detachment

Now to the question about detachment. The first thing to point out is that Stoics recognize what amounts to a very intimate and deep form of attachment as a fundamental mechanism in human psychology, and an indispensable mechanism for the development of virtue. I refer to the ancient discussions of *oikeiōsis* – the appropriation or incorporation of externals so that one's interest in their welfare ceases to be merely instrumental and becomes instead like one's interest in one's own welfare. That is surely the beginning of love: when one cares about another for the other's sake, not one's own. And when this occurs by way of *oikeiōsis* – by way of the psychological incorporation of the beloved's interests into one's own – the attachment is as strong and intimate as can be imagined. The ones we love are literally "parts" of us then, as romantics say. Such attachments occur in the normal course of human events, whether we take further steps toward becoming Stoics or not.

What is distinctive about Stoic love is how Stoics define human welfare, and consequently what our deepest cares and concerns are, both for ourselves and for those we love (for those who have become a part of us, psychologically). Stoics care ultimately only about virtue: excellence in the activity of rational agency. But as I have argued, that entails caring about health – both about physical health and psychological health, including the range and depth of emotional experience necessary for it. It also entails caring about life itself, and liberty, and having the material resources necessary for the exercise of our agency. But we care about those things in a subsidiary way. It would be self-defeating to be concerned about them a way that forces us to compromise virtue. Thus death, disease, discomfort, or even slavery is preferable to a vicious life. Because those we love are a part of us, we love their lives, health, ease, and liberty the way we love our own – as preferable to their opposites, certainly, but as nothing compared to virtue.

That means that a sage will not love others in a way that diminishes her virtue – her excellence in the exercise of her rational agency. She will not, for example, become so attached to others that she literally cannot bear the prospect of losing them, any more than she would be attached to her own life in a way that made the prospect of her own death unbearable. Nor would she wish others to love her in that way – to be desolate and helpless when she is gone, unable to bear the loss. What Stoics wish for others is what we wish for ourselves: good lives; virtuous lives; including the ability to cope with loss. And we add this thought: when a loved one dies, it is literally not possible thereafter to care about his interests for his own sake, because he no longer exists. We must therefore think carefully about the cognitive content of the sorts of attachments and emotions that survive in us after his death. Whatever they are, however appropriate they may be as an extension of the concerns he had during his life, they cannot be the kind of love they once were: caring for another as we care for ourselves. When we pay attention to that, the alienating brutality of some of the ancient texts on the subject of grief, love, and loss will be lessened.

Is Stoic love austere? Not especially. To see this, I think it is only necessary to reflect in a commonsense way on this thought: imagine a person who wants you to be able to say, truthfully, these sentences: "You are my love, my life, my whole life. If I were to lose you my life would be ruined; over." Those sentences are not about loving you for your own sake; they are not ultimately about you at all. They are rather the declaration of a medical emergency and a plea for help (or a threat). So what can it mean when people say that they want *you* to have that kind of emotional attachment to *them*? That they want *you* to lose your life when you lose *them*? Is that compatible with loving you for your own sake? If so, then it is that sort of love that is austere, not the Stoic sort. The only austerity in Stoic love comes not from its lack of attachment (there is plenty of attachment) but rather from its readiness to sacrifice everything *except* virtue for love.

Notes

1. In a famous passage in *Lives of Eminent Philosophers* (7.116), quoted here from LS 65F, Diogenes Laertius says:

   (1) They [the Stoics] say that there are three good feelings: joy, watchfulness, wishing. (2) Joy, they say, is the opposite of pleasure, consisting in well-reasoned swelling [elation]; and watchfulness is the opposite of fear, consisting in well-reasoned shrinking. For the wise man will not be afraid at all, but he will be watchful. (3) They say that wishing is the opposite of appetite, consisting in well-reasoned stretching [desire]. (4) Just as certain passions fall under the primary ones, so too with the primary good feelings. Under wishing: kindness, generosity, warmth, affection. Under watchfulness: respect, cleanliness. Under joy: delight, sociability, cheerfulness.

2. See, for instance, Stockdale 1993.
3. Galen 1981: 2.5.
4. Panksepp 1998.
5. Thayer 1989.
6. Lazarus 1994.
7. Craske 1999.
8. Suppose that affect is a necessary feature of human experience. It does not follow that it suffuses or attaches to every waking thought.
9. References to emotion are often ambiguous, alluding either to some affective quality of experience ("I got angry then – really emotional") or to some persisting disposition ("I'm basically an angry person, and too emotional for my own good"). I focus here on emotions as affective experience, but much of what I have to say depends on the view that such affective experience produces and is produced by underlying mental-neurophysiological

structures – emotional dispositions that often carry the same labels as their counterparts in our affective lives. Stoic therapy clearly has to deal with both emotional states and emotional dispositions, and it is important to consider the possibility that the latter may have consequences for behavior that are not filtered through identifiable emotional states. It is a virtue of psychoanalytic theory, and also of Richard Wollheim's recent book *On the Emotions* that they call our attention to such things. Wollheim goes much farther along these lines than I am prepared to go, however. After sharply distinguishing mental states from mental dispositions, he argues that emotions are dispositions – either conscious, preconscious, or unconscious ones. See Wollheim 1999: 1–8.

10. For explicit consideration of this point by people working in psychiatry, see Nordenfelt 1997, and the extensive series of comments generated in the same journal issue (pp. 292–306). This discussion proceeds without much attention to the theoretical framework of Stoic ethics and goes astray at several points, but is instructive nonetheless.

11. Galen 1981: books 4–5.

12. Panksepp 1998.

13. Panksepp 1998: 206, 217–19.

14. See Sorabji's essay in this volume (Chapter 5).

15. Here is a commonplace model of such change that I assume both ancient Stoics and modern psychologists would accept: Suppose you enter a room in which your lover – whose back is turned to you – is cursing you angrily, shockingly, without warning, blaming you by name for some unnamed injury and breaking off your relationship with finality. You have a rush of sudden feeling and emotion – a rush, bewilderment, anger, hurt. And in the next moment, you see that your lover is reading a script – rehearsing a part in a play that has nothing to do with you. What happens to your emotions? The bewilderment, anger, and hurt drain away immediately, replaced by relief, hilarity, perhaps self-mockery. What happened? What changed? Cognition changed. Beliefs changed, and evidently drove the change in affect, including not only the conative impulse (whatever it was) but even the underlying state of physiological arousal. And we can multiply such examples without end. Psychotherapists quite generally go even farther than this, by acknowledging that many pathological emotional states are also transformable by changes in the subject's beliefs. Consequently, treatment regimes for many sorts of psychological illnesses – including depression, anxiety, phobias of various sorts – rely heavily on what can only be called Stoic principles. (At least one current variety of psychotherapy acknowledges this explicitly: rational emotive behavior therapy. See notes 6 and 17.) This sort of change is commonplace, and naturally enough suggests the Stoic hypothesis – namely, that for rational agents (e.g., humans at or above the age of reason) beliefs underwrite the *original* emotions in such examples as well.

16. Cooper 1999.

17. Contemporary versions of such psychotherapy are quite abundant, the most obvious being rational emotive behavior therapy. See, for example, Ellis 1974 and Lazarus 1995. And see, for the suggestion that some forms of

psychoanalysis might be "Stoic" in a thoroughgoing sense, D. H. Ingram's review of Becker 1998 in the *American Journal of Psychoanalysis* (Ingram 1999).

18. Lazarus 1994.

19. The canonical Stoic remedy would be to crank up the level of one's attention or perceptual ability. But there are physiological limits to sensory perception, and there is no reason to believe that there are not similar limits on the introspection of our mental states.

20. Panksepp 1998: chs. 2–4.

21. Chaplin and Krawiec 1979; Flanagan 1991: ch. 15; Stocker and Hegeman 1996.

22. Stocker and Hegeman 1996: ch. 3.

23. "Blow out your candles and make a wish. Want something. Want *some*thing." Amy, from *Company* (1970), music and lyrics by Stephen Sondheim, based on plays by George Furth.

24. I thank Brad Inwood and Richard Sorabji for suggesting I phrase this point to link it to the Stoic use of *tonos*. See definition II.4 in H. J. Liddell and R. Scott, *A Greek-English Lexicon*, rev. H. S. Jones (Oxford: Clarendon, 1968).

25. Kierkegaard 1993, 152–54: "Purity of Heart Is to Will One Thing."

26. E. E. Cummings 1994:291: "since feeling is first."

27. Personal correspondence, 16 March 1999, from the psychoanalyst Douglas H. Ingram M.D., on an early draft of this paper. "From my perspective . . . it is richness of emotion – including the simultaneous containment of conflicting emotions, layered emotions, and the ironic multiplicity of mingled emotions – that makes for a muscular psychological health. I believe that any suppression of emotion – including that suppression created by calling some emotions 'good' and some 'bad' – leads to a narrowing, even an impoverishment of the capacity for rational agency."

Works Cited

Primary Sources

Abelard, Peter. 1995. *Ethical Writings*. His *Ethics* or *"Know Yourself"* and *Dialogue between a Philosopher, a Jew, and a Christian*. Tr. Paul Vincent Spade. Introd. Marilyn McCord Adams. Indianapolis: Hackett.

    2001. *Collationes*. Ed. and tr. John Marenbon and Giovanni Orlandi. Oxford: Clarendon Press.

Apuleius. 1938. *Opera Quae Supersunt 3*. Ed. P. Thomas. Leipzig: Teubner.

Buridanus, Johannes. 1513. *Quaestiones super Decem Libros Ethicorum Aristotelis ad Nicomachum*. Paris: Ponset le Preux. Rpr. 1968, as *Super Decem Libros Ethicorum*. Frankfurt am Main: Minerva.

    1588 (actually 1518). *In Metaphysicen Aristotelis Quaestiones Argutissimae*, Paris. Rpr. 1964, as *Kommentar zur Aristotelischen Metaphysik*, Frankfurt am Main: Minerva.

Charron, Pierre. 1986. *Les trois vérités* (1595); *Discours* (1600); *De la sagesse* (1601, 1604). Rpr. in Corpus des œuvres de philosophie en langue française. Paris: Fayard.

Chevreau, Urbain. 1652. *L'escole du sage*. Paris. Rpr. Lyon, 1660.

    1656. *Le philosophe moral*. Paris.

    1660. *Suite de l'école du sage*. Paris.

Cicero, Marcus Tullius. 1905. *Tusculanae Disputationes Libri Quinque*. Ed. T. W. Dougan and R. M. Henry. Cambridge: Cambridge University Press.

    1931. *De Finibus Bonorum et Malorum*. 2nd ed. Tr. H. Rackham. Loeb Classical Library. Works of Cicero 17. Cambridge, Mass.: Harvard University Press; London: William Heinemann.

    1951. *De Natura Deorum; Academica*. Tr. H. Rackham. Loeb Classical Library. Works of Cicero 19. Cambridge, Mass.: Harvard University Press; London: William Heinemann.

    1966. *Tusculan Disputations*. Tr. J. E. King. Rev. ed. Loeb Classical Library. Works of Cicero 18. Cambridge, Mass.: Harvard University Press; London: William Heinemann.

1991. *On Duties*. Ed. and tr. Miriam Griffin and Eileen Atkins. Cambridge: Cambridge University Press.

1994. *De Officiis*. Ed. Michael Winterbottom. Oxford: Clarendon Press.

Commentaria in Aristotelem Graeca. 1882–1907. Berlin.

Corpus Christianorum. Series Latina. 1953. Turnhout: Brepols.

Corpus Scriptorum Ecclesiasticorum Latinorum. 1865–. Vienna: Tempsky.

dal Pra, Mario (ed.). 1969. *Pietro Abelardo, Scritti di logica*. Florence: La nouva Italia.

de Balzac, Guez. 1661. *Socrate chrétien*. Paris: A. Courbé.

de Rijk, L. M. (ed.). 1970. *Petrus Abaelardus, Dialectica*. 2nd rev. ed. Assen: Van Gorcum.

(ed.). 1994a. *Nicholas of Autrecourt. His Correspondence with Master Giles and Bernard of Arezzo*. Studien und Texte zur Geistesgeschichte des Mittelalters 42. Leiden: Brill.

(ed.). 1998. *Johannes Buridanus, Summulae, De Suppositionibus*. Artistarium 10-4. Nijmegen: Ingenium.

Descartes, René. 1964–74. *Oeuvres de Descartes*. Ed. Charles Adam and Paul Tannery. 12 vols. Paris: J. Vrin.

1984–91. *The Philosophical Writings of Descartes*. Tr. John Cottingham, Robert Stoothoff, and Dugald Murdoch (vols. 1–2). Tr. John Cottingham, Robert Stoothoff, Dugald Murdoch, and Anthony Kenny (vol. 3). Cambridge: Cambridge University Press.

Diogenes Laertius. 1979–80. *Lives of Eminent Philosophers*. 2 vols. Tr. R. D. Hicks. Loeb Classical Library 184–85. Cambridge, Mass.: Harvard University Press; London: William Heinemann.

du Vair, Guillaume. 1641. *Oeuvres*. Paris. Rpr. 1970, with corrections and additions. 2 vols. Geneva: Slatkine Reprints.

1941. *Traité de la constance et de la consolation es calamités publiques* (1590). Rpr. Paris: La Nef.

1946. *Philosophie morale des Stoïques* (1585); *De la sainte philosophie* (1600). Ed. G. Michaut. Paris: Vrin.

Ebbesen, Sten (ed.). 1977. *Incertorum Auctorum Quaestiones super Sophisticos Elenchos*. Corpus Philosophorum Danicorum Medii Aevi 7. Copenhagen: Det danske Sprog- og Litteraturselskab.

(ed.). 1999a. "Anonymus D'Orvillensis' Commentary on Aristotle's *Categories*." *Cahiers de l'Institut du Moyen Age Grec et Latin* 70: 229–423.

Ebbesen, Sten, K. M. Fredborg, and L. O. Nielsen (eds.). 1983. "*Compendium logicae Porretanum ex codice Oxoniensi Collegii Corporis Christi* 250: A Manual of Porretan Doctrine by a Pupil of Gilbert's." *Cahiers de l'Institut du Moyen Age Grec et Latin* 46: iii–xviii, 1–113.

Ebbesen, Sten, Thomas Izbicki, John Longeway, Francesco del Punta, and Eleonore Stump (eds.). 1984. *Simon of Faversham, Quaestiones super Libro Elenchorum*. Studies and Texts 60. Toronto: Pontifical Institute of Mediaeval Studies.

Ebbesen, Sten, and L. B. Mortensen (eds.). 1985–88. *Andreae Sunonis filii Hexaemeron*. Corpus Philosophorum Danicorum Medii Aevi 11.1–2. Copenhagen: Det danske Sprog- og Litteraturselskab.

Ebbesen, Sten, and Jan Pinborg. 1982. "Gennadios and Western Scholasticism. Radulphus Brito's *Ars Vetus* in Greek Translation." *Classica et Mediaevalia* 33: 263–319.

Epictetus. 1965. *Dissertationes ab Arriani Digestae.* Ed. H. Schenkl. Bibliotheca scriptorum Graecorum et Romanorum Teubneriana. Stuttgart: Teubner.

———. 1995. *The Discourses.* Ed. Christopher Gill. Tr. Elizabeth Carther. Rev. Robin Hard. Everyman Library. London: J. M. Dent; Rutland, Vt.: C. E. Tuttle.

Freud, Sigmund. 1952. *Selected Papers on Hysteria.* In *The Major Works of Sigmund Freud*, ed. and tr. A. A. Brill, pp. 25–118. Chicago: Encyclopedia Brittanica.

Galen. 1896. *Institutio Logica.* Ed. Karl Kalbfleisch. Leipzig: Teubner.

———. 1981. *On the Doctrines of Hippocrates and Plato.* Ed. and tr. Phillip De Lacy. 2nd ed. Corpus Medicorum Graecorum 5.4, 1–2. Berlin: Akademie-Verlag.

Gellius, Aulus. 1990. *Noctes Atticae.* Ed. Peter K. Marshall. 2 vols. Scriptorum classicorum bibliotheca Oxoniensis. Oxford: Clarendon Press.

Goulart, Simon. 1596. *Œuvres morales et mêlées.* Geneva. Rpr. Geneva, 1606.

———. 1612. *Le sage vieillard.* Tr. by Joseph Hall as *The Wise Old Man.* London: 1621.

Green-Pedersen, Niels Jørgen (ed.). 1976. *Boethii Daci Opera: Opuscula.* Corpus Philosophorum Danicorum Medii Aevi 6.2. Copenhagen: Det danske Sprog- og Litteraturselskab.

[Hall, Joseph]. 1596. *Remedies against Discontentment, or Treatise on Contentment under Any Circumstances.* London. Tr. by Théodore Jaquemot as *Remèdes contre les mécontentements ou Traité du contentement en quelque condition que ce soit.* Geneva, 1664.

Hall, Joseph. 1605. *The Christian Seneca.* Tr. by Théodore Jaquemot as *Le Sénèque chrétien.* Geneva, 1628.

———. 1608. *Characters of Virtues and Vices.* London. Tr. by Théodore Jaquemot as *Les caractères des vertus et des vices.* Geneva, 1628.

———. 1609. *Solomon's Divine Arts, or Ethics, Politics, and Economics.* London. Tr. by Théodore Jaquemot as *Les arts divins de Salomon ou ethiques, politiques & economiques.* Geneva, 1632.

———. 1620. *Heaven upon Earth or True Peace and Tranquillity of Mind.* London. Tr. by Théodore Jaquemot as *Le ciel sur la terre ou discours sur la vraie tranquillité de l'esprit.* Geneva, 1629.

Hamesse, Jacqueline (ed.). 1974. *Les auctoritates Aristotelis.* Philosophes Médiévaux 17. Louvain: Publications Universitaires; Paris: Béatrice-Nauwelaerts.

Häring, N. M. (ed.). 1953. "A Latin Dialogue on the Doctrine of Gilbert of Poitiers." *Mediaeval Studies* 15: 243–89.

———. (ed.). 1966. *The Commentaries on Boethius by Gilbert of Poitiers.* Studies and Texts 13. Toronto: Pontifical Institute of Mediaeval Studies.

———. (ed.). 1971. *Thierry of Chartres, Tractatus de sex dierum operibus.* Studies and Texts 20. Toronto: Pontifical Institute of Mediaeval Studies.

Hülser, Karlheinz (ed.). 1987–88. *Die Fragmente zur Dialektik der Stoiker.* 4 vols. Stuttgart-Bad Cannstatt: Frommann-Holzboog.

Iwakuma, Yukio (ed.). Forthcoming. *Ars Meliduna.*

Kant, Immanuel. 1991. *Political Writings.* Ed. Hans Reiss. 2nd ed. Cambridge: Cambridge University Press.

Kierkegaard, Søren. 1993. *Upbuilding Discourses in Various Spirits.* In *Kierkegaard's Writings*, ed. and tr. Howard V. Hong and Edna H. Hong, vol. 15. Princeton: Princeton University Press.

Le Grand, Antoine. 1663. *Les caractères de l'homme sans passion selon les sentiments de Sénèque.* Paris.

Leibniz, Gottfried Wilhem. 1875–90. *Die philosophische schriften.* Ed. C. I. Gerhardt. 7 vols. Berlin: Weidmann.

Lipsius, Justus. 1584. *De Constantia libri duo qui alloquium praecipue continent in publicis malis.* Anvers. Rpr. 1873, in Lucien du Bois (tr.), *Traité de la Constance* (Latin text with facing French). Brussels: Merzbach.

Long, A. A., and David Sedley (ed.). 1987. *The Hellenistic Philosophers.* 2 vols. Cambridge: Cambridge University Press.

Luscombe, David E. (ed.). 1971. *Peter Abelard's Ethics.* Oxford: Clarendon Press.

Meiser, Karl (ed.). 1880. *Anicii Manlii Severini Boethii Commentarii in librum Aristotelis PERI ERMHNEIAS, pars 2.* Leipzig: Teubner.

Montaigne, Michel de. 1965. *Essais.* Ed. P. Villey. Paris: PUF.

Nikitas, D. Z. (ed.). 1990. *Boethius, De topicis differentiis kai hoi Byzantinos metaphraseis ton Manouel Holovolou kai Prochorou Kydone.* Philosophi Byzantini 5. Athens: Academy of Athens; Paris: Vrin; Brussels: Ousia.

Migne, J. P. (ed.). 1844–64. *Patrologiae Cursus Completus, Series Latina.* Paris.
   (ed.). 1857–66. *Patrologiae Cursus Completus, Series Graeca.* Paris.

Obertello, L. (ed.). 1969. *A. M. Severino Boezio, De hypotheticis syllogismis.* Brescia: Istituto di filosofia.

Olympiodorus of Alexandria. 1970. *In Platonis Gorgiam Commentaria.* Ed. L. Westerink. Leipzig: Teubner.

Origen. 1966. *On First Principles. Being Koetschau's Text of the "De Principiis."* Tr. G. W. Butterworth. Harper Torchbooks. Cathedral Library. New York: Harper and Row.

Peter Lombard. 1971–81. *Sententiae in IV libris distinctae.* 3rd ed. Spicilegium Bonaventurianum 4–5. Grottaferrata: Editiones Collegii S. Bonaventurae ad Claras Aquas.

Philo of Alexandria. 1929. *Every Good Man Is Free; The Contemplative Life; The Eternity of the World; Against Flaccus; Apology for the Jews; On Providence.* Tr. F. H. Colson. Loeb Classical Library. Works of Philo of Alexandria 9. Cambridge, Mass.: Harvard University Press; London: William Heinemann.
   1953. *Philo Supplement.* Tr. Ralph Marcus. 2 vols. Loeb Classical Library. Works of Philo of Alexandria. Cambridge, Mass.: Harvard University Press; London: William Heinemann.

Pinborg, Jan (ed.). 1975. *Augustine, De dialectica.* Dordrecht: Reidel.

Plato. 1962. *Timaeus a Calcidio translatus.* Ed. J. H. Waszink. Plato Latinus 4. London: Warburg Institute.
   1979. *Gorgias.* Tr. T. H. Irwin. Oxford: Clarendon Press.

Senault, Jean-François. 1641. *De l'usage des passions.* Paris.
   1644. *L'homme criminel.* Paris.
   1648. *L'homme chrétien.* Paris.

Seneca, Lucius Annaeus. 1917–20. *Epistles.* Tr. Richard M. Gummere. 2 vols. Loeb
   Classical Library. Works of Seneca 4–5. Cambridge, Mass.: Harvard University
   Press; London: William Heinemann.
   1963–65. *Moral Essays.* Tr. John W. Basore. 3 vols. Loeb Classical Library. Works
   of Seneca 1–3. Cambridge, Mass.: Harvard University Press; London: William
   Heinemann.
   1965. *Ad Lucilium Epistulae Morales.* 2 vols. Ed. L. D. Reynolds. Oxford: Clarendon Press.
   1977. *Dialogorum libri decimi.* Ed. L. D. Reynolds. Oxford: Clarendon Press.
   1994. *Four Dialogues.* Tr. C. D. N. Costa. Warminster: Aris and Phillips.
   1995. *Moral and Political Essays.* Ed. J. M. Cooper and J. F. Procopé. Cambridge:
   Cambridge University Press.
Sheldon-Williams, I. P. (ed.). 1968. *Johannes Scottus Eriugena, Periphyseon I.* Scrip-
   tores Latini Hiberniae 7. Dublin: Institute for Advanced Studies.
Simplicius. 1907. In *Aristotelis Categorias Commentarium.* Ed. Karl Kalbfleisch. Com-
   mentaria in Aristotelem Graeca 8. Berlin: Reimer.
Smith, Adam. 1982. *The Theory of Moral Sentiments.* Ed. D. D. Raphael and A. L.
   Macfie. Indianapolis: Liberty Classics.
Spinoza, Benedictus de. 1951. *Works.* Tr. R. H. M. Elwes. 2 vols. New York: Dover.
   1992. *The Ethics; Treatise on the Emendation of the Intellect; Selected Letters.* Tr. Samuel
   Shirley. Ed. Seymour Feldman. Indianapolis: Hackett.
Stobaeus, John. 1974. *Anthologium.* Ed. C. Wachsmuth and Otto Hense. Berlin:
   Weidmann.
von Arnim, H. (ed.). 1968. *Stoicorum Veterum Fragmenta.* 4 vols. Stuttgart: Teubner.
William of Ockham. 1967–85. *Opera Philosophica et Theologica.* 17 vols. Ed.
   Gedeon Gál. St. Bonaventure, N.Y.: St. Bonaventure University Press and
   the Franciscan Institute.
Yves de Paris. 1638. *De l'indifférence.* Modern edition by René Bady. 1966. Paris:
   Les Belles Lettres.

Secondary Sources

Annas, Julia. 1993. *The Morality of Happiness.* Cambridge, Mass.: Harvard University
   Press.
Appiah, Kwame Anthony. 1996. *For Love of Country.* Boston: Beacon Press.
Barnes, Jonathan. 1997. *Logic and the Imperial Stoa.* Leiden: Brill.
Becker, Ernest. 1973. *The Denial of Death.* New York: Free Press.
Becker, Lawrence C. 1998. *A New Stoicism.* Princeton: Princeton University Press.
Beitz, Charles. 1979. *Political Theory and International Relations.* Princeton: Prince-
   ton University Press.
Bellincioni, Maria Scarpat. 1984a. "Clementia Liberum Arbitrium Habet." *Paideia*
   39: 173–83. Rpr. 1986, in *Studi Senecani e Altri Scritti,* ed. Maria Scarpat
   Bellincioni, pp. 113–25. Brescia: Paideia Editrice.
   1984b. *Potere ed etica in Seneca: Clementia e voluntas amica.* Brescia: Paideia
   Editrice.
Bennett, Jonathan. 1984. *A Study of Spinoza's "Ethics."* Indianapolis: Hackett.

Benson, Hugh H. 1995. "The Dissolution of the Problem of the *Elenchus*." *Oxford Studies in Ancient Philosophy* 13: 45–112.

Blomme, Robert. 1958. *La doctrine du péché dans les écoles théologiques de la première moitié du XIIe siècle.* Publications Universitaires de Louvain. Louvain: Gembloux.

Bobzien, Susanne. 1998. *Determinism and Freedom in Stoic Philosophy.* Oxford: Clarendon Press.

Bonhöffer, Adolf Friedrich. 1890. *Epictet und die Stoa. Untersuchungen zur stoischen Philosophie.* Stuttgart: F. Enke.

    1894. *Die Ethik des Stoikers Epictet.* Stuttgart: F. Enke. Tr. 1996, by W. O. Stephens as *The Ethics of the Stoic Epictetus.* Revisioning Philosophy 2. New York: Peter Lang.

Brennan, Tad. 1998. "The Old Stoic Theory of the Emotions." In *The Emotions in Hellenistic Philosophy*, ed. J. Sihvola and T. Engberg-Pedersen, pp. 21–70. Dordrecht: Kluwer.

Carnois, Bernard. 1980. "Le désir selon les Stoïciens et selon Spinoza." *Dialogue* 19: 255–77.

Carraud, Vincent. 1997. "Morale par provision et probabilité." In *Descartes et le Moyen Age*, ed. Joël Biard and Roshdi Rashed, pp. 259–79. Paris: Vrin.

Chaplin, James P., and T. S. Krawiec. 1979. *Systems and Theories of Psychology.* 4th ed. New York: Holt, Rinehart, and Winston.

Chomsky, Noam. 1966. *Cartesian Linguistics.* New York: Harper and Row.

Cooper, John M. 1998. "Posidonius on Emotions." In *The Emotions in Hellenistic Philosophy*, ed. J. Sihvola and T. Engberg-Pedersen, pp. 71–111. Dordrecht: Kluwer.

    1999. *Reason and Emotion: Essays on Ancient Moral Psychology and Ethical Theory.* Princeton: Princeton University Press.

Craske, Michelle G. 1999. *Anxiety Disorders.* Boulder, Colo.: Westview Press.

Cummings, E. E. 1994. *Complete Poems, 1904–1962.* New York: Liveright.

DeDijn, Herman. 1993. "Knowledge, Anthropocentrism and Salvation." *Studia Spinozana* 9: 247–62.

Deleuze, Gilles. 1981. *Spinoza: Philosophie Pratique.* Paris: Éditions de Minuit.

de Rijk, L. M. 1962–67. *Logica Modernorum: A Contribution to the History of Early Terminist Logic.* 2 vols. Assen: Van Gorcum.

    1994b. "John Buridan on Man's Capability of Grasping the Truth." *Miscellanea Mediaevalia* 22: 281–303.

Donagan, Alan. 1977. *The Theory of Morality.* Chicago: University of Chicago Press.

Döring, Klaus. 1979. *Exemplum Socratis: Studien zur Sokratesnachwirkung in der kynisch-stoischen Popularphilosophie der frühen Kaiserzeit und im frühen Christentum.* Hermes, Zeitschrift für klassische Philologie, Einzelschriften 42. Wiesbaden: F. Steiner.

Düll, Rudolf. 1976. "Seneca Iurisconsultus." *Aufstieg und Niedergang der römischen Welt* 2.15: 365–80.

Dyck, Andrew R. 1996. *A Commentary on Cicero, "De officiis."* Ann Arbor: University of Michigan Press.

Ebbesen, Sten. 1981. *Commentators and Commentaries on Aristotle's Sophistici Elenchi: A Study of Post-Aristotelian Ancient and Medieval Writings on Fallacies.* 3 vols.

Corpus Latinum Commentariorum in Aristotelem Graecorum, 7.1–3. Leiden: Brill.

1984. "Proof and Its Limits according to Buridan, *Summulae* 8." In *Preuve et raisons à l'Université de Paris. Logique, ontologie et théologie au XIVe siècle*, ed. Z. Kaluza and P. Vignaux, pp. 97–110. Paris: Vrin.

1989. "Three 13th-Century Sophismata about Beginning and Ceasing." *Cahiers de l'Institut du Moyen Age Grec et Latin* 59: 121–80.

1992. "What Must One Have an Opinion About?" *Vivarium* 30: 62–79.

1993. "The Theory of *loci* in Antiquity and the Middle Ages." In *Argumentationstheorie. Scholastische Forschungen zu den logischen und semantischen Regeln korrekten Folgerns*, ed. Klaus Jacobi, pp. 15–39. Leiden: Brill.

1997. "Doing Theology with Sophismata." In *Vestigia, imagines, verba. Semiotics and Logic in Medieval Theological Texts (XIIth–XIVth Century)*, ed. C. Marmo, pp. 151–69. Semiotic and Cognitive Studies 4. Turnhout: Brepols.

1999. "Radulphus Brito. The Last of the Great Arts Masters. Or: Philosophy and Freedom." *Miscellanea Mediaevalia* 27: 231–51.

Ellis, Albert. 1974. *Humanistic Psychotherapy: The Rational-Emotive Approach*. New York: McGraw-Hill.

Engberg-Pedersen, Troels. 1990. *The Stoic Theory of Oikeiōsis: Moral Development and Social Interaction in Early Stoic Philosophy*. Studies in Hellenistic Civilization 2. Aarhus: Aarhus University Press.

2000. *Paul and the Stoics*. Edinburgh: T & T Clark; Louisville, Ky.: Westminster John Knox.

(ed.). 2001. *Paul beyond the Judaism/Hellenism Divide*. Louisville, Ky.: Westminster John Knox.

Eymard d'Angers, Julien (Charles Chesneau). 1951–52. "Le stoïcisme en France dans la première moitié du XXVIIIe siècle." In *Études franciscaines* 2:287–97 and 389–410; 3:5–19 and 133–57. This study was originally published as a series of five articles: "Les origines (1575–1616)"; "Pierre Charron"; "Le stoïcisme chrétien"; "Le stoïcisme et les protestants"; and "L'humanisme chrétien." All five articles were reprinted in 1976 as *Recherches sur le stoïcisme au XVIe et XVIIe siècles*. Hildesheim: Georg Olms Verlag.

1964. "Le renouveau du stoïcisme au XVIe et au XVIIe siècles." In *Actes du VIIè Congrès de l'Association Guillaume Budé*, pp. 122–52. Paris: Les Belles Lettres.

Fillion-Lahille, Janine. 1984. *Le De Ira de Sénèque et la philosophie stoïcienne des passions*. Paris: Klincksieck.

Flanagan, Owen. 1991. *Varieties of Moral Personality*. Cambridge, Mass.: Harvard University Press.

Frede, Michael. 1974. *Die stoische Logik*. Göttingen: Wandenhoeck and Ruprecht.

1986. "The Stoic Doctrine of the Affections of the Soul." In *The Norms of Nature*, ed. Malcolm Schofield and Gisela Striker, pp. 93–110. Cambridge: Cambridge University Press.

Gewirth, Alan. 1985. *Human Rights: Essays on Justification and Applications*. Chicago: University of Chicago Press.

1996. *The Community of Rights*. Chicago: University of Chicago Press.

Gill, Christopher. 1983. "Did Chrysippus Understand Medea?" *Phronesis* 28: 136–49.

Goodin, Robert. 1985. *Protecting the Vulnerable*. Chicago: University of Chicago Press.

1988. "What Is So Special about Our Fellow Countrymen?" *Ethics* 98: 663–86.

Gourinat, Jean-Baptiste. 1999. "La définition et les propriétés de la proposition dans le stoïcisme ancien." In *Théories de la phrase et de la proposition de Platon à Averroès*, ed. Philippe Büttgen, Stéphane Diebler, and Marwan Rashed, pp. 133–50. Études de littérature ancienne 10. Paris: Éditions Rue d'Ulm and Presses de l'école normale supérieure.

2001. "Le Socrate d'Épictète." *Philosophie Antique* 1: 137–65.

Griffin, Miriam. 1992. *Seneca: A Philosopher in Politics*. 2nd ed. Oxford: Clarendon Press.

Gueroult, Martial. 1985. *Descartes's Philosophy Interpreted according to the Order of Reasons*. Tr. Roger Ariew. Minneapolis: University of Minnesota Press.

Hadot, Pierre. 1992. *La citadelle intérieure: Introduction aux Pensées de Marc Aurèle*. Paris: Fayard.

Hampshire, Stuart. 1956. *Spinoza*. London: Faber and Faber.

Holmes, Stephen, and Cass R. Sunstein. 1999. *The Cost of Rights: Why Liberty Depends on Taxes*. New York: W. W. Norton.

Ildefonse, Frédérique. 1999. "La théorie stoïcienne de la phrase (énoncé, proposition) et son influence chez les grammariens." In *Théories de la phrase et de la proposition de Platon à Averroès*, ed. Philippe Büttgen, Stéphane Diebler, and Marwan Rashed, pp. 151–70. Études de littérature ancienne 10. Paris: Éditions Rue d'Ulm and Presses de l'école normale supérieure.

Ingram, D. H. 1999. Review of Becker 1998. *American Journal of Psychoanalysis* 59: 292–94.

Inwood, Brad. 1985. *Ethics and Human Action in Early Stoicism*. Oxford: Clarendon Press.

1993. "Seneca and Psychological Dualism." In *Passions and Perceptions: Studies in Hellenistic Philosophy of Mind*, ed. Jacques Brunschwig and Martha Nussbaum, pp. 150–83. Cambridge: Cambridge University Press.

1995. "Politics and Paradox in Seneca's *De Beneficiis*." In *Justice and Generosity*, ed. A. Laks and M. Schofield, pp. 241–65. Cambridge: Cambridge University Press.

1999a. "God and Human Knowledge in Seneca's *Natural Questions*." *Proceedings of the Boston Area Colloquium in Ancient Philosophy* 15: 23–43.

1999b. "Rules and Reasoning in Stoic Ethics." In *Topics in Stoic Philosophy*, ed. K. Ierodiakonou, pp. 95–127. Oxford: Clarendon Press.

Iwakuma, Yukio. 1999. "Logic, Grammar, and Theology in the 11th and 12th Centuries." In *Medieval Analyses in Language and Cognition*, ed. Sten Ebbesen and R. L. Friedman, pp. 165–89. Det Kongelige Danske Videnskabernes Selskab, Historisk-filosofiske Meddelelser 77. Copenhagen.

Iwakuma, Yukio, and Sten Ebbesen. 1992. "Logico-Theological Schools from the Second Half of the Twelfth Century: A List of Sources." *Vivarium* 30: 173–210.

Jacobi, Klaus. 1987. "Kategorien der Sittenlehre. Gedanken zur Sprache der Moral in einem Logik-Kompendium des 12. Jahrhunderts." In *Philosophie im Mittelalter. Entwicklungslinien und Paradigmen*, ed. J. P. Beckmann and Wolfgang Kluxen, pp. 103–24. Hamburg: Felix Meiner.

Jagu, Amand. 1946. *Épictète et Platon*. Paris: J. Vrin.

James, Susan. 1993. "Spinoza the Stoic." In *The Rise of Modern Philosophy*, ed. Tom Sorell, pp. 289–316. Oxford: Clarendon Press.

——— 1994. "Internal and External in the Work of Descartes." In *Philosophy in the Age of Pluralism*, ed. James Tully, pp. 7–19. Cambridge: Cambridge University Press.

James, William. 1890. *The Principles of Psychology*. New York: Henry Holt.

Jolivet, Jean. 1963. "Abélard et le philosophe (Occident et Islam au XIIe siècle)." *Revue de l'histoire des religions* 164: 181–89.

——— 1980. "Doctrines et figures de philosophes chez Abélard." In *Petrus Abaelardus (1079–1142): Person, Werk und Wirkung*, ed. Rudolf Thomas, pp. 103–20. Trier theologische Studien 38. Trier: Paulinus.

Jolivet, Jean, and A. de Libera (eds.). 1987. *Gilbert de Poitiers et ses contemporains*. History of Logic 5. Naples: Bibliopolis.

Kagan, Shelly. 1989. *The Limits of Morality*. Oxford: Clarendon Press.

King, Peter. 1999. "Ockham's Ethical Theory." In *The Cambridge Companion to Ockham*, ed. Paul Vincent Spade, pp. 227–44. Cambridge: Cambridge University Press.

Lagrée, Jacqueline. 1994. *Juste Lipse et la restauration du stoïcisme*. With Latin text and French translation of *Constance, Manuel de philosophie stoïcienne*, and *Physique des stoïciens*. Collection Philologie et Mercure. Paris: Vrin.

——— 1995. "Le sage, le prince et la foule." In *L'individu dans la pensée moderne, XVIe – XVIIIe siècles*, ed. G. M. Cazzaniaga and Y. C. Zavka, pp. 513–26. Pisa: Università di Pisa.

——— 1998. "Juste Lipse, l'âme et la vertu." In *Iustus Lipsius: Europae lumen et columen*, pp. 90–106. *Supplementa Humanistica Lovaniensia*, vol. 15. Leuven: Leuven University Press.

——— 1999. "Juste Lipse et la conception stoïcienne de l'âme" (with a translation of chaps. 17–19 of book 3 of *Physique des stoïciens*). In *Les âmes*, ed. J. Robelin and C. Duflo, pp. 63–79. Besançon: PU Franc-Comtoises.

——— 1999b. "La vertu stoïcienne de constance." In *Le stoïcisme au XVIe et au XVIIe siècle*, ed. P. F. Moreau and A. Michel, pp. 94–116. Paris: Albin Michel.

Lambertini, Roberto. 1989. "*Resurgant entia rationis*. Matthaeus de Augubio on the Object of Logic." *Cahiers de l'Institut du Moyen Age Grec et Latin* 59: 3–60.

Landis, Michele L. 1998. "Let Me Next Time Be 'Tried by Fire': Disaster Relief and the Origins of the American Welfare State, 1789–1874." *Northwestern Law Review* 92: 967–1034.

Lapidge, Michael. 1988. "The Stoic Inheritance." In *A History of Twelfth-Century Western Philosophy*, ed. Peter Dronke, pp. 81–112. Cambridge: Cambridge University Press.

Lauterpacht, Hersch. 1946. "The Grotian Tradition in International Law." *British Yearbook of International Law* 23: 1–53. Rpr. 1975, in *International Law: Collected Papers*, ed. H. Lauterpacht, 2.1: 307–65. Cambridge: Cambridge University Press.

Lazarus, Richard S. 1994. *Emotion and Adaptation*. New York: Oxford University Press.

1995. "Cognition and Emotion from the RET Standpoint." *Journal of Rational-Emotive and Cognitive-Behavior Therapy* 13: 29–54.

Levi, Anthony. 1964. *French Moralists: The Theory of the Passions, 1585–1649.* Oxford: Clarendon Press.

Lloyd, Genevieve. 1996. *Spinoza and the Stoics.* London: Routledge.

Long, A. A. 1971. *Problems in Stoicism.* London: Ashgate.

1988. "Socrates in Hellenistic Philosophy." *Classical Quarterly 38: 150–71.* Rpr. in Long 1996: 1–34.

1996. *Stoic Studies.* Cambridge: Cambridge University Press.

2000. "Epictetus as Socratic Mentor." *Proceedings of the Cambridge Philological Society* 41: 79–98.

2002. *Epictetus: A Stoic and Socratic Guide to Life.* Oxford: Clarendon Press.

Lottin, Odon. 1942–60. *Psychologie et morale aux XIIe et XIIIe siècles.* 6 vols. Louvain: Abbaye du Mont César.

Malherbe, Abraham J. 1986. *Moral Exhortation: A Greco-Roman Sourcebook.* Ed. Wayne A. Meeks. Library of Early Christianity 4. Philadelphia: Westminster.

1987. *Paul and the Thessalonians: The Philosophic Tradition of Pastoral Care.* Philadelphia: Fortress.

1989. *Paul and the Popular Philosophers.* Minneapolis: Fortress.

1992. "Hellenistic Moralists and the New Testament." *Aufstieg und Niedergang der römischen Welt* II. 2.16.1: 268–333.

1994. "Determinism and Free Will in Paul: The Argument of 1 Corinthians 8 and 9." In *Paul in His Hellenistic Context,* ed. T. Engberg-Pedersen, pp. 231–55. Edinburgh: T&T Clark; Minneapolis: Fortress.

Marenbon, John. 1997. *The Philosophy of Peter Abelard.* Cambridge: Cambridge University Press.

Marshall, John. 1998. *Descartes's Moral Theory.* Ithaca, N.Y.: Cornell University Press, 1998.

Matheron, Alexandre. 1994. "Le moment stoïcien de l'*Éthique* de Spinoza." In *Le Stoïcisme aux XVIe et XVIIe Siècles,* ed. Jacqueline Lagrée, pp. 147–62. Caen: Presses Universitaires de Caen. Rpr., Matheron 1999.

1999. "Le moment stoïcien de l'*Éthique* de Spinoza." In *Le stoïcisme au XVIe et au XVIIe Siècle,* ed. P. F. Moreau and A. Michel, pp. 302–16. Paris: Albin Michel.

Maurach, Gregor. 1965. "Zur Eigenart and Herkunft von Senecas Methode in den *Naturales Quaestiones.*" *Hermes* 93: 357–69. Rpr. 1975, in *Seneca als Philosoph,* ed. G. Maurach, pp. 305–22. Wege der Forschung 414. Darmstadt.

McGrade, A. S. 1999. "Natural Law and Moral Omnipotence." In *The Cambridge Companion to Ockham,* ed. Paul Vincent Spade, pp. 273–301. Cambridge: Cambridge University Press.

Mehl, Edouard. 1999. "Les Méditations stoïciennes de Descartes." In *Le stoïcisme au XVIè et au XVIIè siècle,* ed. P. F. Moreau and A. Michel, pp. 251–80. Paris: Albin Michel.

Mesnard, P. 1928. "Du Vair et le néo-stoïcisme." *Revue histoire de la Philosophie* 2: 142–66.

Millar, Fergus. 1977. *The Emperor in the Roman World (31 BC–AD 337).* Ithaca, N.Y.: Cornell University Press.

Murphy, Liam B. 1993. "The Demands of Beneficence." *Philosophy and Public Affairs* 22: 267–92.

2000. *Moral Demands in Nonideal Theory.* New York: Oxford University Press.

Nagel, Thomas. 1991. *Equality and Partiality.* New York: Oxford University Press.

Nielsen, Lauge Olaf. 1982. *Theology and Philosophy in the Twelfth Century.* Acta Theologica Danica 15. Leiden: Brill.

Nordenfelt, Lennart. 1997. "The Stoic Conception of Mental Disorder: The Case of Cicero." *Philosophy, Psychiatry and Psychology* 4: 285–91.

Nozick, Robert. 1974. *Anarchy, State, and Utopia.* New York: Basic Books.

Nuchelmans, Gabriel. 1973. *Theories of the Proposition: Ancient and Medieval Conceptions of the Bearers of Truth and Falsity.* Amsterdam: North-Holland.

Nussbaum, Martha. 1994. *The Therapy of Desire: Theory and Practice in Hellenistic Ethics.* Princeton: Princeton University Press.

1995. "*Erōs* and the Wise: The Stoic Response to a Cultural Dilemma." *Oxford Studies in Ancient Philosophy* 13: 231–67.

1997. "Kant and Stoic Cosmopolitanism." In *Perpetual Peace*, ed. J. Bohmann, pp. 25–38. Cambridge, Mass.: MIT Press. Rpr. 1997, in *Journal of Political Philosophy* 5: 1–25.

2000. *Women and Human Development: The Capabilities Approach.* Cambridge: Cambridge University Press.

2001. *Upheavals of Thought: The Intelligence of Emotions.* Cambridge: Cambridge University Press.

2002. *For Love of Country: A New Democracy Forum on the Limits of Patriotism.* Ed. Joshua Cohen and Joel Rogers. Boston: Beacon Press.

Nussbaum, Martha, and Juha Sihvola (eds.). 2002. *The Sleep of Reason: Erotic Experience and Sexual Ethics in Ancient Greece and Rome.* Chicago: University of Chicago Press.

Olivo, Gilles. 1999. "Une patience sans espérance? Descartes et le stoïcisme." In *Le stoïcisme au XVIè et au XVIIè siècle*, ed. P. F. Moreau and A. Michel, pp. 234–50. Paris: Albin Michel.

Panksepp, Jaak. 1998. *Affective Neuroscience: The Foundations of Human and Animal Emotions.* New York: Oxford University Press.

Pereboom, Derk. 1994. "Stoic Psychotherapy in Descartes and Spinoza." *Faith and Philosophy* 11: 592–625.

Pinborg, Jan. 1962. "Das Sprachdenken der Stoa und Augustins Dialektik." *Classica et Mediaevalia* 23: 148–77.

Pohlenz, Max. 1949. "Paulus und die Stoa." *Zeitschrift für die neutestamentliche Wissenschaft* 42: 69–104.

Pogge, Thomas. 1989. *Realizing Rawls.* Ithaca, N.Y.: Cornell University Press.

Rawls, John. 1993. "The Law of Peoples." In *On Human Rights: The Oxford Amnesty Lectures 1993*, ed. Stephen Shute and Susan Hurley, pp. 41–82. New York: Basic Books.

Reich, Klaus. 1939. "Kant and Greek Ethics." *Mind* 48: 338–54, 446–63.

Rodis-Lewis, Geneviève. 1962. *La morale de Descartes.* Paris: PUF.

Roques, P. 1957. "La philosophie morale des Stoïques de Guillaume du Vair." *Archives de philosophie* 20: 226–39, 379–91.

Rutherford, Donald. 2001. "Leibniz and the Stoics: The Consolations of Theodicy." In *The Problem of Evil in Early Modern Philosophy*, ed. E. Kremer and M. Latzer, pp. 138–64. Toronto: University of Toronto Press.

———. 2003. "Patience sans espérance: Leibniz's Critique of Stoicism." In *Hellenistic and Early Modern Philosophy*, ed. Brad Inwood and Jon Miller. Cambridge: Cambridge University Press.

Scheffler, Samuel. 1982. *The Rejection of Consequentialism.* Oxford: Clarendon Press.

Schneewind, J. B. 1998. *The Invention of Autonomy.* Cambridge: Cambridge University Press.

Schofield, Malcolm. 1999. *The Stoic Idea of the City.* Rev. ed. with a new introduction by Martha Nussbaum. Chicago: University of Chicago Press.

Schrijvers, P. H. 1986. "Literary and Philosophical Aspects of Lipsius's *De Constantia in publicis malis.*" In *Acta conventus neolatini Sanctandreani*, cd. I. D. McFarlane, pp. 275–82. Medieval and Renaissance Texts and Studies 38. Binghamton, N.Y.: Center for Medieval and Early Renaissance Studies.

Sedley, D. N. 1993. "Chrysippus on Psychophysical Causality." In *Passions and Perceptions: Studies in Hellenistic Philosophy of Mind*, ed. Jacques Brunschwig and Martha Nussbaum, pp. 313–31. Cambridge: Cambridge University Press.

Sen, Amartya. 1981. *Poverty and Famines.* Oxford: Clarendon Press.

Sen, Amartya, and Jean Drèze. 1995. *India: Economic Development and Social Opportunity.* Delhi: Oxford University Press.

Shklar, Judith. 1990. *The Faces of Injustice.* New Haven: Yale University Press.

Shue, Henry. 1980. *Basic Rights: Subsistence, Affluence, and U.S. Foreign Policy.* Princeton: Princeton University Press.

———. 1988. "Mediating Duties." *Ethics* 98: 687–704.

Simmons, Alison. 2001. "Sensible Ends: Latent Telology in Descartes' Account of Sensation." *Journal of the History of Philosophy* 39: 49–75.

Singer, Peter. 1972. "Famine, Affluence, and Morality." *Philosophy and Public Affairs* 1: 229–43.

Sorabji, Richard. 2000. *Emotion and Peace of Mind: From Stoic Agitation to Christian Temptation.* Gifford Lectures. Oxford: Oxford University Press.

Sorell, Tom. 1993. "Morals and Modernity in Descartes." In *The Rise of Modern Philosophy: The Tension between the New and Traditional Philosophies from Machiavelli to Descartes*, ed. T. Sorell, pp. 273–88. Oxford: Clarendon Press.

Spade, Paul Vincent. 1982. "Insolubilia." In *The Cambridge History of Later Medieval Philosophy*, ed. Norman Kretzmann, Anthony Kenny, and Jan Pinborg, pp. 46–53. Cambridge: Cambridge University Press.

Spanneut, Michel. 1957. *Le stoïcisme des Pères de l'Eglise, de Clément de Rome à Clément d'Alexandrie.* Paris: Seuil.

———. 1964. "Le stoïcisme au Moyen Age et Recherches sur le stoïcisme aux XVIe et XVIIe siècle." In *Actes du VIIè Congrès de l'Association Guillaume Budé*, pp. 118–19. Paris: Les Belles Lettres.

———. 1973. *Le permanence du stoïcisme de Zénon à Malraux.* Gembloux: Duculot.

Stockdale, James. 1993. *Courage under Fire: A Test of Epictetus' Doctrines in a Laboratory of Human Behavior.* Stanford: Hoover Institution Press.

Stocker, Michael, and Elizabeth Hegeman. 1996. *Valuing Emotions*. Cambridge: Cambridge University Press.

Striker, Gisela. 1996. "*Ataraxia*: Happiness as Tranquillity." In *Essays on Hellenistic Epistemology and Ethics*, ed. G. Striker, pp. 183–95. Cambridge: Cambridge University Press.

Taranto, Domenico. 1990. "Studi sulla crisi del neostoicismo nella Francia del Grand Siècle." In *Tra antichi e moderni, Antropologia e stato tra disciplinamento e morale privata*, Atti del Convegno di studi Solerno, 20–21 ottobre 1987, ed. I. Cappiello, pp. 341–90. Naples: Edizioni Scientifiche Italiane.

Tarrant, Harold. 2000. *Plato's First Interpreters*. Ithaca, N.Y.: Cornell University Press.

Taylor, Charles. 1989. *The Sources of the Self: The Making of the Modern Identity*. Cambridge, Mass.: Harvard University Press.

Tesón, Fernando R. 1992. "The Kantian Theory of International Law." *Columbia Law Review* 92: 53–102.

Thayer, Robert E. 1989. *The Biopsychology of Mood and Arousal*. New York: Oxford University Press.

Treggiari, Susan. 1991. *Roman Marriage: Iusti Coniuges from the Time of Cicero to the Time of Ulpian*. Oxford: Clarendon Press.

Unger, Peter. 1996. *Living High and Letting Die*. New York: Oxford University Press.

United Nations Development Program. 1998. *Human Development Report 1998*. New York: Oxford University Press.

Vlastos, Gregory. 1991. *Socrates, Ironist and Moral Philosopher*. Cambridge: Cambridge University Press.

1994. *Socratic Studies*. Cambridge: Cambridge University Press.

Verbeke, Gerard. 1983. *The Presence of Stoicism in Medieval Thought*. Washington, D.C.: Catholic University of America Press.

van der Waerdt, Paul (ed.). 1994. *The Socratic Movement*. Ithaca, N.Y.: Cornell University Press.

Wollheim, Richard. 1999. *On the Emotions*. New Haven: Yale University Press.

Willing, Anthony. 1999. "Unheard of Objects of Knowledge: A Controversial Principle of Buridan's Epistemic Logic." *Franciscan Studies* 57: 203–24.

Wolfson, Harry. 1934. *The Philosophy of Spinoza: Unfolding the Latent Processes of His Reasoning*. Cambridge, Mass.: Harvard University Press.

Yovel, Yirmiyahu. 1989. *Spinoza and Other Heretics: The Adventures of Immanence*. Princeton: Princeton University Press.

Zupko, Jack. 2003. *John Buridan: Portrait of a Fourteenth-Century Arts Master*. Publications in Medieval Studies. Notre Dame, Ind.: University of Notre Dame Press.

Name Index

Abelard, Peter, 6, 117, 119, 121–122, 132–145
Adam of Balsham, 119
Adams, Marilyn McCord, 137
Annas, Julia, 196
Apuleius, 116
Appiah, Kwame Anthony, 217, 246
Aristotelians, 109, 118, 123
Aristotle, 33, 40, 42, 43–45, 48–49, 50, 51, 77, 98, 108, 116, 195
Augustine, 32, 34, 103–106, 193

Barnes, Jonathan, 25
Beitz, Charles, 215, 245
Bellincioni, Maria, 92–93
Bennett, Jonathan, 205
Bobzien, Susanne, 50
Boethius, 109, 112, 119
Boethius of Dacia, 124–125
Brown, Eric, 247

Calvin, John, 7
Carraud, Vincent, 167
Cassian, 102
Cato the Younger, 226
Chanut, Pierre, 193
Charron, Pierre, 148
Chevreau, Urbain, 160
Christina, queen of Sweden, 193, 195
Chomsky, Noam, 249
Chrysippus, 3, 4, 9, 36, 39, 40, 41, 45–46, 49, 50, 51, 52, 97, 98, 112, 197, 200, 251, 255, 256
Cicero, 8–9, 33, 37, 43, 49, 97, 112, 123, 155, 178, 196, 202, 208, 214–245
Cleanthes, 39, 46, 187, 196
Corneille, Pierre, 167

Cynics, 238
Cummings, E. E., 270

de Balzac, Guez, 158
Deleuze, Gilles, 208
Descartes, René, 7, 32, 148, 159, 167–168, 177–193, 203
Dewar, Michael, 92
Didymus the Blind, 99, 104
Diogenes Laertius, 37, 273
Donagan, Alan, 136
du Vair, Guillaume, 7, 155, 156, 160–162, 177–178
Dyck, Andrew R., 247

Elisabeth, princess of Bohemia, 125, 167, 178–182, 185, 186, 189–190, 193, 194–195, 196
Engberg-Pedersen, Troels, 44
Epictetus, 3, 10–29, 36, 45, 50, 104, 178, 202, 250–251, 253
Epicurus, 181–182
Epstein, Richard, 240
Essenes, 58, 60
Euripides, 45
Evagrius, 5, 100–103

Frede, Michael, 49, 117, 202
Freud, Sigmund, 210

Galen, 39, 41, 45, 50, 98, 250–251, 253, 255
Gellius, Aulus, 49, 104–106
Gentili, Alberico, 215
Gewirth, Alan, 248
Gilbert of Poitiers, 110
Godfrey of Poitiers, 143
Goldsmith, Jack, 245

Subject Index

affect, 148, 159, 203, 206–207, 250–251, 253, 258–261, 262, 273
appearance. *See* impression
appropriation (*oikeiōsis*)
    process of, 35, 44, 272
    theory of, 67, 71
Aristotelianism, 56, 70–71, 72, 109, 110, 113, 115–122, 125, 167, 208
    and Platonism, 32, 112, 208, 251, 268
assent (*sunkatathesis; adsensus mentis*)
    act of, 5, 35, 47–48, 50, 121, 156
    connection with sin, 100
    and consent, 142
    doctrine of, 6, 141, 202

beatitude. *See* happiness
beginnings. *See* prepassions

catharsis, 98
certainty
    moral vs. metaphysical, 167
clemency, 5, 78–80
conation, 252–253
conditionals, theory of, 115–118
concepts, natural. *See* preconceptions
consent
    and assent, 142
    distinct from will, 143
    doctrine of, 6, 121–122, 132–145
    and intention, 134–136, 146
    as locus of sin, 140
consequence
    logical, 6, 128, 158
consolation, 237
    Christian, 7, 160–162
cosmopolitanism, 155
creative fire (*ignis artifex*), 111

deliberation, 264–265
determinism, 49, 140, 203, 205–206
diatribe, 26

elenchus
    in Epictetus, 18–19, 22
    Socratic, 11, 12, 14, 20, 21, 23, 24, 25
emotion. *See* passions
Epicureanism, 7, 53, 143, 169, 170, 172, 181, 182, 247
ethics
    Aristotelian, 70–71, 123
    Cartesian, 167
    Socratic, 12
evils
    public vs. private, 156, 160, 162

faith (*pistis*)
    Christian, 4, 70, 71
first movements. *See* prepassions
freedom (*eleutheria*), 7, 8, 52–53, 56, 59–61, 62, 70, 123, 155, 157, 185, 202–203, 204
friendship, 224

God, 38, 59–74, 104, 135–145, 189–190, 192, 198–211
goodness
    intrinsic, 145
    metaphysical, 138–140
    of possible worlds, 145
grammar, 118–119

happiness (*eudaimonia*), 7, 21, 168, 177–181, 182–183, 184–185, 188, 189–190, 193, 198–211, 213, 263–264

and self-preservation 199, 201
theological, 7, 161–162

war, 148, 150, 156, 198, 215, 220
wisdom (*sophia*), 4, 48, 70, 73, 164, 186,
    187, 189, 190, 193, 207

will (*boulēsis; voluntas*), 33, 34, 36, 73, 97,
    143, 188. *See also* freedom
weakness of (*akrasia*), 44–45, 64, 65, 66,
    68, 69, 70
words, 72, 110–122
imposition of, 110